A SIGN OF AFFECTION

suu Morishita

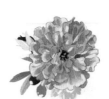

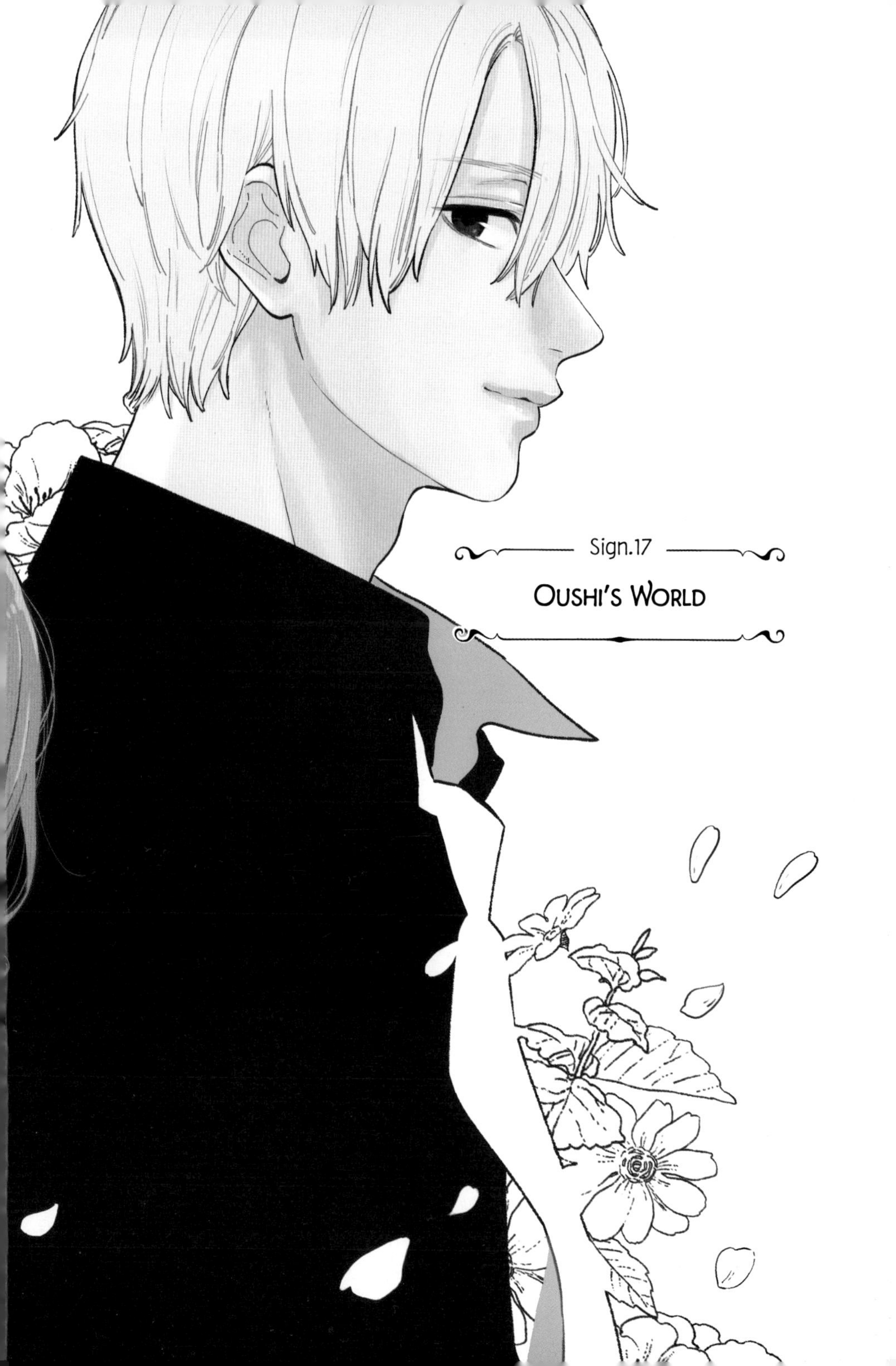
Sign.17
Oushi's World

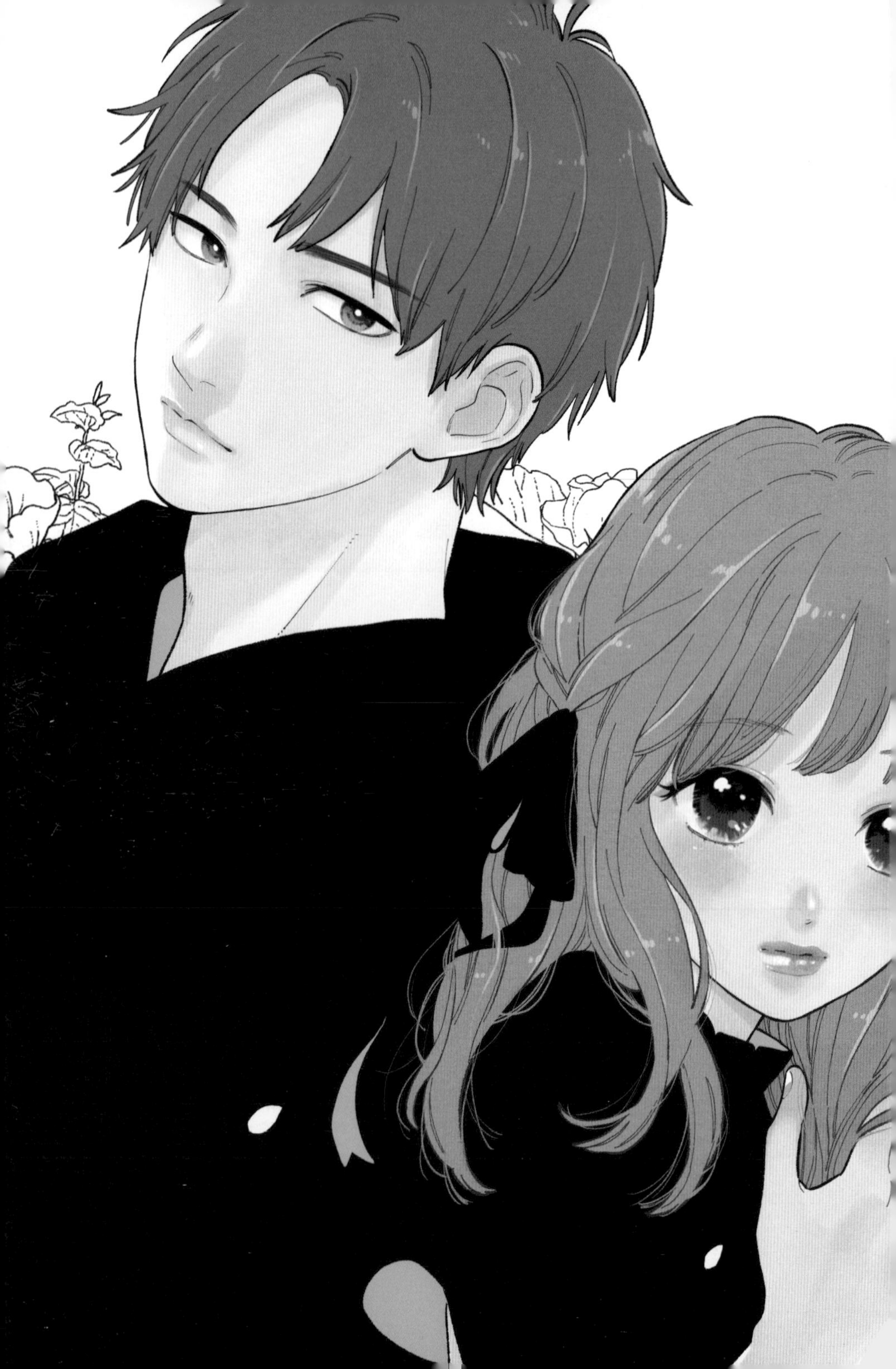

CONTENTS

*When the letters in the bubbles are washed out, it means that Yuki is reading the speaker's lips and discerning words from the context of the conversation. When the letters are shown sideways, it means she's having difficulty figuring out a word.

CHARACTERS

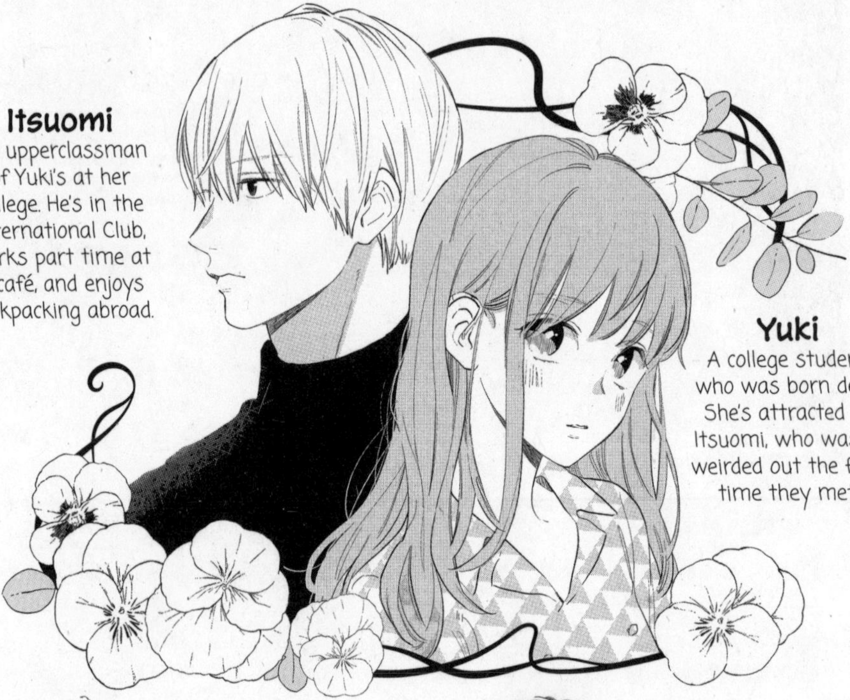

Itsuomi
An upperclassman of Yuki's at her college. He's in the International Club, works part time at a café, and enjoys backpacking abroad.

Yuki
A college student who was born deaf. She's attracted to Itsuomi, who wasn't weirded out the first time they met.

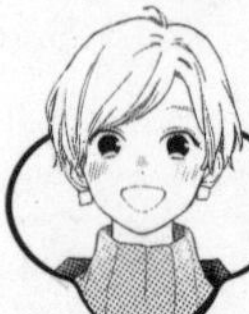

Rin-chan
A friend of Yuki's and a member of the same club as Itsuomi. She's crushing on Kyouya.

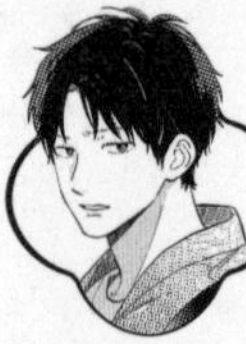

Oushi
A childhood friend of Yuki's. He can use sign language and somehow always ends up giving her a hard time.

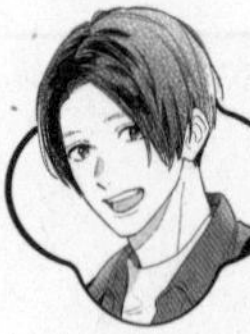

Kyouya
Itsuomi's cousin and owner of the café where Itsuomi works part time.

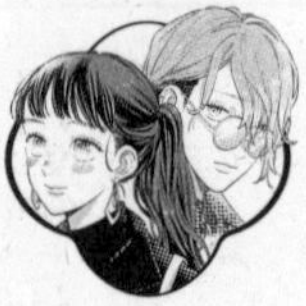

Emma & Shin
Classmates of Itsuomi from high school.

STORY

Yuki is a college student who was born deaf. One day, a classmate named Itsuomi helped her out of an awkward situation, and she was immediately fascinated with him. Eventually, Yuki realized that her fascination was really love, which she decided to pursue in earnest. Itsuomi asked her to be his girlfriend, and the two started going out. Right away, he introduced her to his best friends, and Yuki started to feel just how much she meant to him.

A SIGN OF AFFECTION

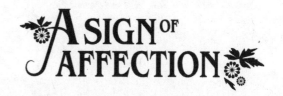

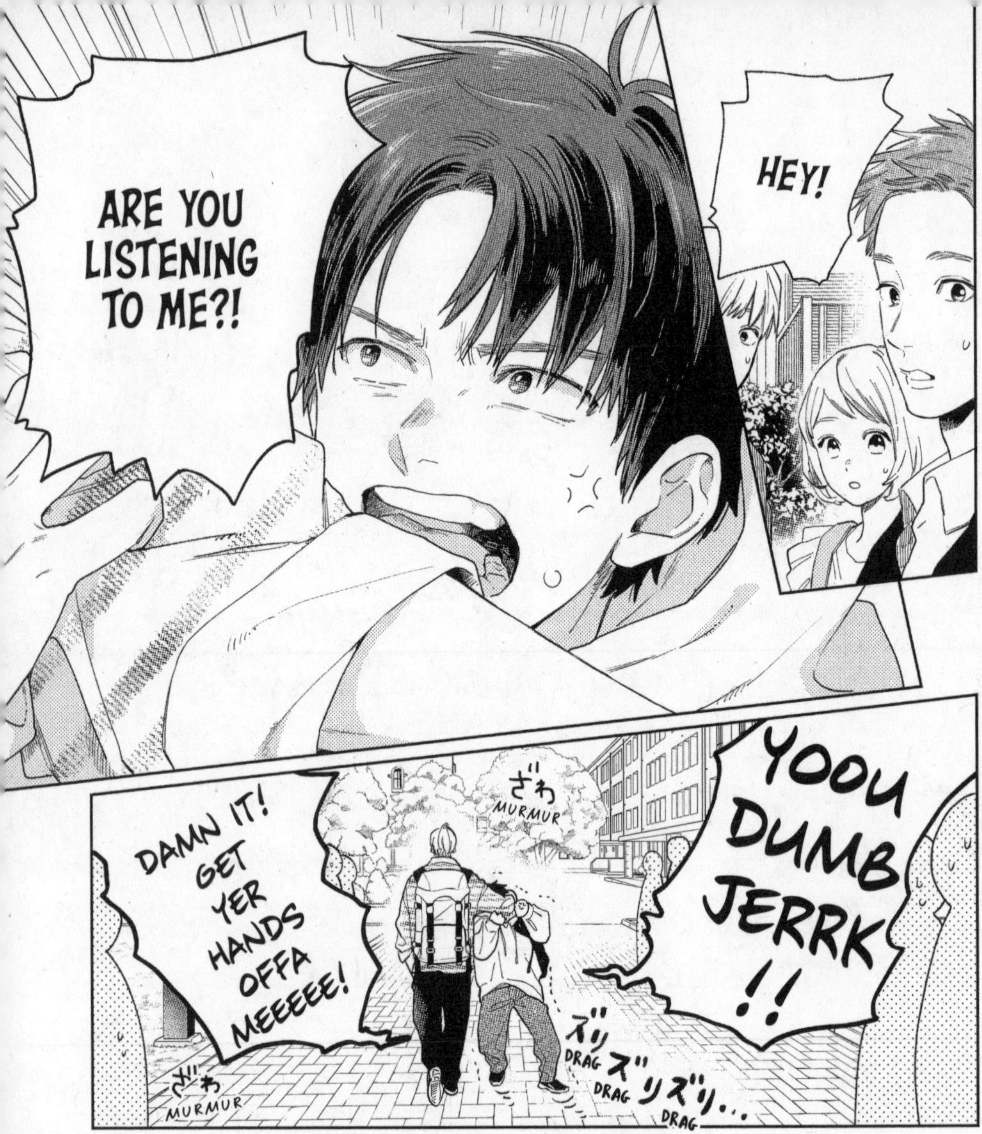
HEY!
ARE YOU LISTENING TO ME?!
YOOU DUMB JERRK!!
ざわ MURMUR
DAMN IT! GET YER HANDS OFFA MEEEEE!
ズリ DRAG
ズリズリ... DRAG DRAG
ざわ MURMUR

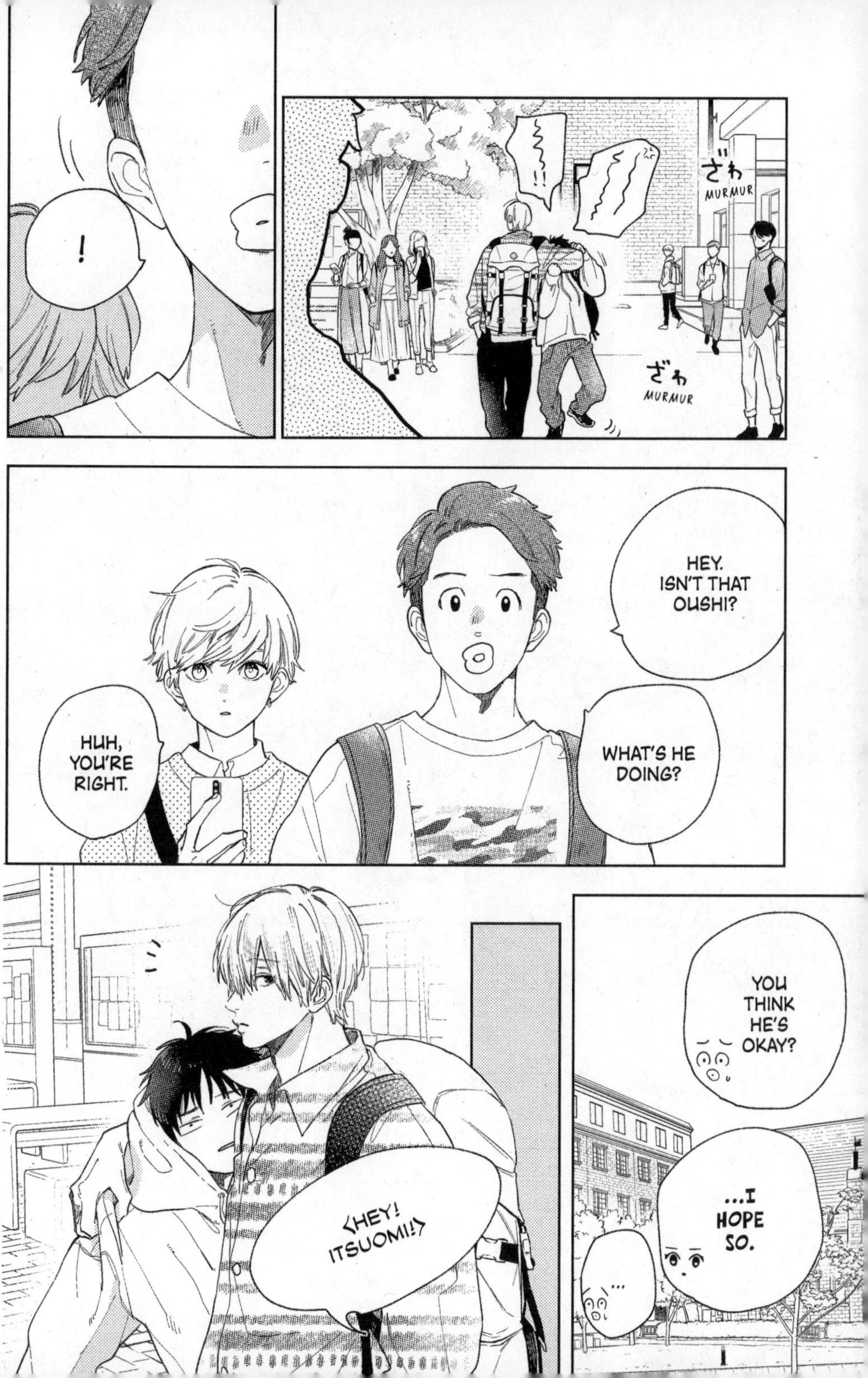

ざわ
MURMUR
ざわ
MURMUR
!
HEY. ISN'T THAT OUSHI?
WHAT'S HE DOING?
HUH, YOU'RE RIGHT.
YOU THINK HE'S OKAY?
...I HOPE SO.
...
<HEY! ITSUOMI!!>

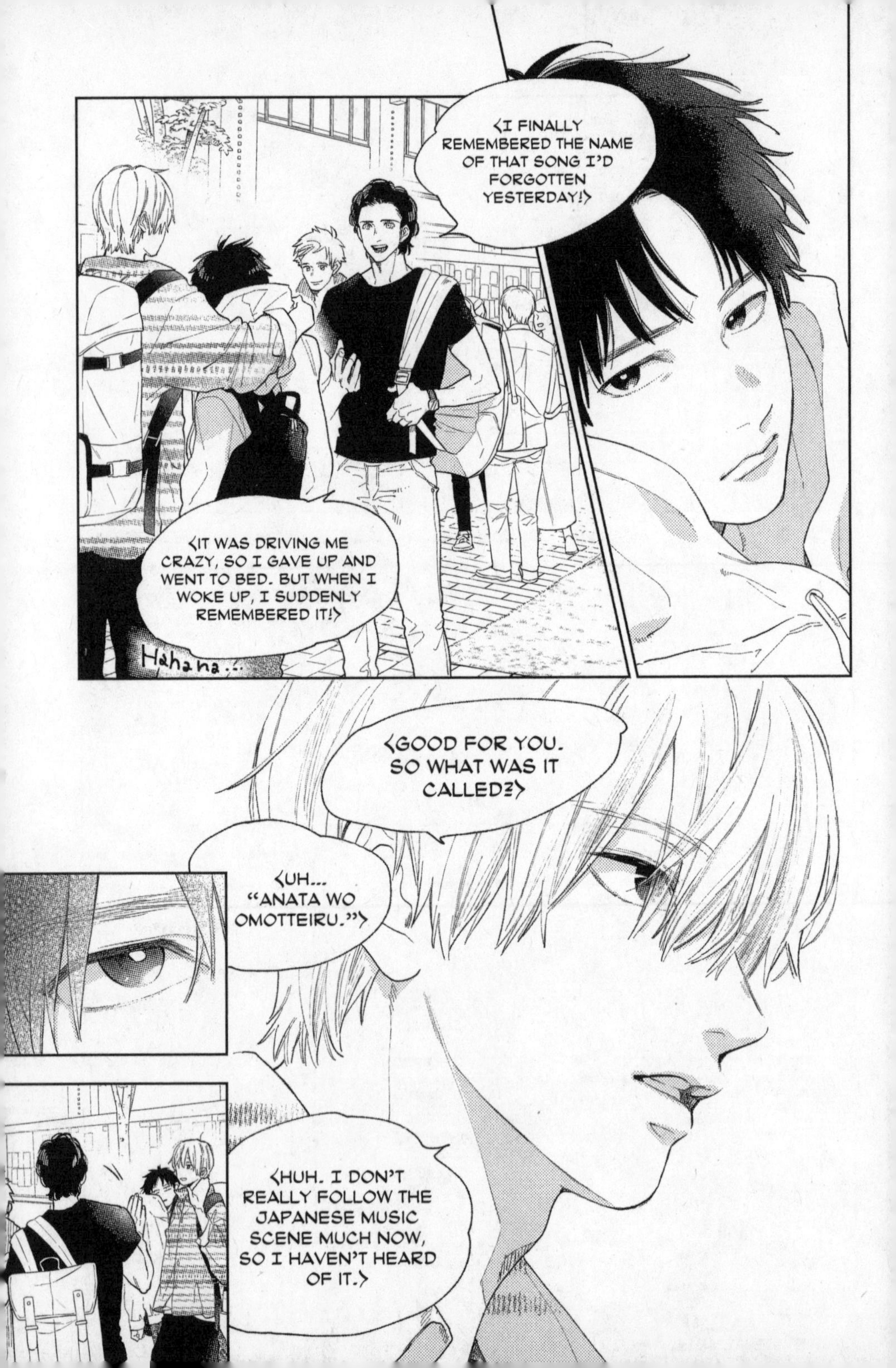

<I FINALLY REMEMBERED THE NAME OF THAT SONG I'D FORGOTTEN YESTERDAY!>
<IT WAS DRIVING ME CRAZY, SO I GAVE UP AND WENT TO BED. BUT WHEN I WOKE UP, I SUDDENLY REMEMBERED IT!>
Hahaha...
<GOOD FOR YOU. SO WHAT WAS IT CALLED?>
<UH... "ANATA WO OMOTTEIRU.">
<HUH. I DON'T REALLY FOLLOW THE JAPANESE MUSIC SCENE MUCH NOW, SO I HAVEN'T HEARD OF IT.>

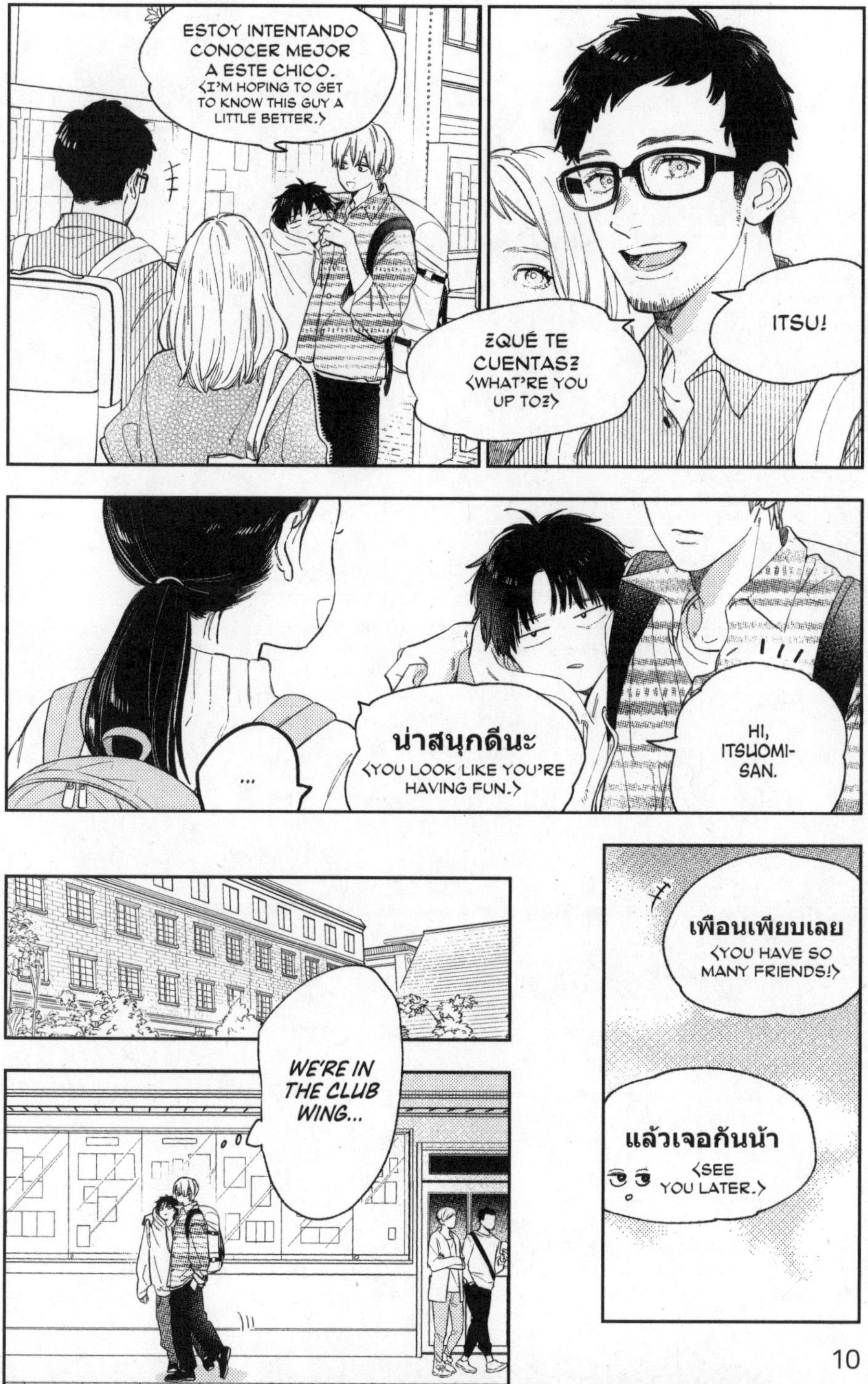

ITSU!
¿QUÉ TE CUENTAS? <WHAT'RE YOU UP TO?>
ESTOY INTENTANDO CONOCER MEJOR A ESTE CHICO. <I'M HOPING TO GET TO KNOW THIS GUY A LITTLE BETTER.>
HI, ITSUOMI-SAN.
น่าสนุกดีนะ <YOU LOOK LIKE YOU'RE HAVING FUN.>
...
เพือนเพียบเลย <YOU HAVE SO MANY FRIENDS!>
แล้วเจอกันน้า <SEE YOU LATER.>
WE'RE IN THE CLUB WING...

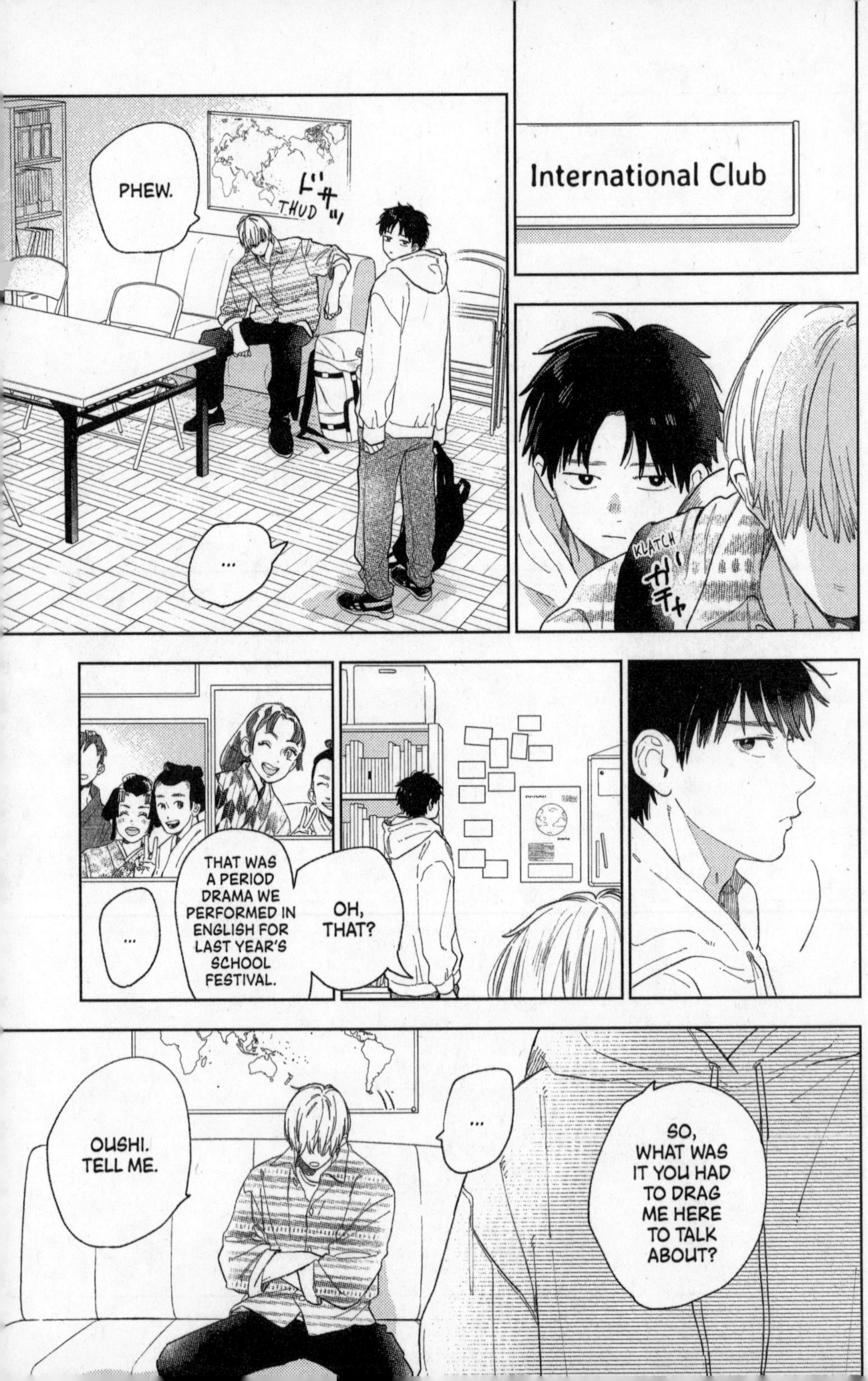
International Club
KLATCH
ガチャ
PHEW.
ドサッ
THUD
...
OH, THAT?
THAT WAS A PERIOD DRAMA WE PERFORMED IN ENGLISH FOR LAST YEAR'S SCHOOL FESTIVAL.
...
SO, WHAT WAS IT YOU HAD TO DRAG ME HERE TO TALK ABOUT?
...
OUSHI. TELL ME.

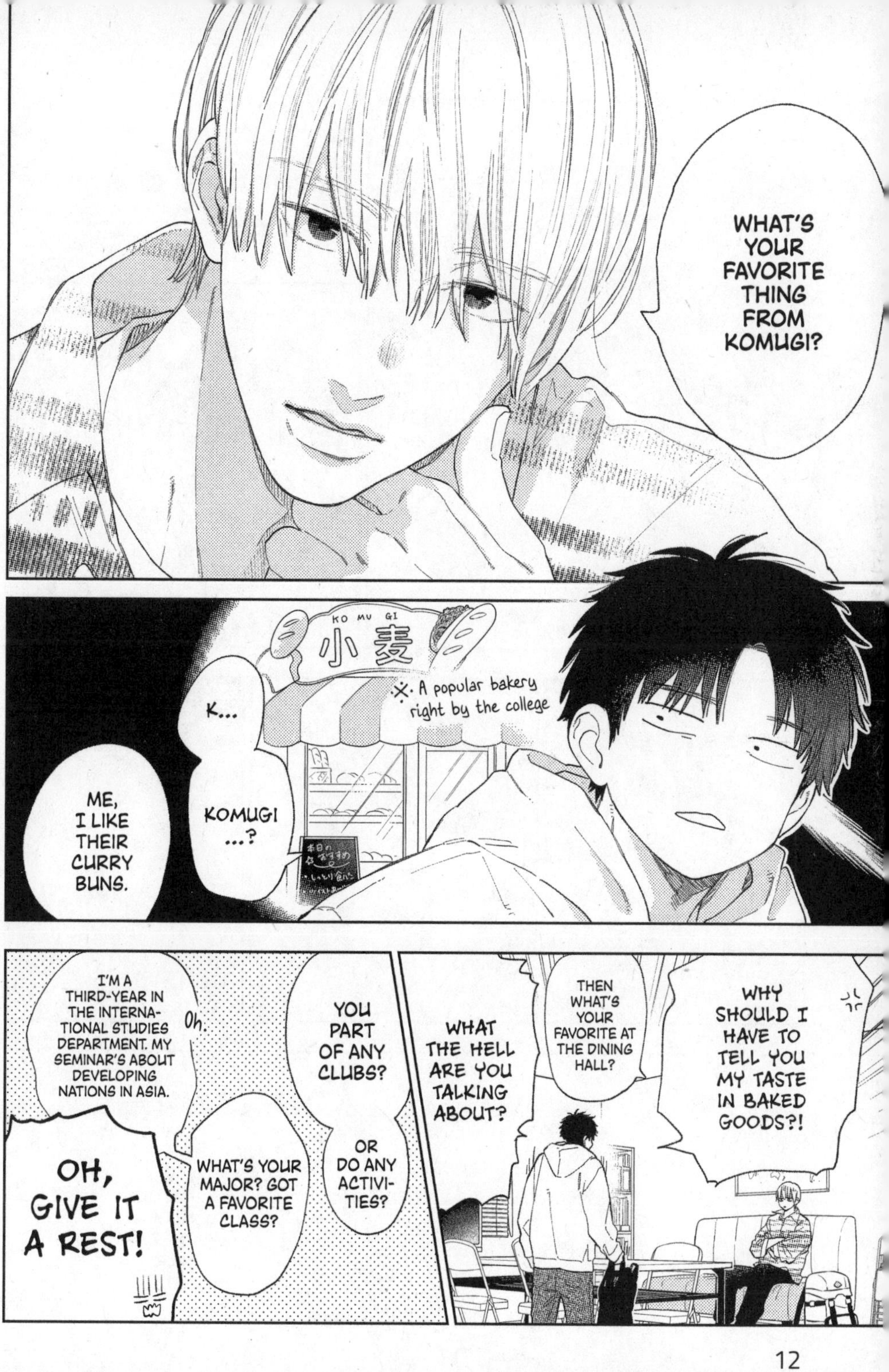
WHAT'S YOUR FAVORITE THING FROM KOMUGI?
KO MU GI
小麦
※: A popular bakery right by the college
K...
KOMUGI ...?
ME, I LIKE THEIR CURRY BUNS.
WHY SHOULD I HAVE TO TELL YOU MY TASTE IN BAKED GOODS?!
THEN WHAT'S YOUR FAVORITE AT THE DINING HALL?
WHAT THE HELL ARE YOU TALKING ABOUT?
YOU PART OF ANY CLUBS?
OR DO ANY ACTIVITIES?
Oh.
I'M A THIRD-YEAR IN THE INTERNATIONAL STUDIES DEPARTMENT. MY SEMINAR'S ABOUT DEVELOPING NATIONS IN ASIA.
WHAT'S YOUR MAJOR? GOT A FAVORITE CLASS?
OH, GIVE IT A REST!

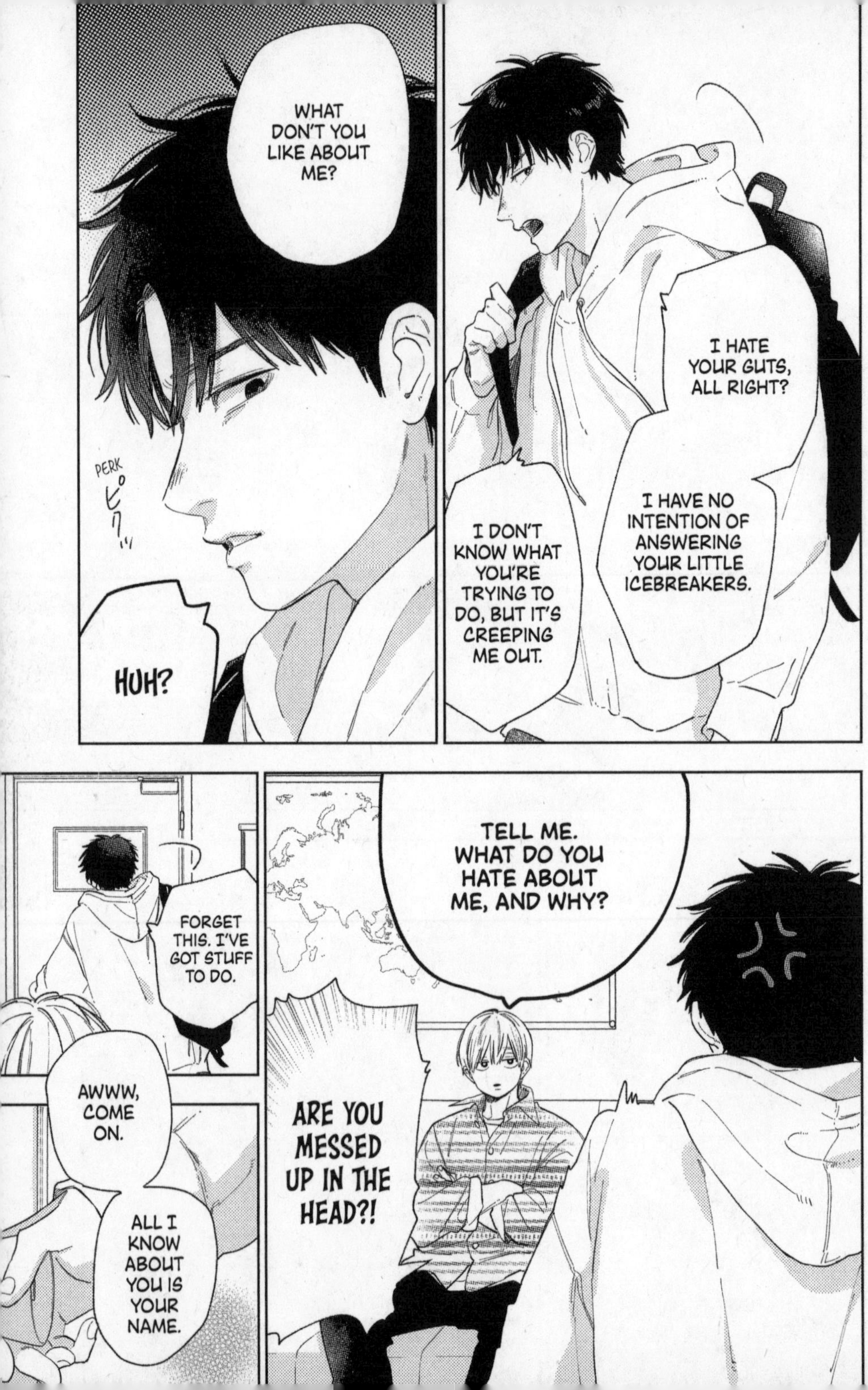
I HATE YOUR GUTS, ALL RIGHT?
I HAVE NO INTENTION OF ANSWERING YOUR LITTLE ICEBREAKERS.
I DON'T KNOW WHAT YOU'RE TRYING TO DO, BUT IT'S CREEPING ME OUT.
WHAT DON'T YOU LIKE ABOUT ME?
PERK
ピクッ
HUH?
TELL ME. WHAT DO YOU HATE ABOUT ME, AND WHY?
ARE YOU MESSED UP IN THE HEAD?!
FORGET THIS. I'VE GOT STUFF TO DO.
AWWW, COME ON.
ALL I KNOW ABOUT YOU IS YOUR NAME.

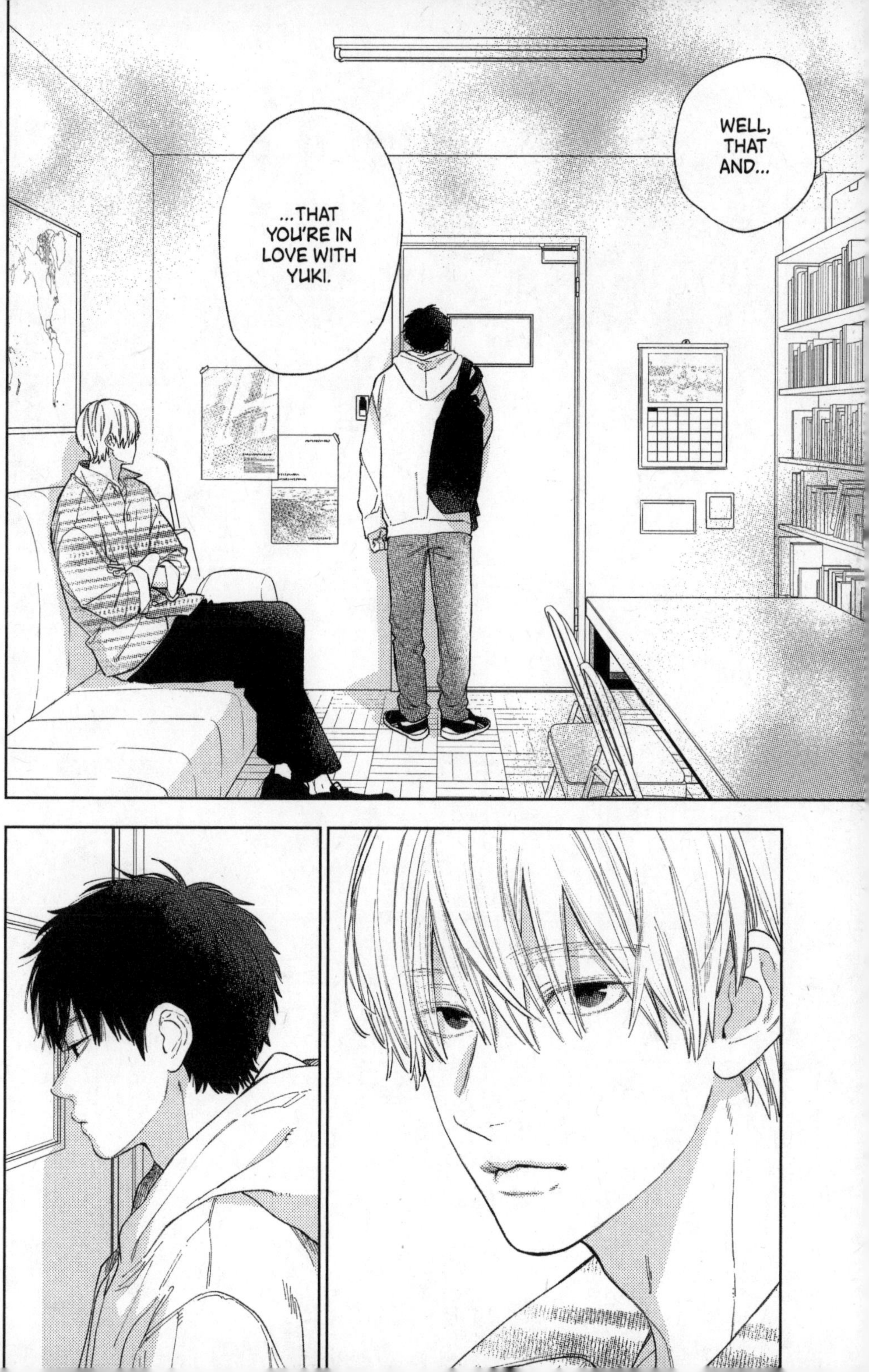
WELL, THAT AND...
...THAT YOU'RE IN LOVE WITH YUKI.

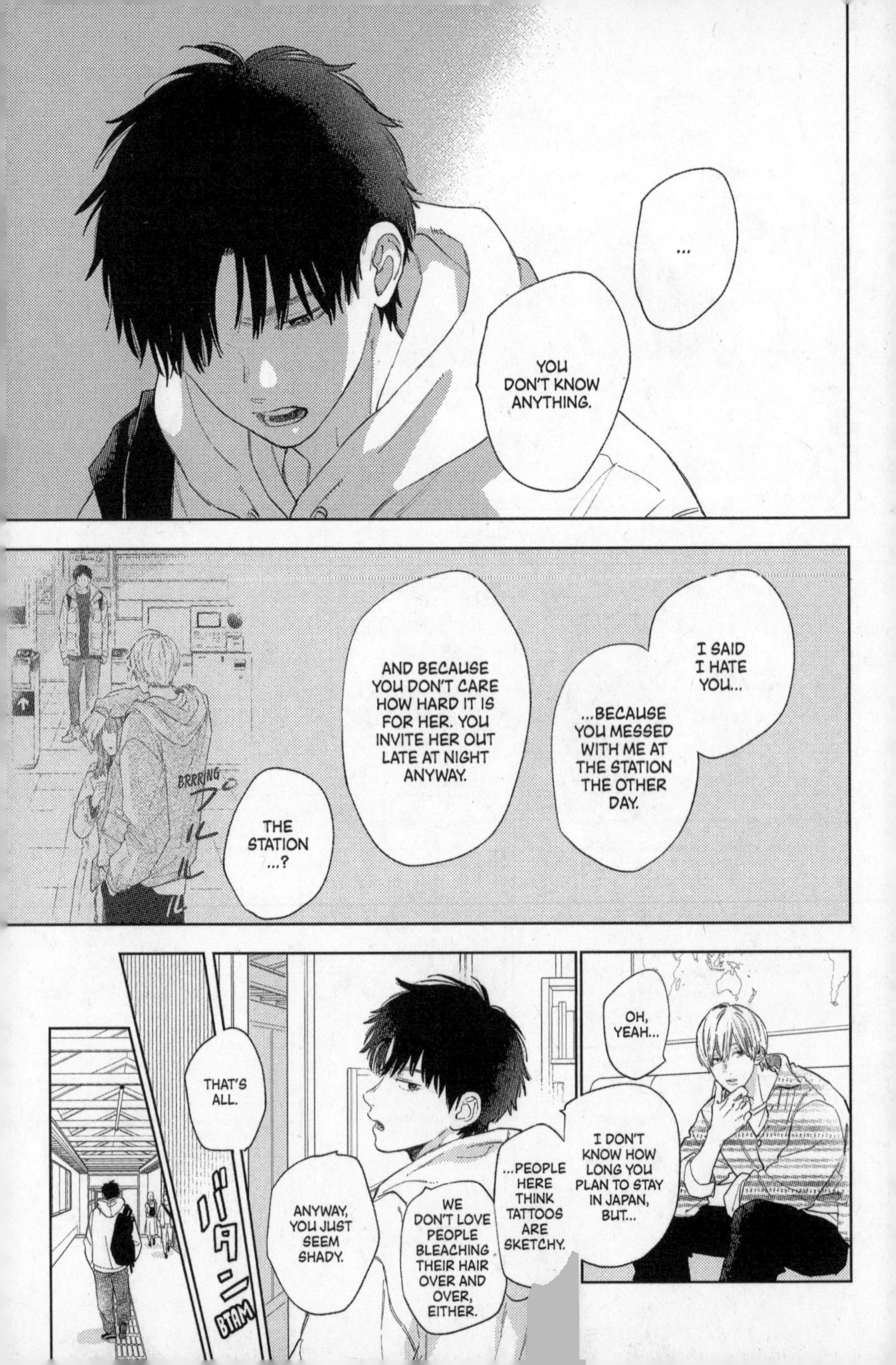
...
YOU DON'T KNOW ANYTHING.
I SAID I HATE YOU...
...BECAUSE YOU MESSED WITH ME AT THE STATION THE OTHER DAY.
AND BECAUSE YOU DON'T CARE HOW HARD IT IS FOR HER. YOU INVITE HER OUT LATE AT NIGHT ANYWAY.
BRRRING
THE STATION ...?
OH, YEAH...
I DON'T KNOW HOW LONG YOU PLAN TO STAY IN JAPAN, BUT...
...PEOPLE HERE THINK TATTOOS ARE SKETCHY.
WE DON'T LOVE PEOPLE BLEACHING THEIR HAIR OVER AND OVER, EITHER.
ANYWAY, YOU JUST SEEM SHADY.
THAT'S ALL.
BTAM

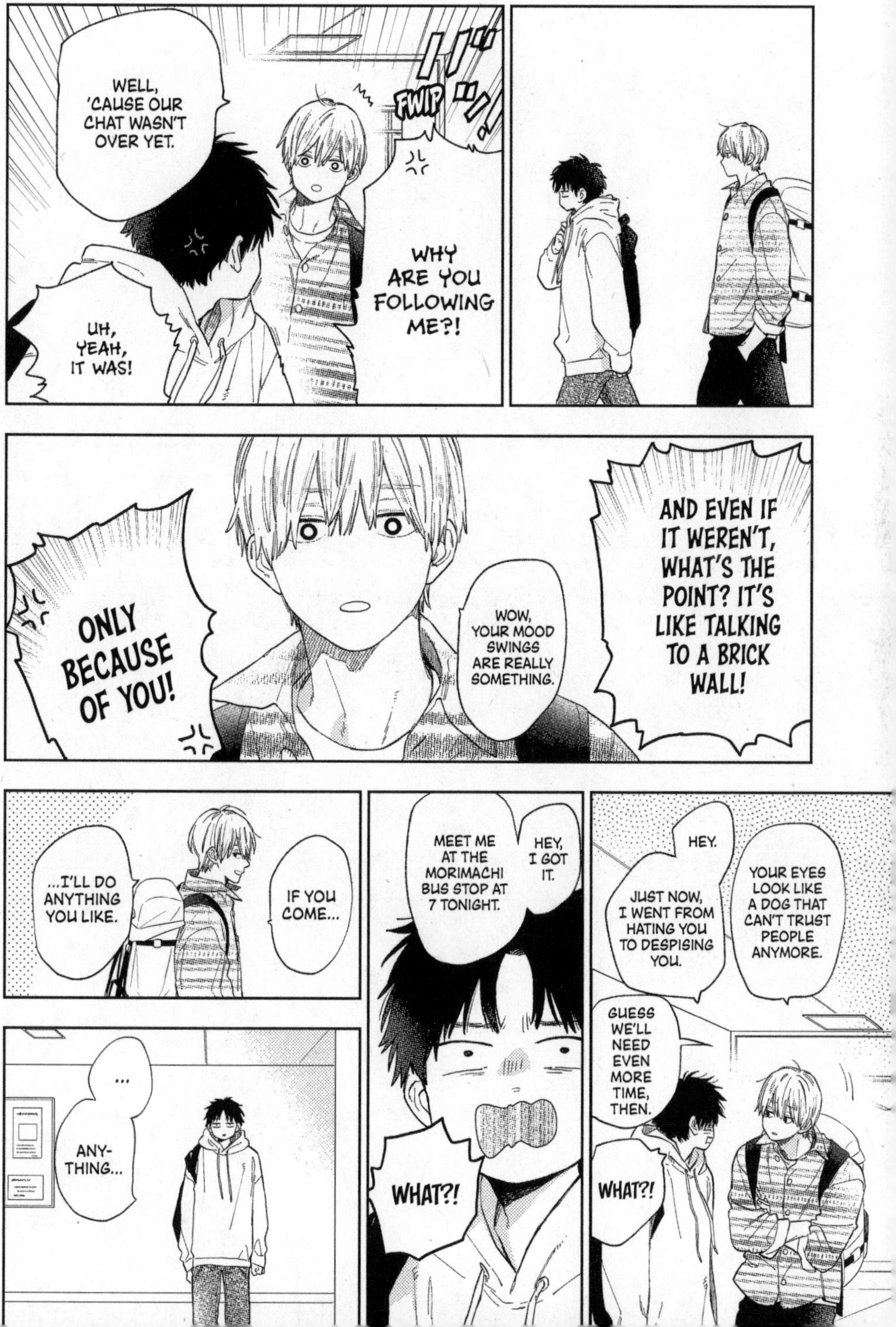
FWIP
WHY ARE YOU FOLLOWING ME?!
WELL, 'CAUSE OUR CHAT WASN'T OVER YET.
UH, YEAH, IT WAS!
AND EVEN IF IT WEREN'T, WHAT'S THE POINT? IT'S LIKE TALKING TO A BRICK WALL!
WOW, YOUR MOOD SWINGS ARE REALLY SOMETHING.
ONLY BECAUSE OF YOU!
HEY.
YOUR EYES LOOK LIKE A DOG THAT CAN'T TRUST PEOPLE ANYMORE.
JUST NOW, I WENT FROM HATING YOU TO DESPISING YOU.
GUESS WE'LL NEED EVEN MORE TIME, THEN.
WHAT?!
HEY, I GOT IT.
MEET ME AT THE MORIMACHI BUS STOP AT 7 TONIGHT.
WHAT?!
IF YOU COME...
...I'LL DO ANYTHING YOU LIKE.
...
ANY-THING...

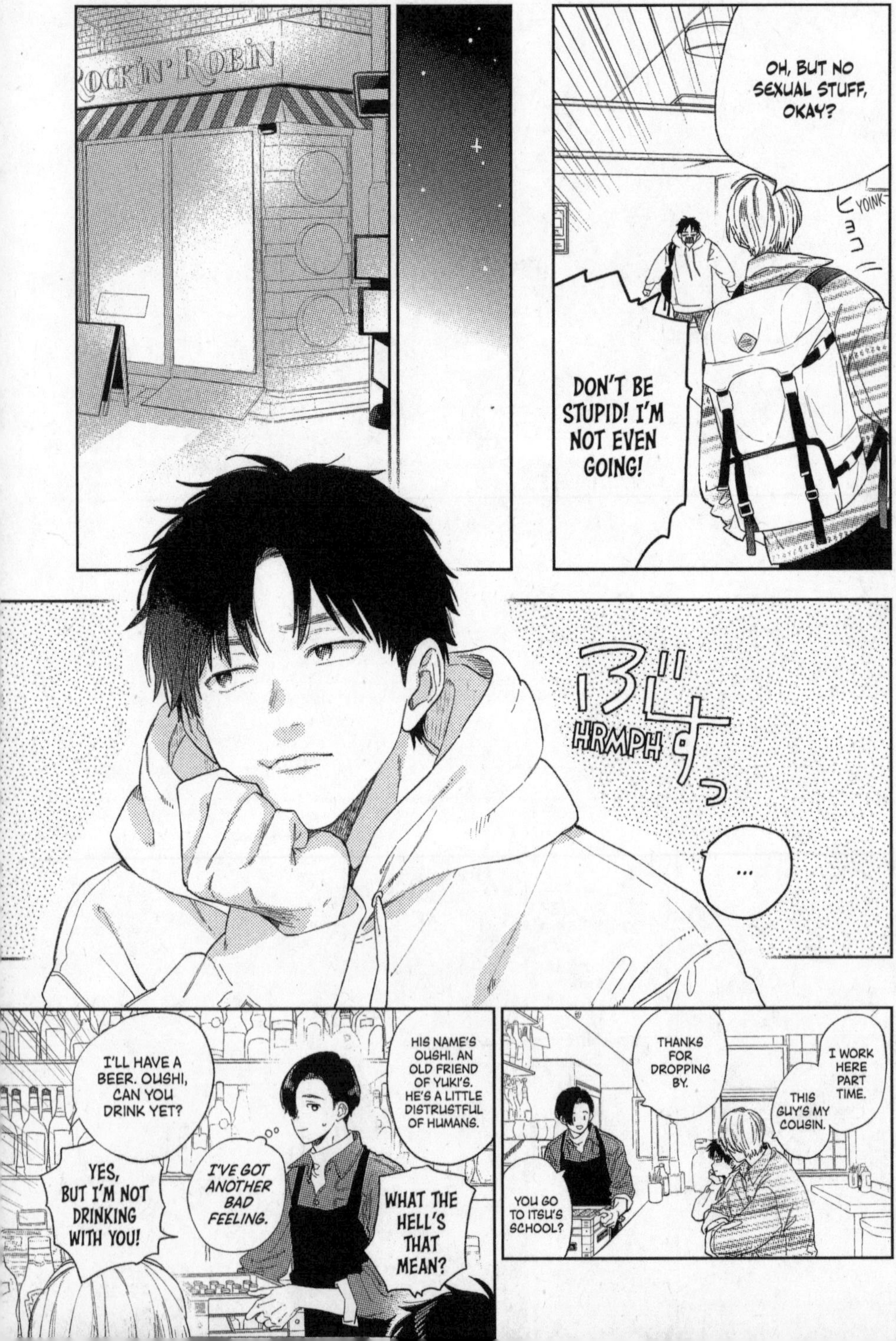
OH, BUT NO SEXUAL STUFF, OKAY?
ヒョコ YOINK
DON'T BE STUPID! I'M NOT EVEN GOING!
ROCKIN' ROBIN
HRMPH
...
I WORK HERE PART TIME. THIS GUY'S MY COUSIN.
THANKS FOR DROPPING BY.
YOU GO TO ITSU'S SCHOOL?
HIS NAME'S OUSHI. AN OLD FRIEND OF YUKI'S. HE'S A LITTLE DISTRUSTFUL OF HUMANS.
WHAT THE HELL'S THAT MEAN?
I'LL HAVE A BEER. OUSHI, CAN YOU DRINK YET?
I'VE GOT ANOTHER BAD FEELING.
YES, BUT I'M NOT DRINKING WITH YOU!

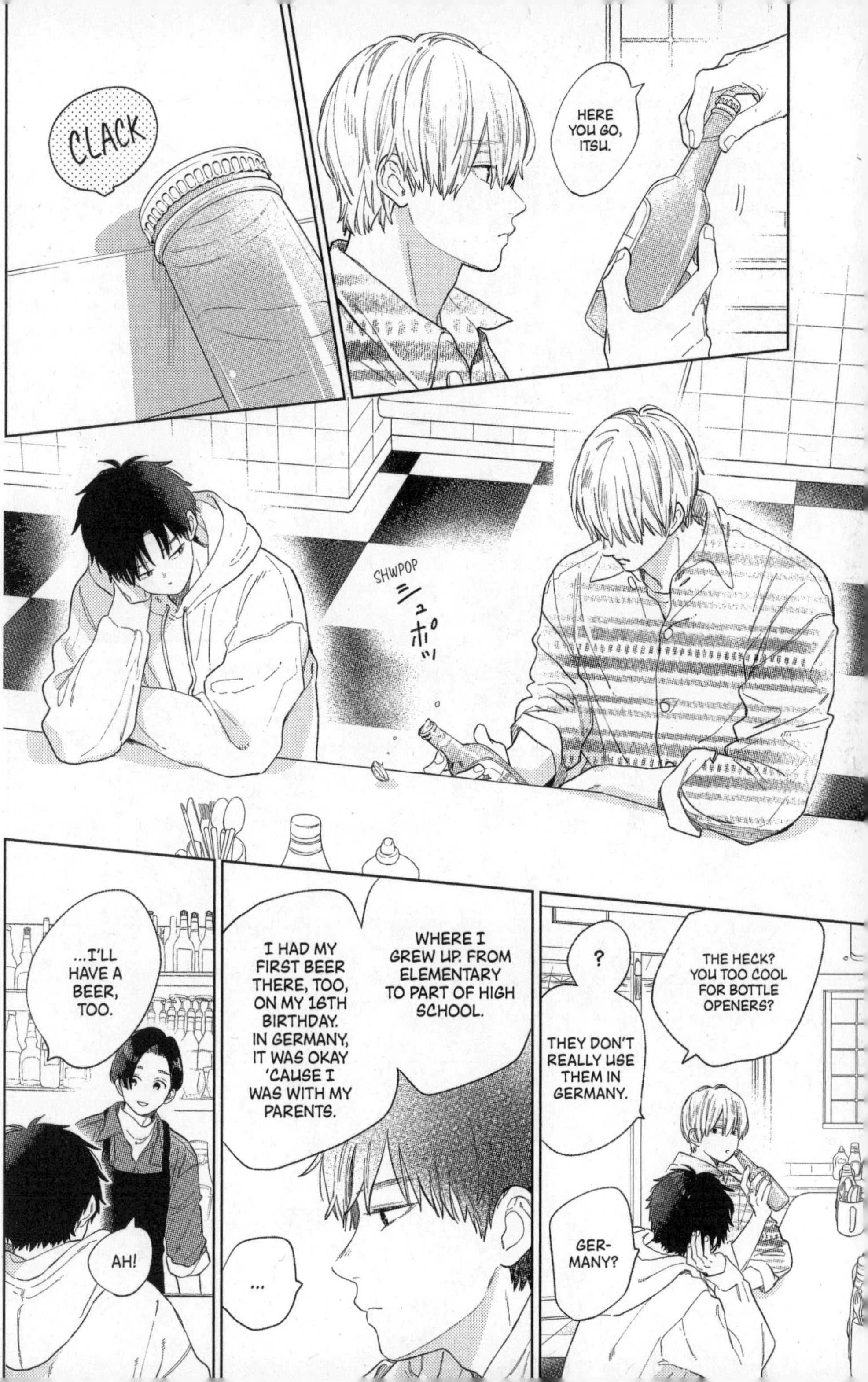
HERE YOU GO, ITSU.
CLACK
SHWPOP
シュポッ
THE HECK? YOU TOO COOL FOR BOTTLE OPENERS?
?
THEY DON'T REALLY USE THEM IN GERMANY.
GER-MANY?
WHERE I GREW UP. FROM ELEMENTARY TO PART OF HIGH SCHOOL.
I HAD MY FIRST BEER THERE, TOO, ON MY 16TH BIRTHDAY. IN GERMANY, IT WAS OKAY 'CAUSE I WAS WITH MY PARENTS.
...
...I'LL HAVE A BEER, TOO.
AH!

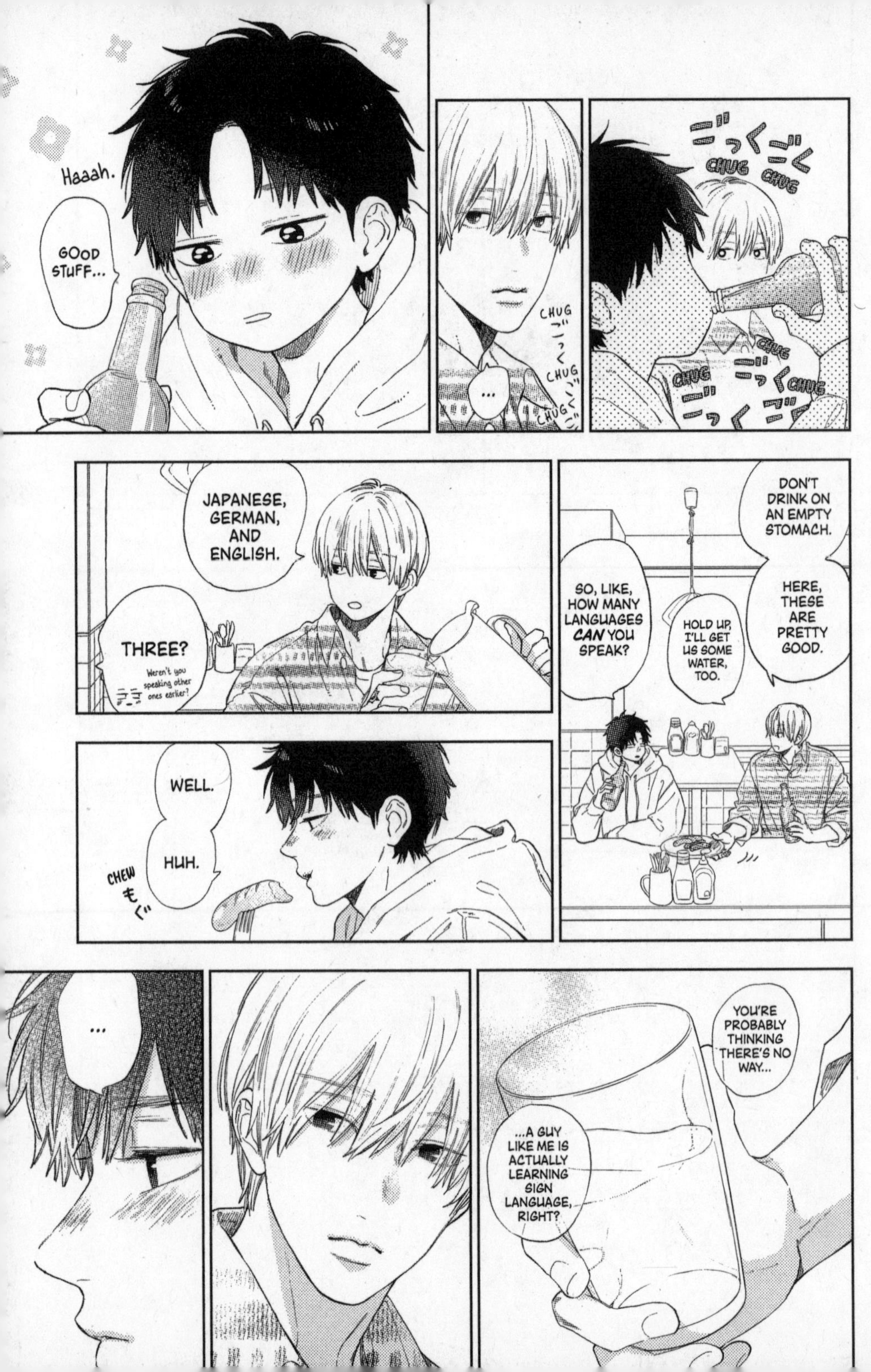
ごっくごく
CHUG CHUG
CHUG ごっく CHUG
ごっく CHUG ごく
CHUG
ごっく
CHUG
ごく
CHUG
ごく
...
Haaah.
GOOD STUFF...
DON'T DRINK ON AN EMPTY STOMACH.
HERE, THESE ARE PRETTY GOOD.
HOLD UP, I'LL GET US SOME WATER, TOO.
SO, LIKE, HOW MANY LANGUAGES **CAN** YOU SPEAK?
JAPANESE, GERMAN, AND ENGLISH.
THREE?
Weren't you speaking other ones earlier?
WELL.
HUH.
CHEW
もぐ
YOU'RE PROBABLY THINKING THERE'S NO WAY...
...A GUY LIKE ME IS ACTUALLY LEARNING SIGN LANGUAGE, RIGHT?
...

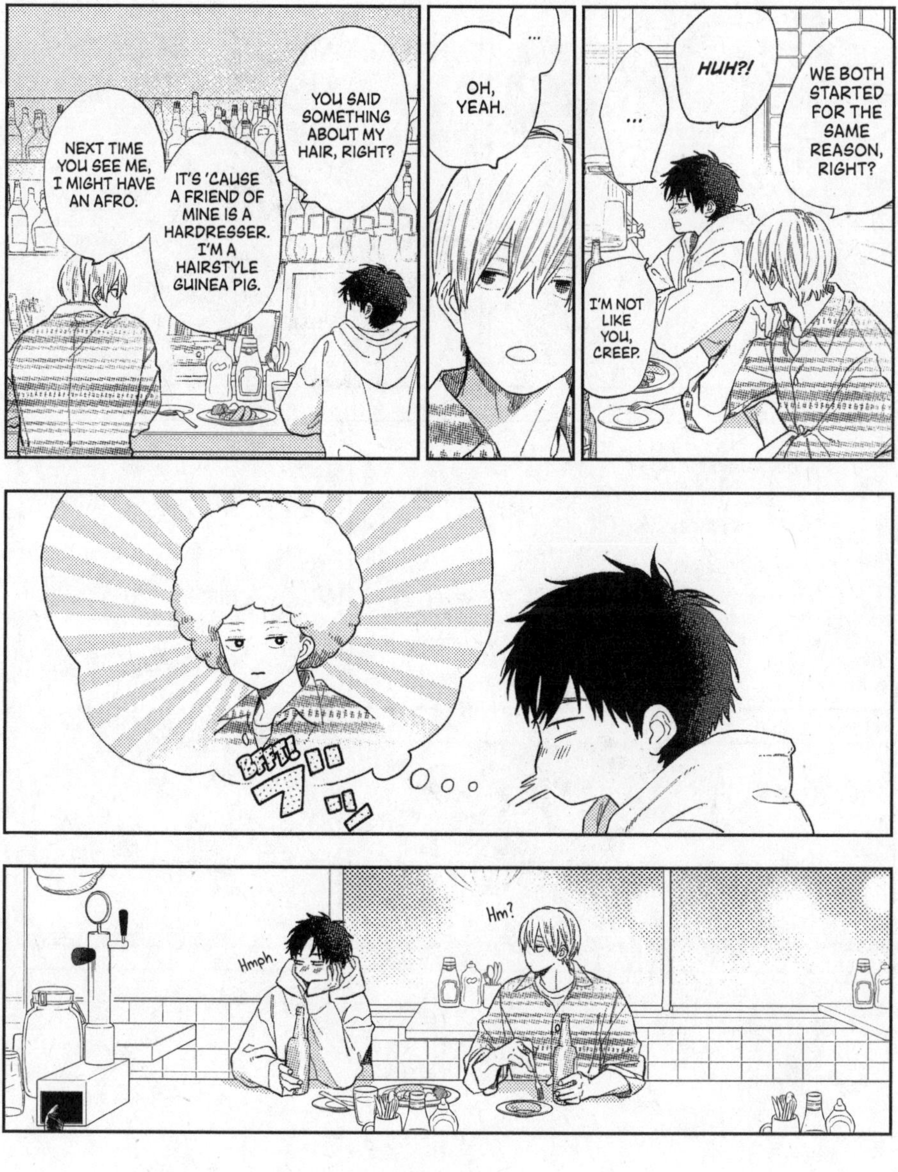
WE BOTH STARTED FOR THE SAME REASON, RIGHT?
HUH?!
...
I'M NOT LIKE YOU, CREEP.
...
OH, YEAH.
YOU SAID SOMETHING ABOUT MY HAIR, RIGHT?
IT'S 'CAUSE A FRIEND OF MINE IS A HARDRESSER. I'M A HAIRSTYLE GUINEA PIG.
NEXT TIME YOU SEE ME, I MIGHT HAVE AN AFRO.
BFFT!
Hm?
Hmph.

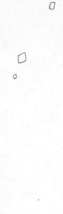

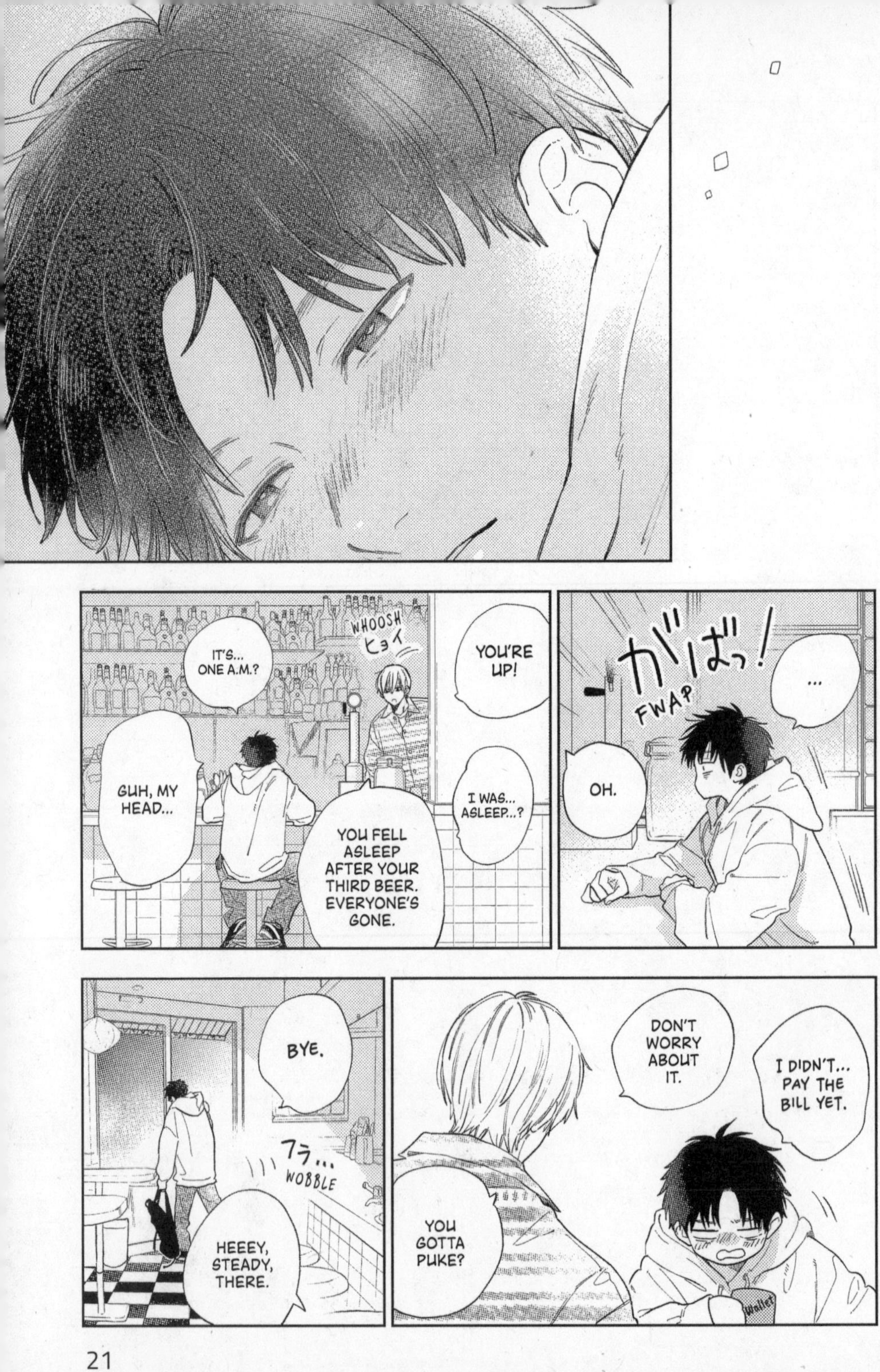
がばっ！
FWAP
...
OH.
YOU'RE UP!
WHOOSH
ヒョイ
IT'S... ONE A.M.?
I WAS... ASLEEP...?
YOU FELL ASLEEP AFTER YOUR THIRD BEER. EVERYONE'S GONE.
GUH, MY HEAD...
I DIDN'T... PAY THE BILL YET.
DON'T WORRY ABOUT IT.
YOU GOTTA PUKE?
Wallet
BYE.
フラ...
WOBBLE
HEEEY, STEADY, THERE.

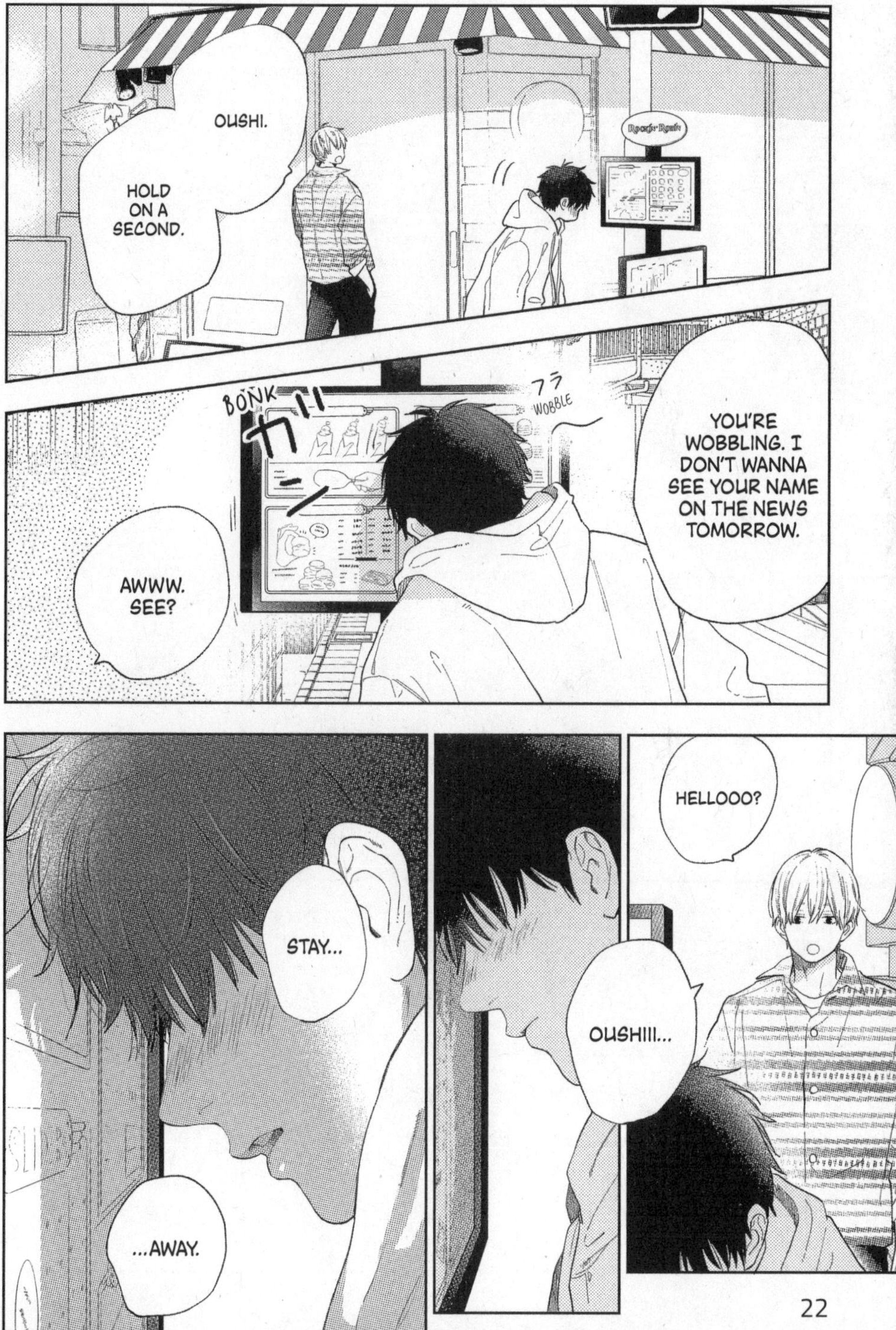
OUSHI.
HOLD ON A SECOND.
YOU'RE WOBBLING. I DON'T WANNA SEE YOUR NAME ON THE NEWS TOMORROW.
フラ
WOBBLE
BONK
AWWW. SEE?
HELLOOO?
OUSHIII...
STAY...
...AWAY.

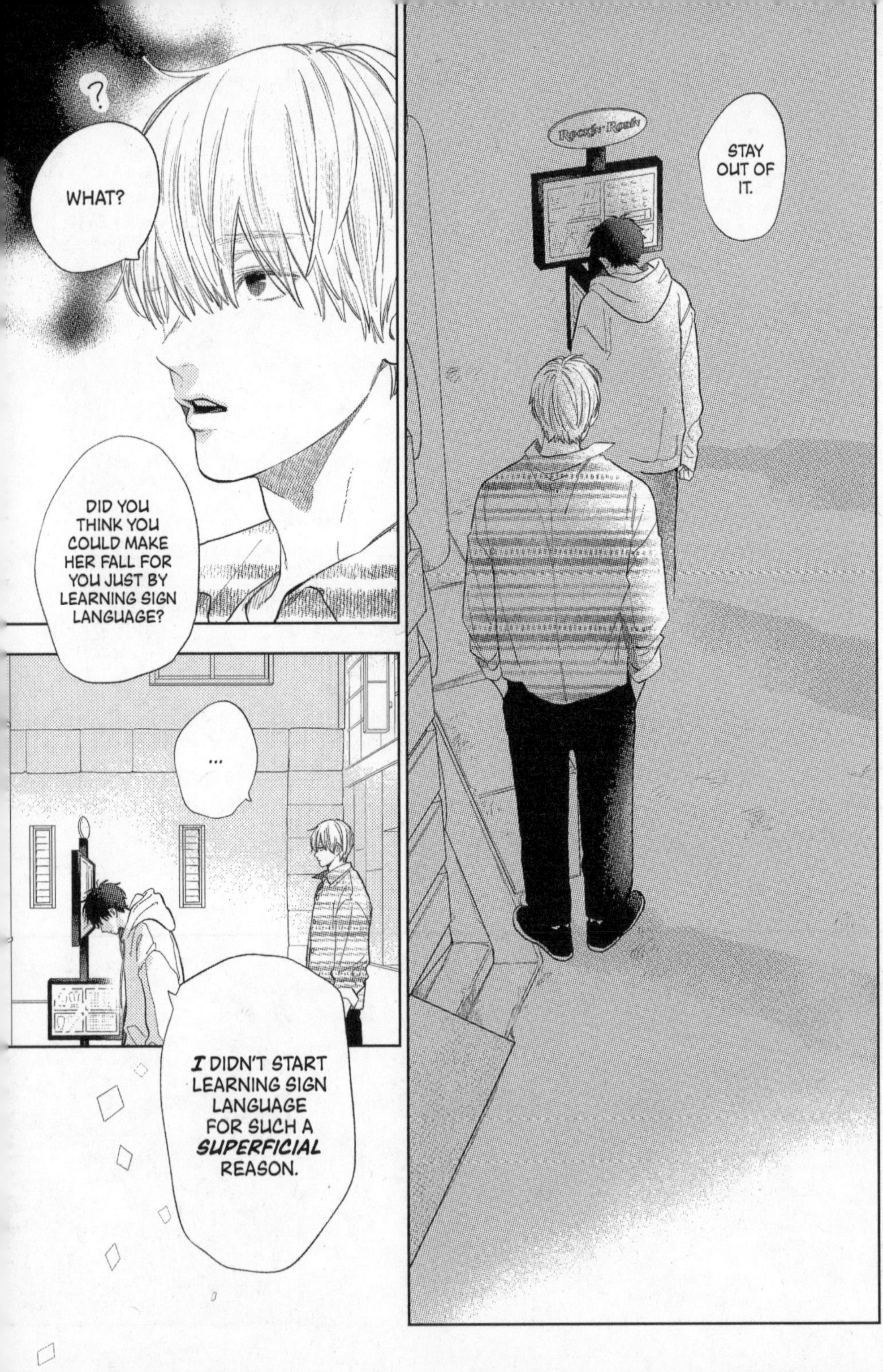
STAY OUT OF IT.
?
WHAT?
DID YOU THINK YOU COULD MAKE HER FALL FOR YOU JUST BY LEARNING SIGN LANGUAGE?
...
I DIDN'T START LEARNING SIGN LANGUAGE FOR SUCH A SUPERFICIAL REASON.

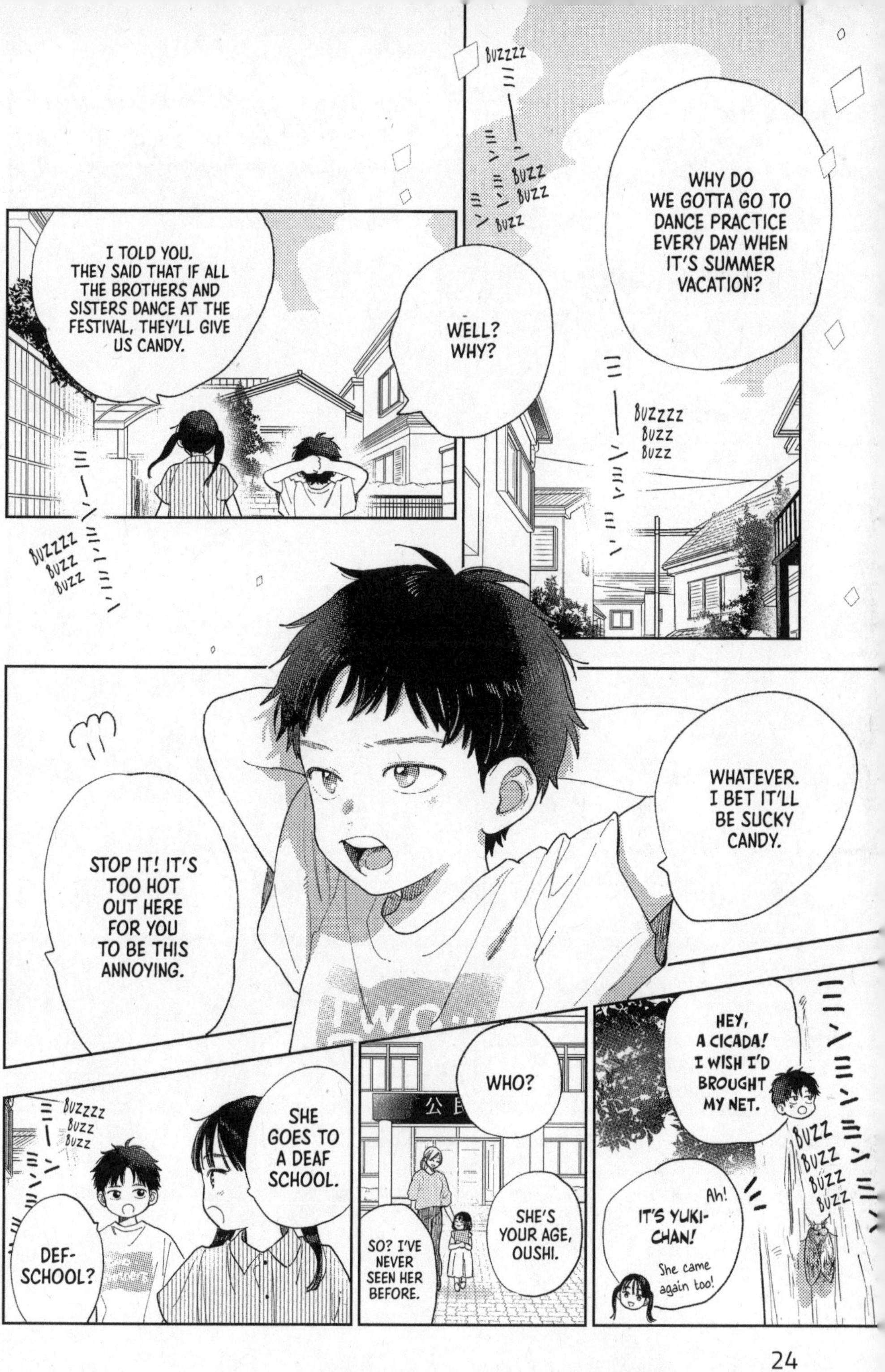
BUZZZZ
BUZZ
BUZZ
BUZZ
WHY DO WE GOTTA GO TO DANCE PRACTICE EVERY DAY WHEN IT'S SUMMER VACATION?
WELL? WHY?
BUZZZZ
BUZZ
BUZZ
I TOLD YOU. THEY SAID THAT IF ALL THE BROTHERS AND SISTERS DANCE AT THE FESTIVAL, THEY'LL GIVE US CANDY.
BUZZZZ
BUZZ
BUZZ
WHATEVER. I BET IT'LL BE SUCKY CANDY.
STOP IT! IT'S TOO HOT OUT HERE FOR YOU TO BE THIS ANNOYING.
HEY, A CICADA! I WISH I'D BROUGHT MY NET.
BUZZ
BUZZ
BUZZ
BUZZ
Ah!
IT'S YUKI-CHAN!
She came again too!
WHO?
SHE'S YOUR AGE, OUSHI.
SO? I'VE NEVER SEEN HER BEFORE.
SHE GOES TO A DEAF SCHOOL.
BUZZZZ
BUZZ
BUZZ
DEF-SCHOOL?

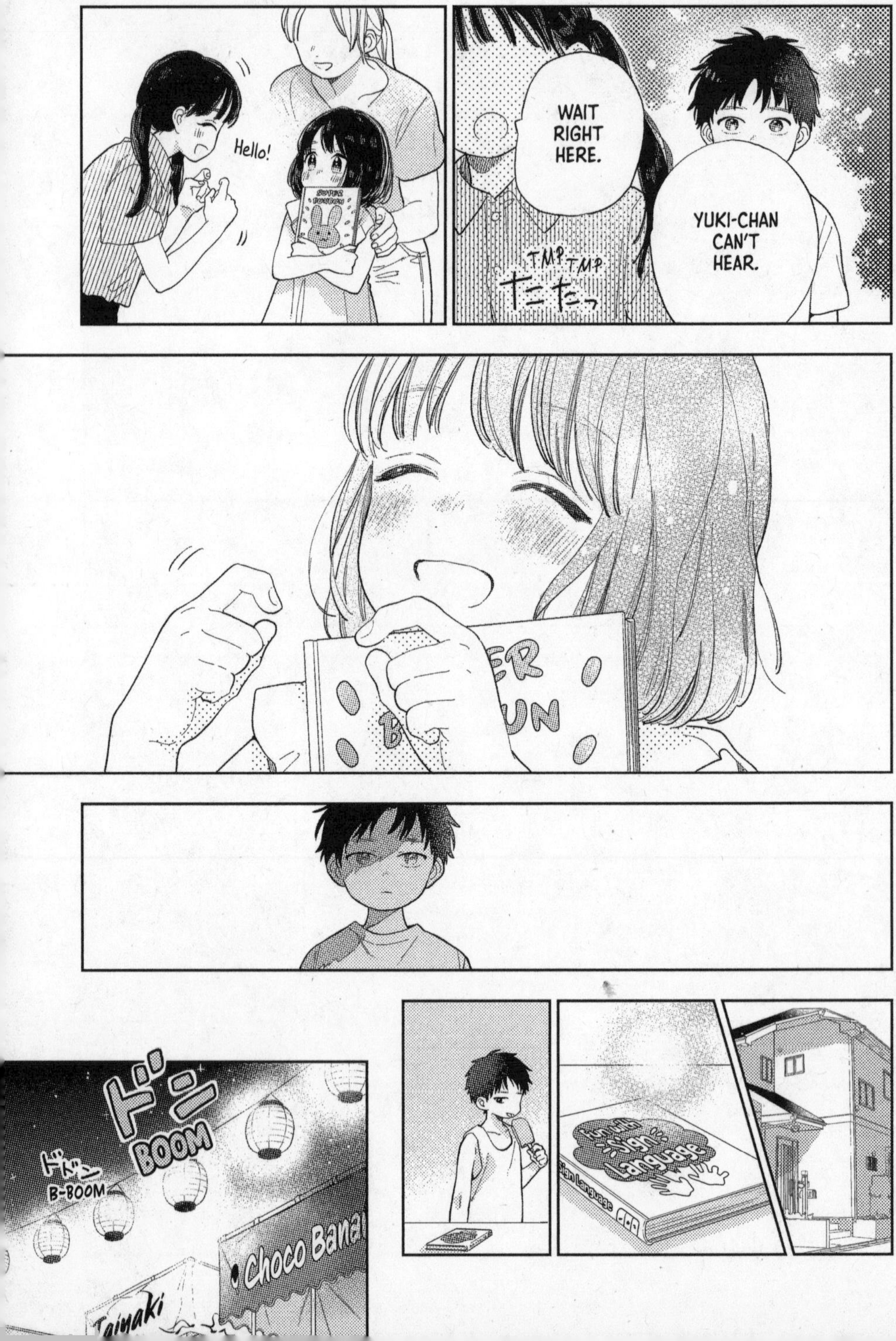
WAIT RIGHT HERE.
YUKI-CHAN CAN'T HEAR.
TMP TMP
Hello!
Fun with Sign Language
Sign Language
ドン
BOOM
ドドン
B-BOOM
Choco Bana
Taiyaki

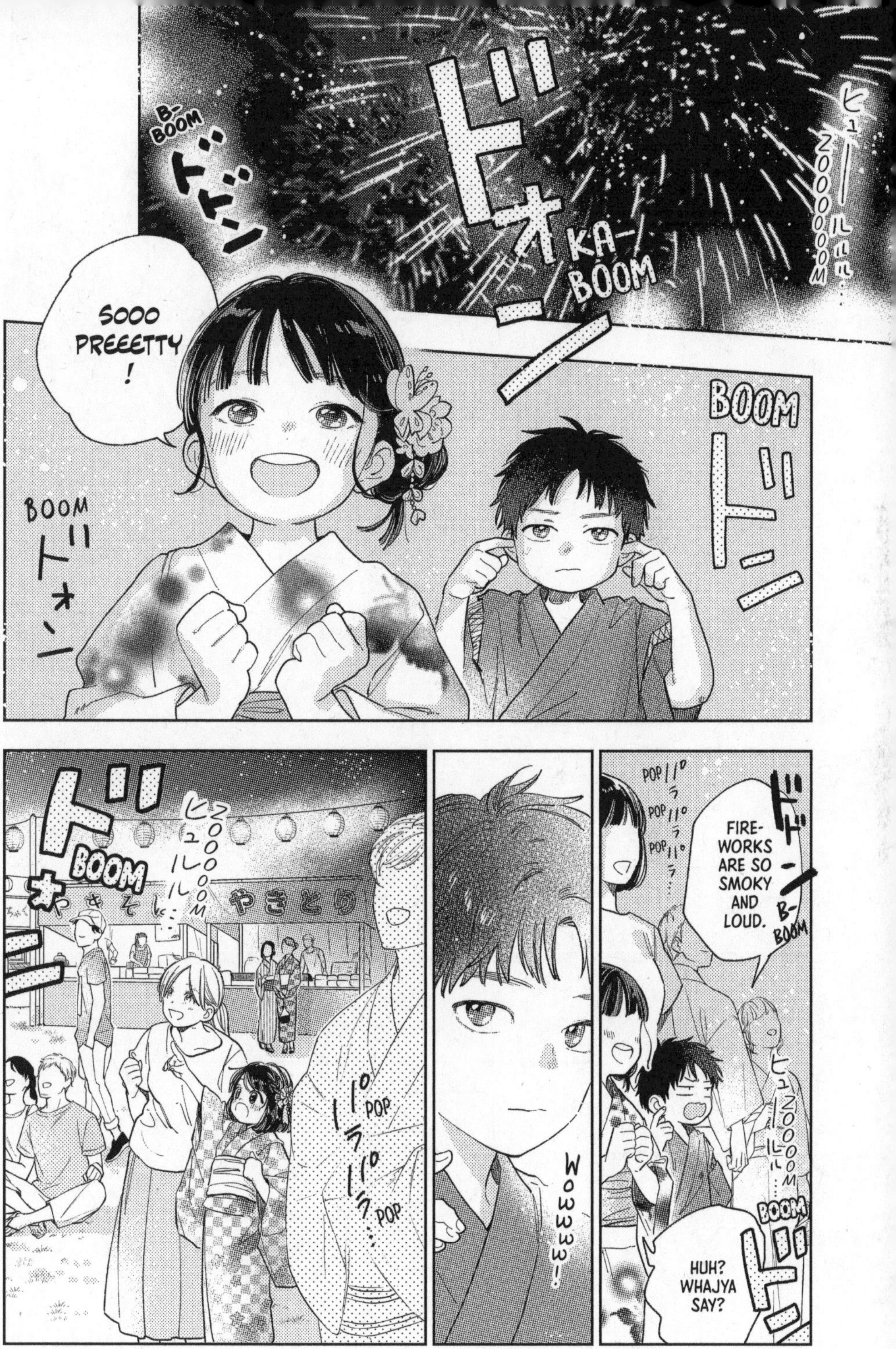
ZOOOOOOOM
KA-BOOM
B-BOOM
SOOO PREEETTY!
BOOM
BOOM
POP
POP
POP
FIRE-WORKS ARE SO SMOKY AND LOUD.
B-BOOM
ZOOOOOM
BOOM
HUH? WHAJYA SAY?
WOWWWW!
BOOM
ZOOOOOOOM
やきとり
POP
POP

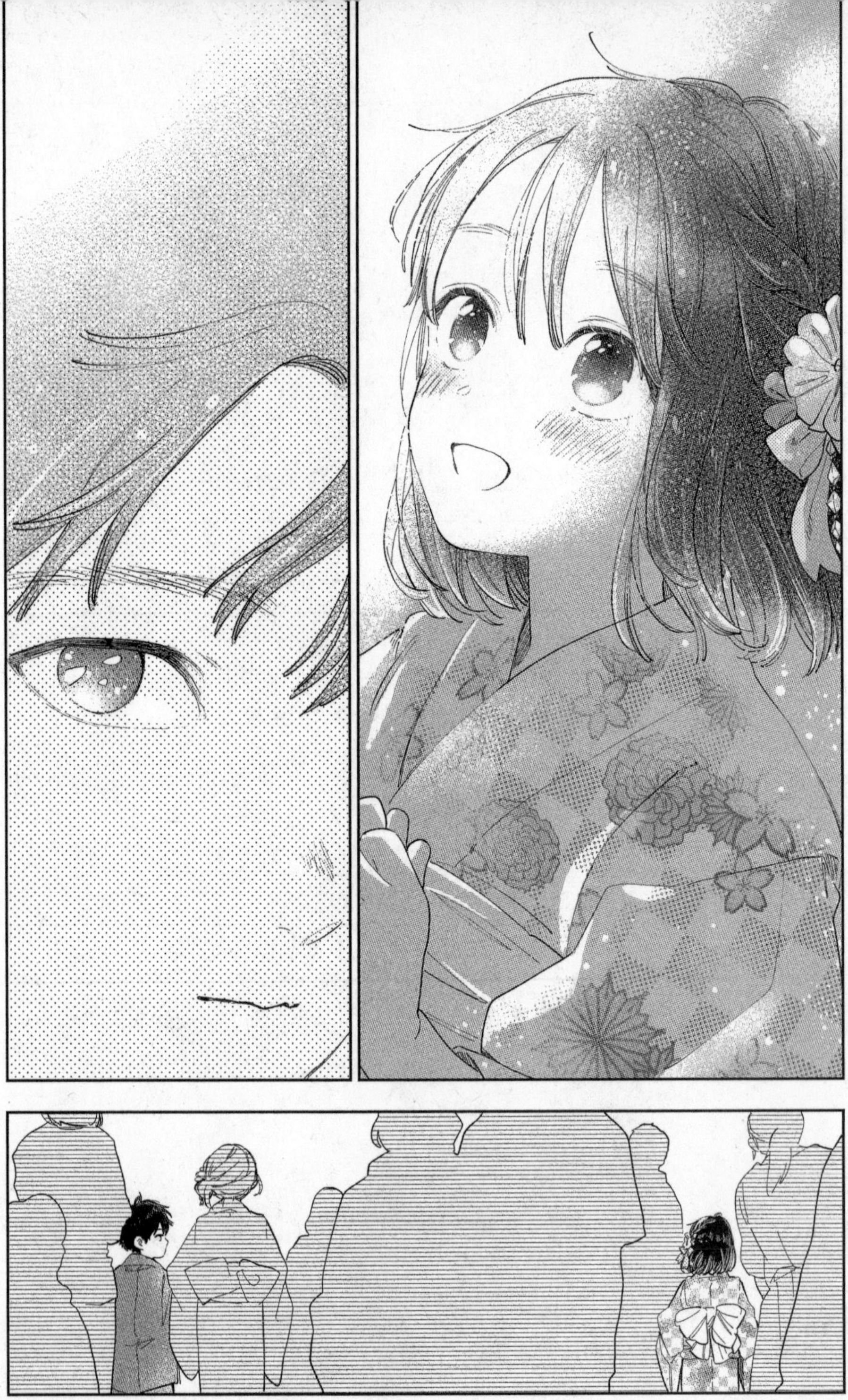

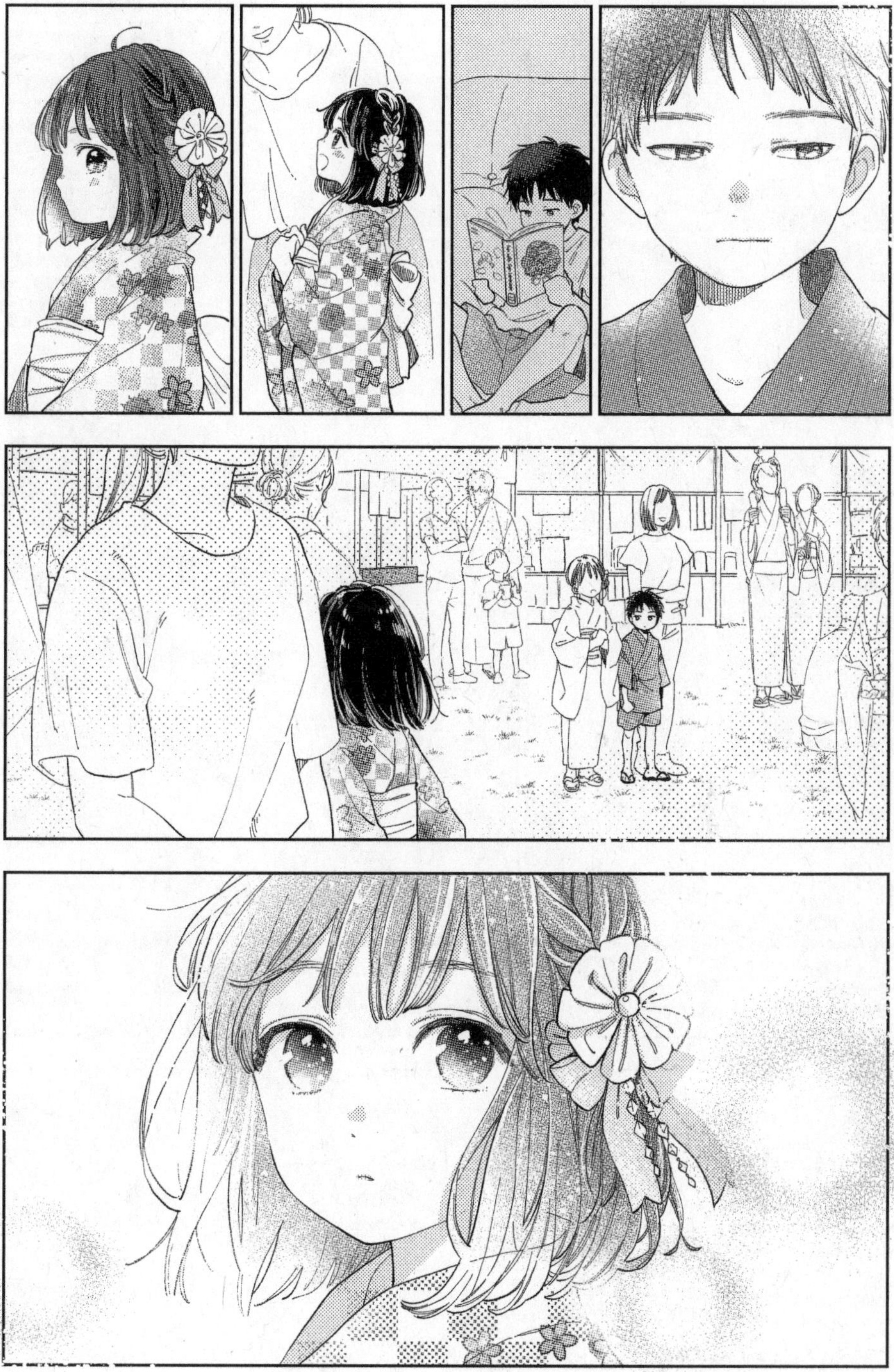

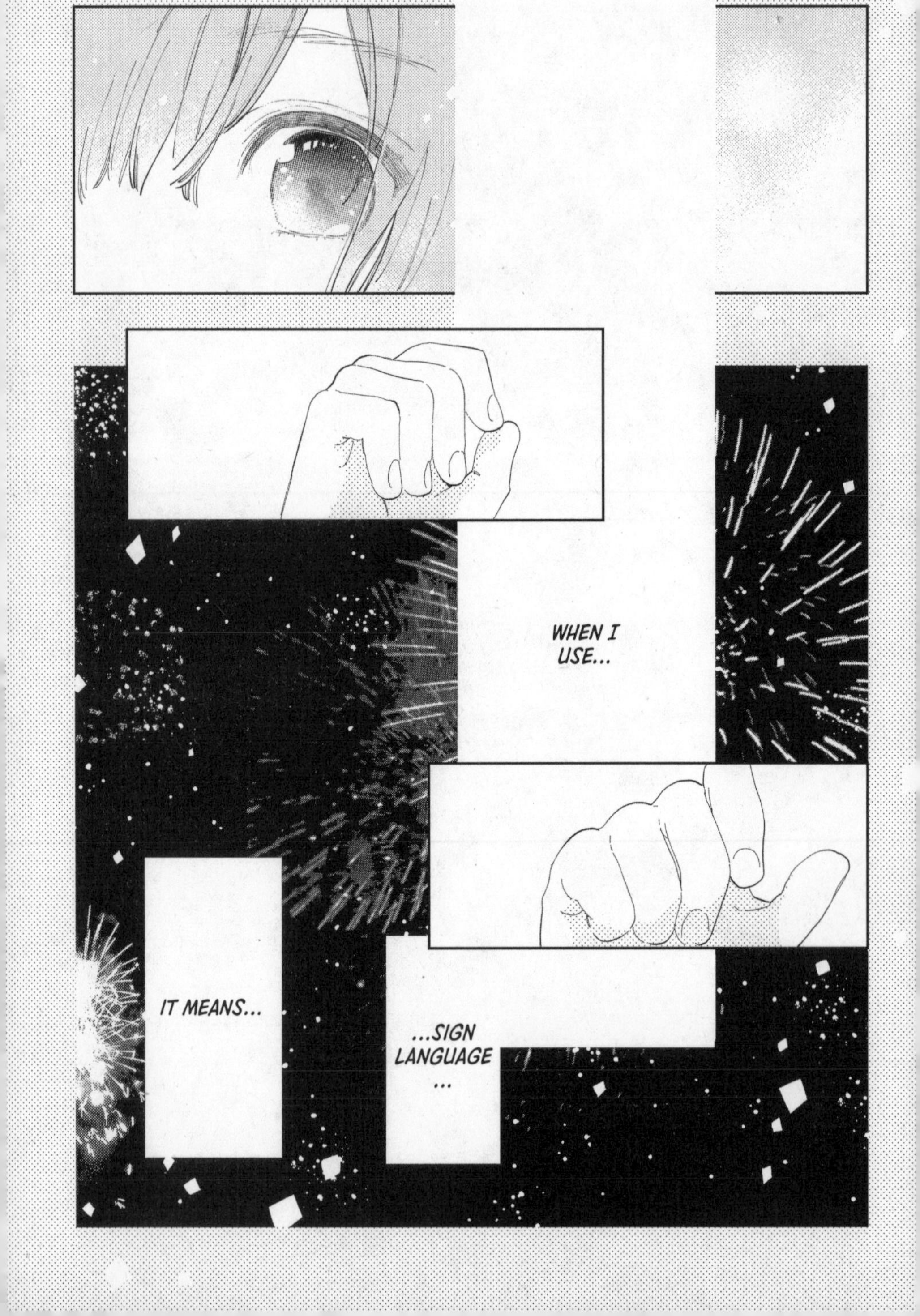
WHEN I USE...
...SIGN LANGUAGE ...
IT MEANS...

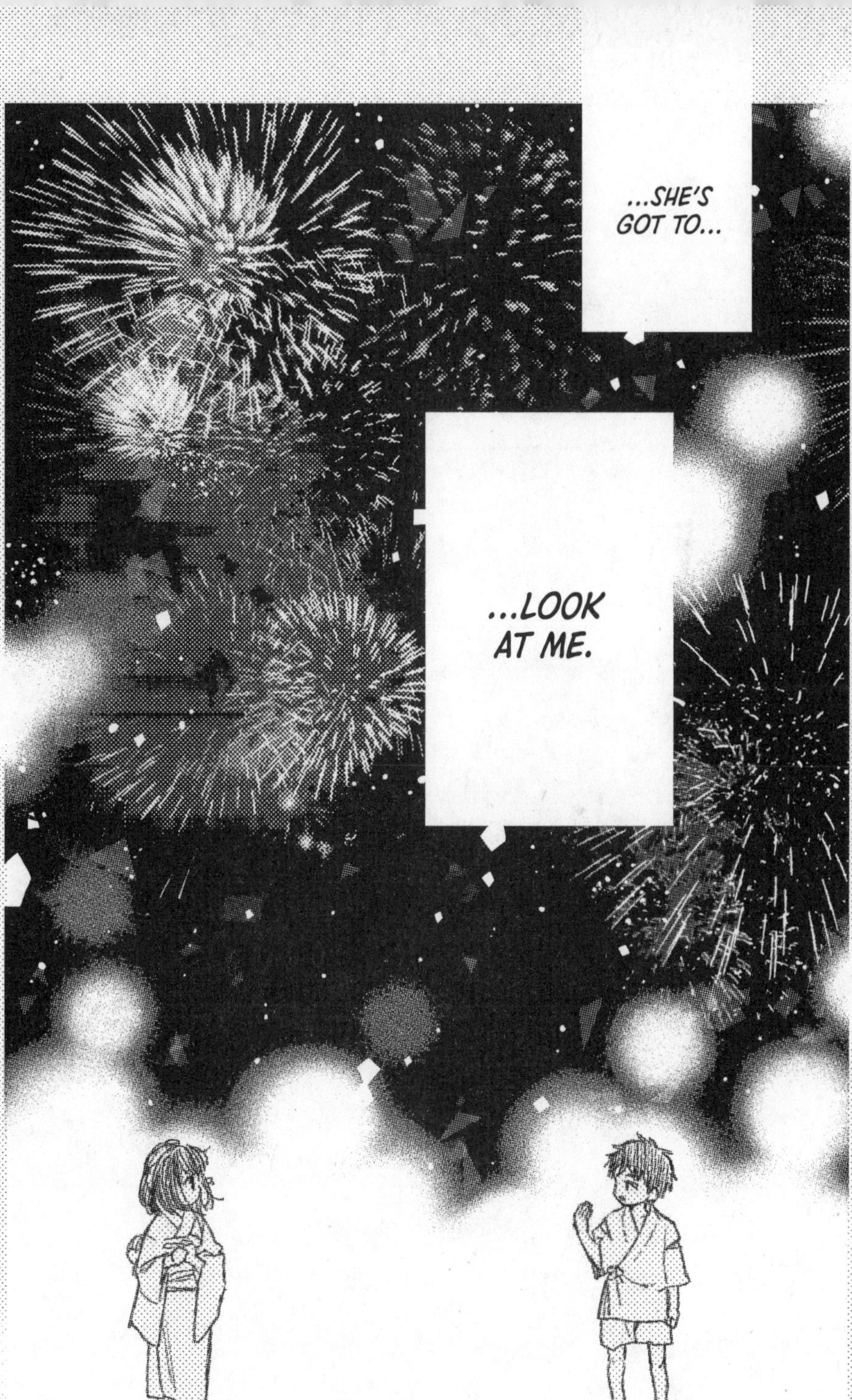
...SHE'S GOT TO...
...LOOK AT ME.

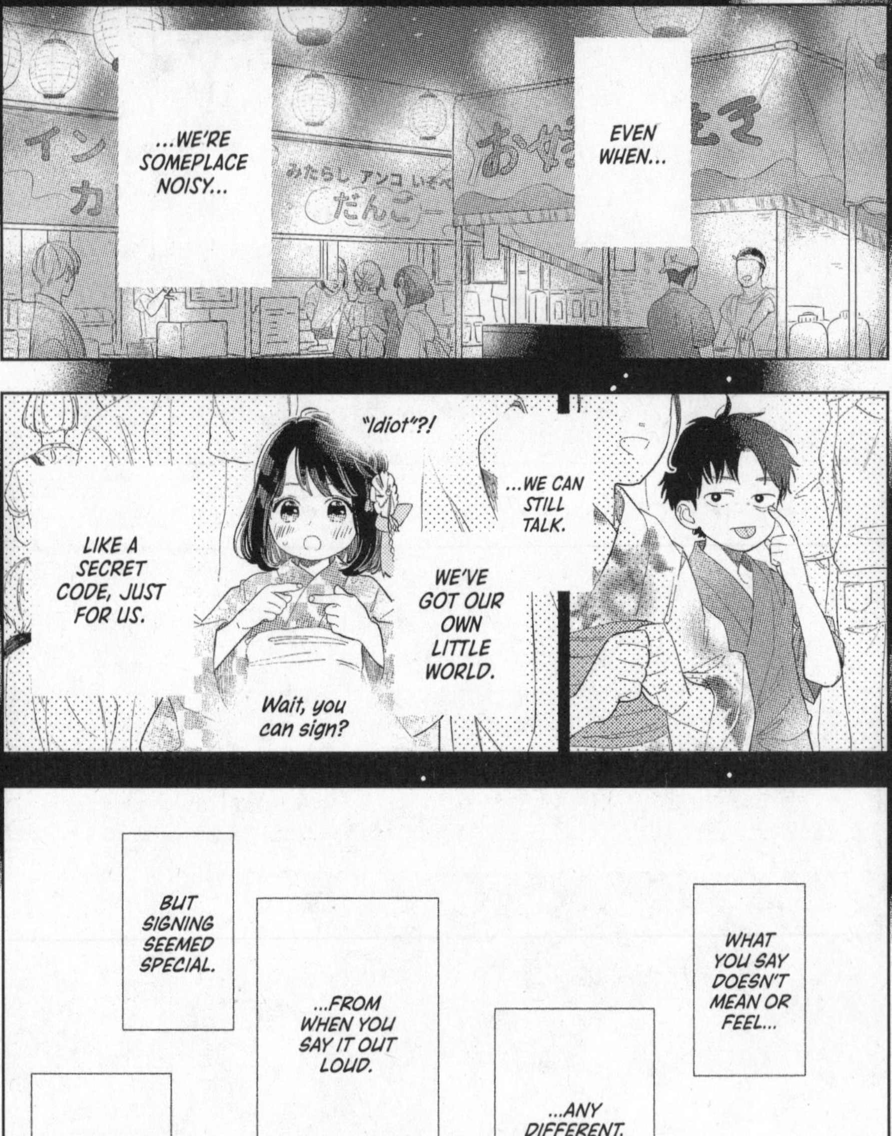
EVEN WHEN...
...WE'RE SOMEPLACE NOISY...
...WE CAN STILL TALK.
"Idiot"?!
WE'VE GOT OUR OWN LITTLE WORLD.
LIKE A SECRET CODE, JUST FOR US.
Wait, you can sign?
WHAT YOU SAY DOESN'T MEAN OR FEEL...
...ANY DIFFERENT, WHEN YOU SIGN IT...
...FROM WHEN YOU SAY IT OUT LOUD.
BUT SIGNING SEEMED SPECIAL.
AND THAT'S WHY I GOT INTO SIGN LANGUAGE.

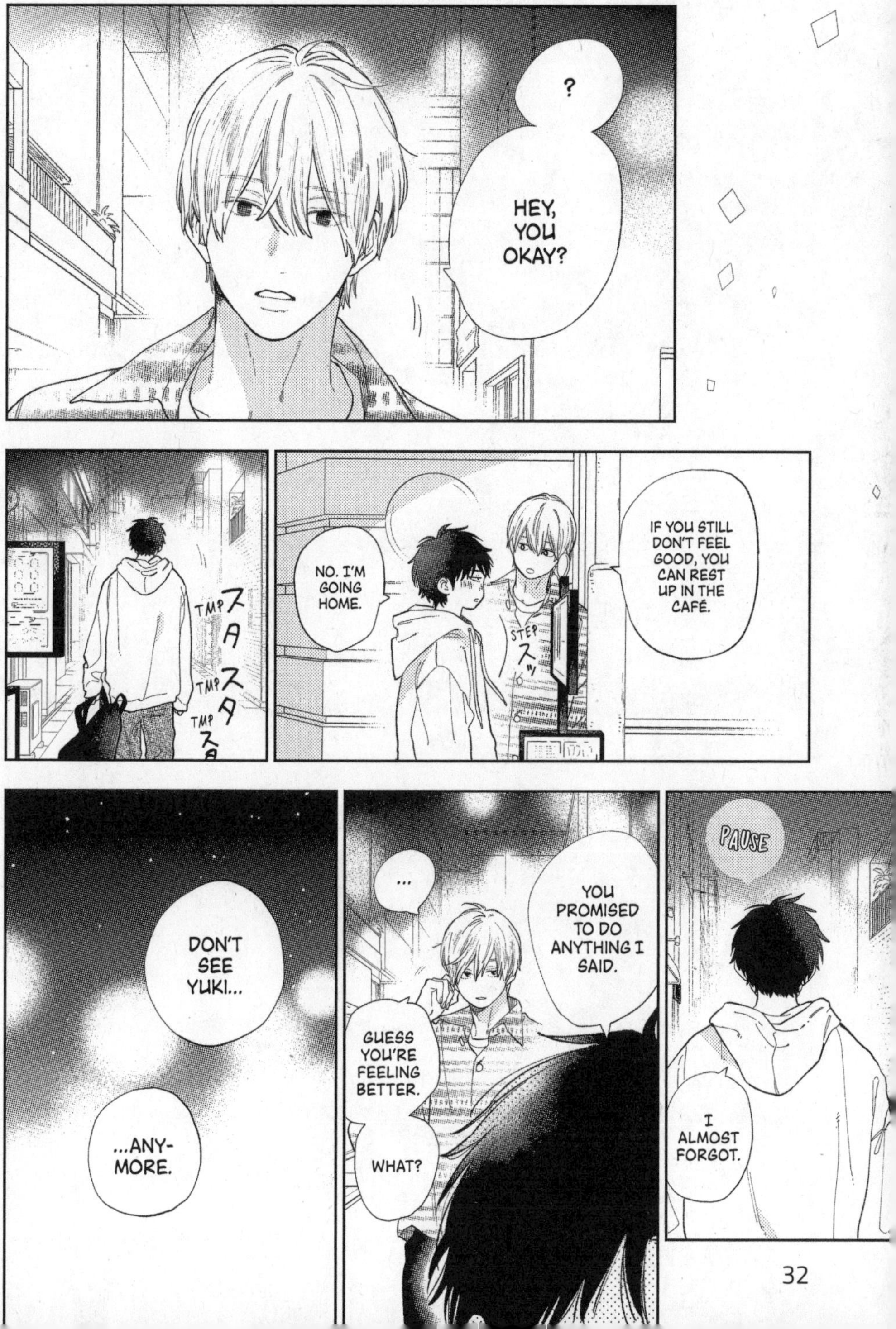
?
HEY, YOU OKAY?
IF YOU STILL DON'T FEEL GOOD, YOU CAN REST UP IN THE CAFÉ.
NO. I'M GOING HOME.
STEP
TMP TMP TMP
PAUSE
I ALMOST FORGOT.
YOU PROMISED TO DO ANYTHING I SAID.
...
GUESS YOU'RE FEELING BETTER.
WHAT?
DON'T SEE YUKI...
...ANY-MORE.

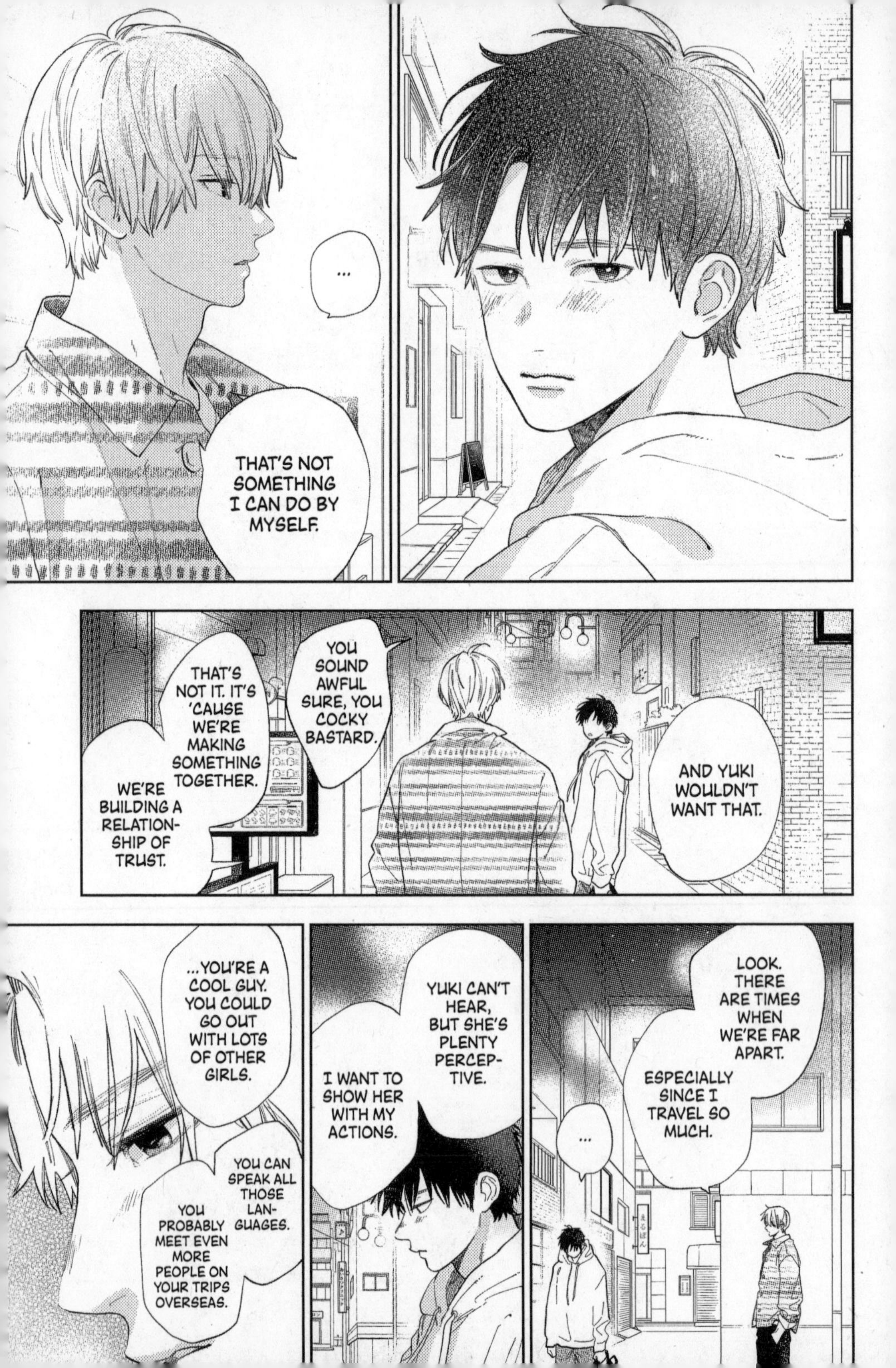
...
THAT'S NOT SOMETHING I CAN DO BY MYSELF.
AND YUKI WOULDN'T WANT THAT.
YOU SOUND AWFUL SURE, YOU COCKY BASTARD.
THAT'S NOT IT. IT'S 'CAUSE WE'RE MAKING SOMETHING TOGETHER.
WE'RE BUILDING A RELATIONSHIP OF TRUST.
LOOK. THERE ARE TIMES WHEN WE'RE FAR APART.
ESPECIALLY SINCE I TRAVEL SO MUCH.
...
YUKI CAN'T HEAR, BUT SHE'S PLENTY PERCEPTIVE.
I WANT TO SHOW HER WITH MY ACTIONS.
...YOU'RE A COOL GUY. YOU COULD GO OUT WITH LOTS OF OTHER GIRLS.
YOU CAN SPEAK ALL THOSE LANGUAGES.
YOU PROBABLY MEET EVEN MORE PEOPLE ON YOUR TRIPS OVERSEAS.

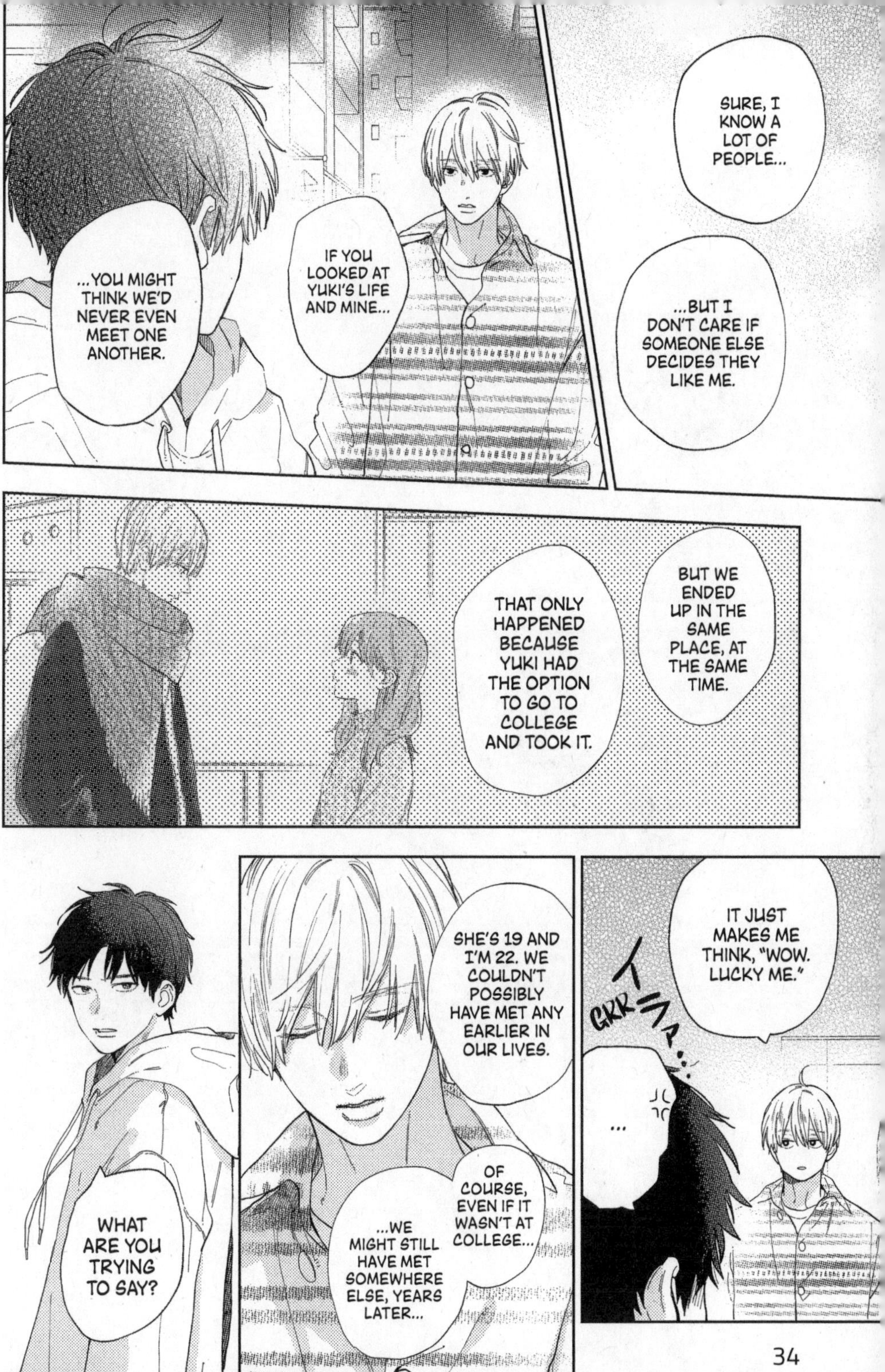
SURE, I KNOW A LOT OF PEOPLE...
...BUT I DON'T CARE IF SOMEONE ELSE DECIDES THEY LIKE ME.
IF YOU LOOKED AT YUKI'S LIFE AND MINE...
...YOU MIGHT THINK WE'D NEVER EVEN MEET ONE ANOTHER.
BUT WE ENDED UP IN THE SAME PLACE, AT THE SAME TIME.
THAT ONLY HAPPENED BECAUSE YUKI HAD THE OPTION TO GO TO COLLEGE AND TOOK IT.
IT JUST MAKES ME THINK, "WOW. LUCKY ME."
GRR
...
SHE'S 19 AND I'M 22. WE COULDN'T POSSIBLY HAVE MET ANY EARLIER IN OUR LIVES.
OF COURSE, EVEN IF IT WASN'T AT COLLEGE...
...WE MIGHT STILL HAVE MET SOMEWHERE ELSE, YEARS LATER...
WHAT ARE YOU TRYING TO SAY?

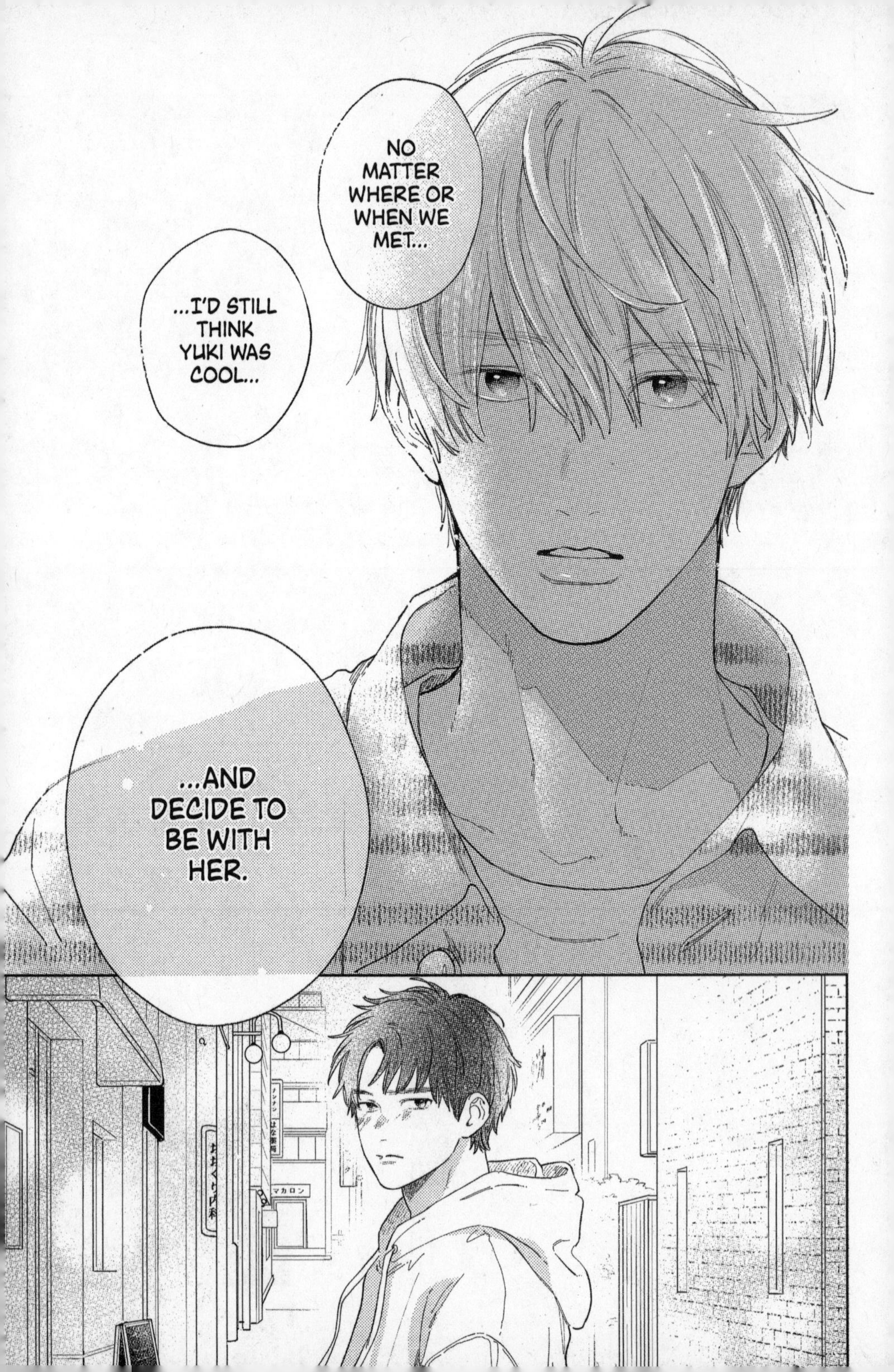
NO MATTER WHERE OR WHEN WE MET...
...I'D STILL THINK YUKI WAS COOL...
...AND DECIDE TO BE WITH HER.
マカロン

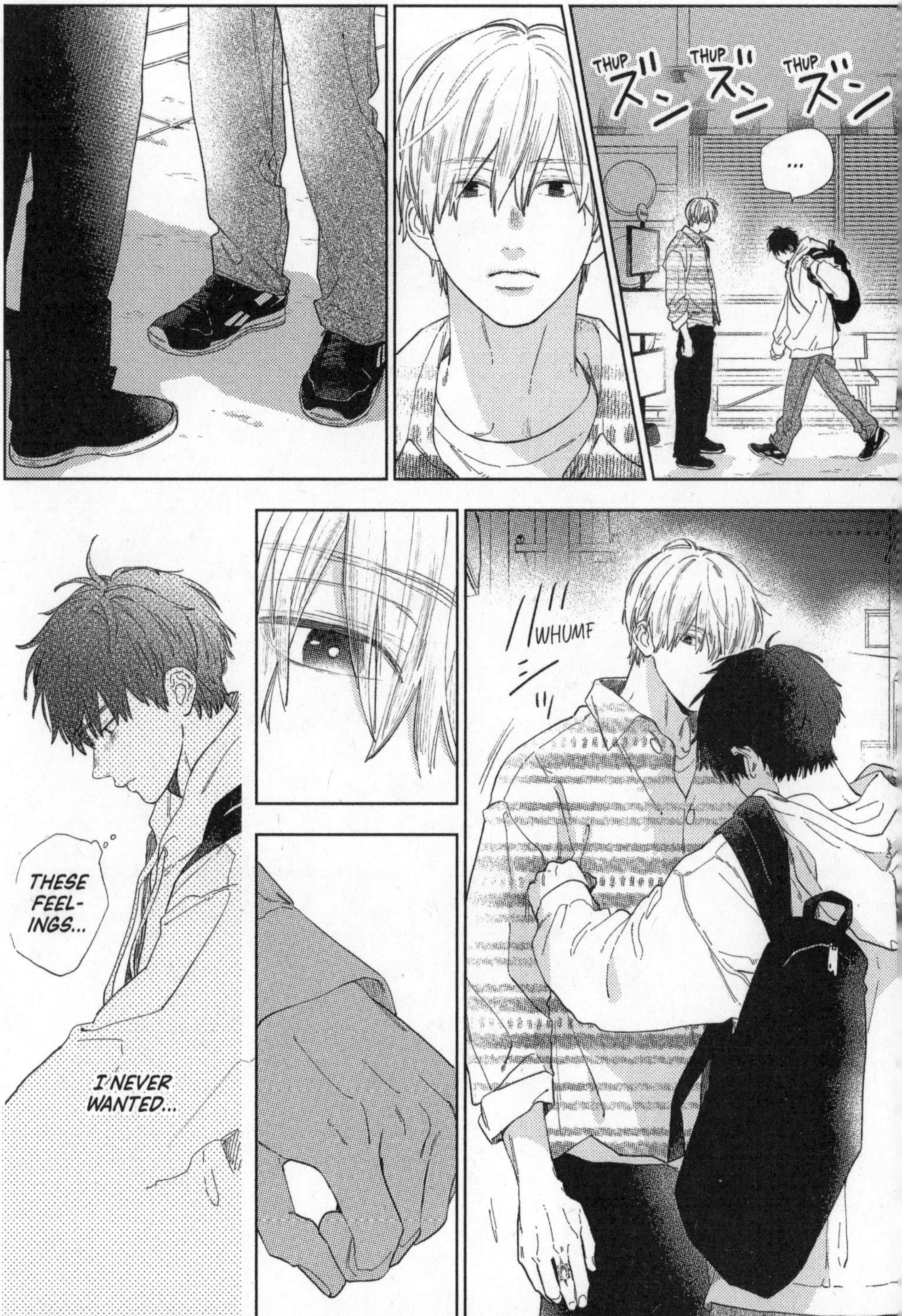
THUP ズン
THUP ズン
THUP ズン
...
WHUMF
THESE FEEL-INGS...
I NEVER WANTED...

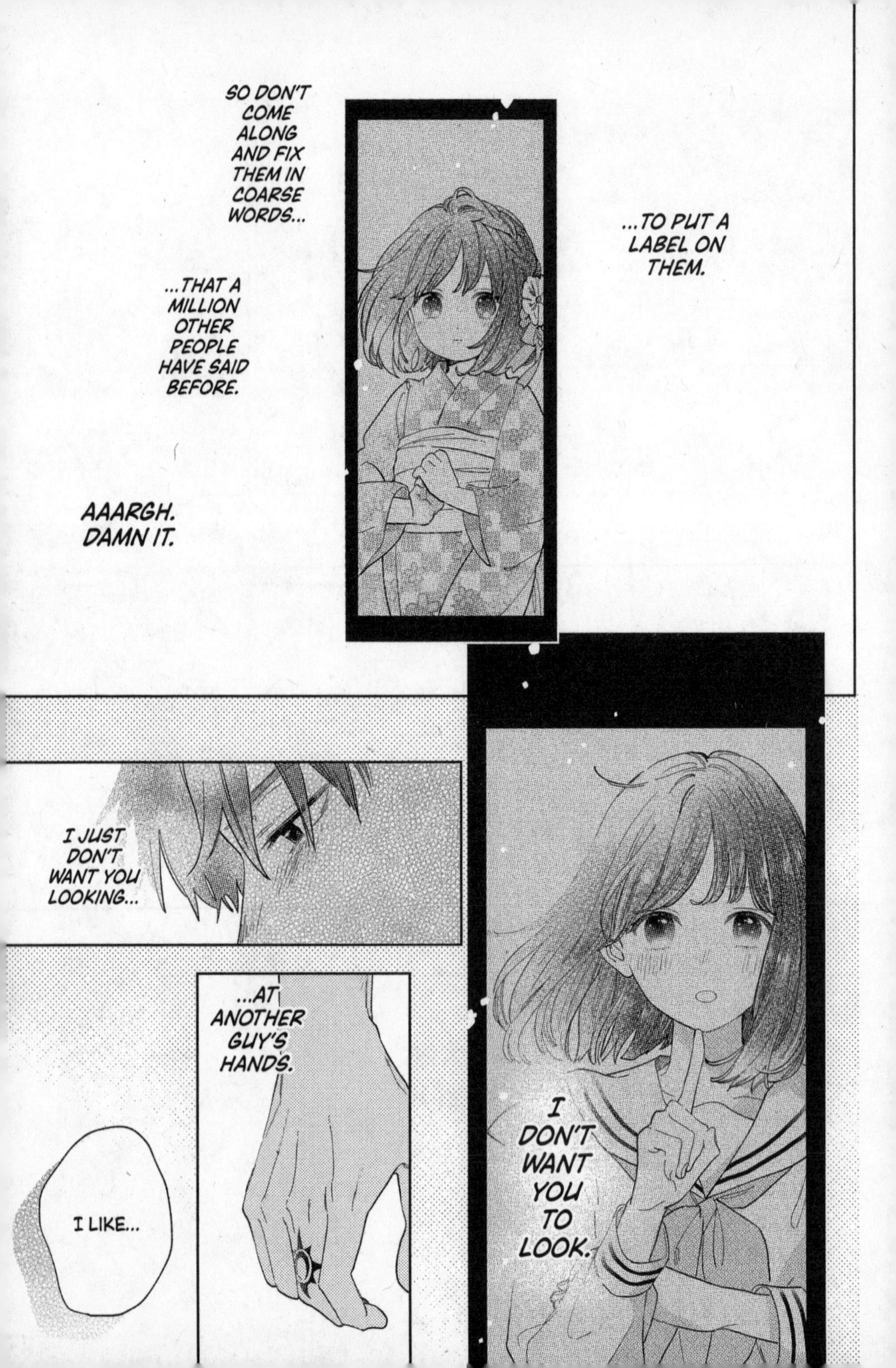
...TO PUT A LABEL ON THEM.
SO DON'T COME ALONG AND FIX THEM IN COARSE WORDS...
...THAT A MILLION OTHER PEOPLE HAVE SAID BEFORE.
AAARGH. DAMN IT.
I DON'T WANT YOU TO LOOK.
I JUST DON'T WANT YOU LOOKING...
...AT ANOTHER GUY'S HANDS.
I LIKE...

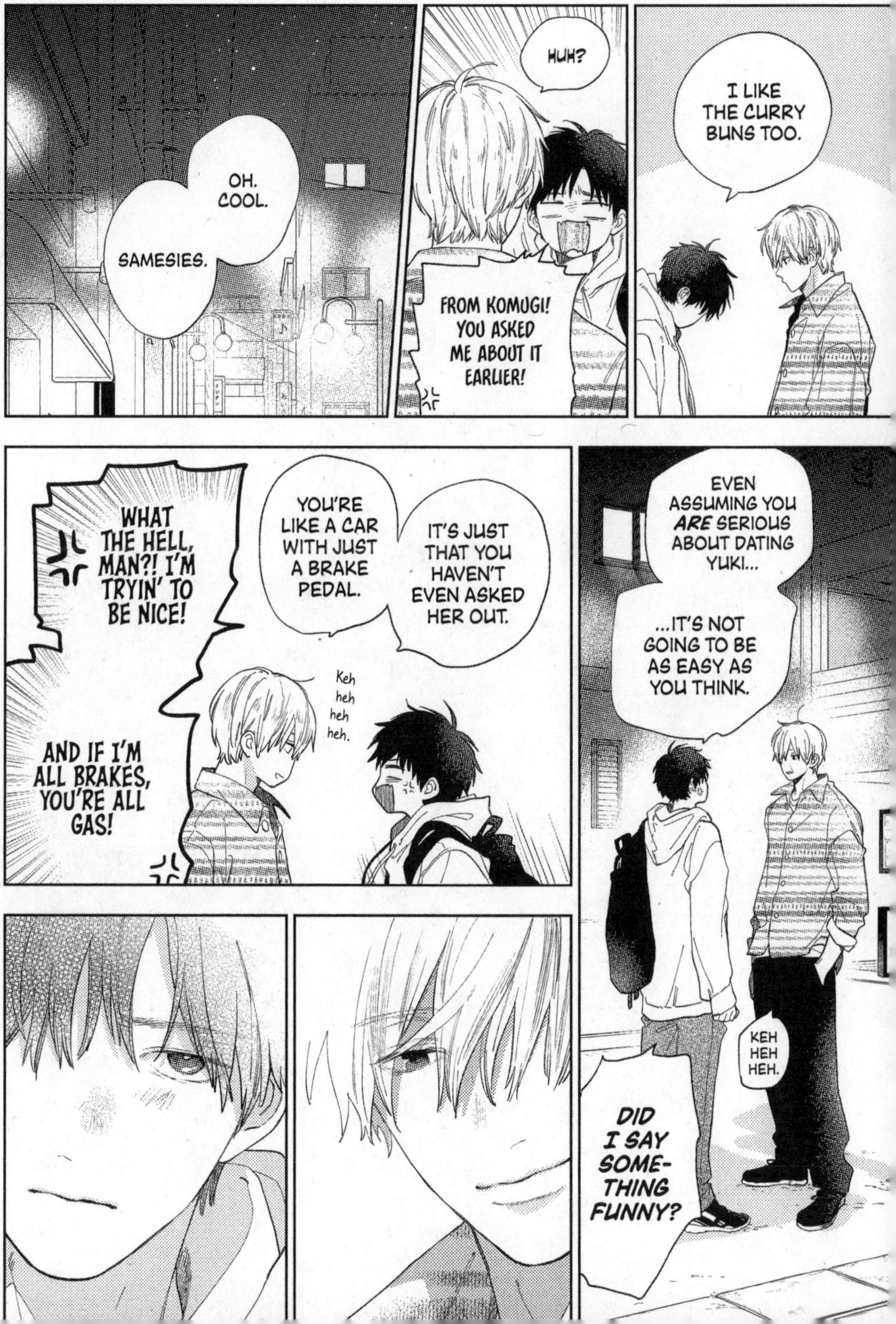
I LIKE THE CURRY BUNS TOO.
HUH?
FROM KOMUGI! YOU ASKED ME ABOUT IT EARLIER!
OH. COOL.
SAMESIES.
EVEN ASSUMING YOU *ARE* SERIOUS ABOUT DATING YUKI...
...IT'S NOT GOING TO BE AS EASY AS YOU THINK.
KEH HEH HEH.
DID I SAY SOMETHING FUNNY?
IT'S JUST THAT YOU HAVEN'T EVEN ASKED HER OUT.
YOU'RE LIKE A CAR WITH JUST A BRAKE PEDAL.
Keh heh heh heh.
WHAT THE HELL, MAN?! I'M TRYIN' TO BE NICE!
AND IF I'M ALL BRAKES, YOU'RE ALL GAS!

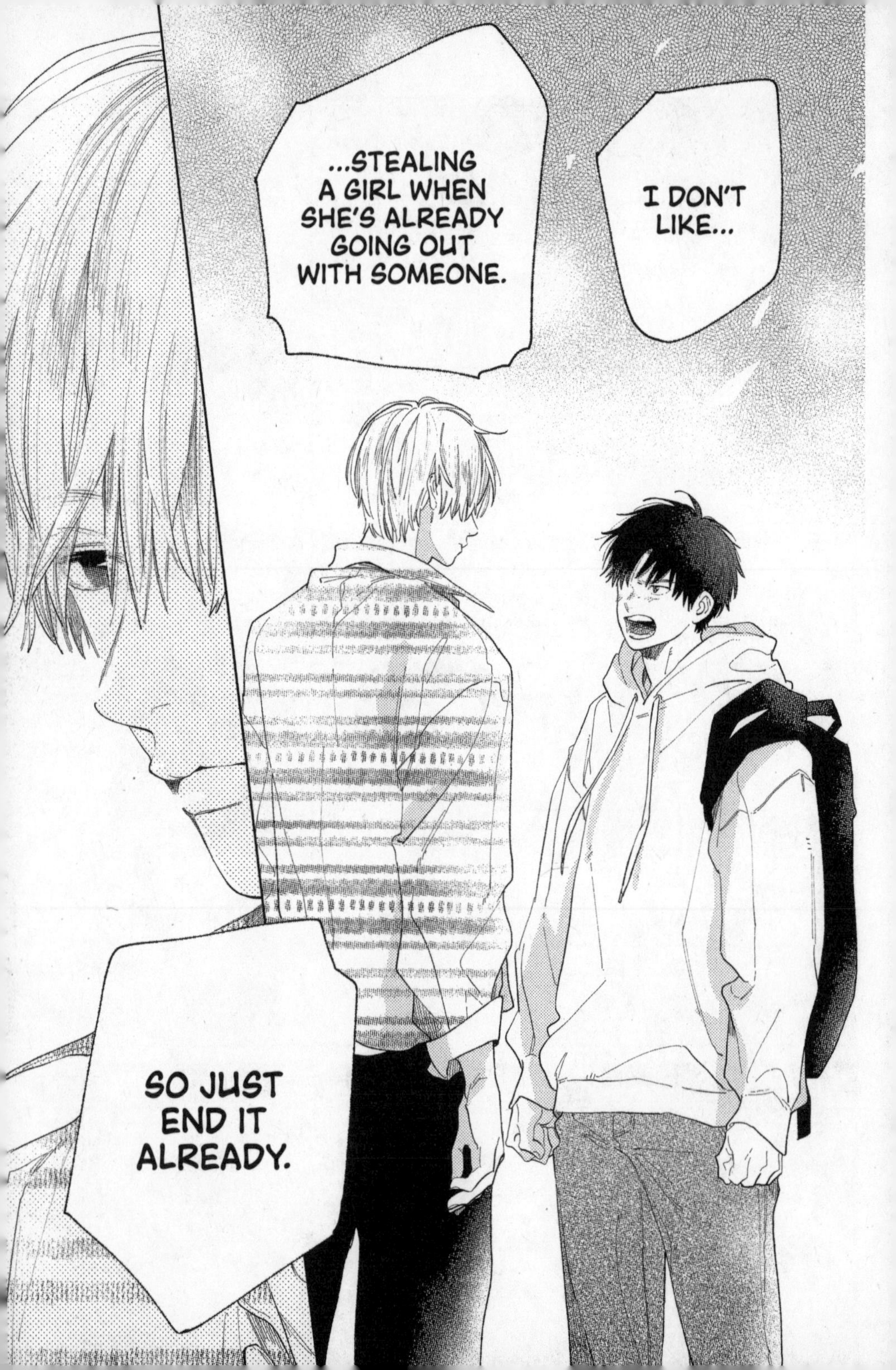
I DON'T LIKE...
...STEALING A GIRL WHEN SHE'S ALREADY GOING OUT WITH SOMEONE.
SO JUST END IT ALREADY.

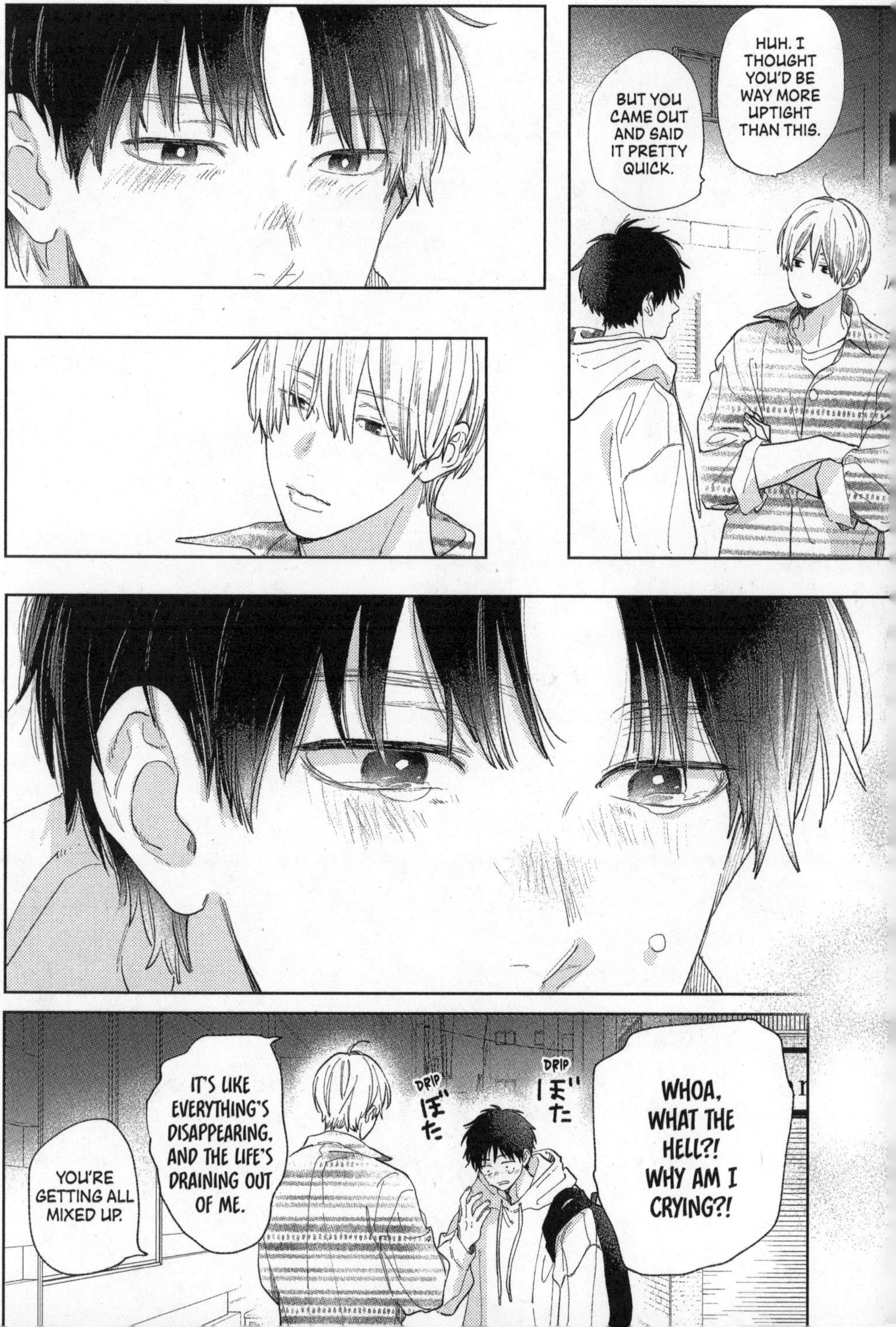
HUH. I THOUGHT YOU'D BE WAY MORE UPTIGHT THAN THIS.
BUT YOU CAME OUT AND SAID IT PRETTY QUICK.
WHOA, WHAT THE HELL?! WHY AM I CRYING?!
DRIP
ぼた
DRIP
ぼた
IT'S LIKE EVERYTHING'S DISAPPEARING, AND THE LIFE'S DRAINING OUT OF ME.
YOU'RE GETTING ALL MIXED UP.

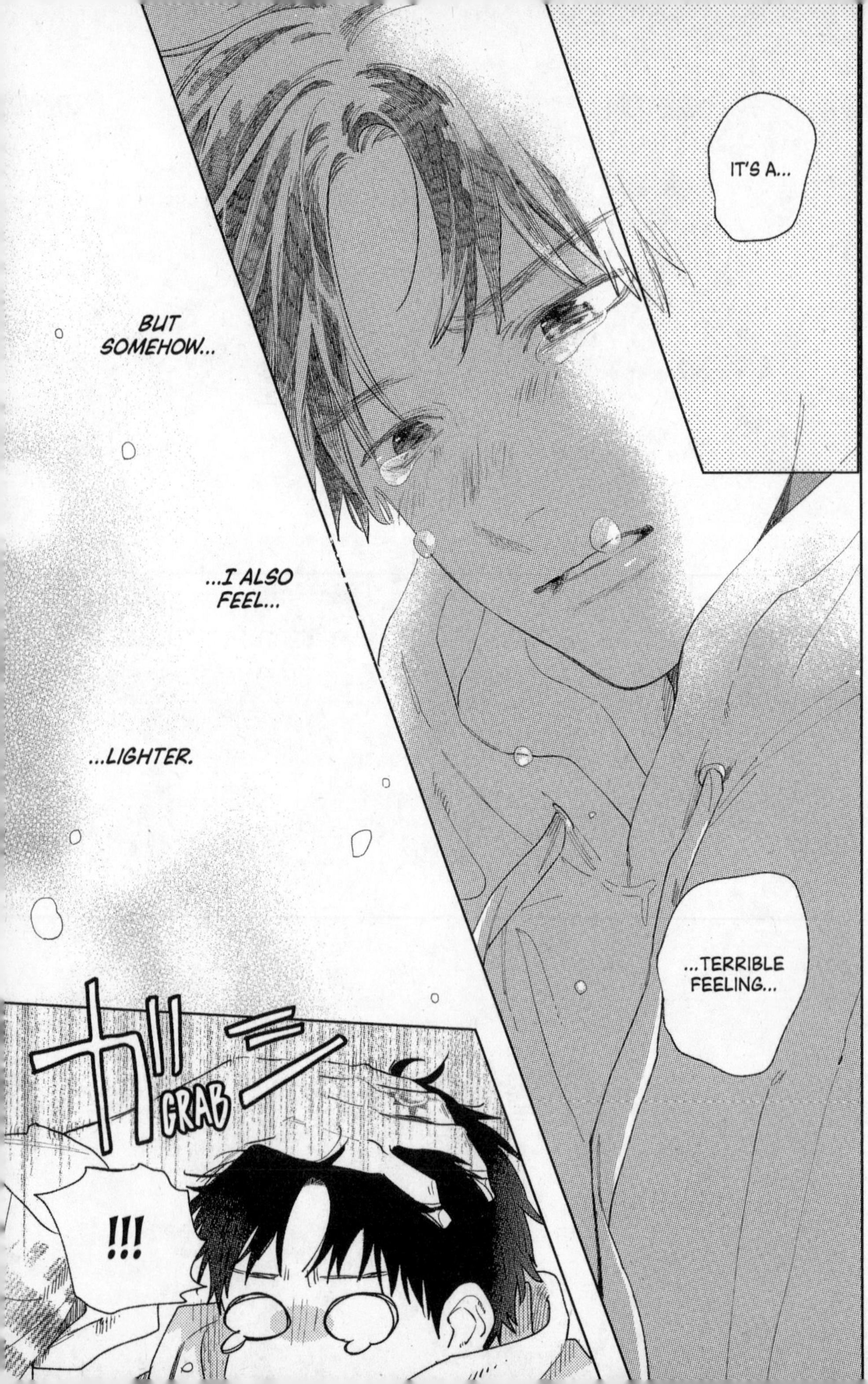

IT'S A...
...TERRIBLE FEELING...
BUT SOMEHOW...
...I ALSO FEEL...
...LIGHTER.
GRAB
!!!

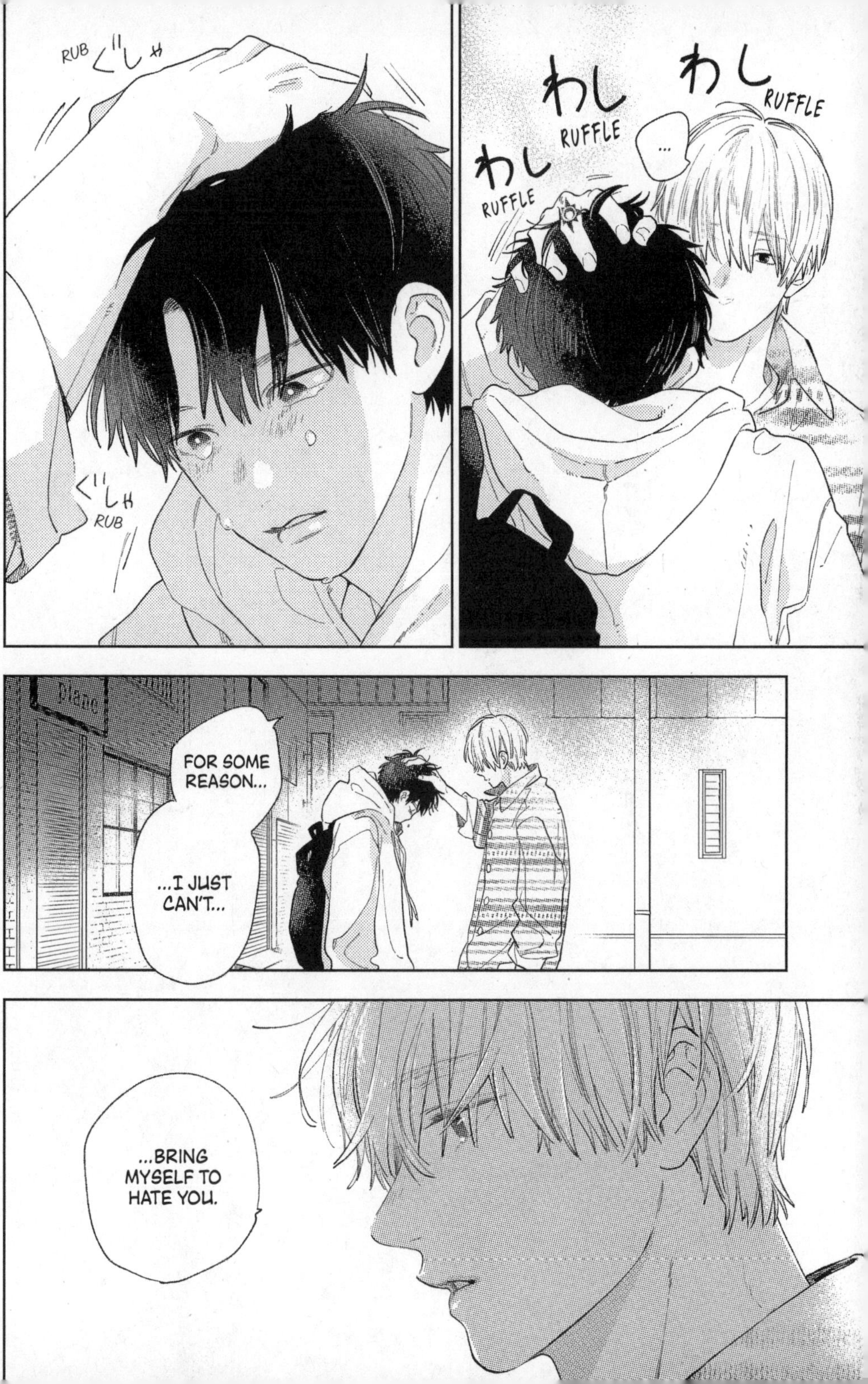
わし
RUFFLE
...
わし
RUFFLE
わし
RUFFLE
RUB
ぐしゃ
ぐしゃ
RUB
FOR SOME REASON...
...I JUST CAN'T...
...BRING MYSELF TO HATE YOU.

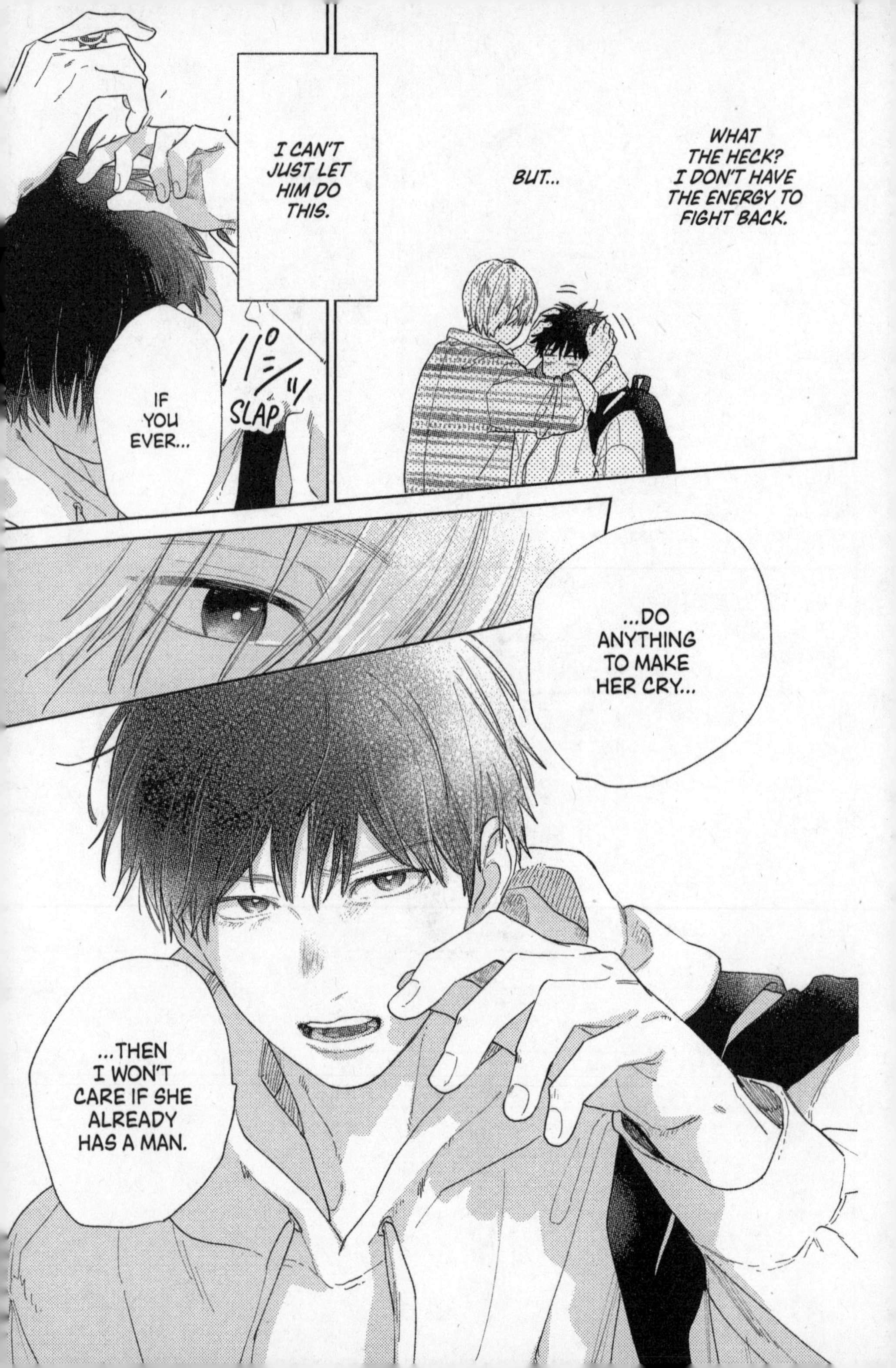
WHAT THE HECK? I DON'T HAVE THE ENERGY TO FIGHT BACK.
BUT...
I CAN'T JUST LET HIM DO THIS.
SLAP
IF YOU EVER...
...DO ANYTHING TO MAKE HER CRY...
...THEN I WON'T CARE IF SHE ALREADY HAS A MAN.

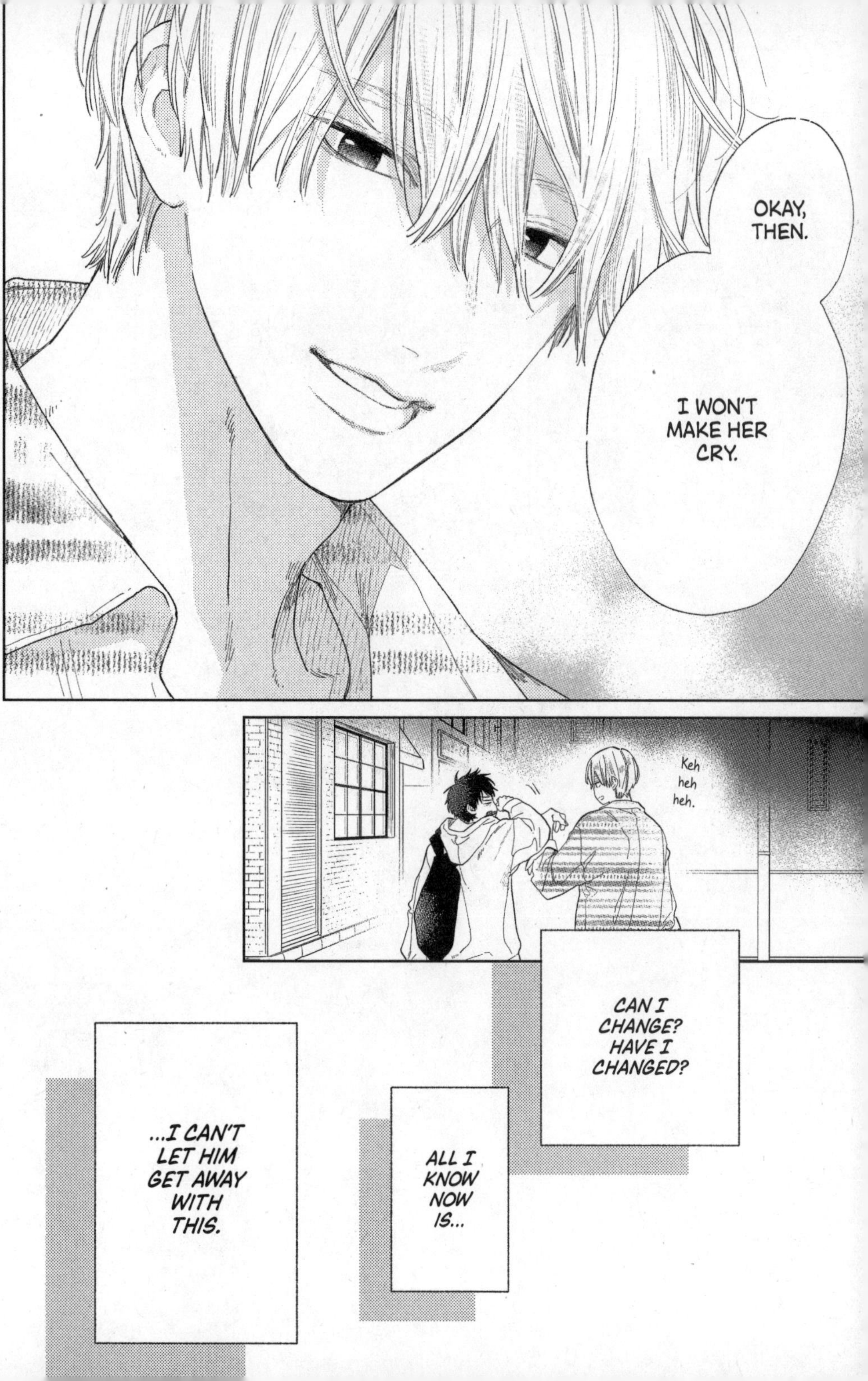
OKAY, THEN.
I WON'T MAKE HER CRY.
Keh heh heh.
CAN I CHANGE? HAVE I CHANGED?
ALL I KNOW NOW IS...
...I CAN'T LET HIM GET AWAY WITH THIS.

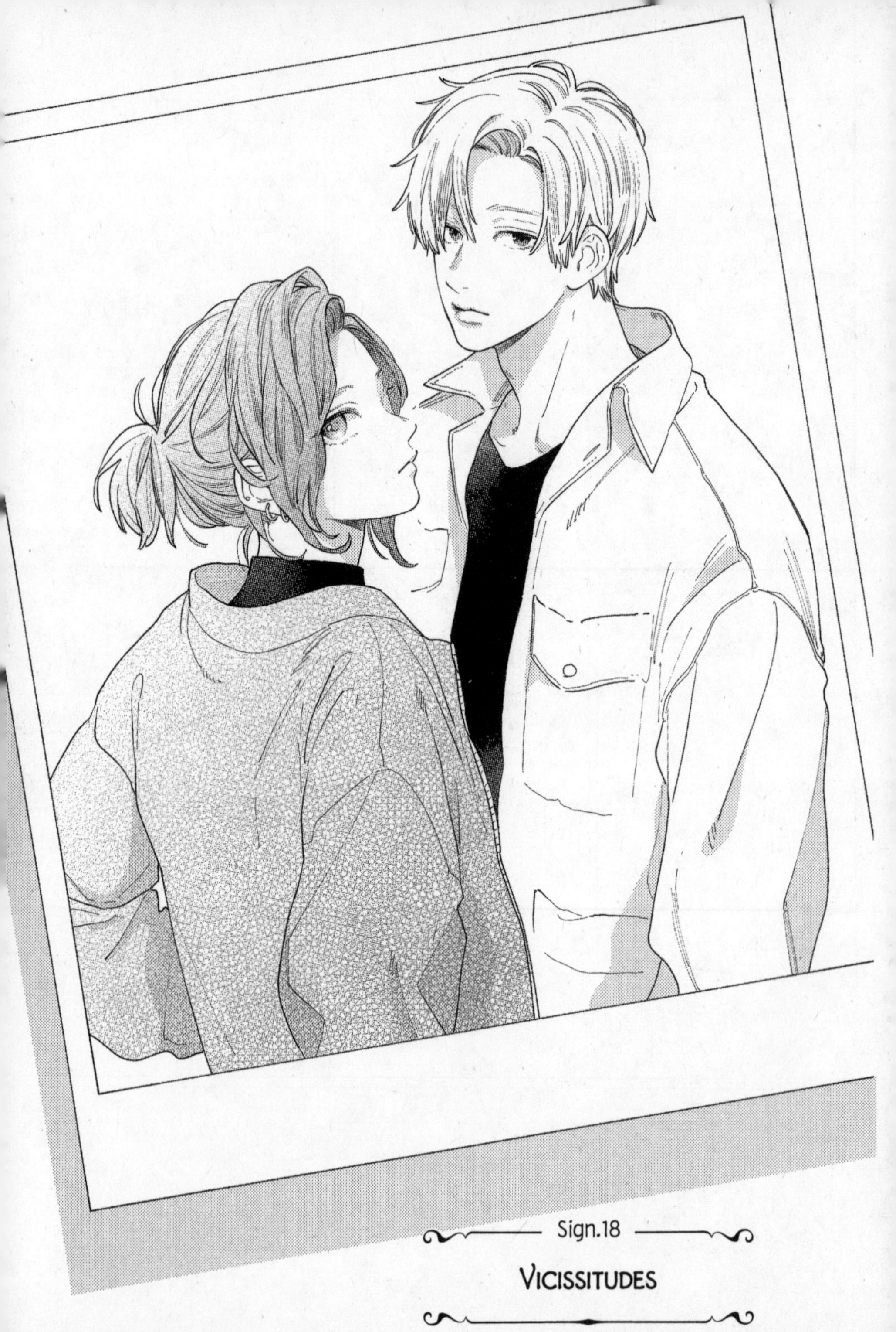

Sign.18

Vicissitudes

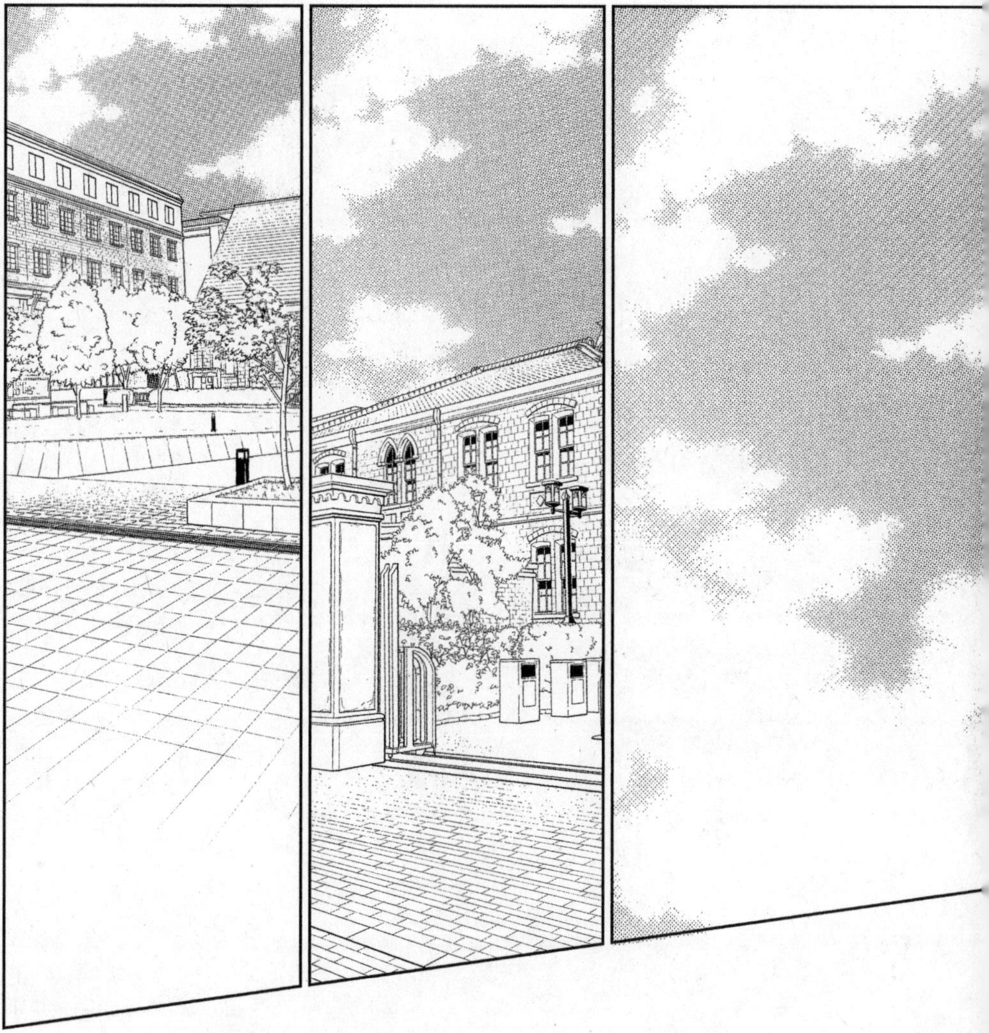

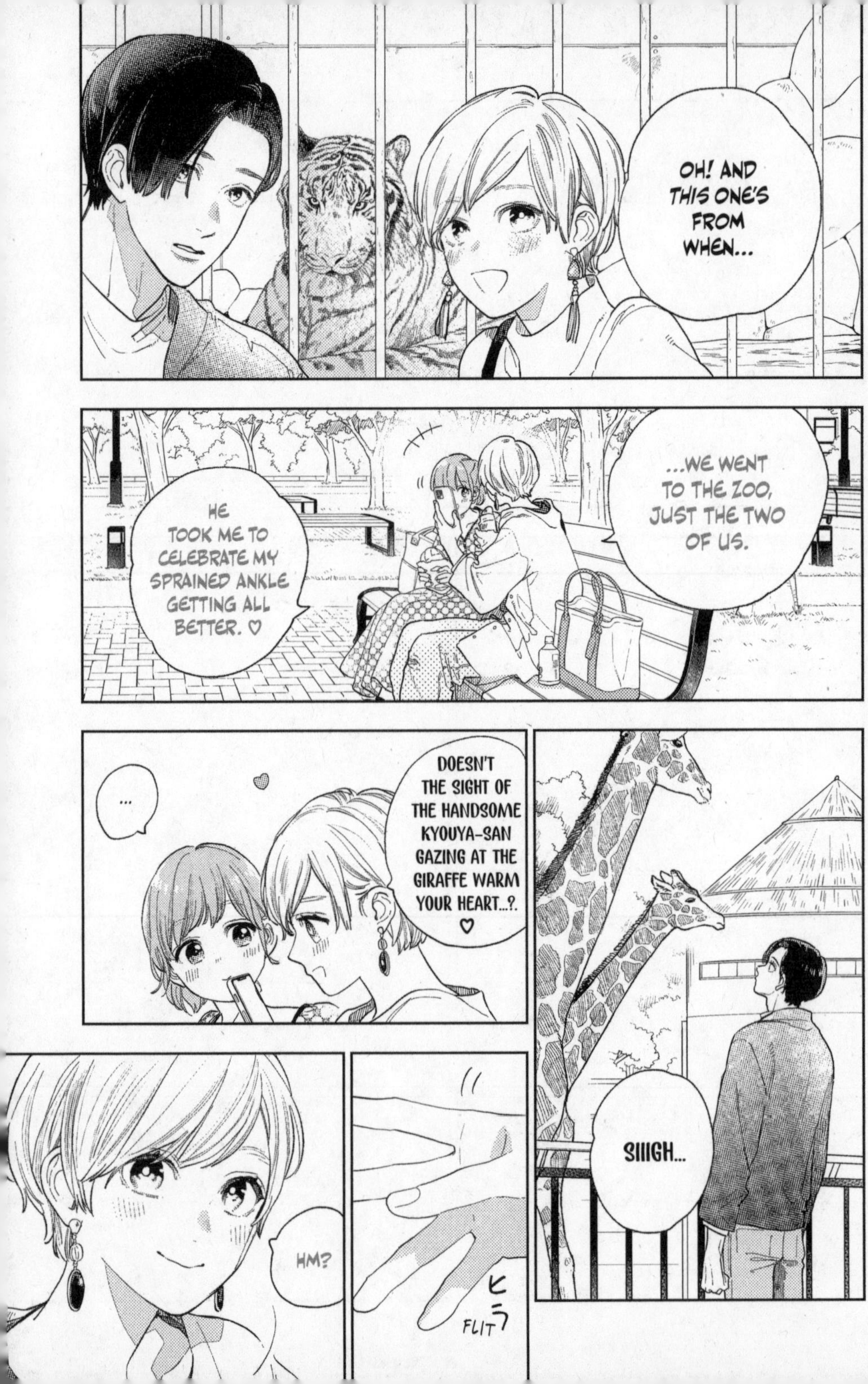
OH! AND THIS ONE'S FROM WHEN...
...WE WENT TO THE ZOO, JUST THE TWO OF US.
HE TOOK ME TO CELEBRATE MY SPRAINED ANKLE GETTING ALL BETTER. ♡
SIIIGH...
DOESN'T THE SIGHT OF THE HANDSOME KYOUYA-SAN GAZING AT THE GIRAFFE WARM YOUR HEART...?. ♡
...
ヒラ
FLIT
HM?

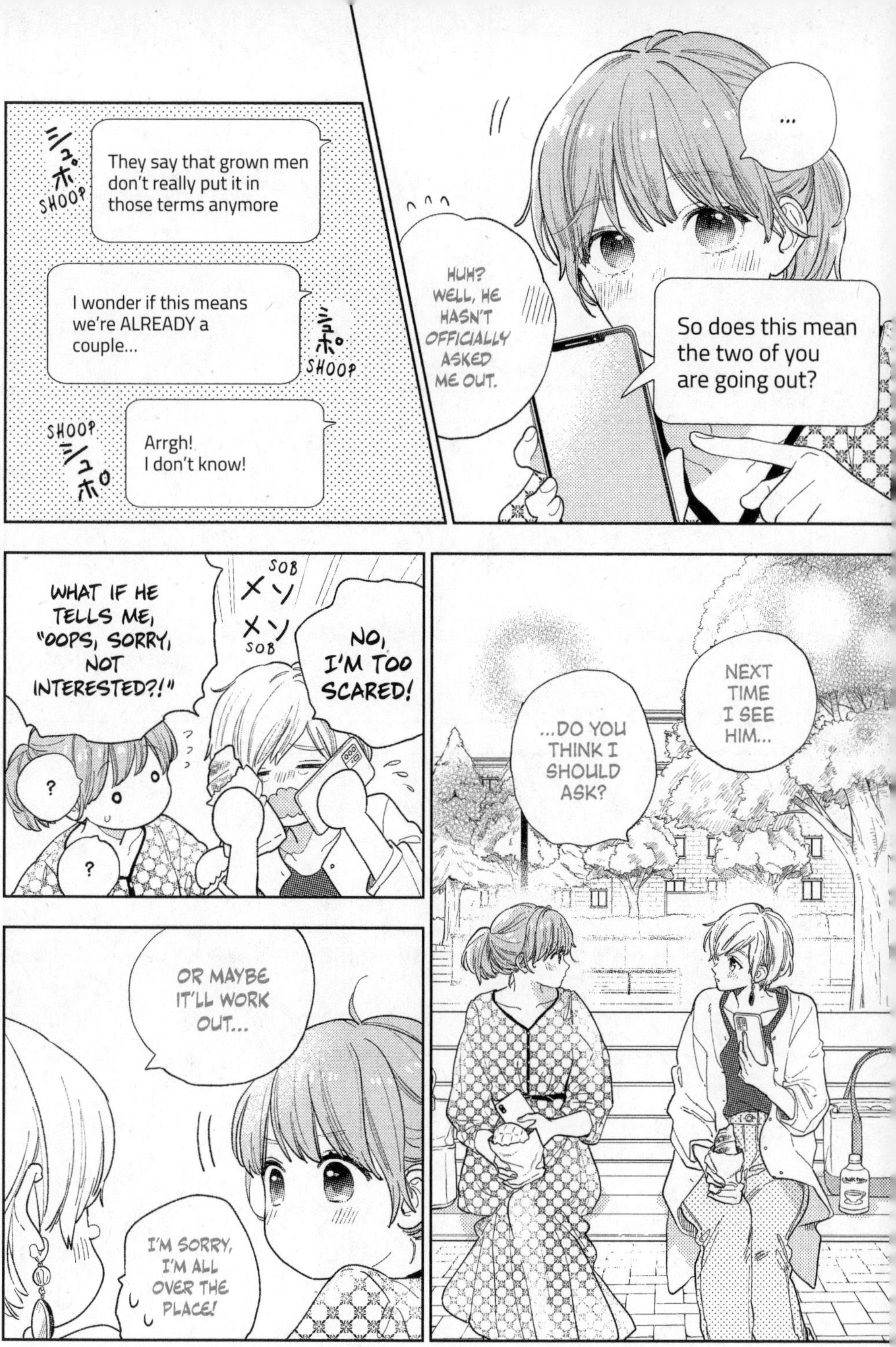
...
So does this mean the two of you are going out?
HUH? WELL, HE HASN'T OFFICIALLY ASKED ME OUT.
They say that grown men don't really put it in those terms anymore
シュポ SHOOP
I wonder if this means we're ALREADY a couple...
シュポ SHOOP
Arrgh! I don't know!
SHOOP シュポ
NEXT TIME I SEE HIM...
...DO YOU THINK I SHOULD ASK?
NO, I'M TOO SCARED!
メソ SOB メソ SOB
WHAT IF HE TELLS ME, "OOPS, SORRY, NOT INTERESTED?!"
?
?
OR MAYBE IT'LL WORK OUT...
I'M SORRY, I'M ALL OVER THE PLACE!

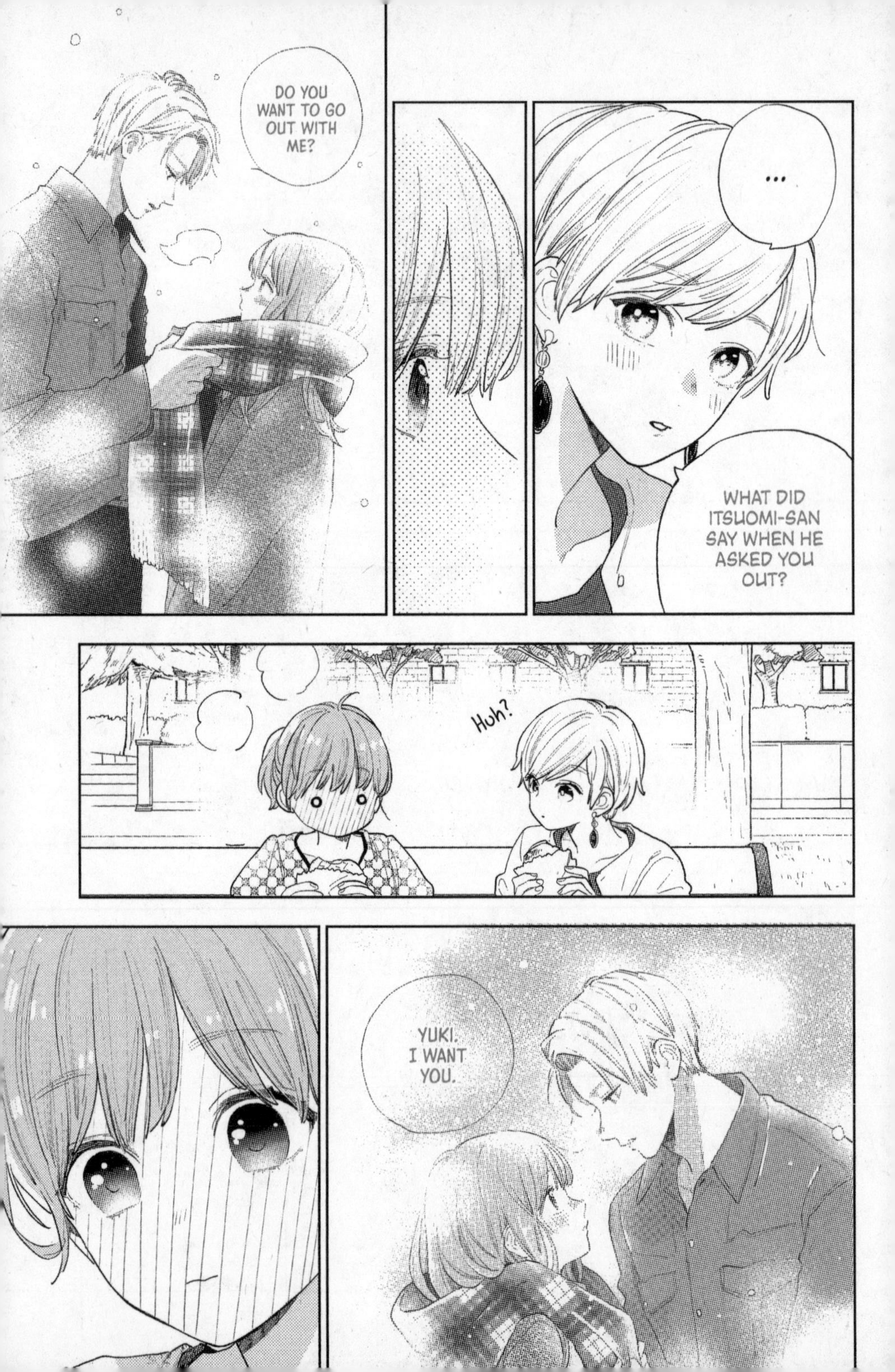
...
WHAT DID ITSUOMI-SAN SAY WHEN HE ASKED YOU OUT?
DO YOU WANT TO GO OUT WITH ME?
Huh?
YUKI. I WANT YOU.

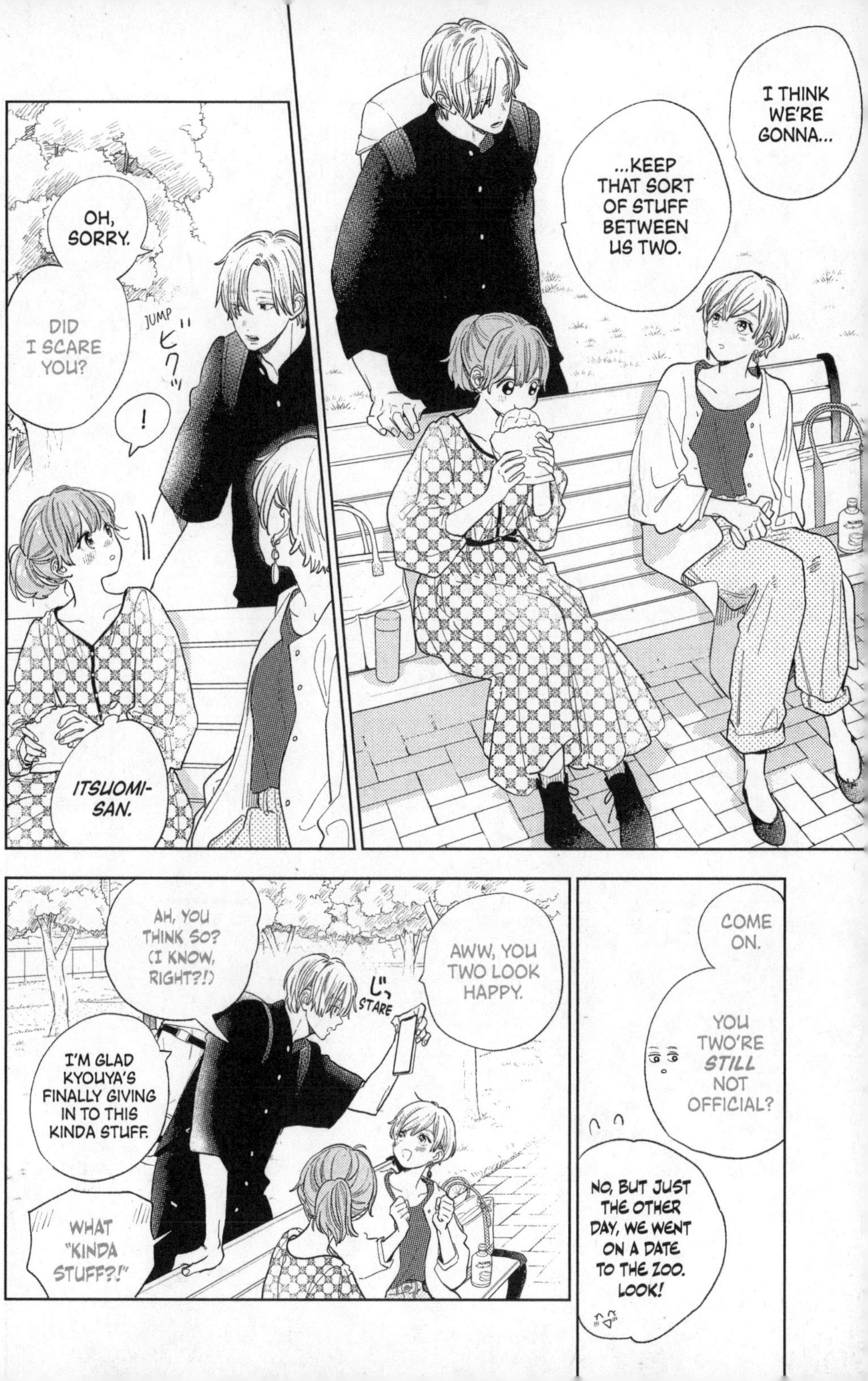

I THINK WE'RE GONNA...
...KEEP THAT SORT OF STUFF BETWEEN US TWO.
OH, SORRY.
JUMP
DID I SCARE YOU?
!
ITSUOMI-SAN.
COME ON.
YOU TWO'RE STILL NOT OFFICIAL?
NO, BUT JUST THE OTHER DAY, WE WENT ON A DATE TO THE ZOO. LOOK!
AWW, YOU TWO LOOK HAPPY.
STARE
AH, YOU THINK SO? (I KNOW, RIGHT?!)
I'M GLAD KYOUYA'S FINALLY GIVING IN TO THIS KINDA STUFF.
WHAT "KINDA STUFF?!"

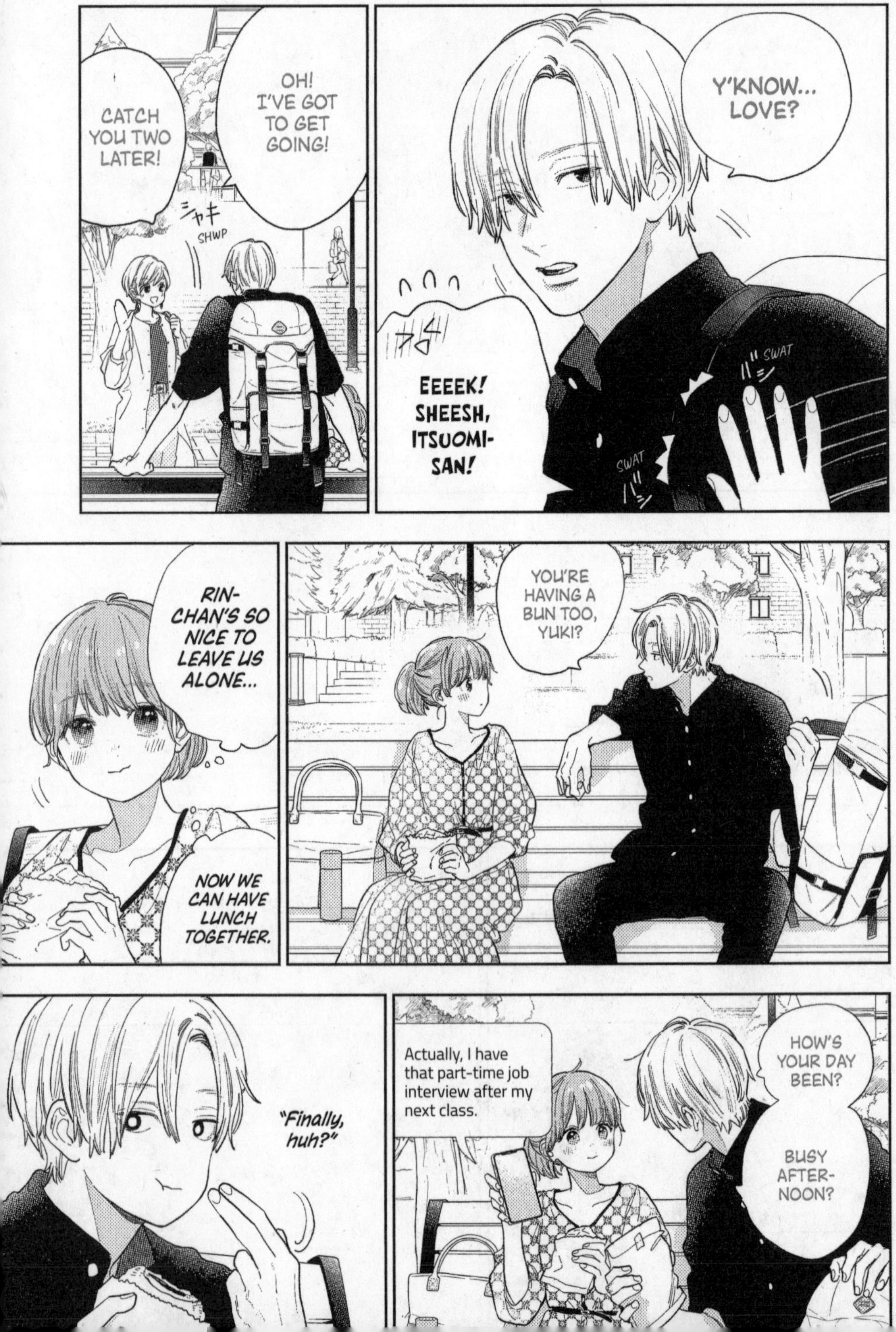
Y'KNOW... LOVE?
EEEEK! SHEESH, ITSUOMI-SAN!
SWAT
SWAT
OH! I'VE GOT TO GET GOING!
CATCH YOU TWO LATER!
SHWP
YOU'RE HAVING A BUN TOO, YUKI?
RIN-CHAN'S SO NICE TO LEAVE US ALONE...
NOW WE CAN HAVE LUNCH TOGETHER.
HOW'S YOUR DAY BEEN?
BUSY AFTERNOON?
Actually, I have that part-time job interview after my next class.
"Finally, huh?"

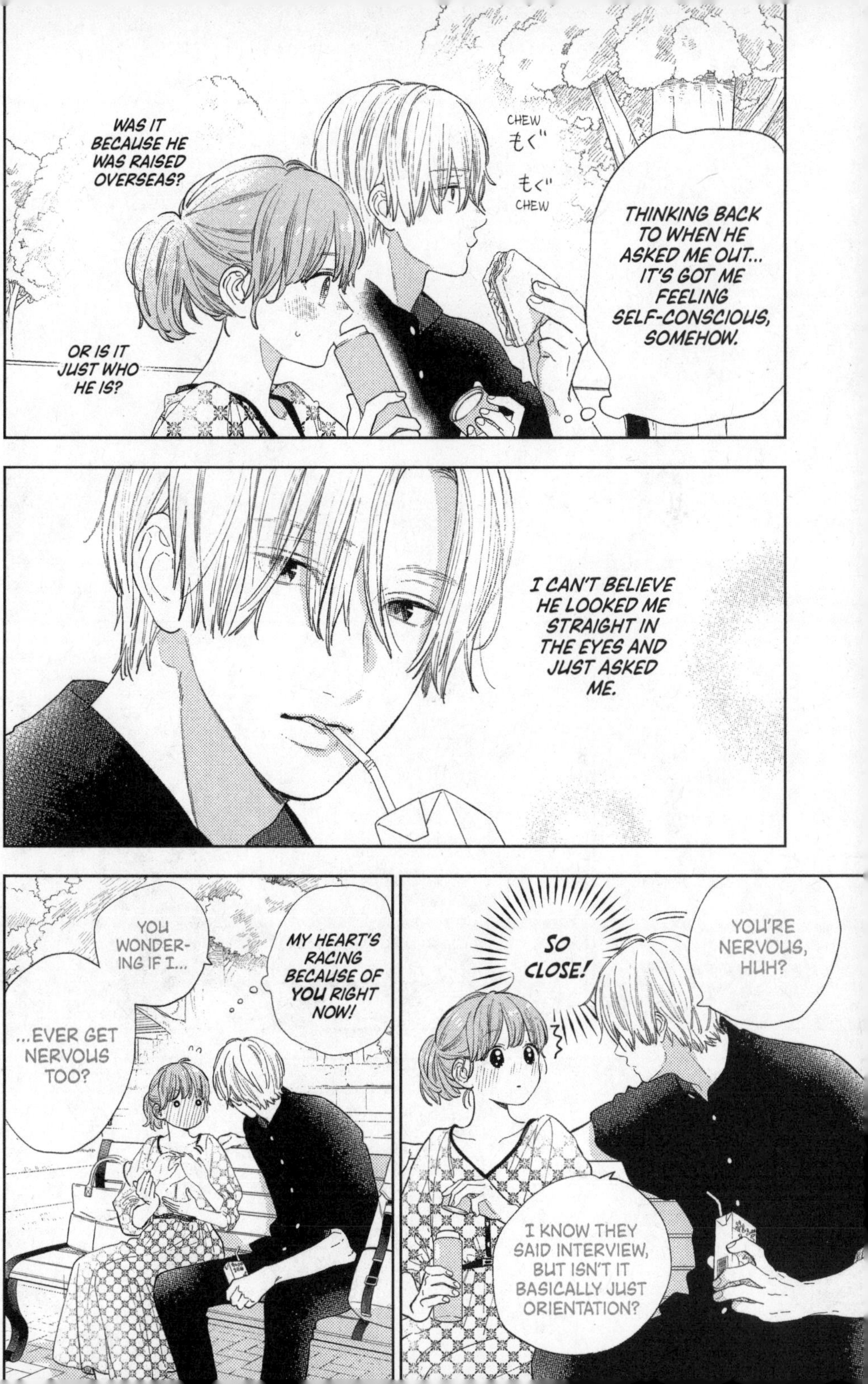
THINKING BACK TO WHEN HE ASKED ME OUT... IT'S GOT ME FEELING SELF-CONSCIOUS, SOMEHOW.
CHEW もぐ
もぐ CHEW
WAS IT BECAUSE HE WAS RAISED OVERSEAS?
OR IS IT JUST WHO HE IS?
I CAN'T BELIEVE HE LOOKED ME STRAIGHT IN THE EYES AND JUST ASKED ME.
YOU'RE NERVOUS, HUH?
SO CLOSE!
I KNOW THEY SAID INTERVIEW, BUT ISN'T IT BASICALLY JUST ORIENTATION?
YOU WONDERING IF I...
...EVER GET NERVOUS TOO?
MY HEART'S RACING BECAUSE OF YOU RIGHT NOW!

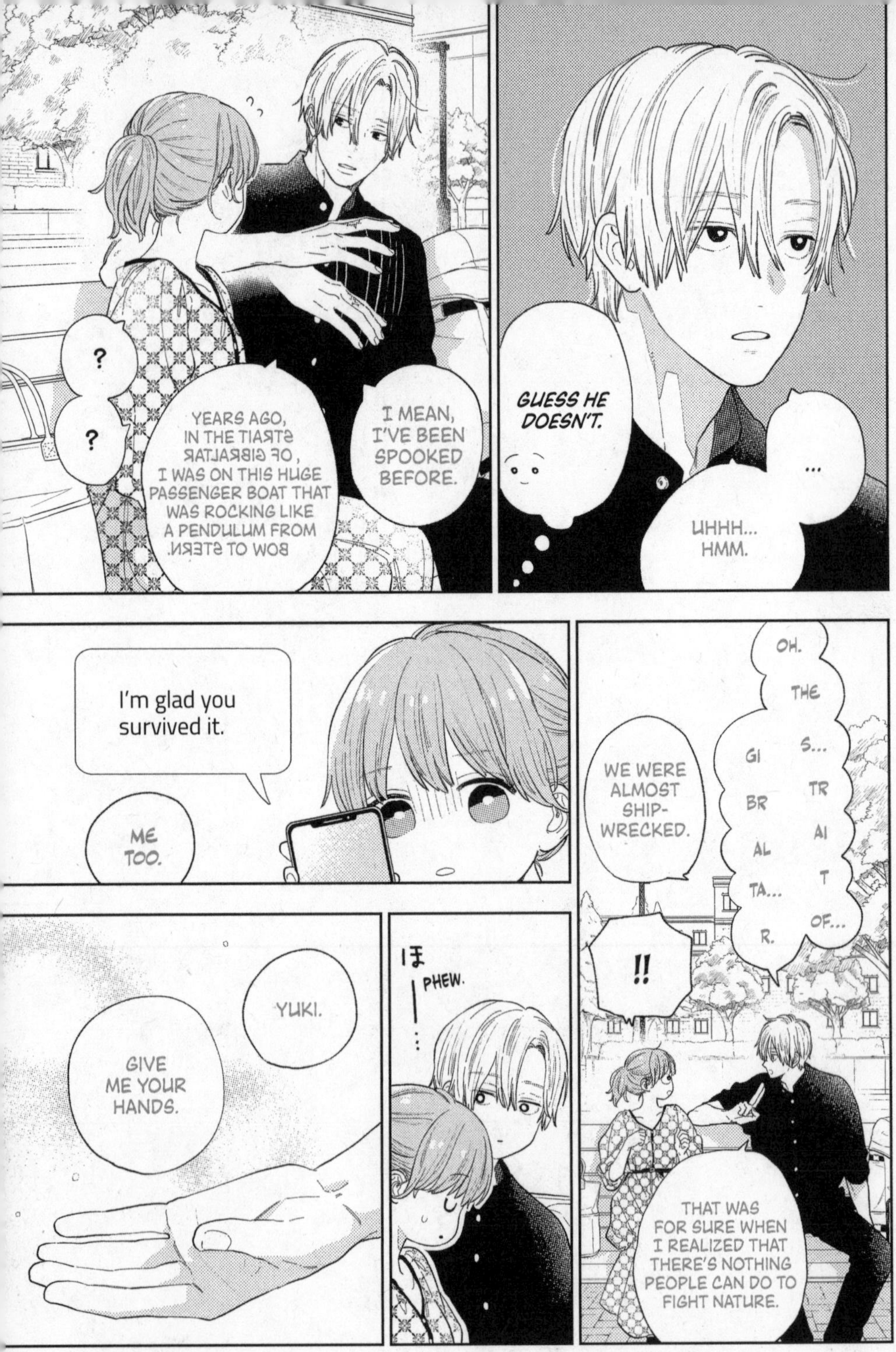
GUESS HE DOESN'T.
...
UHHH... HMM.
I MEAN, I'VE BEEN SPOOKED BEFORE.
YEARS AGO, IN THE STRAIT OF GIBRALTAR, I WAS ON THIS HUGE PASSENGER BOAT THAT WAS ROCKING LIKE A PENDULUM FROM BOW TO STERN.
?
?
OH. THE S... TR AI T OF... GI BR AL TA... R.
WE WERE ALMOST SHIP-WRECKED.
!!
THAT WAS FOR SURE WHEN I REALIZED THAT THERE'S NOTHING PEOPLE CAN DO TO FIGHT NATURE.
I'm glad you survived it.
ME TOO.
ほ
PHEW.
—…
YUKI.
GIVE ME YOUR HANDS.

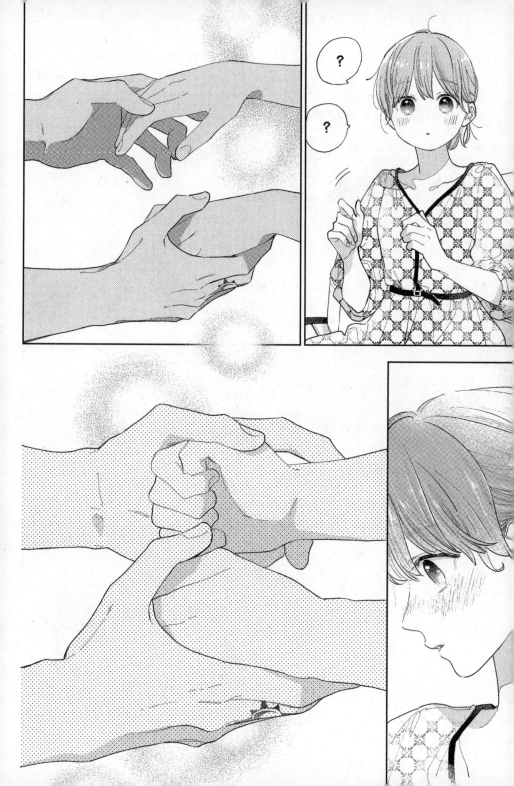

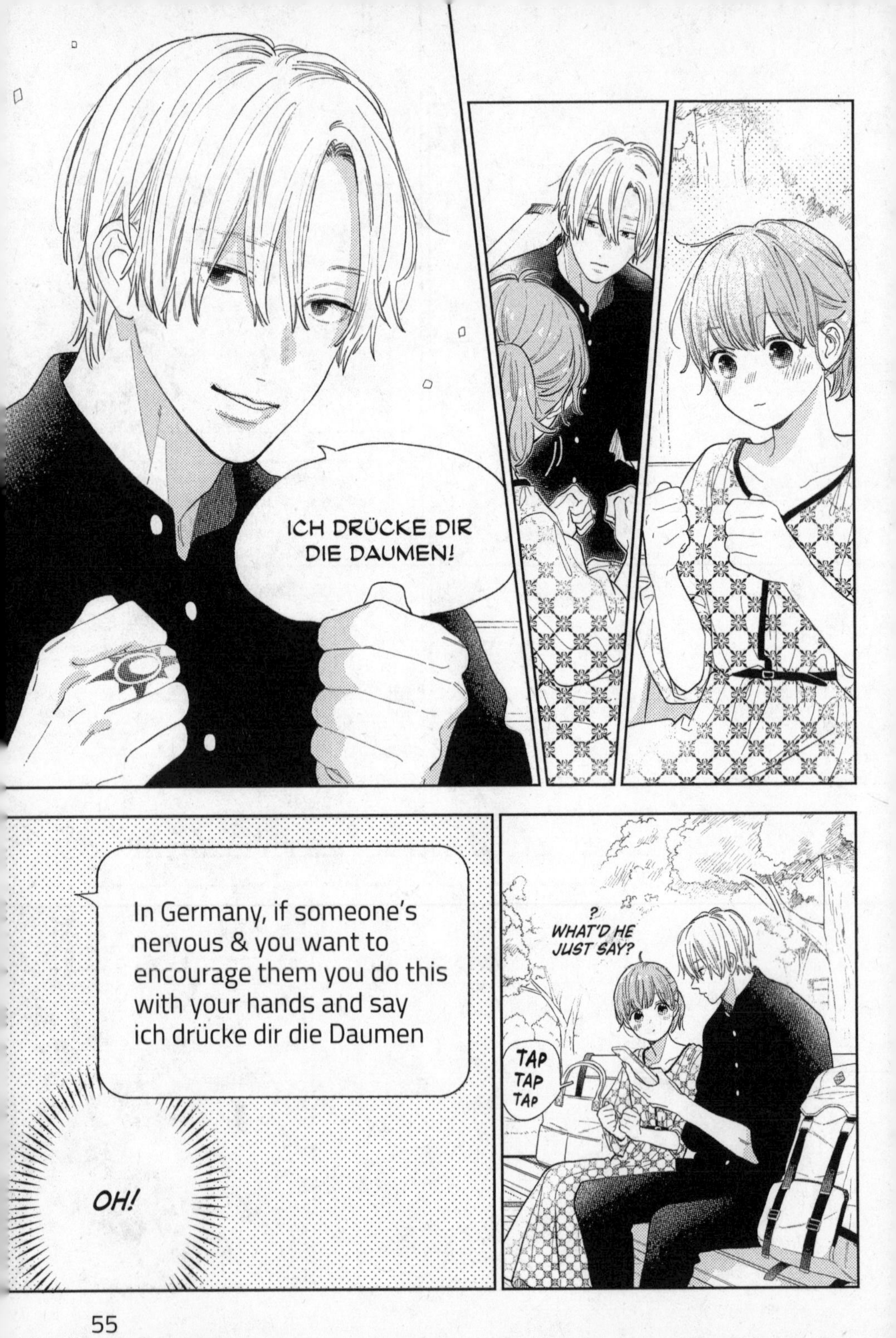
ICH DRÜCKE DIR DIE DAUMEN!
? WHAT'D HE JUST SAY?
TAP TAP TAP
In Germany, if someone's nervous & you want to encourage them you do this with your hands and say ich drücke dir die Daumen
OH!

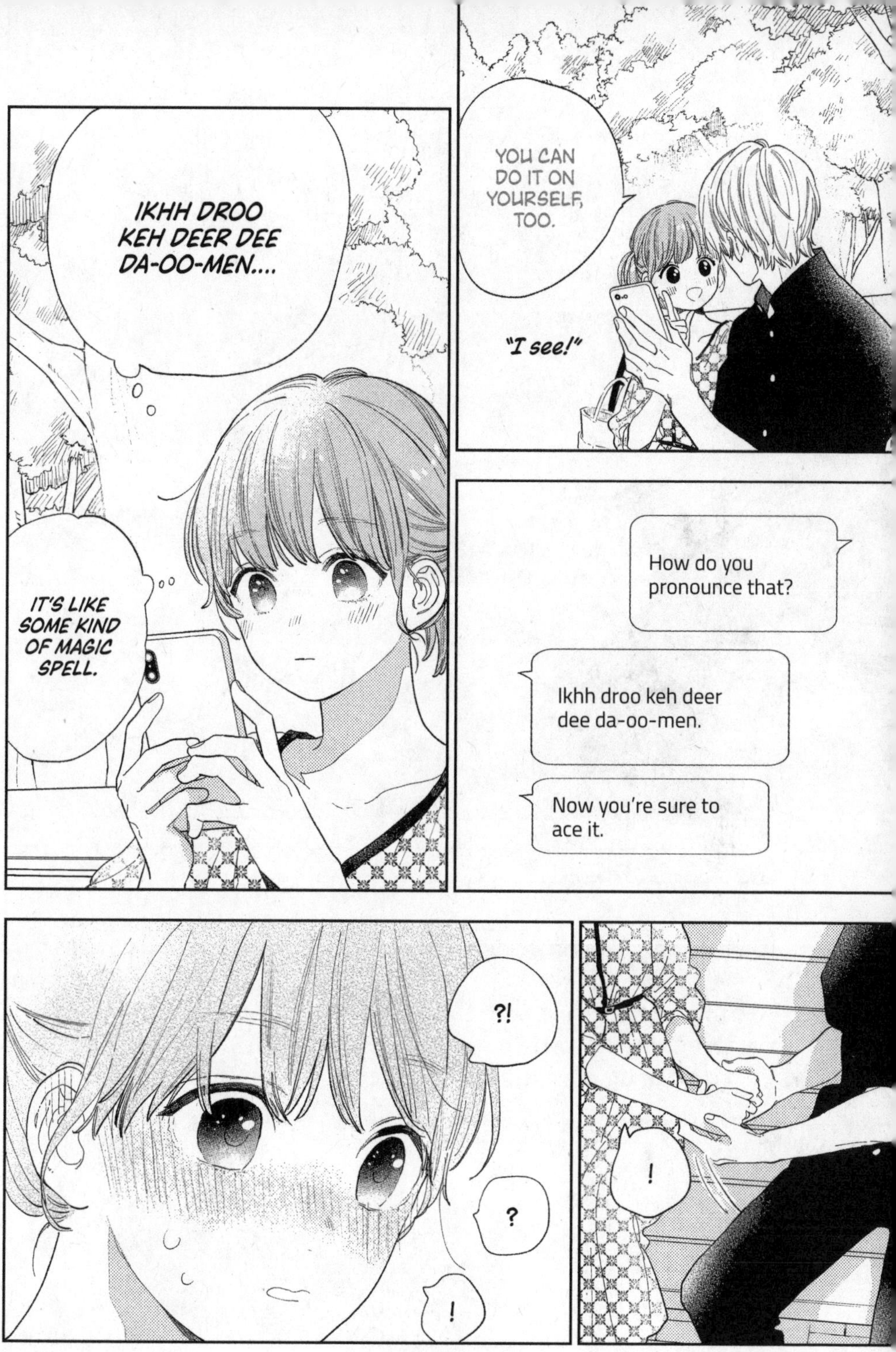
YOU CAN DO IT ON YOURSELF, TOO.
"I see!"
How do you pronounce that?
Ikhh droo keh deer dee da-oo-men.
Now you're sure to ace it.
IKHH DROO KEH DEER DEE DA-OO-MEN....
IT'S LIKE SOME KIND OF MAGIC SPELL.
!
?!
?
!

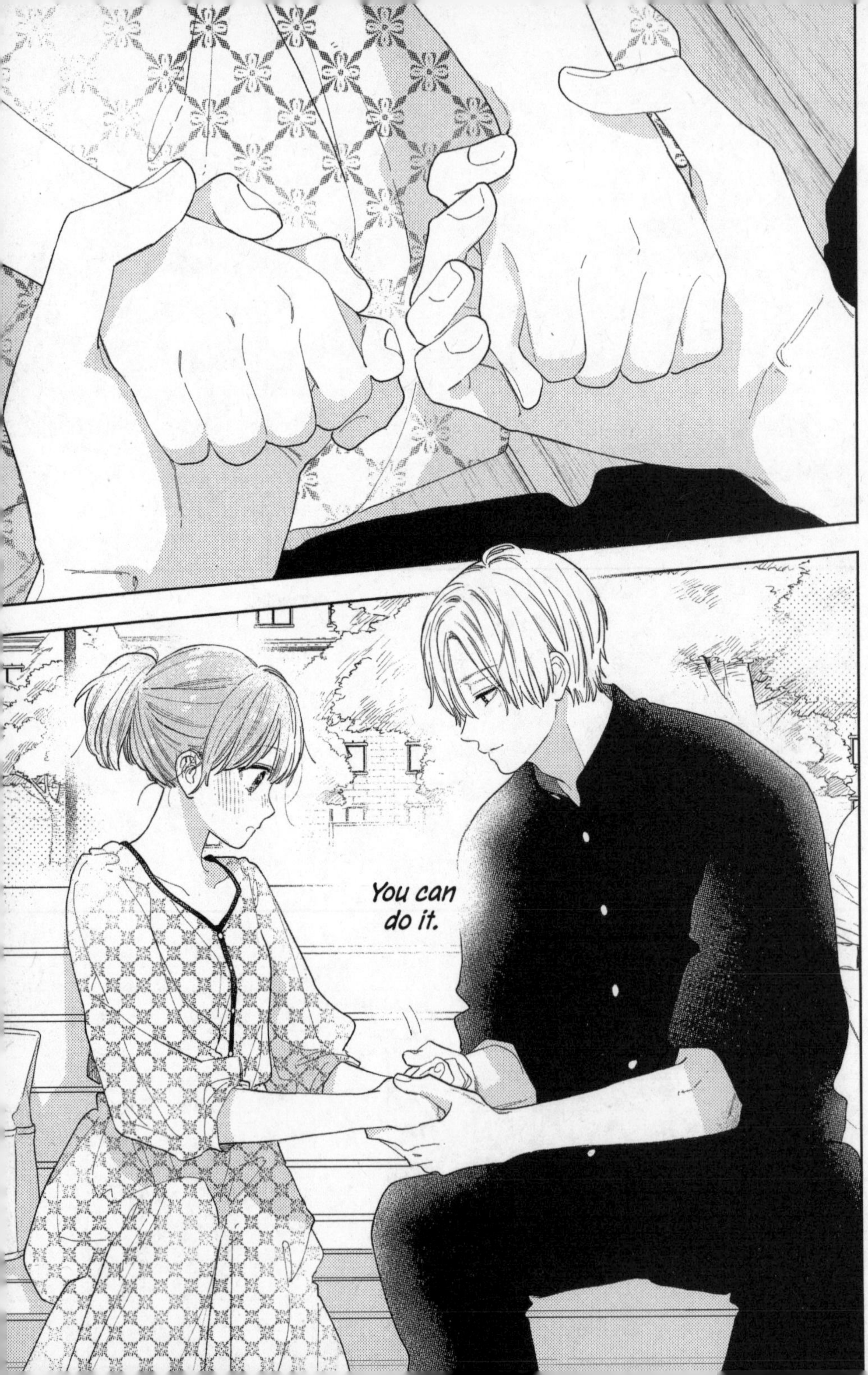
You can do it.

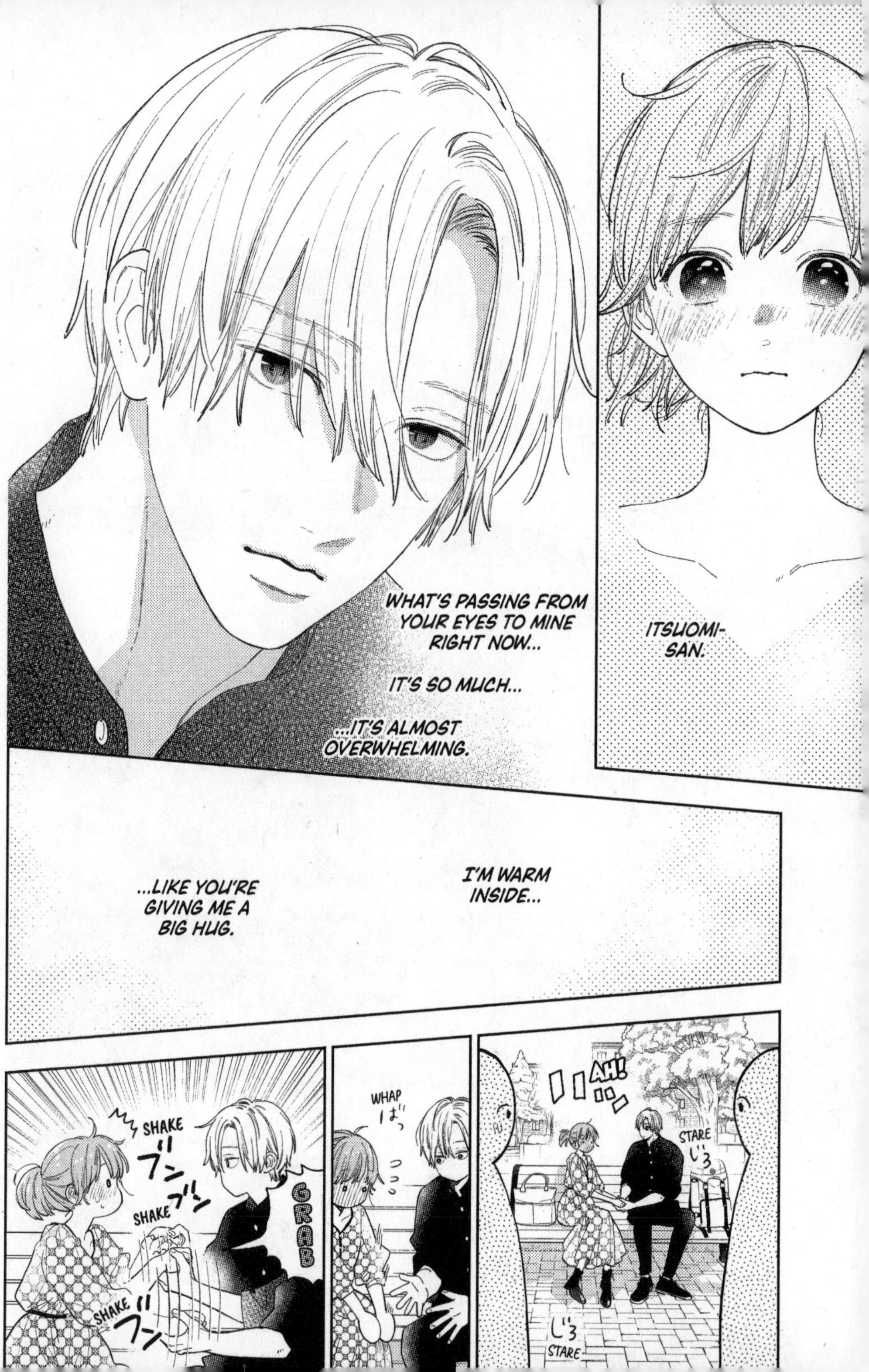
ITSUOMI-SAN.
WHAT'S PASSING FROM YOUR EYES TO MINE RIGHT NOW...
IT'S SO MUCH...
...IT'S ALMOST OVERWHELMING.
I'M WARM INSIDE...
...LIKE YOU'RE GIVING ME A BIG HUG.
AH!
STARE じろ
じろ STARE
WHAP ぱっ
SHAKE ブン
SHAKE ブン
GRAB
SHAKE ブン

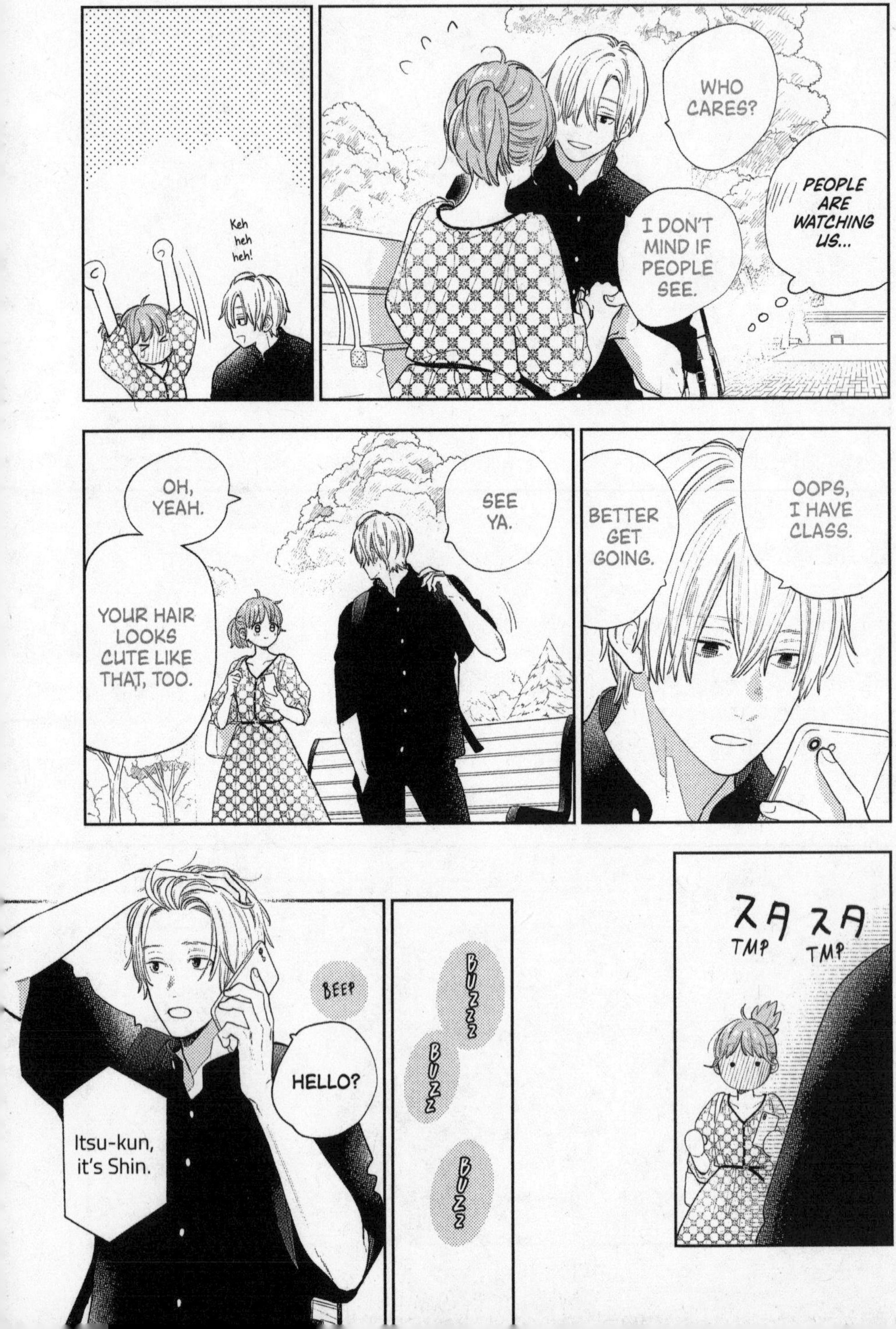
WHO CARES?
PEOPLE ARE WATCHING US...
I DON'T MIND IF PEOPLE SEE.
Keh heh heh!
OOPS, I HAVE CLASS.
BETTER GET GOING.
SEE YA.
OH, YEAH.
YOUR HAIR LOOKS CUTE LIKE THAT, TOO.
スタ TMP
スタ TMP
BUZZZ
BUZZ
BUZZ
BEEP
HELLO?
Itsu-kun, it's Shin.

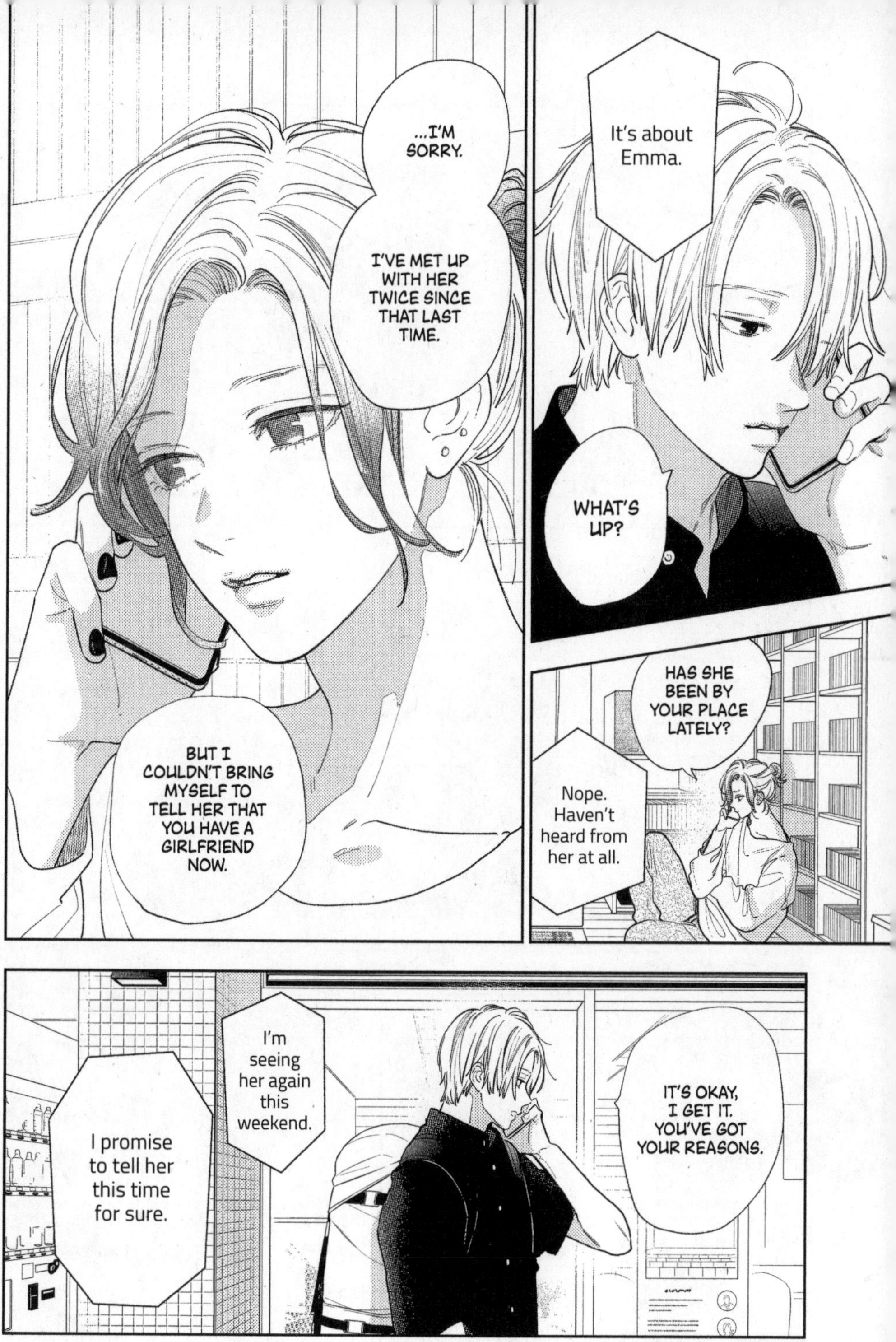
It's about Emma.
WHAT'S UP?
HAS SHE BEEN BY YOUR PLACE LATELY?
Nope. Haven't heard from her at all.
...I'M SORRY.
I'VE MET UP WITH HER TWICE SINCE THAT LAST TIME.
BUT I COULDN'T BRING MYSELF TO TELL HER THAT YOU HAVE A GIRLFRIEND NOW.
IT'S OKAY, I GET IT. YOU'VE GOT YOUR REASONS.
I'm seeing her again this weekend.
I promise to tell her this time for sure.

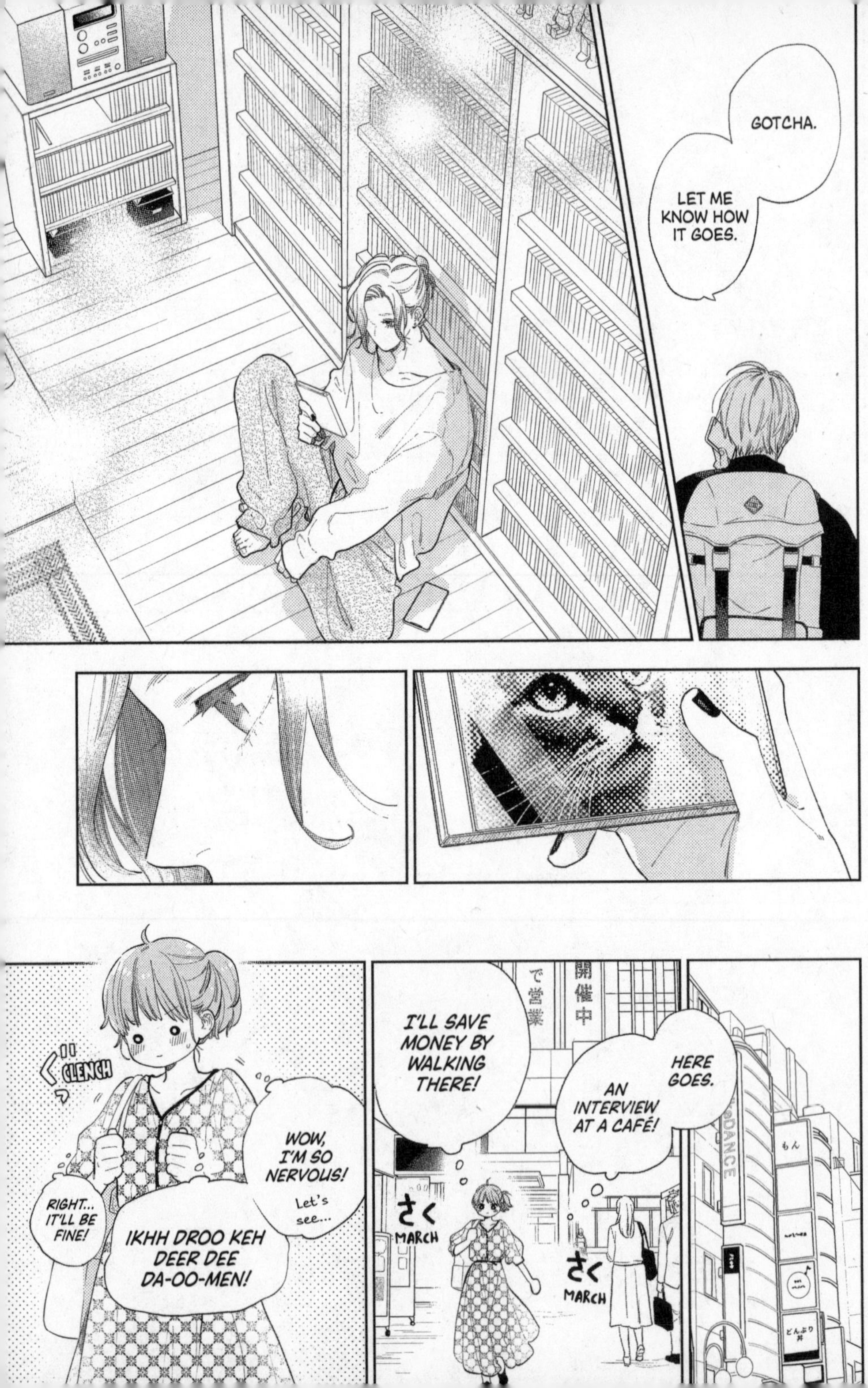

GOTCHA.
LET ME KNOW HOW IT GOES.
開催中
で営業
HERE GOES.
AN INTERVIEW AT A CAFÉ!
I'LL SAVE MONEY BY WALKING THERE!
さく MARCH
さく MARCH
どんぶり 丼
WOW, I'M SO NERVOUS!
Let's see...
IKHH DROO KEH DEER DEE DA-OO-MEN!
RIGHT... IT'LL BE FINE!
CLENCH

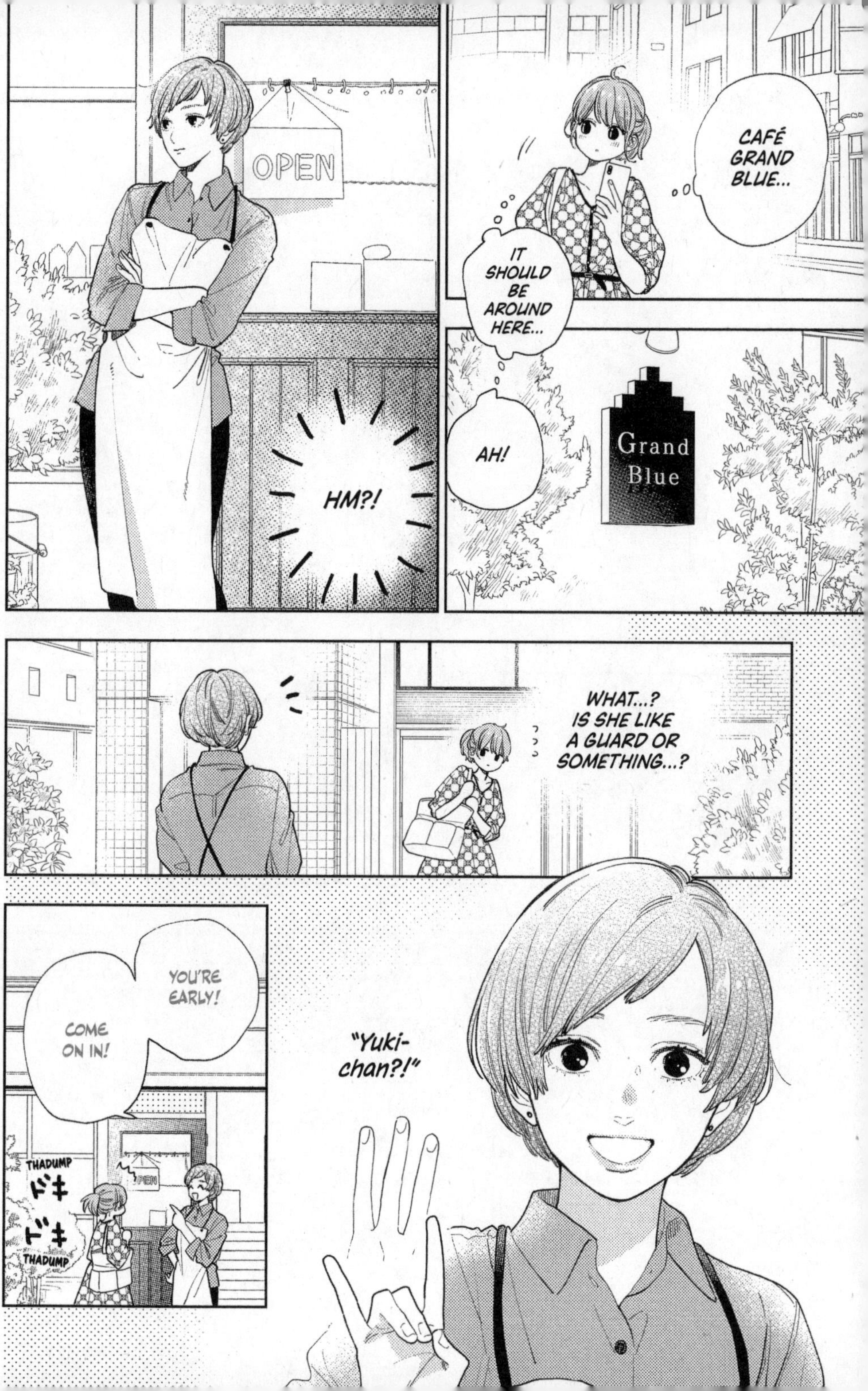
CAFÉ GRAND BLUE...
IT SHOULD BE AROUND HERE...
AH!
Grand Blue
HM?!
OPEN
WHAT...? IS SHE LIKE A GUARD OR SOMETHING...?
"Yuki-chan?!"
YOU'RE EARLY!
COME ON IN!
THADUMP
ドキ
ドキ
THADUMP
OPEN

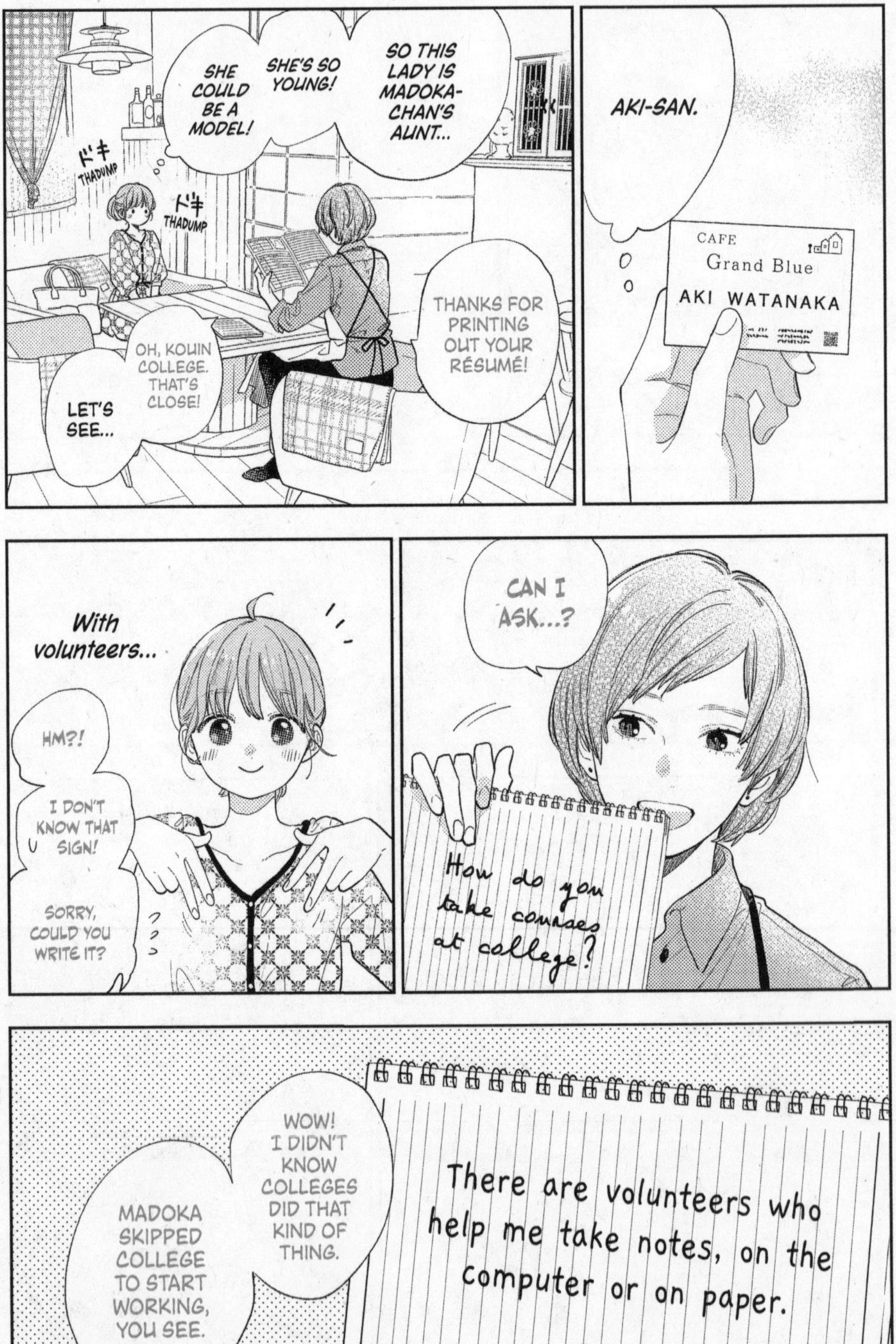
AKI-SAN.
CAFE
Grand Blue
AKI WATANAKA
SO THIS LADY IS MADOKA-CHAN'S AUNT...
SHE'S SO YOUNG!
SHE COULD BE A MODEL!
ドキ THADUMP
ドキ THADUMP
THANKS FOR PRINTING OUT YOUR RÉSUMÉ!
OH, KOUIN COLLEGE. THAT'S CLOSE!
LET'S SEE...
CAN I ASK...?
How do you take courses at college?
With volunteers...
HM?!
I DON'T KNOW THAT SIGN!
SORRY, COULD YOU WRITE IT?
There are volunteers who help me take notes, on the computer or on paper.
WOW! I DIDN'T KNOW COLLEGES DID THAT KIND OF THING.
MADOKA SKIPPED COLLEGE TO START WORKING, YOU SEE.

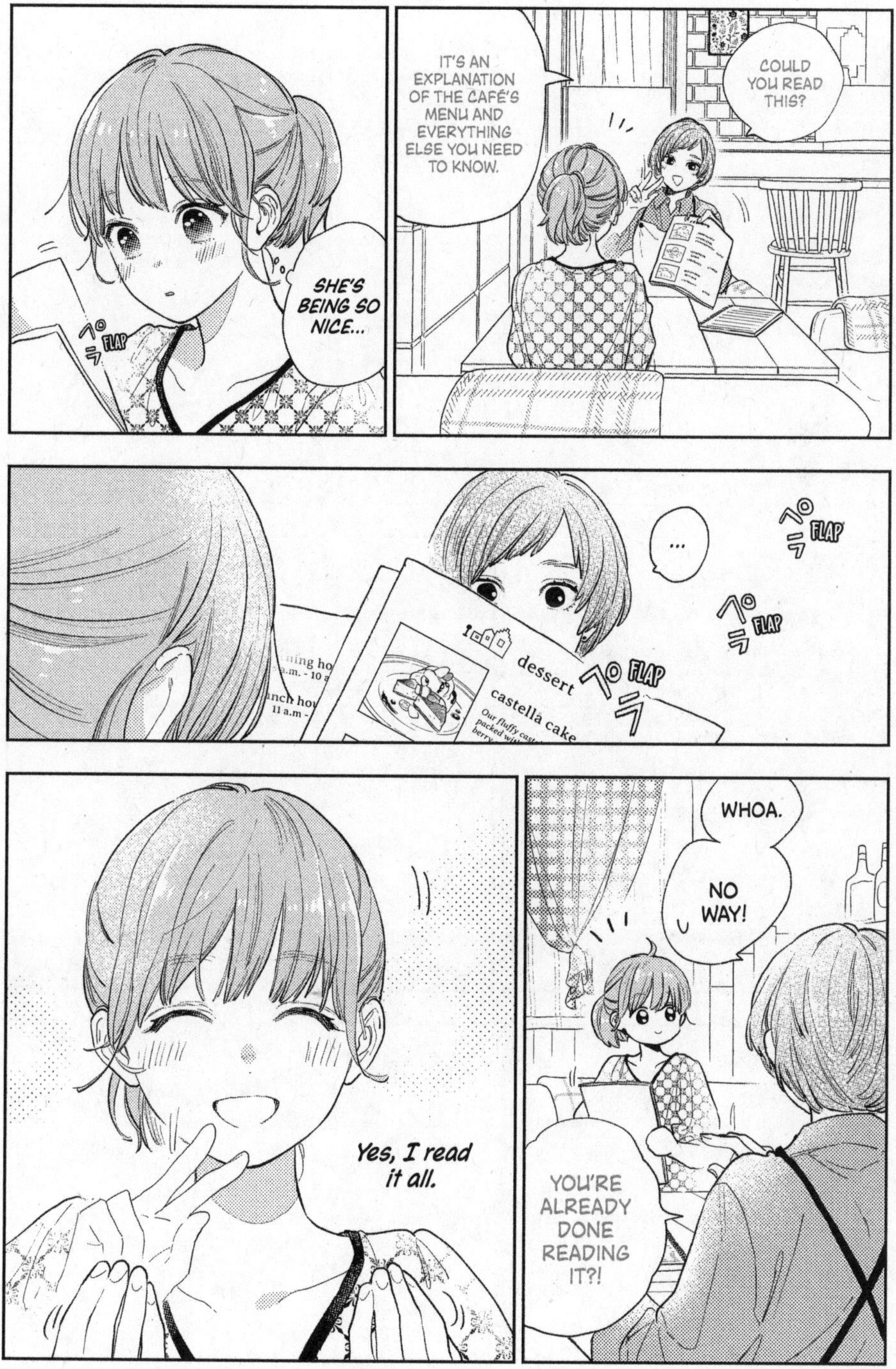
COULD YOU READ THIS?
IT'S AN EXPLANATION OF THE CAFÉ'S MENU AND EVERYTHING ELSE YOU NEED TO KNOW.
ペラ FLAP
SHE'S BEING SO NICE...
...
ペラ FLAP
ペラ FLAP
dessert
castella cake
ペラ FLAP
WHOA.
NO WAY!
YOU'RE ALREADY DONE READING IT?!
Yes, I read it all.

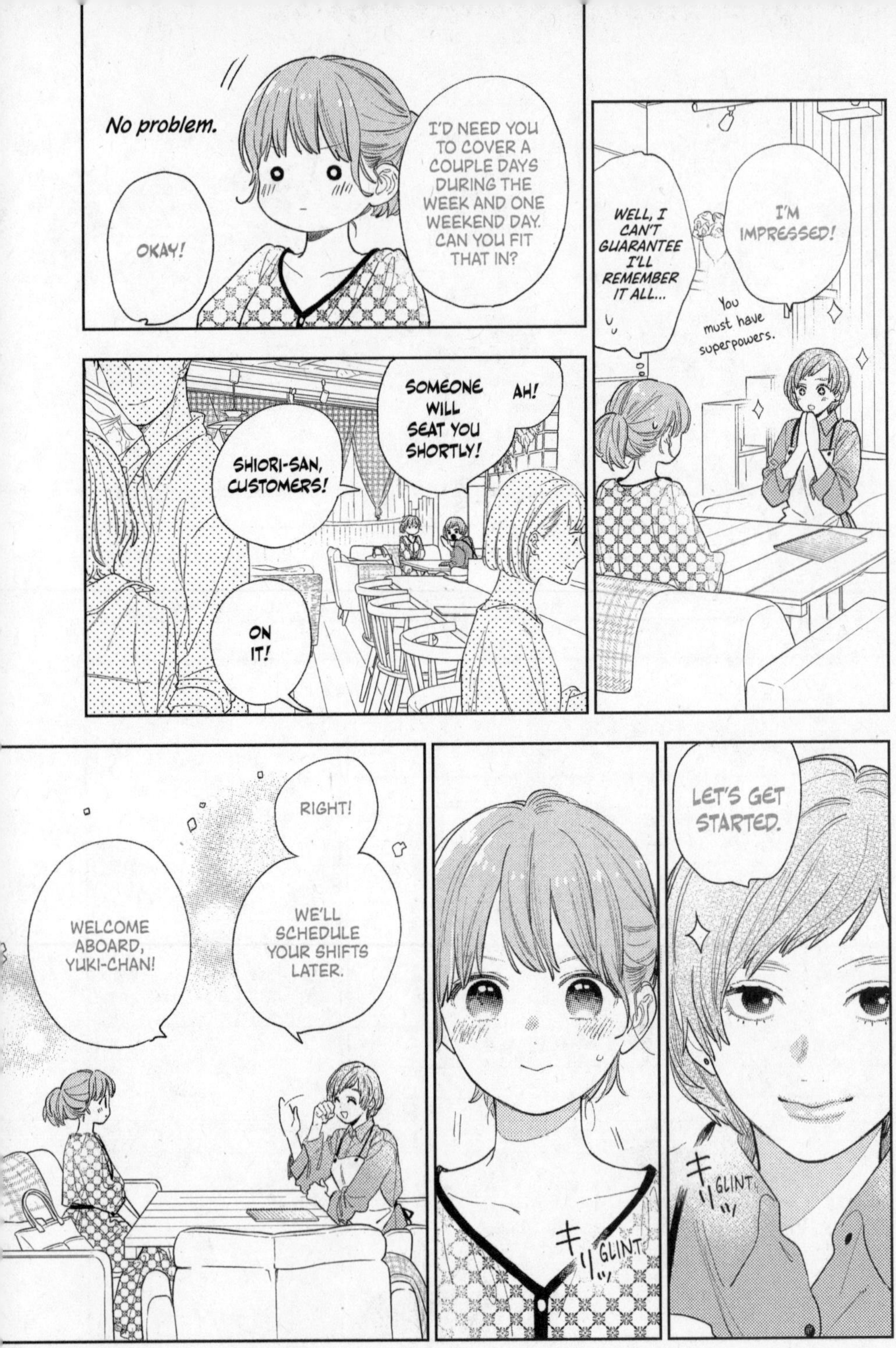
I'D NEED YOU TO COVER A COUPLE DAYS DURING THE WEEK AND ONE WEEKEND DAY. CAN YOU FIT THAT IN?
OKAY!
No problem.
I'M IMPRESSED!
You must have superpowers.
WELL, I CAN'T GUARANTEE I'LL REMEMBER IT ALL...
AH!
SOMEONE WILL SEAT YOU SHORTLY!
SHIORI-SAN, CUSTOMERS!
ON IT!
LET'S GET STARTED.
GLINT
GLINT
RIGHT!
WE'LL SCHEDULE YOUR SHIFTS LATER.
WELCOME ABOARD, YUKI-CHAN!

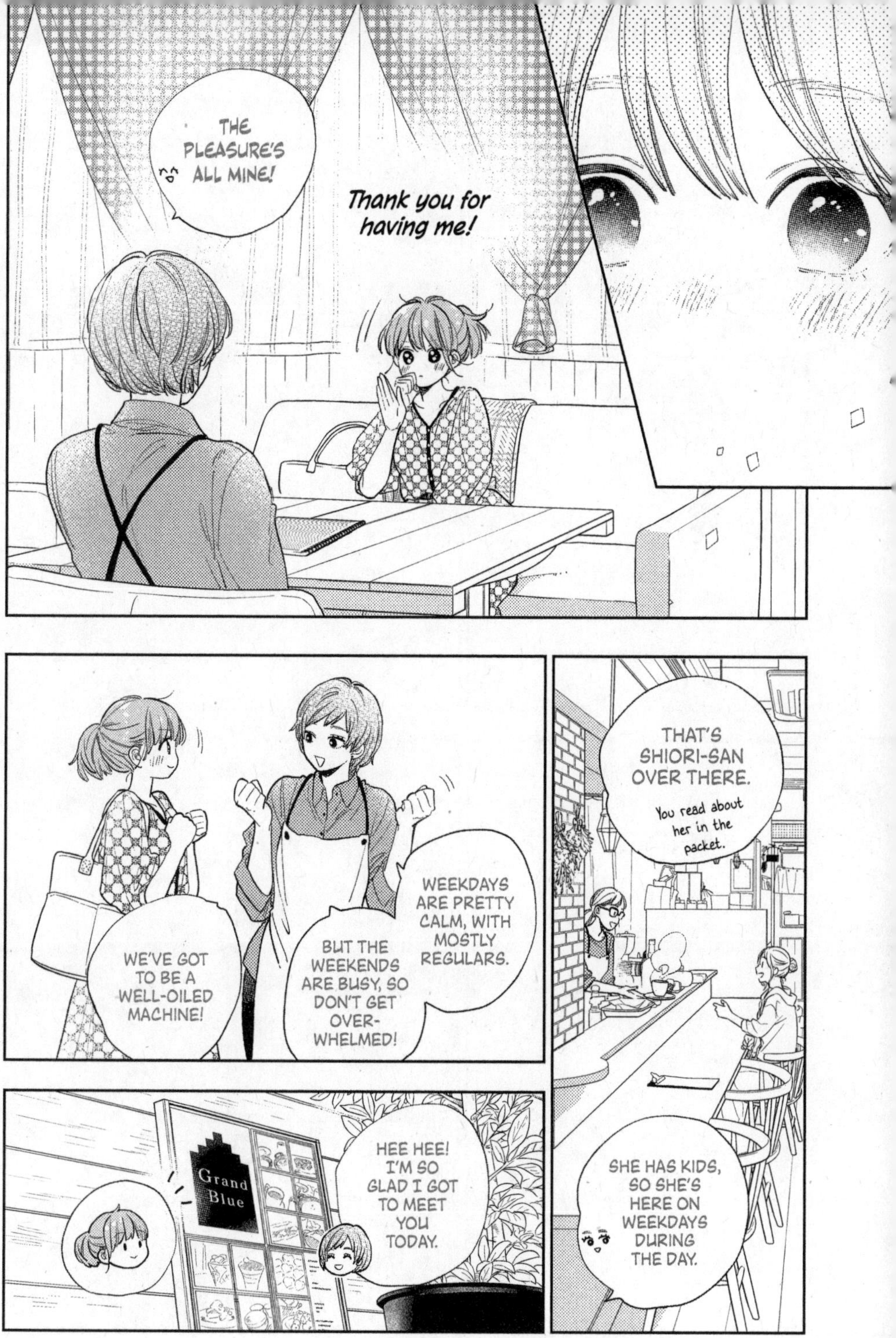
Thank you for having me!
THE PLEASURE'S ALL MINE!
THAT'S SHIORI-SAN OVER THERE.
You read about her in the packet.
SHE HAS KIDS, SO SHE'S HERE ON WEEKDAYS DURING THE DAY.
WEEKDAYS ARE PRETTY CALM, WITH MOSTLY REGULARS.
BUT THE WEEKENDS ARE BUSY, SO DON'T GET OVER-WHELMED!
WE'VE GOT TO BE A WELL-OILED MACHINE!
Grand Blue
HEE HEE! I'M SO GLAD I GOT TO MEET YOU TODAY.

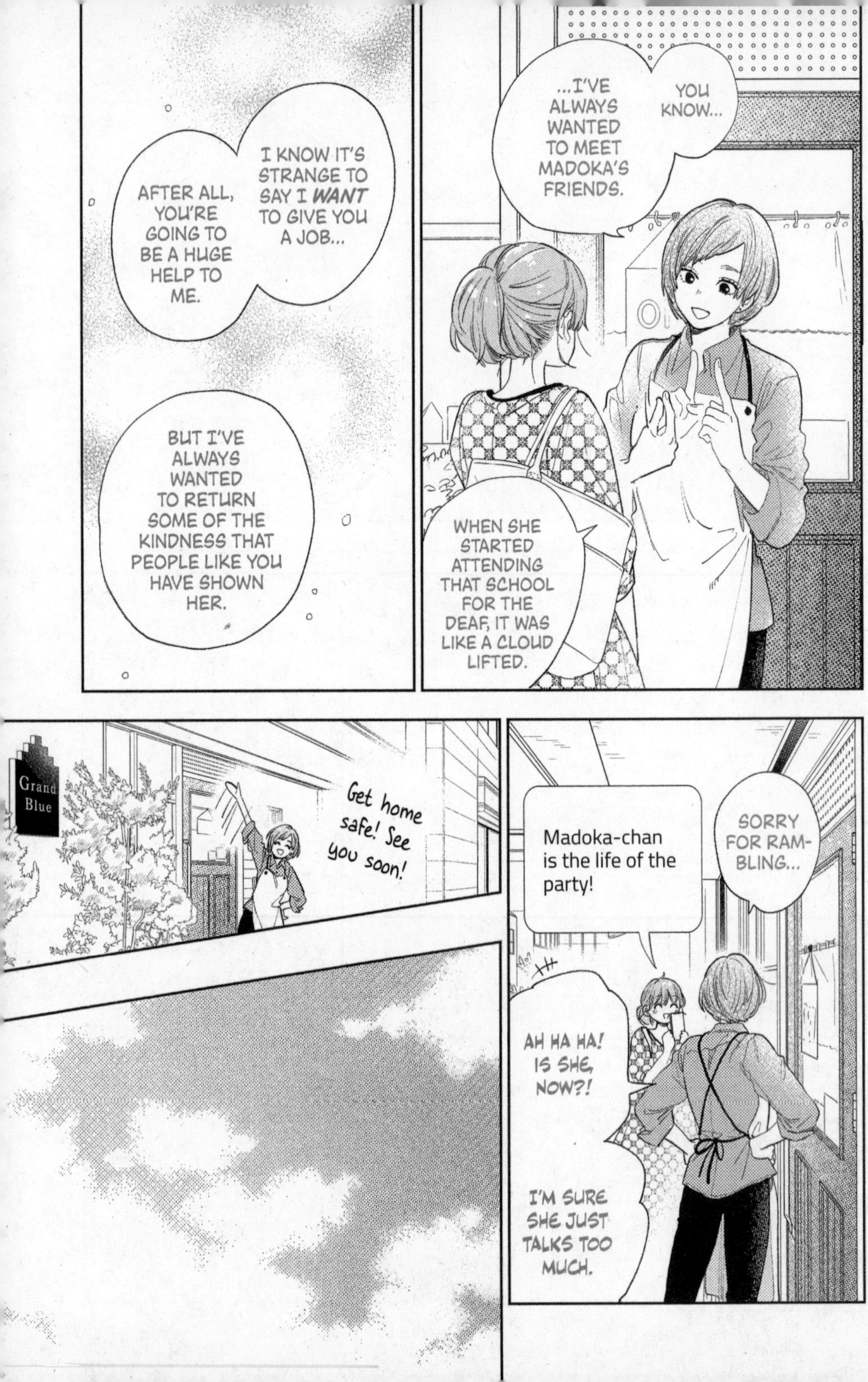
YOU KNOW...
...I'VE ALWAYS WANTED TO MEET MADOKA'S FRIENDS.
WHEN SHE STARTED ATTENDING THAT SCHOOL FOR THE DEAF, IT WAS LIKE A CLOUD LIFTED.
I KNOW IT'S STRANGE TO SAY I *WANT* TO GIVE YOU A JOB...
AFTER ALL, YOU'RE GOING TO BE A HUGE HELP TO ME.
BUT I'VE ALWAYS WANTED TO RETURN SOME OF THE KINDNESS THAT PEOPLE LIKE YOU HAVE SHOWN HER.
SORRY FOR RAM-BLING...
Madoka-chan is the life of the party!
AH HA HA! IS SHE, NOW?!
I'M SURE SHE JUST TALKS TOO MUCH.
Grand Blue
Get home safe! See you soon!

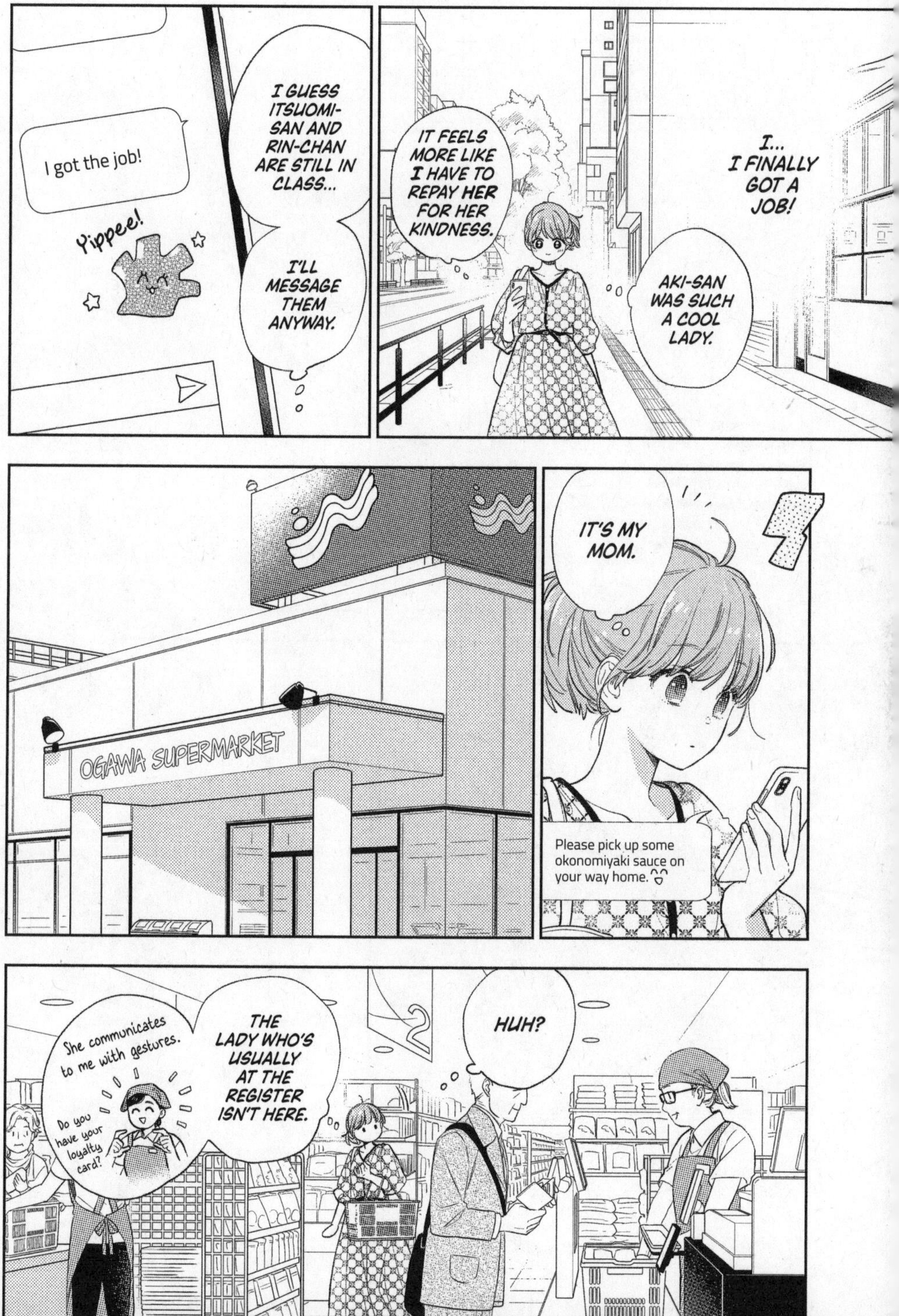
I... I FINALLY GOT A JOB!
AKI-SAN WAS SUCH A COOL LADY.
IT FEELS MORE LIKE I HAVE TO REPAY HER FOR HER KINDNESS.
I GUESS ITSUOMI-SAN AND RIN-CHAN ARE STILL IN CLASS...
I'LL MESSAGE THEM ANYWAY.
I got the job!
Yippee!
IT'S MY MOM.
Please pick up some okonomiyaki sauce on your way home.
OGAWA SUPERMARKET
HUH?
THE LADY WHO'S USUALLY AT THE REGISTER ISN'T HERE.
She communicates to me with gestures.
Do you have your loyalty card?

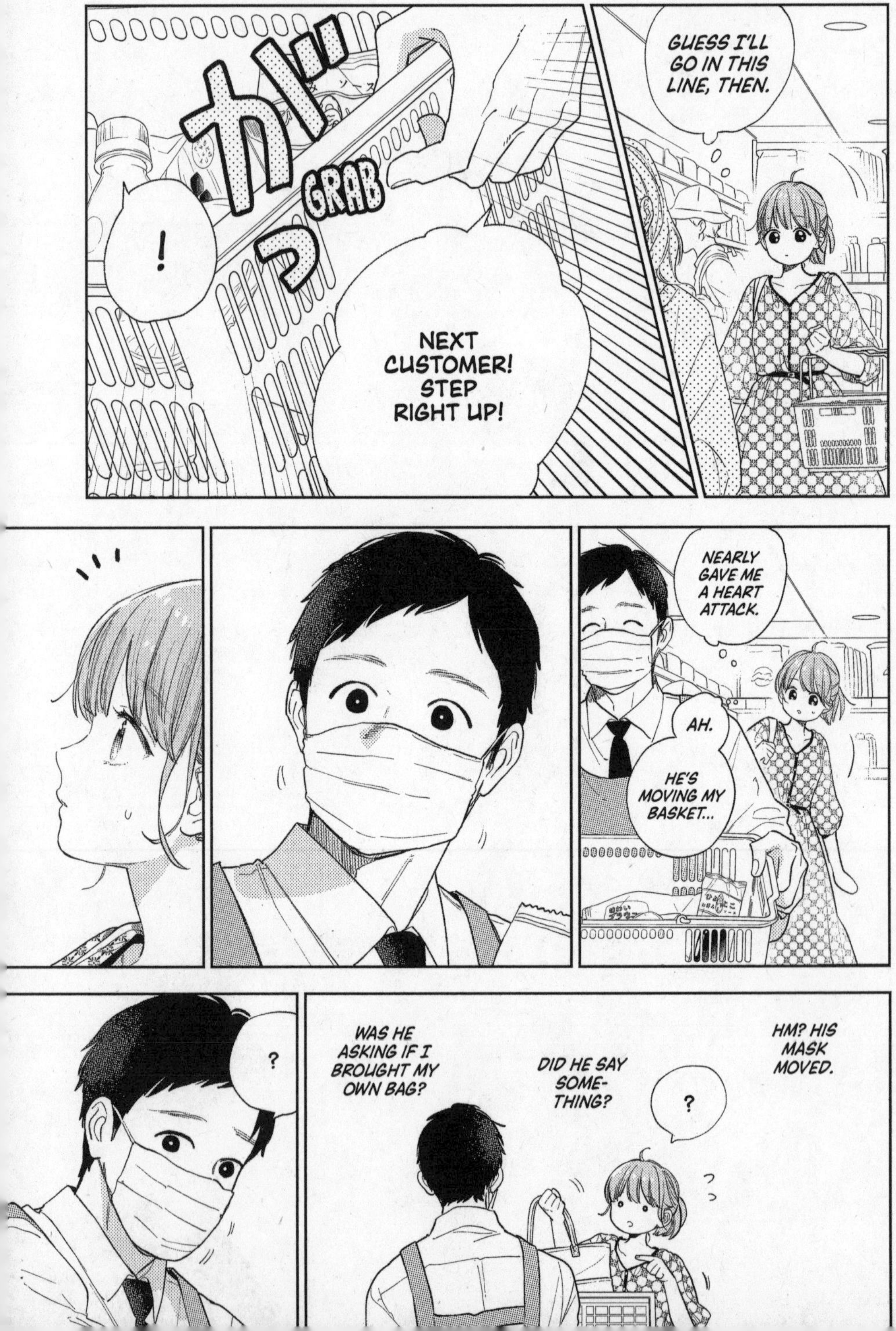
GUESS I'LL GO IN THIS LINE, THEN.
カドっ
GRAB
!
NEXT CUSTOMER! STEP RIGHT UP!
NEARLY GAVE ME A HEART ATTACK.
AH.
HE'S MOVING MY BASKET...
HM? HIS MASK MOVED.
DID HE SAY SOME-THING?
?
WAS HE ASKING IF I BROUGHT MY OWN BAG?
?

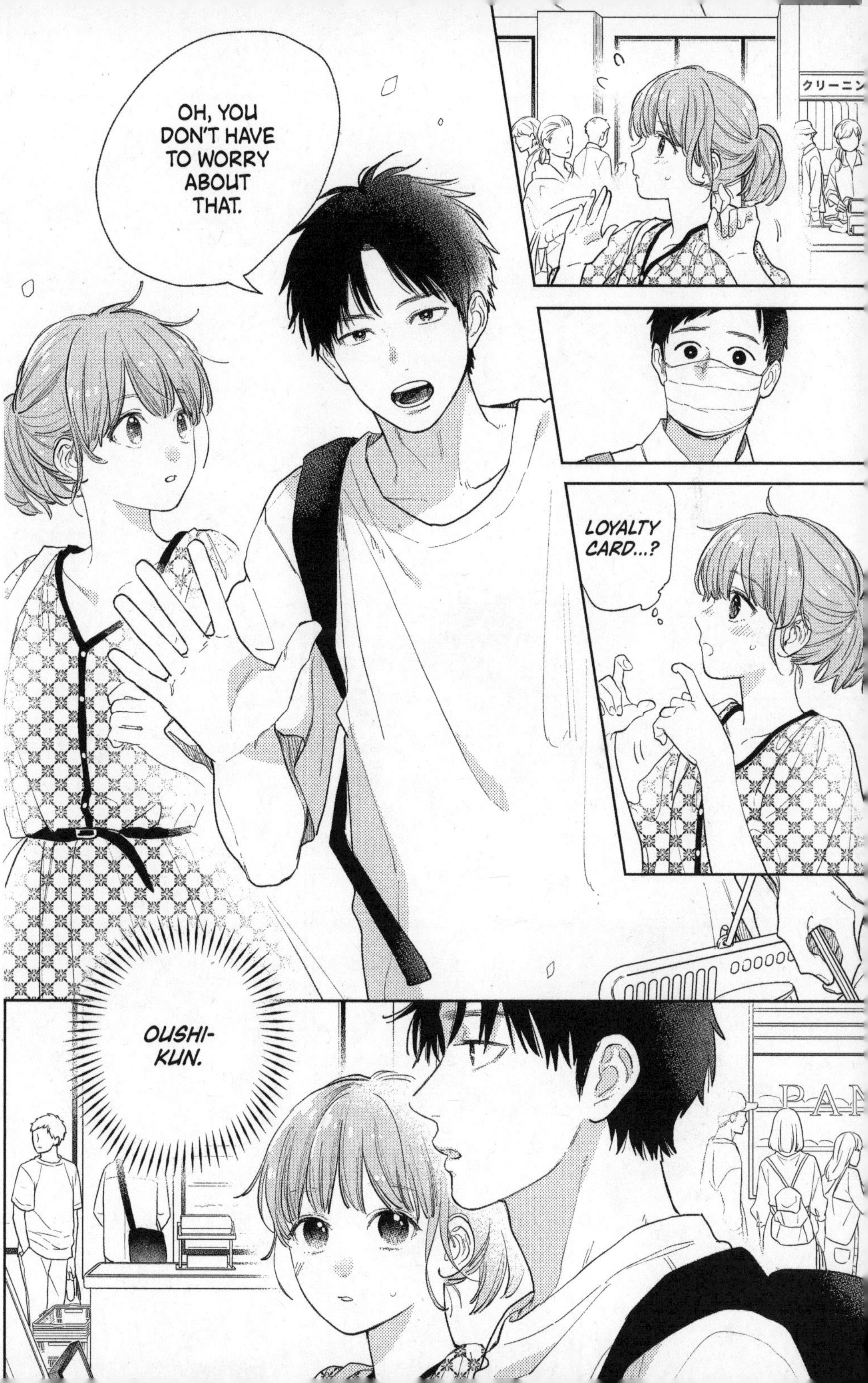
クリーニン
LOYALTY CARD...?
OH, YOU DON'T HAVE TO WORRY ABOUT THAT.
OUSHI-KUN.

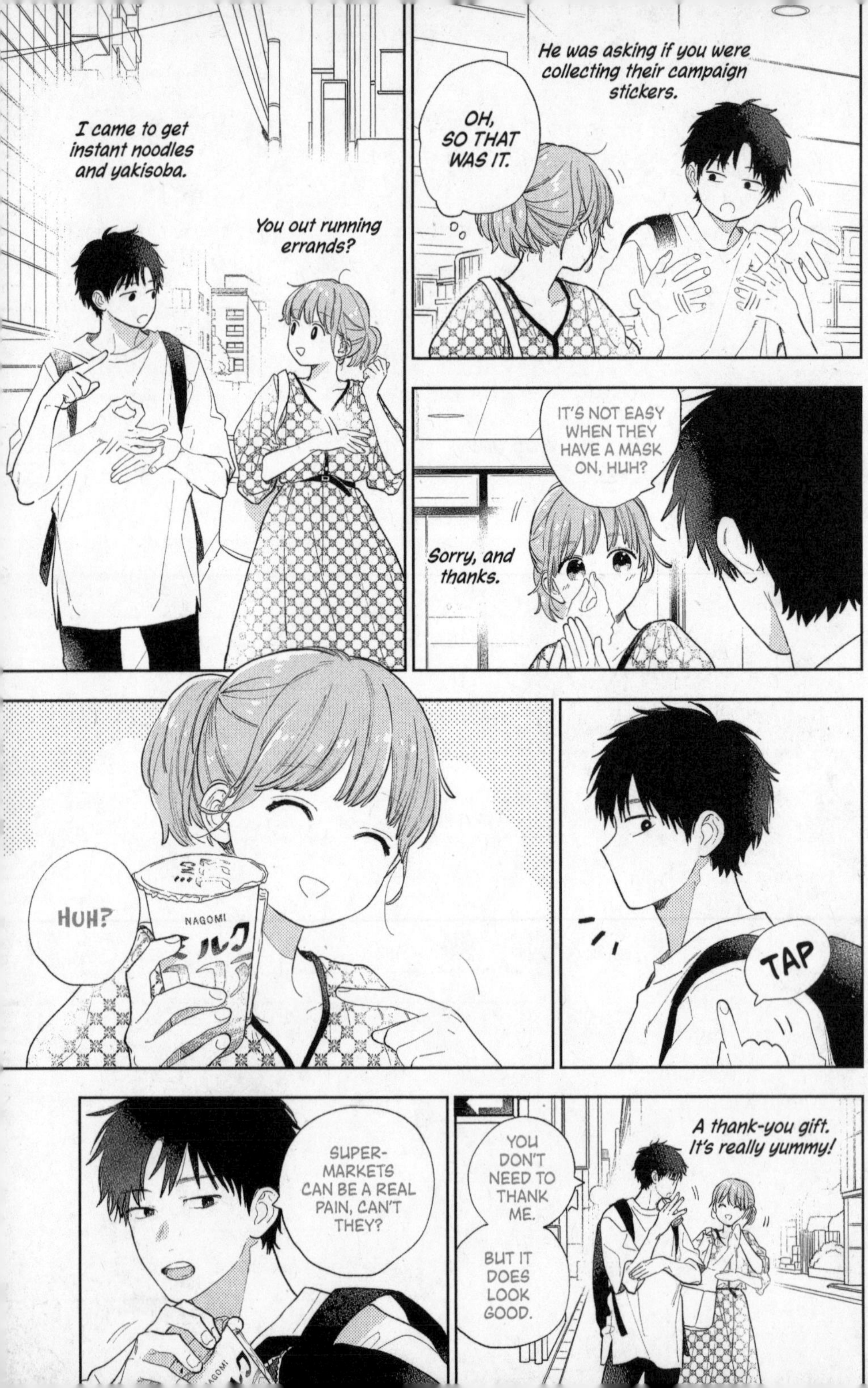
He was asking if you were collecting their campaign stickers.
OH, SO THAT WAS IT.
IT'S NOT EASY WHEN THEY HAVE A MASK ON, HUH?
Sorry, and thanks.
You out running errands?
I came to get instant noodles and yakisoba.
TAP
HUH?
NAGOMI
ミルク
A thank-you gift. It's really yummy!
YOU DON'T NEED TO THANK ME.
BUT IT DOES LOOK GOOD.
SUPER-MARKETS CAN BE A REAL PAIN, CAN'T THEY?

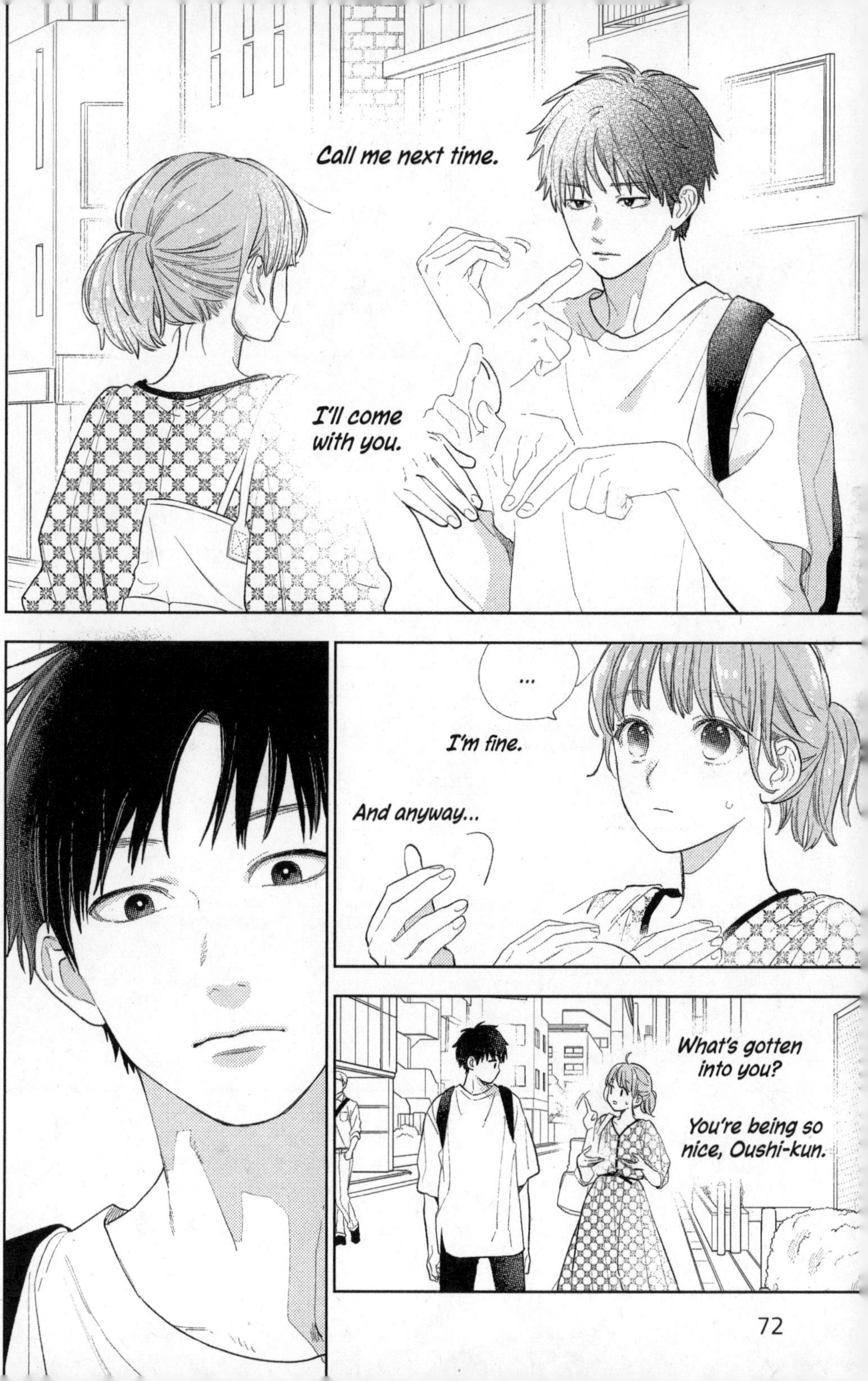

Call me next time.
I'll come with you.
...
I'm fine.
And anyway...
What's gotten into you?
You're being so nice, Oushi-kun.

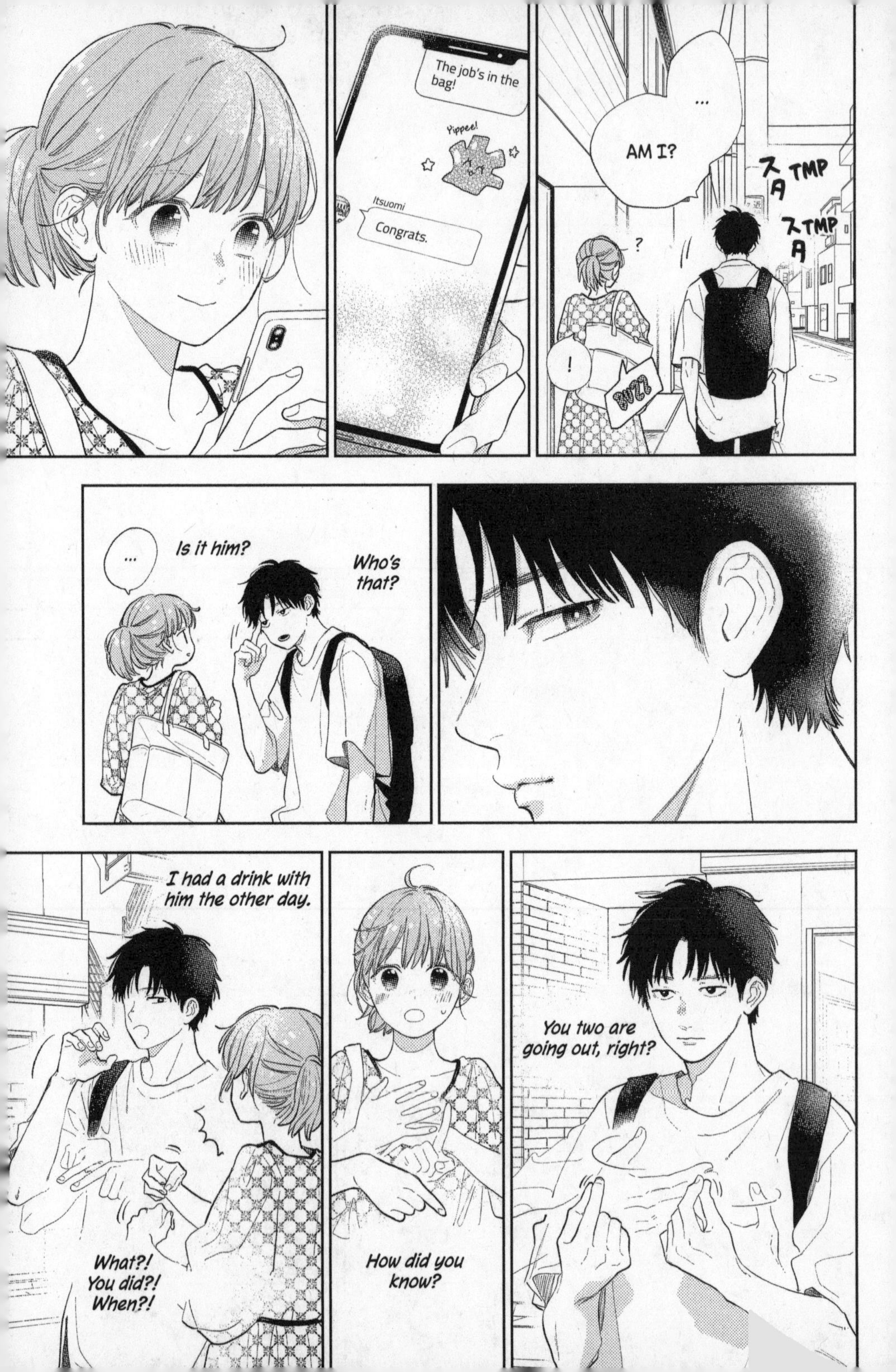
...
AM I?
TMP
TMP
?
!
The job's in the bag!
Yippee!
Itsuomi
Congrats.
Who's that?
Is it him?
...
You two are going out, right?
How did you know?
I had a drink with him the other day.
What?! You did?! When?!

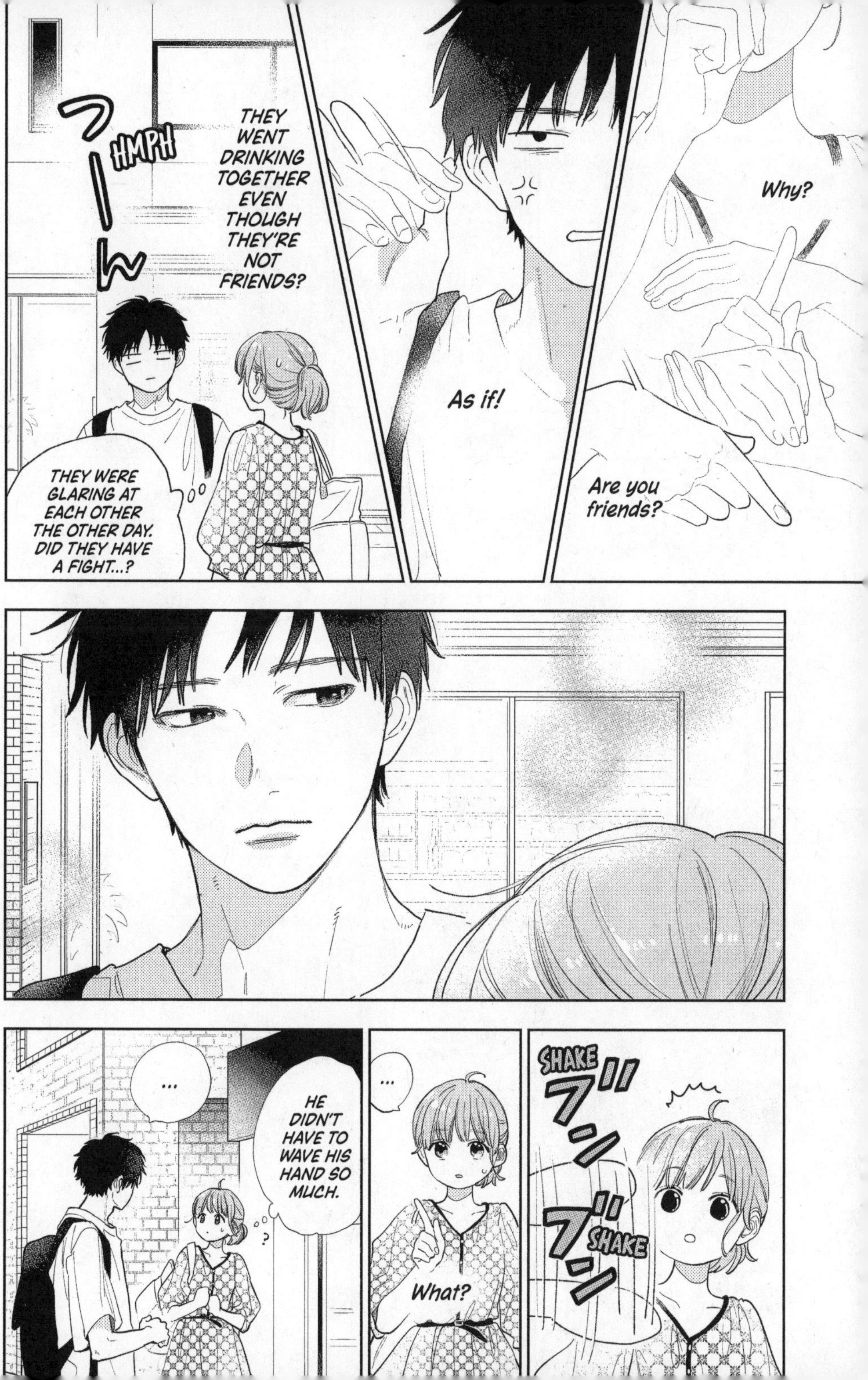
Why?
Are you friends?
As if!
HMPH
THEY WENT DRINKING TOGETHER EVEN THOUGH THEY'RE NOT FRIENDS?
THEY WERE GLARING AT EACH OTHER THE OTHER DAY. DID THEY HAVE A FIGHT...?
SHAKE
SHAKE
...
What?
...
HE DIDN'T HAVE TO WAVE HIS HAND SO MUCH.
?

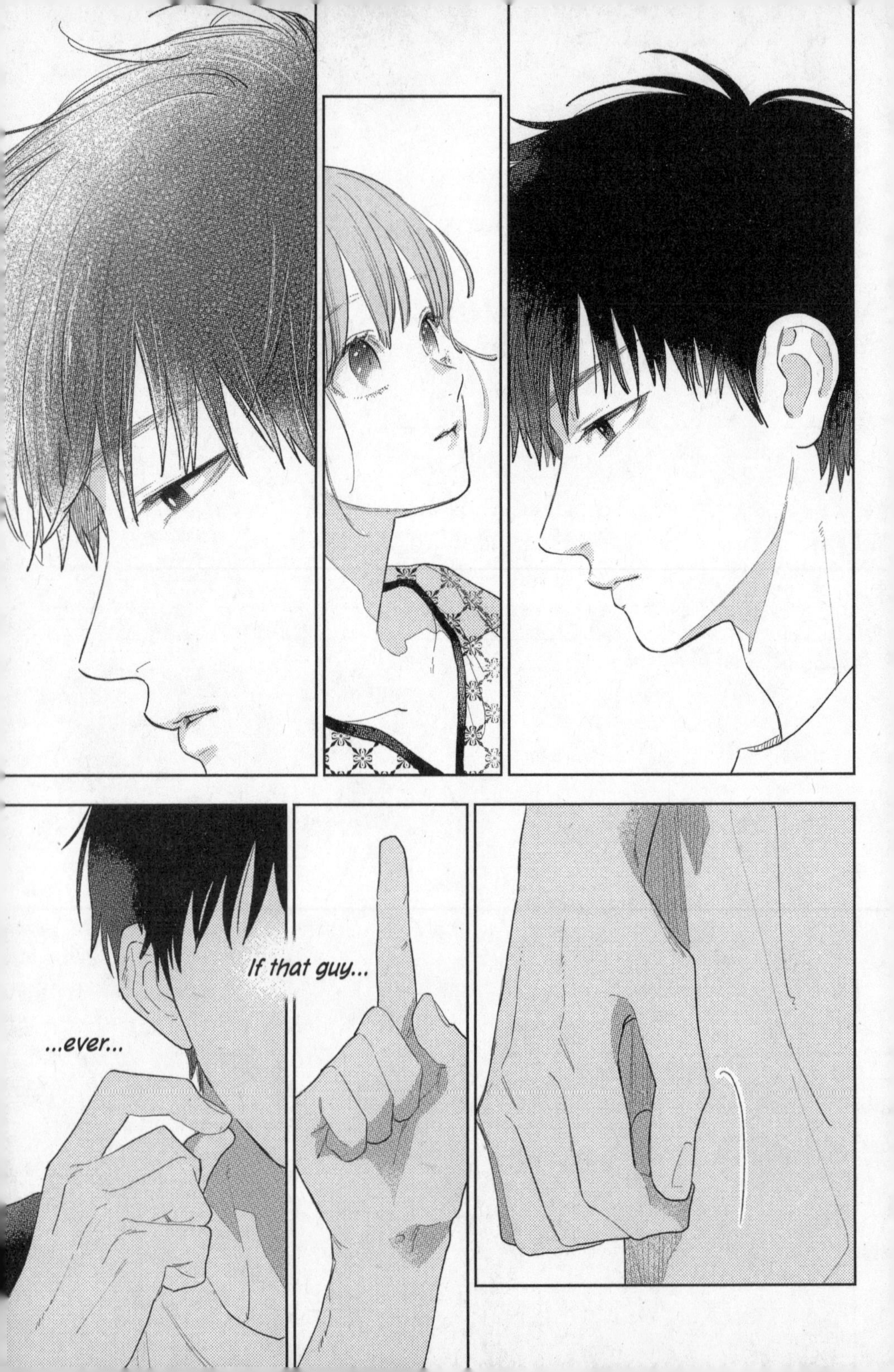
If that guy...
...ever...

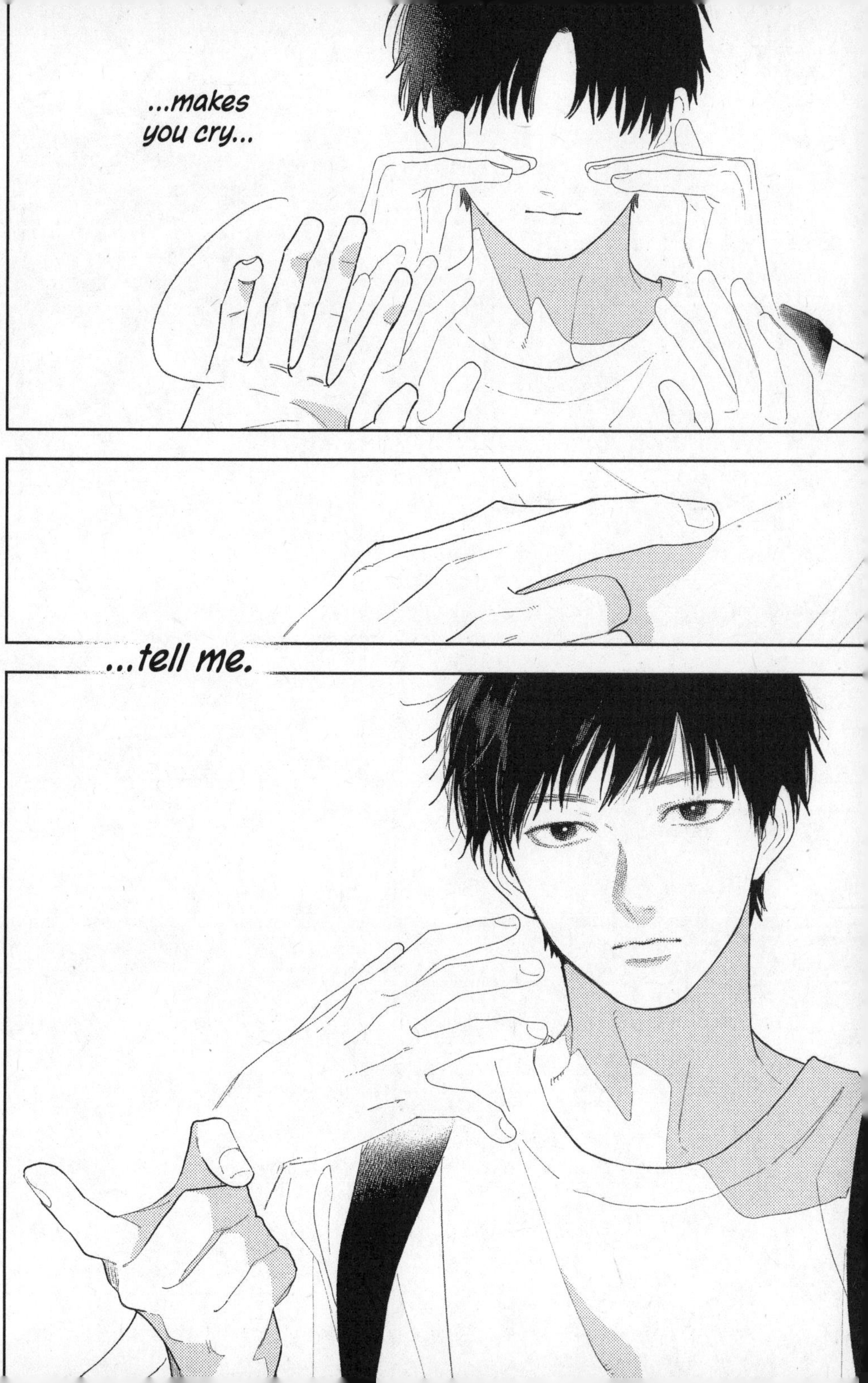
...makes you cry...
...tell me.

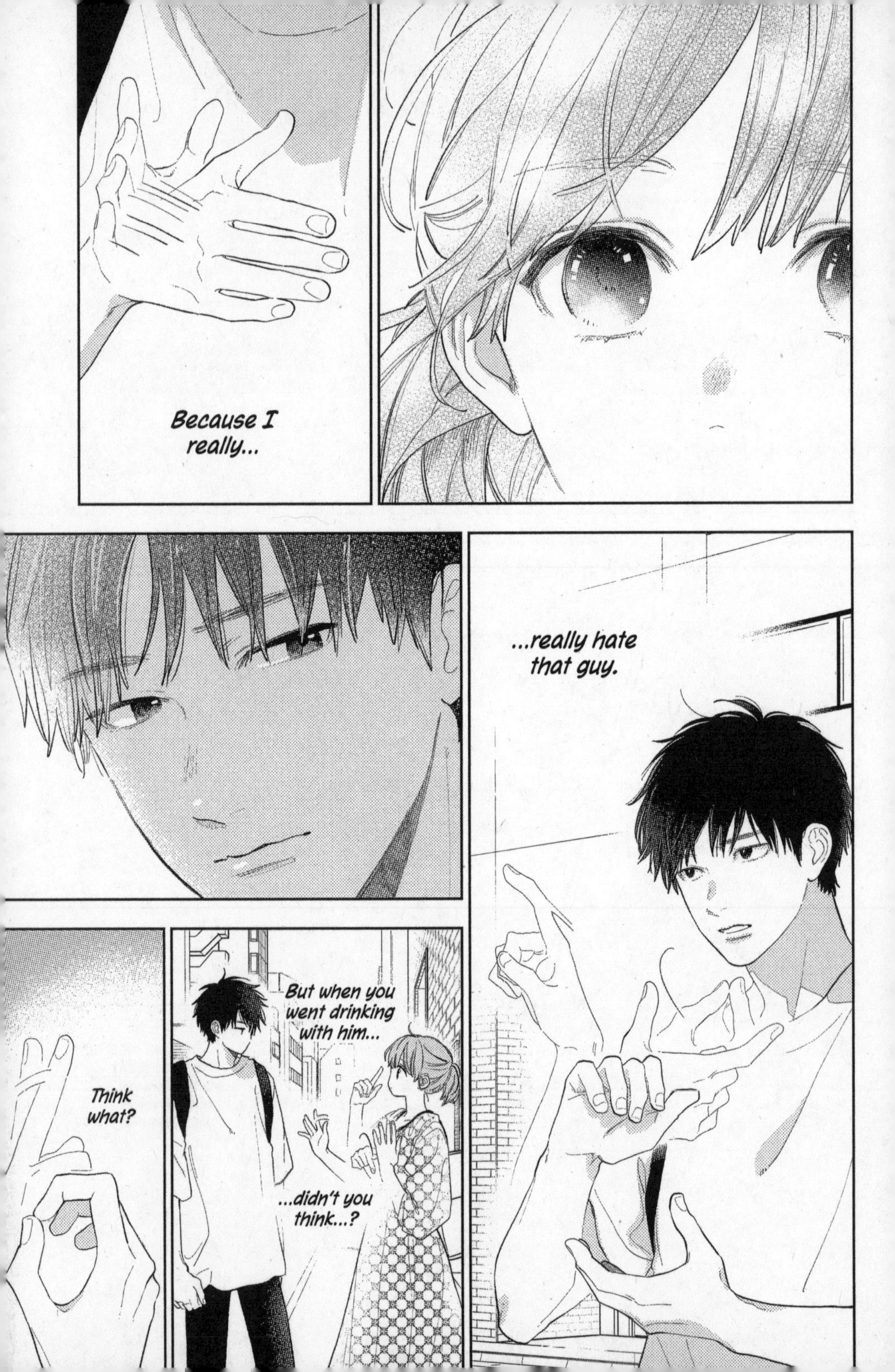
Because I really...
...really hate that guy.
But when you went drinking with him...
...didn't you think...?
Think what?

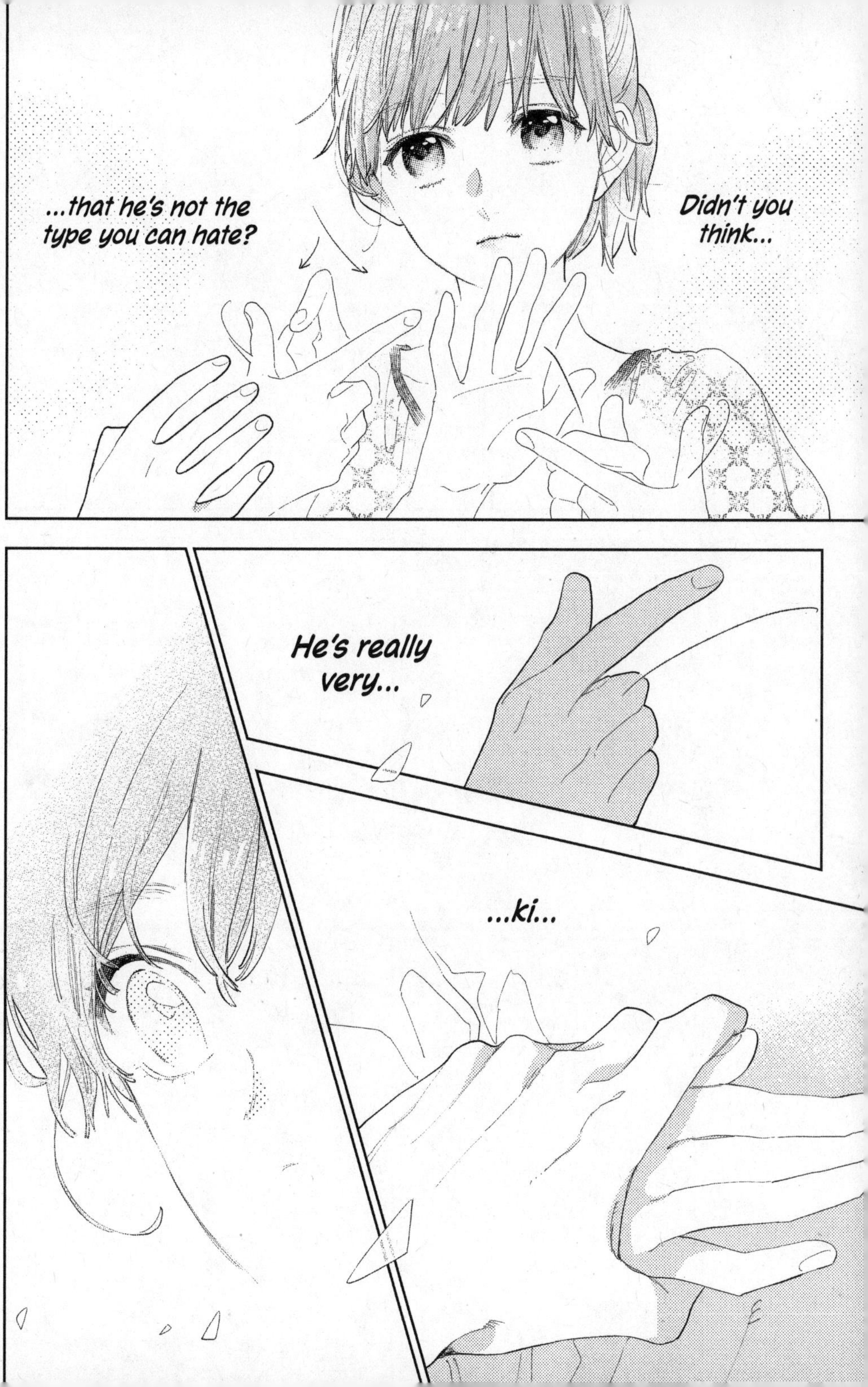
Didn't you think...
...that he's not the type you can hate?
He's really very...
...ki...

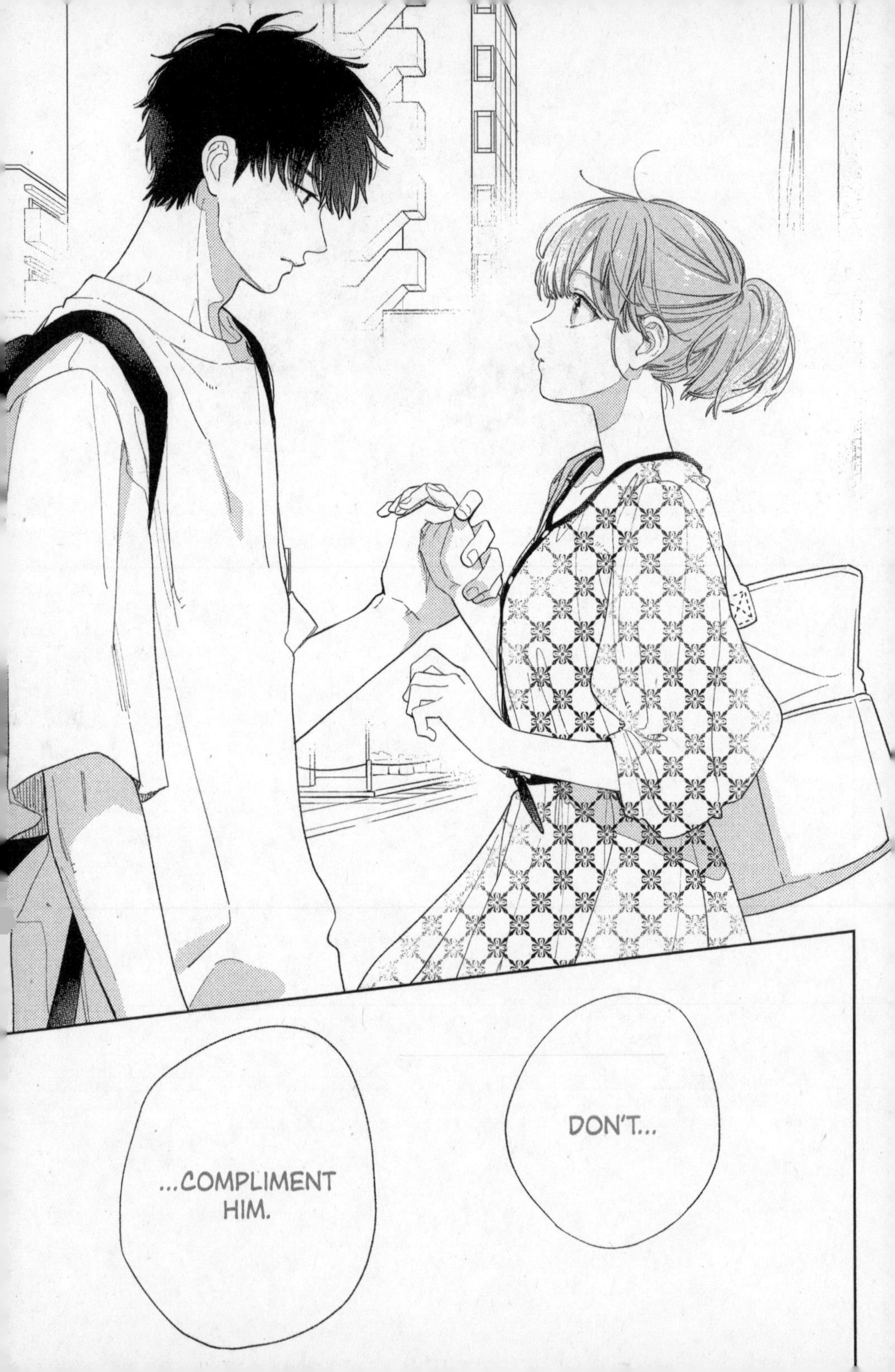
DON'T...
...COMPLIMENT HIM.

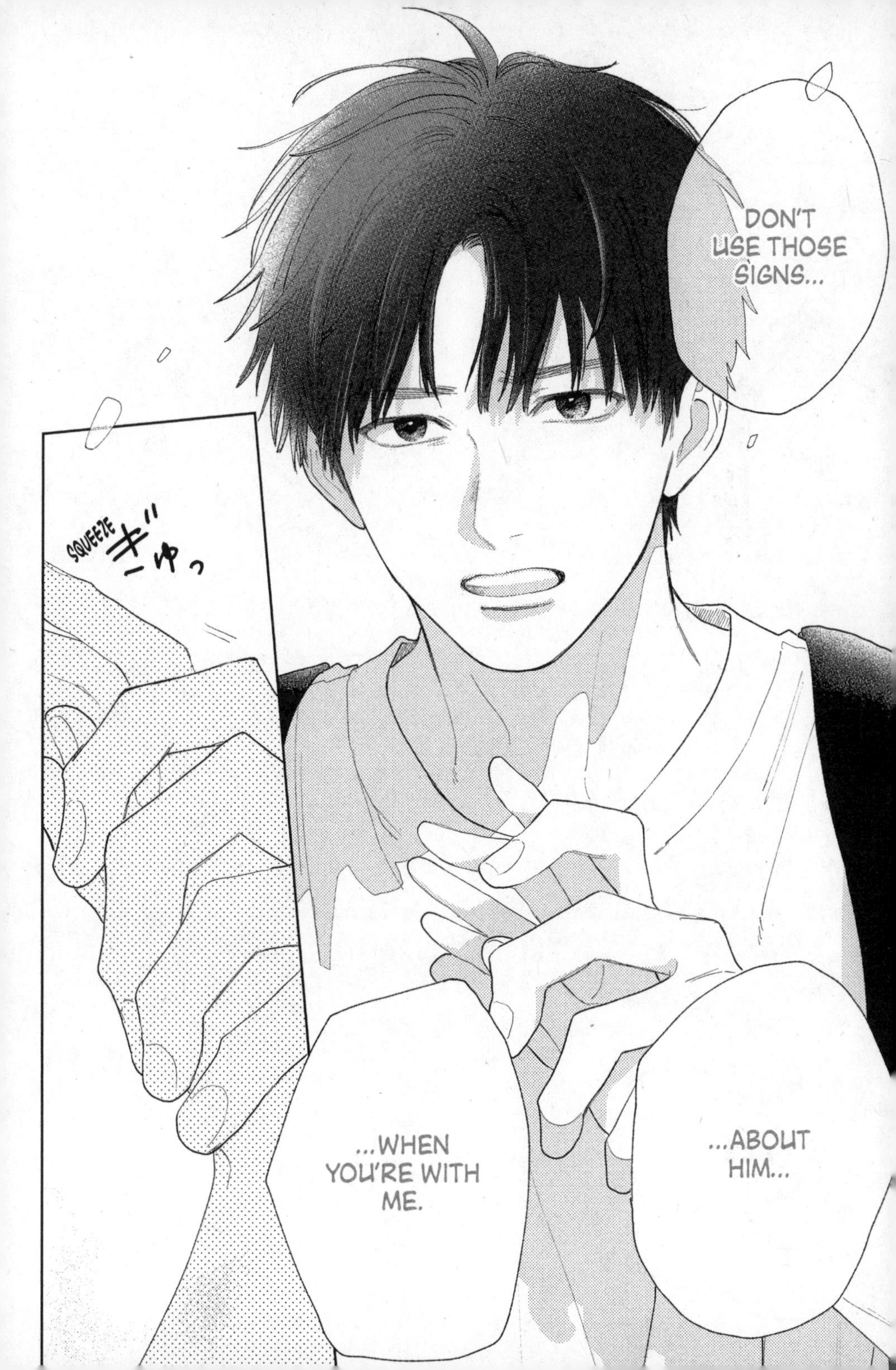
DON'T USE THOSE SIGNS...
...ABOUT HIM...
...WHEN YOU'RE WITH ME.
SQUEEZE
ぎゅっ

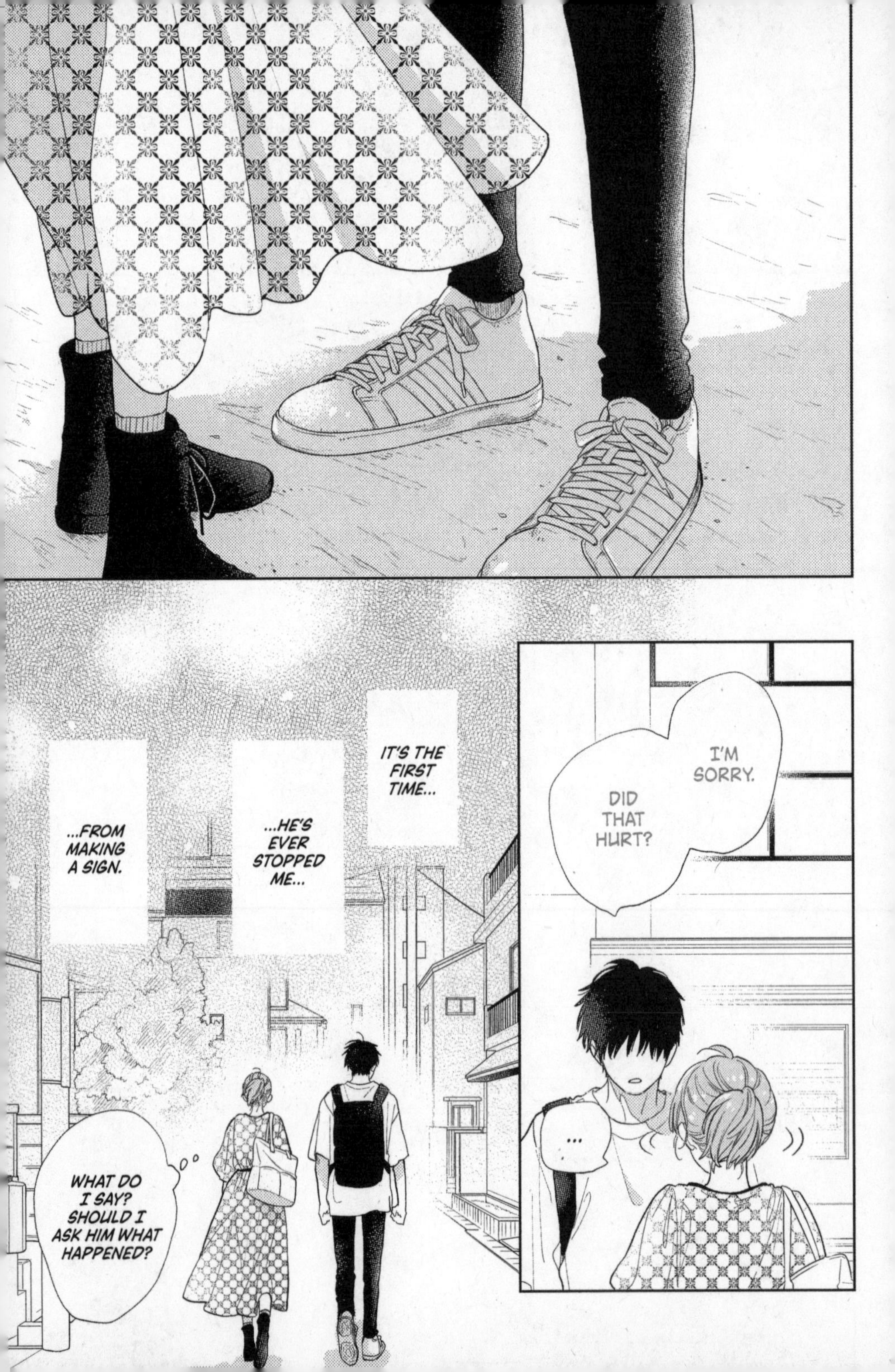
I'M SORRY.
DID THAT HURT?
...
IT'S THE FIRST TIME...
...HE'S EVER STOPPED ME...
...FROM MAKING A SIGN.
WHAT DO I SAY? SHOULD I ASK HIM WHAT HAPPENED?

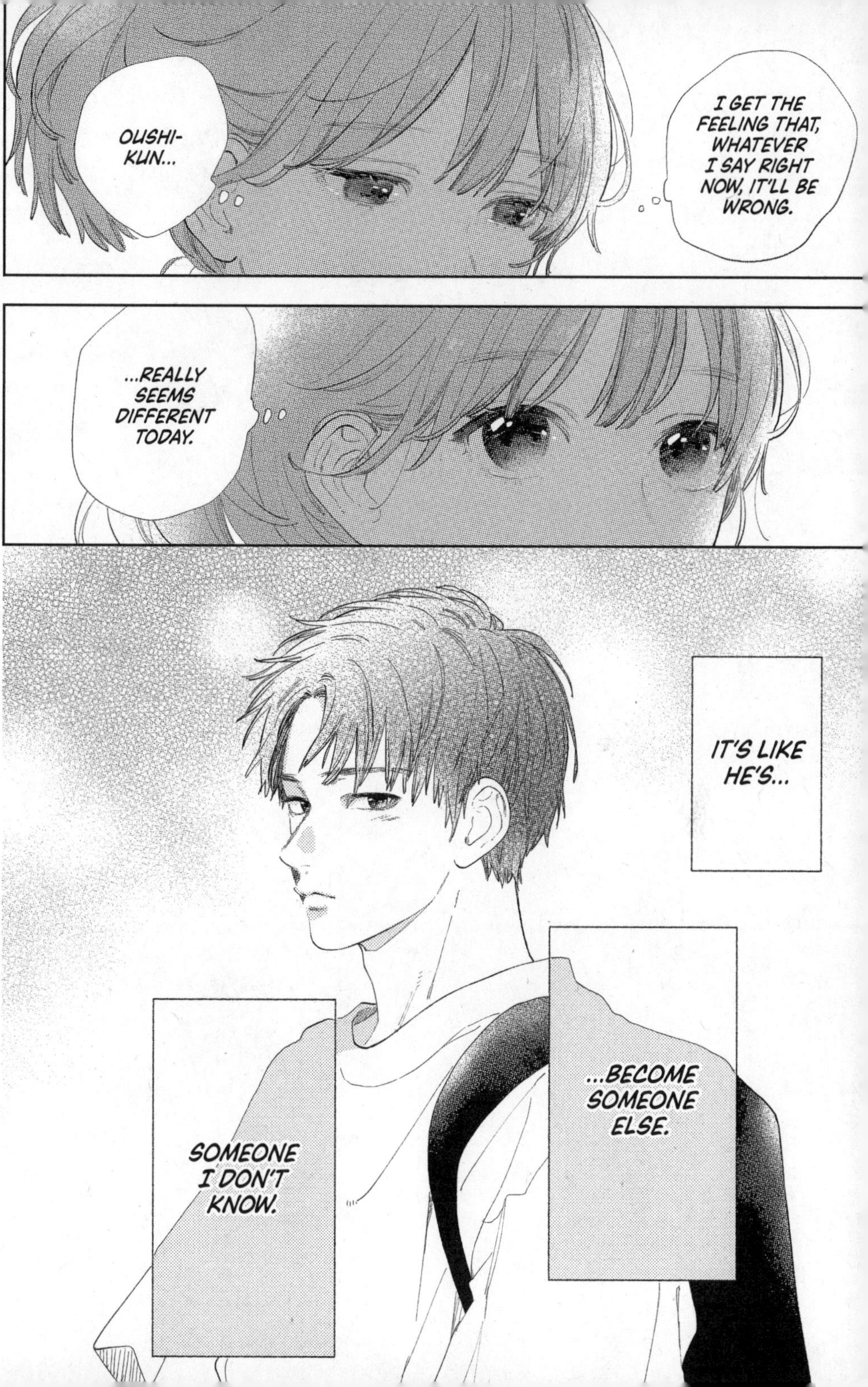
I GET THE FEELING THAT, WHATEVER I SAY RIGHT NOW, IT'LL BE WRONG.
OUSHI-KUN...
...REALLY SEEMS DIFFERENT TODAY.
IT'S LIKE HE'S...
...BECOME SOMEONE ELSE.
SOMEONE I DON'T KNOW.

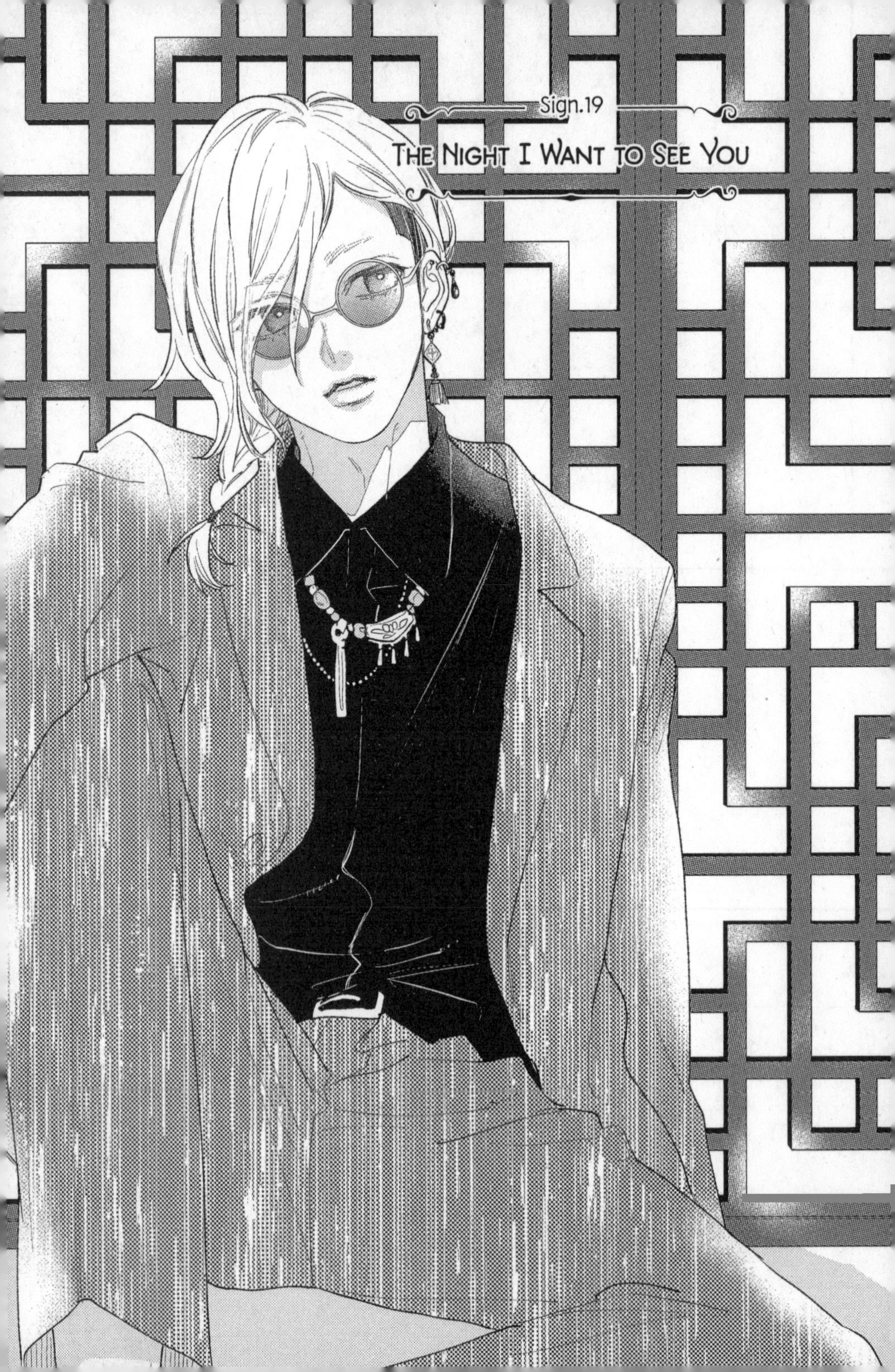
Sign.19
The Night I Want to See You

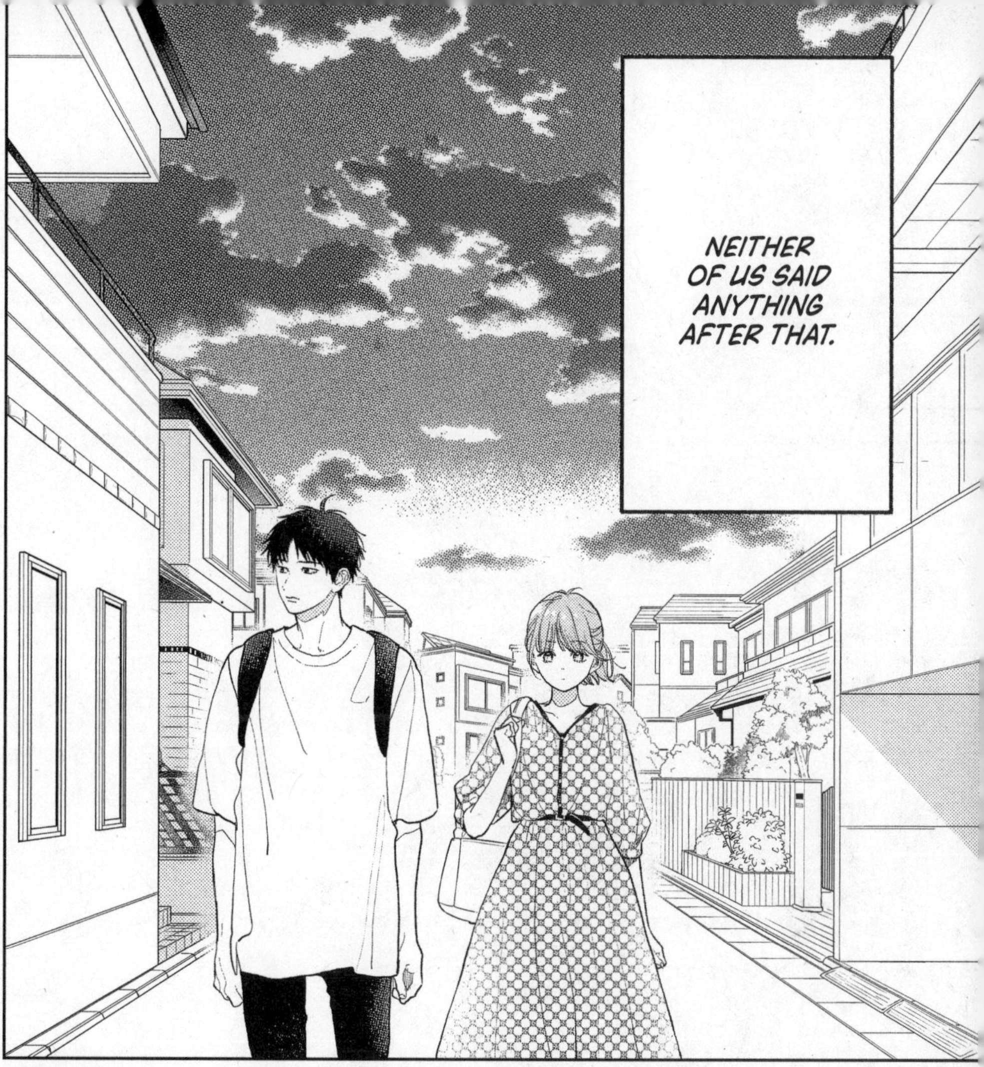
NEITHER OF US SAID ANYTHING AFTER THAT.

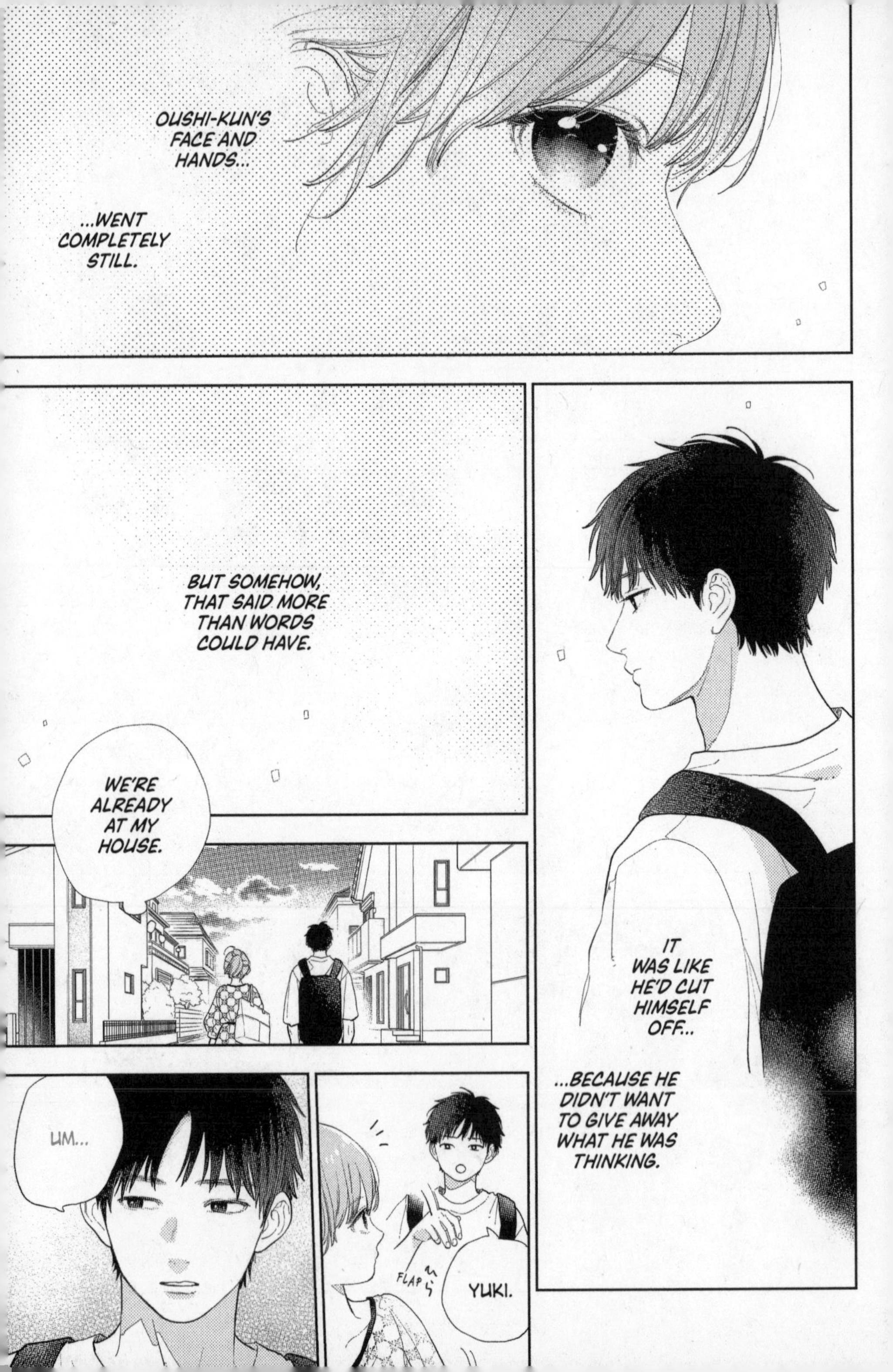
OUSHI-KUN'S FACE AND HANDS...
...WENT COMPLETELY STILL.
IT WAS LIKE HE'D CUT HIMSELF OFF...
...BECAUSE HE DIDN'T WANT TO GIVE AWAY WHAT HE WAS THINKING.
BUT SOMEHOW, THAT SAID MORE THAN WORDS COULD HAVE.
WE'RE ALREADY AT MY HOUSE.
FLAP
YUKI.
UM...

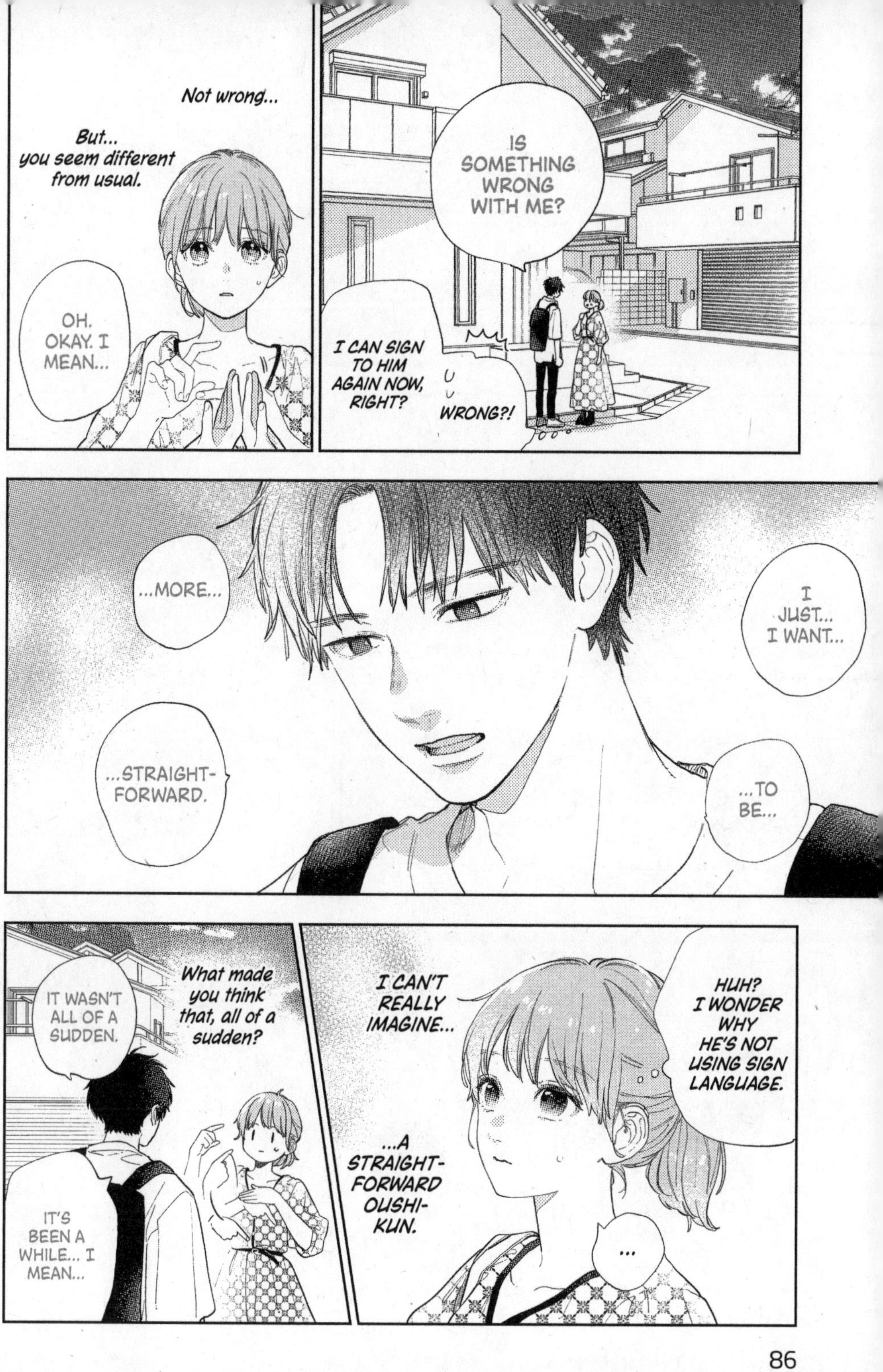
IS SOMETHING WRONG WITH ME?
I CAN SIGN TO HIM AGAIN NOW, RIGHT?
WRONG?!
Not wrong...
But... you seem different from usual.
OH. OKAY. I MEAN...
I JUST... I WANT...
...TO BE...
...MORE...
...STRAIGHT-FORWARD.
HUH? I WONDER WHY HE'S NOT USING SIGN LANGUAGE.
I CAN'T REALLY IMAGINE...
...A STRAIGHT-FORWARD OUSHI-KUN.
...
What made you think that, all of a sudden?
IT WASN'T ALL OF A SUDDEN.
IT'S BEEN A WHILE... I MEAN...

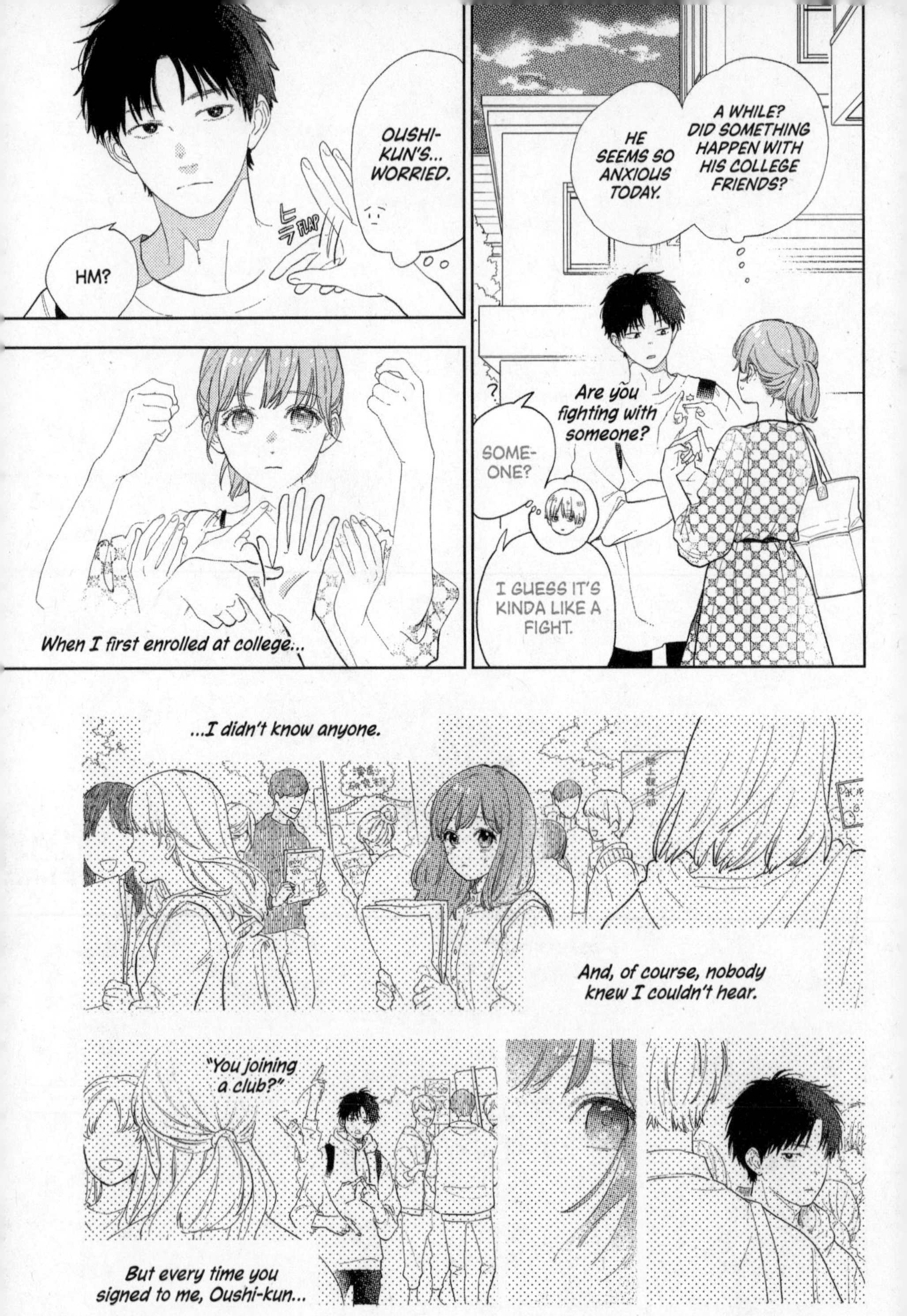
A WHILE? DID SOMETHING HAPPEN WITH HIS COLLEGE FRIENDS?
HE SEEMS SO ANXIOUS TODAY.
Are you fighting with someone?
?
SOME-ONE?
I GUESS IT'S KINDA LIKE A FIGHT.
OUSHI-KUN'S... WORRIED.
FLAP
HM?
When I first enrolled at college...
...I didn't know anyone.
And, of course, nobody knew I couldn't hear.
"You joining a club?"
But every time you signed to me, Oushi-kun...

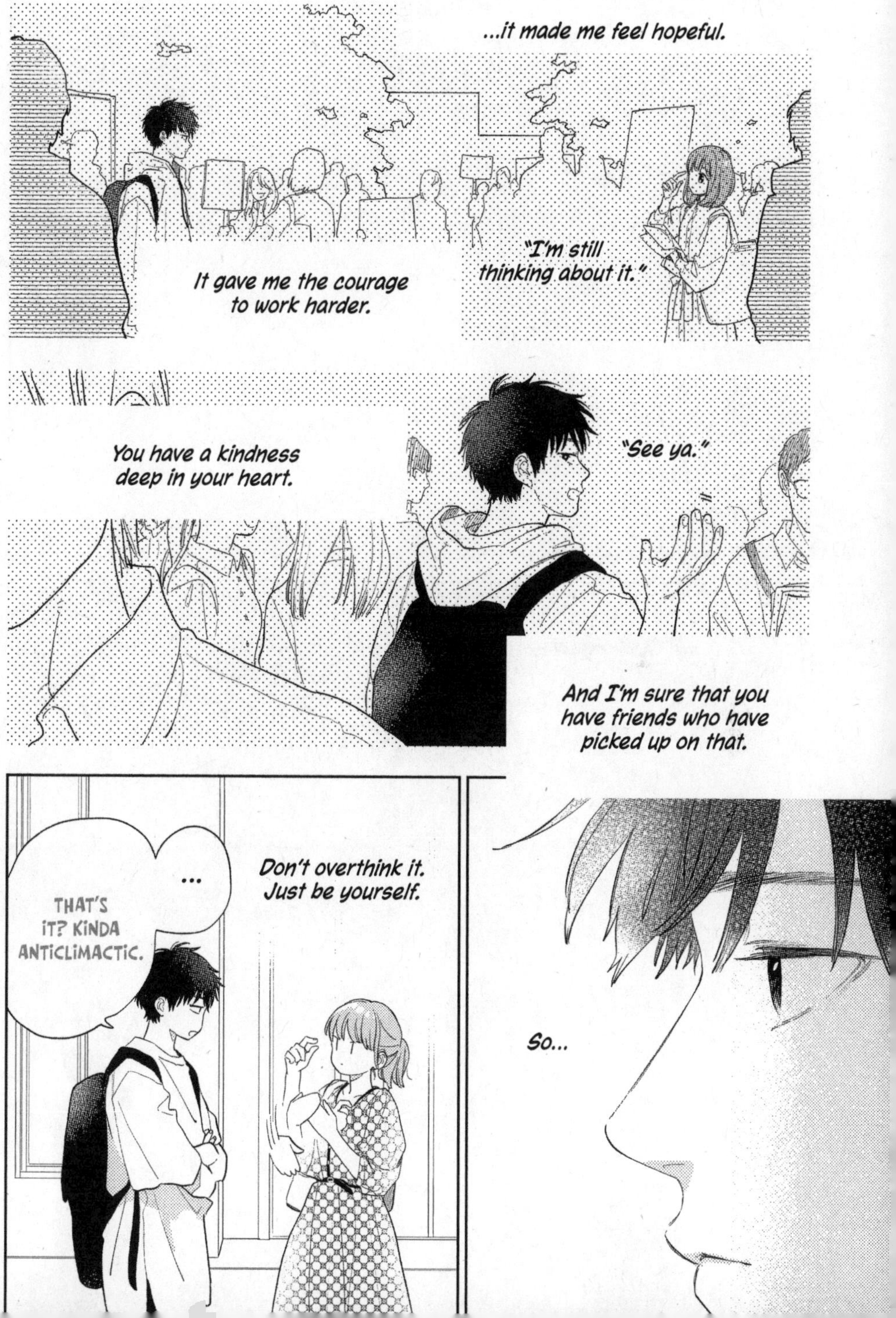
...it made me feel hopeful.
"I'm still thinking about it."
It gave me the courage to work harder.
"See ya."
You have a kindness deep in your heart.
And I'm sure that you have friends who have picked up on that.
So...
Don't overthink it. Just be yourself.
...
THAT'S IT? KINDA ANTICLIMACTIC.

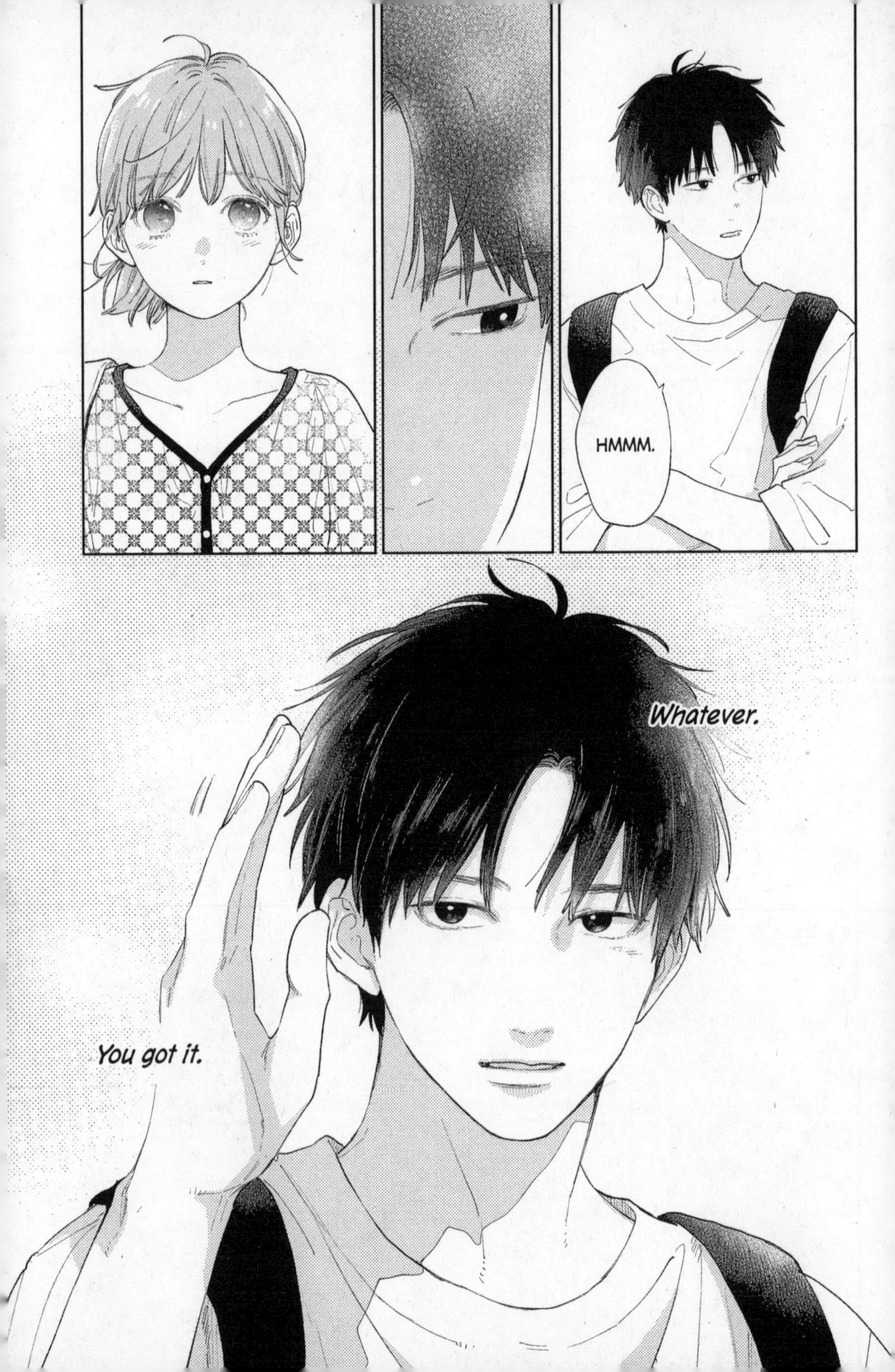
HMMM.
Whatever.
You got it.

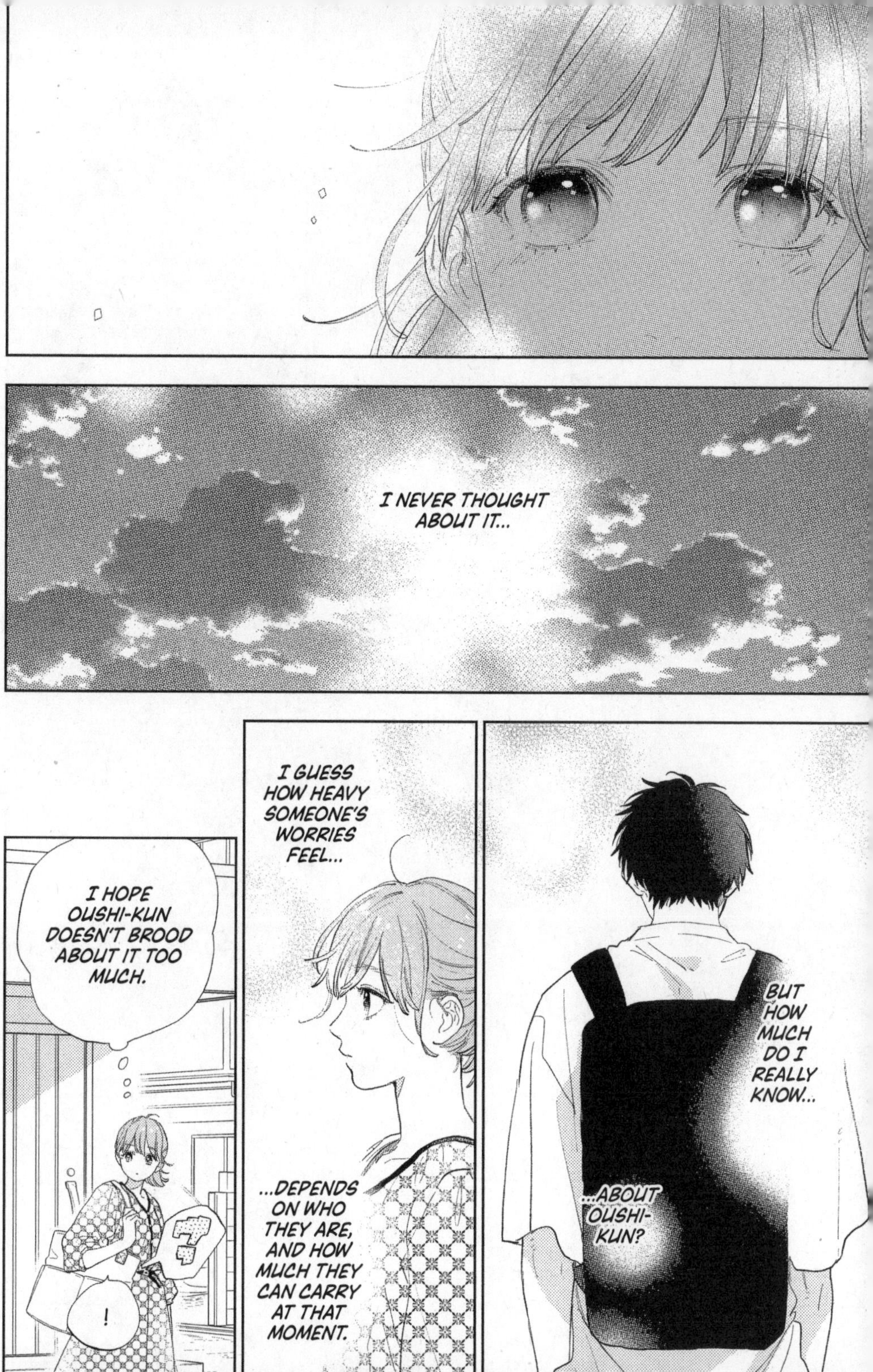
I NEVER THOUGHT ABOUT IT...
BUT HOW MUCH DO I REALLY KNOW...
...ABOUT OUSHI-KUN?
I GUESS HOW HEAVY SOMEONE'S WORRIES FEEL...
...DEPENDS ON WHO THEY ARE, AND HOW MUCH THEY CAN CARRY AT THAT MOMENT.
I HOPE OUSHI-KUN DOESN'T BROOD ABOUT IT TOO MUCH.
!

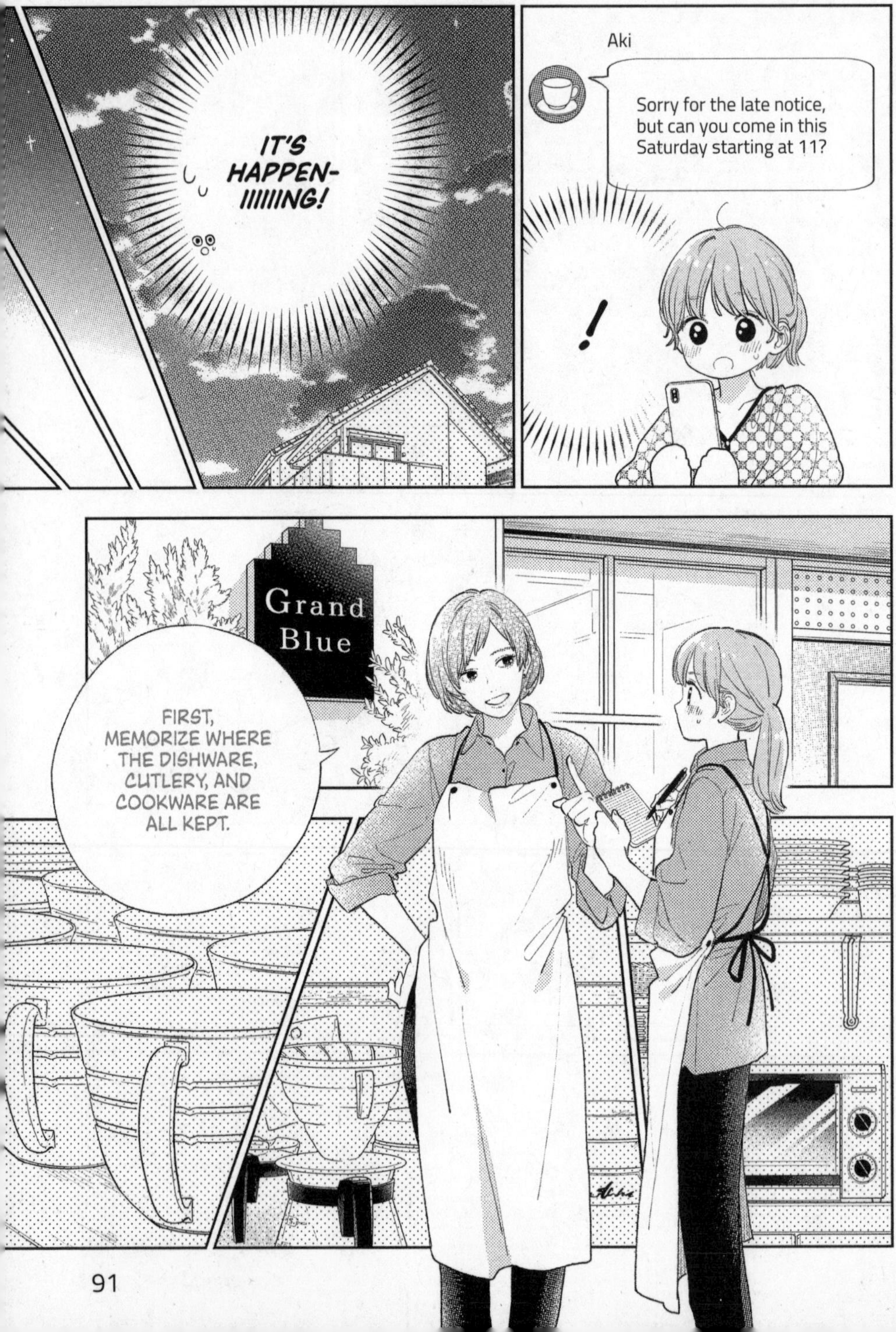
Aki
Sorry for the late notice, but can you come in this Saturday starting at 11?
IT'S HAPPEN-IIIIIING!
Grand Blue
FIRST, MEMORIZE WHERE THE DISHWARE, CUTLERY, AND COOKWARE ARE ALL KEPT.

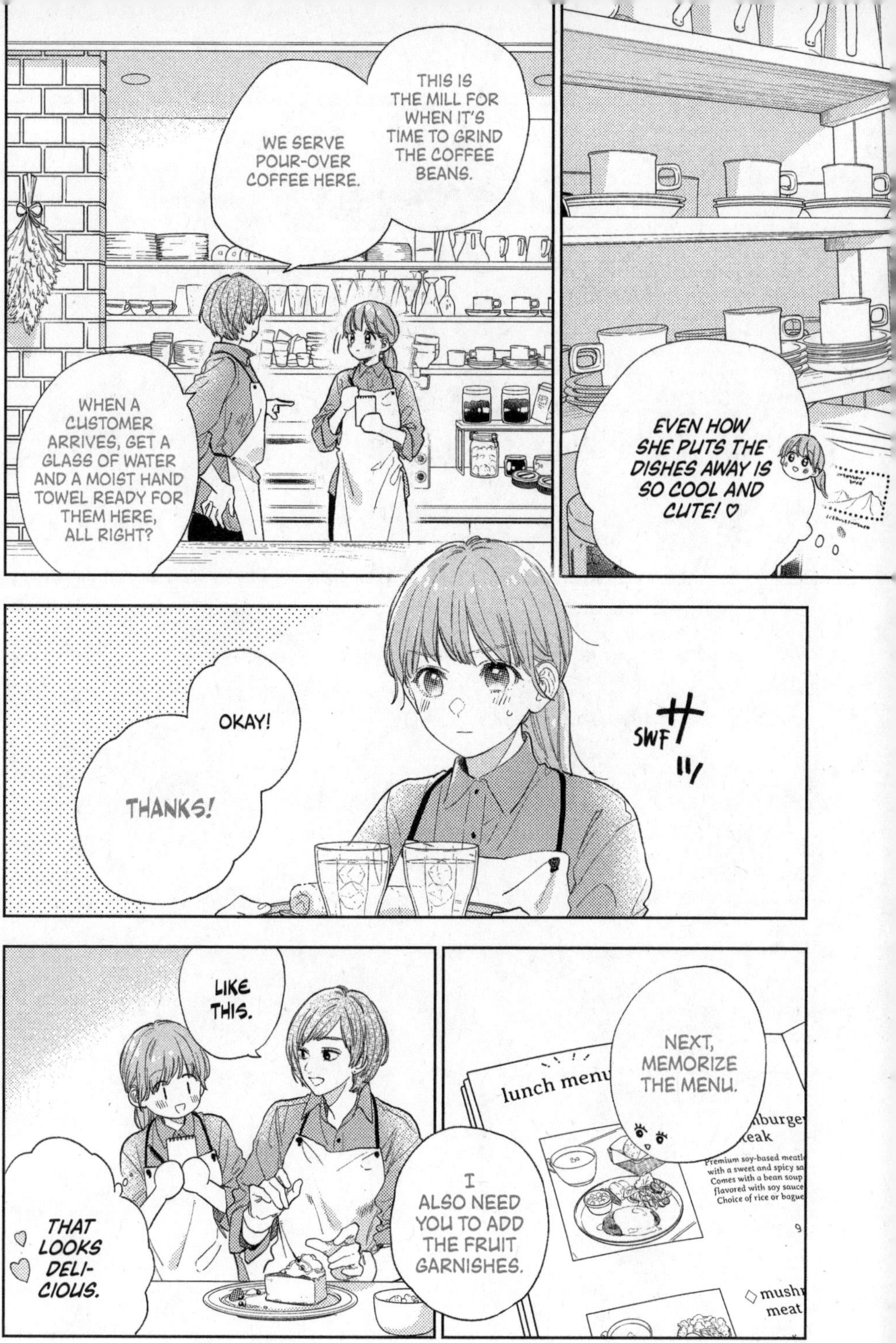
EVEN HOW SHE PUTS THE DISHES AWAY IS SO COOL AND CUTE! ♡
WE SERVE POUR-OVER COFFEE HERE.
THIS IS THE MILL FOR WHEN IT'S TIME TO GRIND THE COFFEE BEANS.
WHEN A CUSTOMER ARRIVES, GET A GLASS OF WATER AND A MOIST HAND TOWEL READY FOR THEM HERE, ALL RIGHT?
SWF
OKAY!
THANKS!
NEXT, MEMORIZE THE MENU.
lunch menu
LIKE THIS.
I ALSO NEED YOU TO ADD THE FRUIT GARNISHES.
THAT LOOKS DELI-CIOUS.

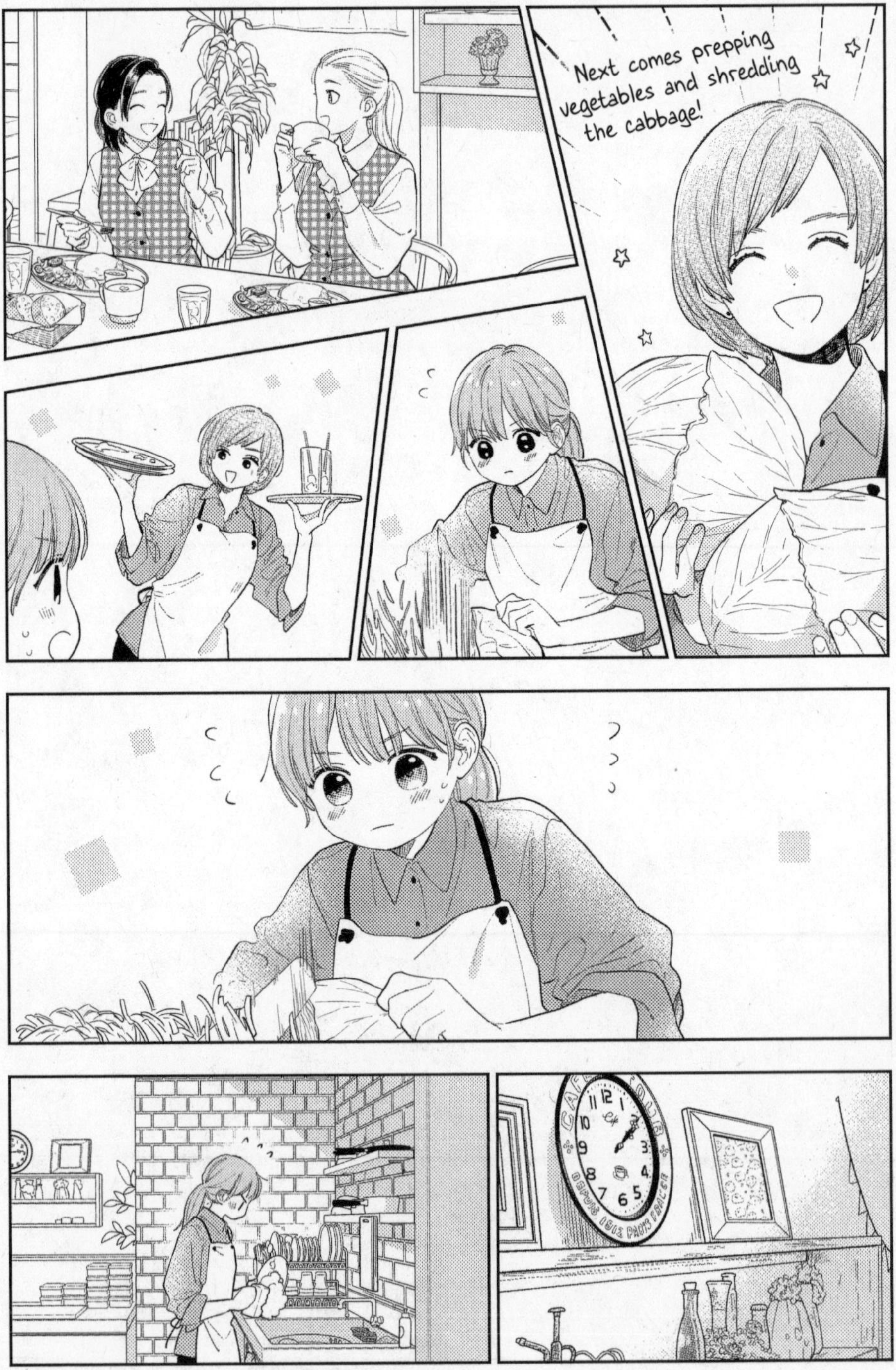
Next comes prepping vegetables and shredding the cabbage!

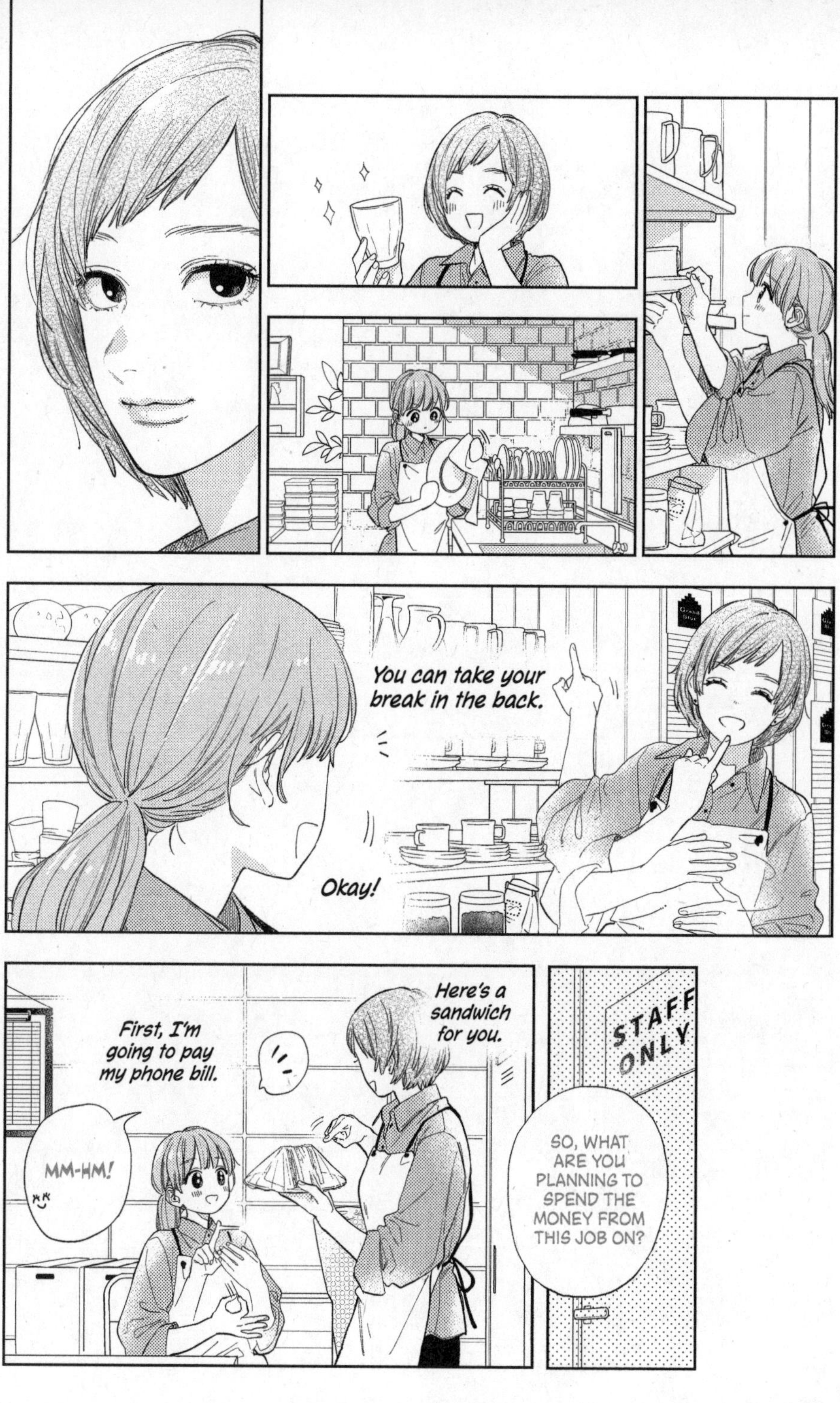
You can take your break in the back.
Okay!
STAFF ONLY
SO, WHAT ARE YOU PLANNING TO SPEND THE MONEY FROM THIS JOB ON?
Here's a sandwich for you.
First, I'm going to pay my phone bill.
MM-HM!

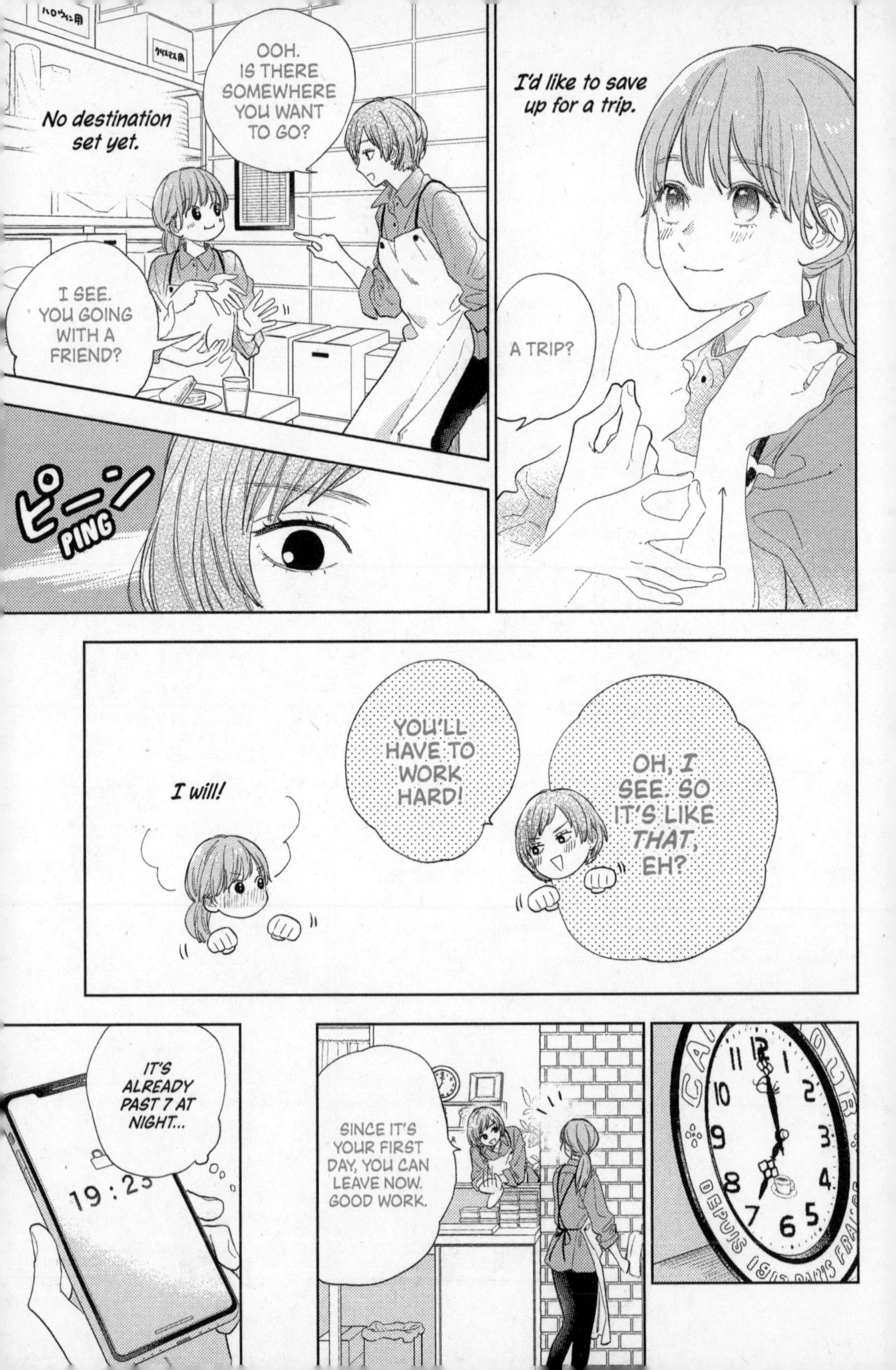
I'd like to save up for a trip.
A TRIP?
OOH. IS THERE SOMEWHERE YOU WANT TO GO?
No destination set yet.
I SEE. YOU GOING WITH A FRIEND?
ピーン
PING
OH, I SEE. SO IT'S LIKE THAT, EH?
YOU'LL HAVE TO WORK HARD!
I will!
SINCE IT'S YOUR FIRST DAY, YOU CAN LEAVE NOW. GOOD WORK.
IT'S ALREADY PAST 7 AT NIGHT...

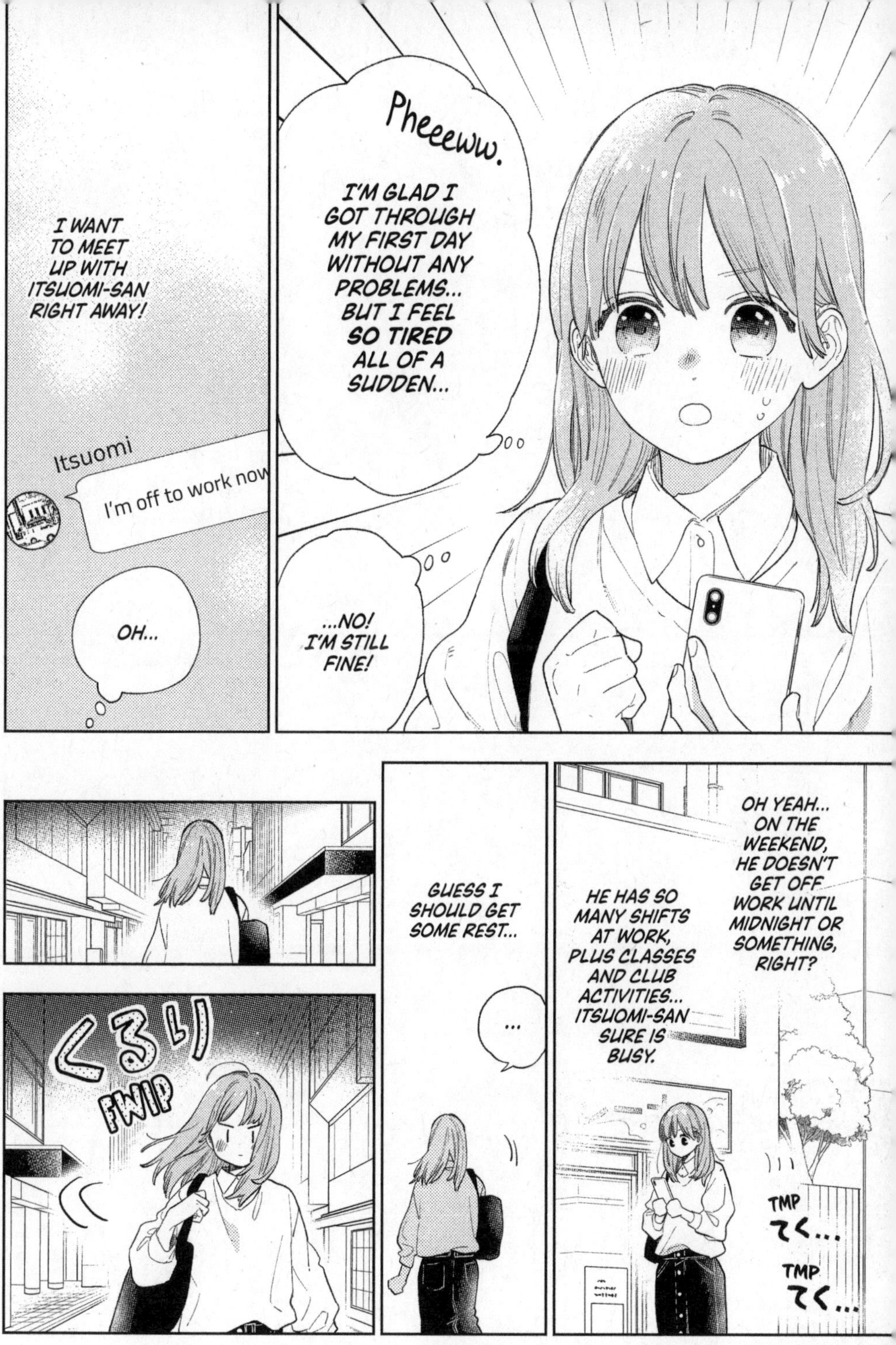
Pheeeww.
I'M GLAD I GOT THROUGH MY FIRST DAY WITHOUT ANY PROBLEMS... BUT I FEEL SO TIRED ALL OF A SUDDEN...
...NO! I'M STILL FINE!
I WANT TO MEET UP WITH ITSUOMI-SAN RIGHT AWAY!
Itsuomi
I'm off to work now
OH...
OH YEAH... ON THE WEEKEND, HE DOESN'T GET OFF WORK UNTIL MIDNIGHT OR SOMETHING, RIGHT?
HE HAS SO MANY SHIFTS AT WORK, PLUS CLASSES AND CLUB ACTIVITIES... ITSUOMI-SAN SURE IS BUSY.
TMP
てく...
TMP
てく...
...
GUESS I SHOULD GET SOME REST...
くるり
FWIP

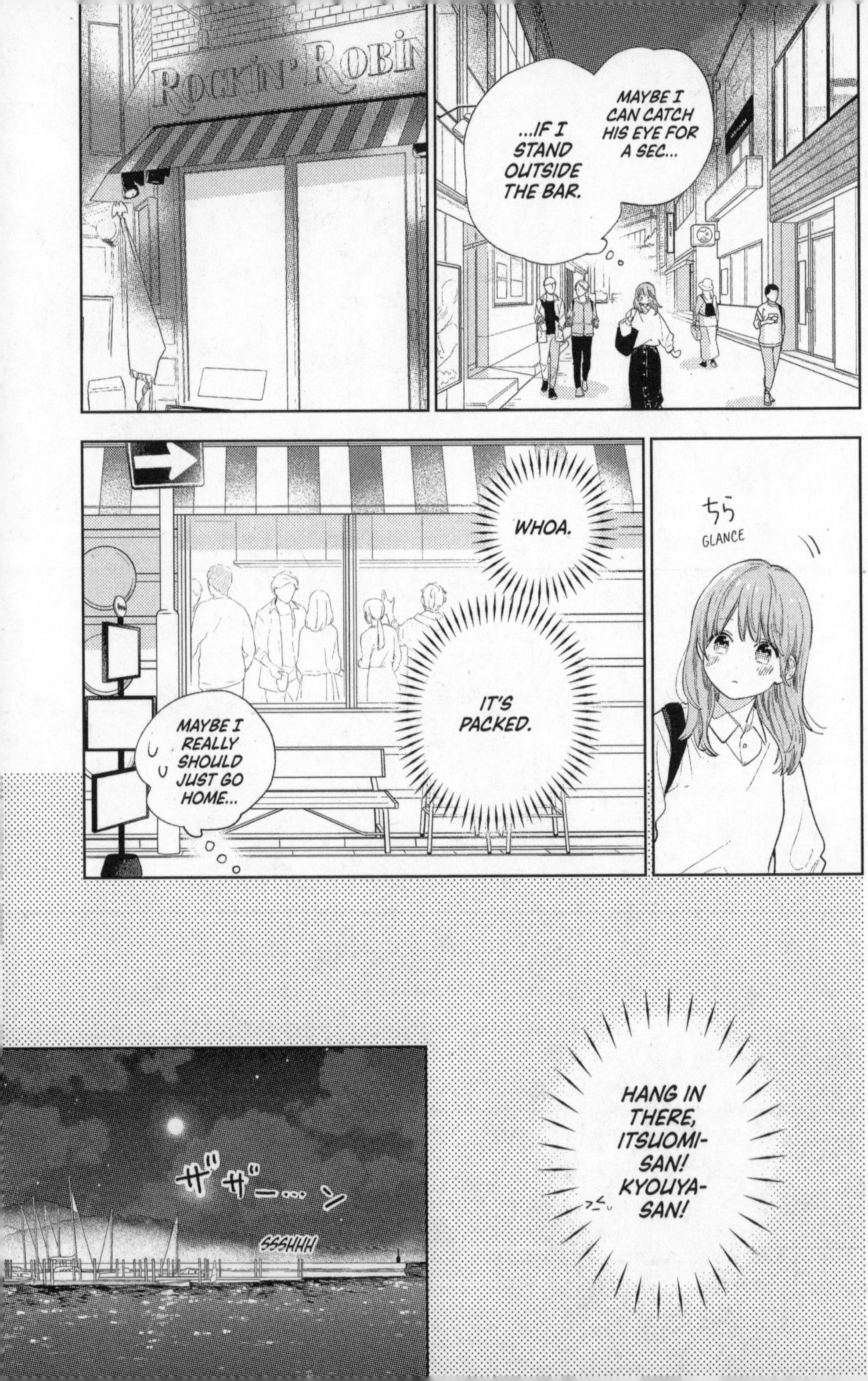
MAYBE I CAN CATCH HIS EYE FOR A SEC...
...IF I STAND OUTSIDE THE BAR.
ROCKIN' ROBI
ちら
GLANCE
WHOA.
IT'S PACKED.
MAYBE I REALLY SHOULD JUST GO HOME...
HANG IN THERE, ITSUOMI-SAN! KYOUYA-SAN!
ザザー… ン
SSSHHH

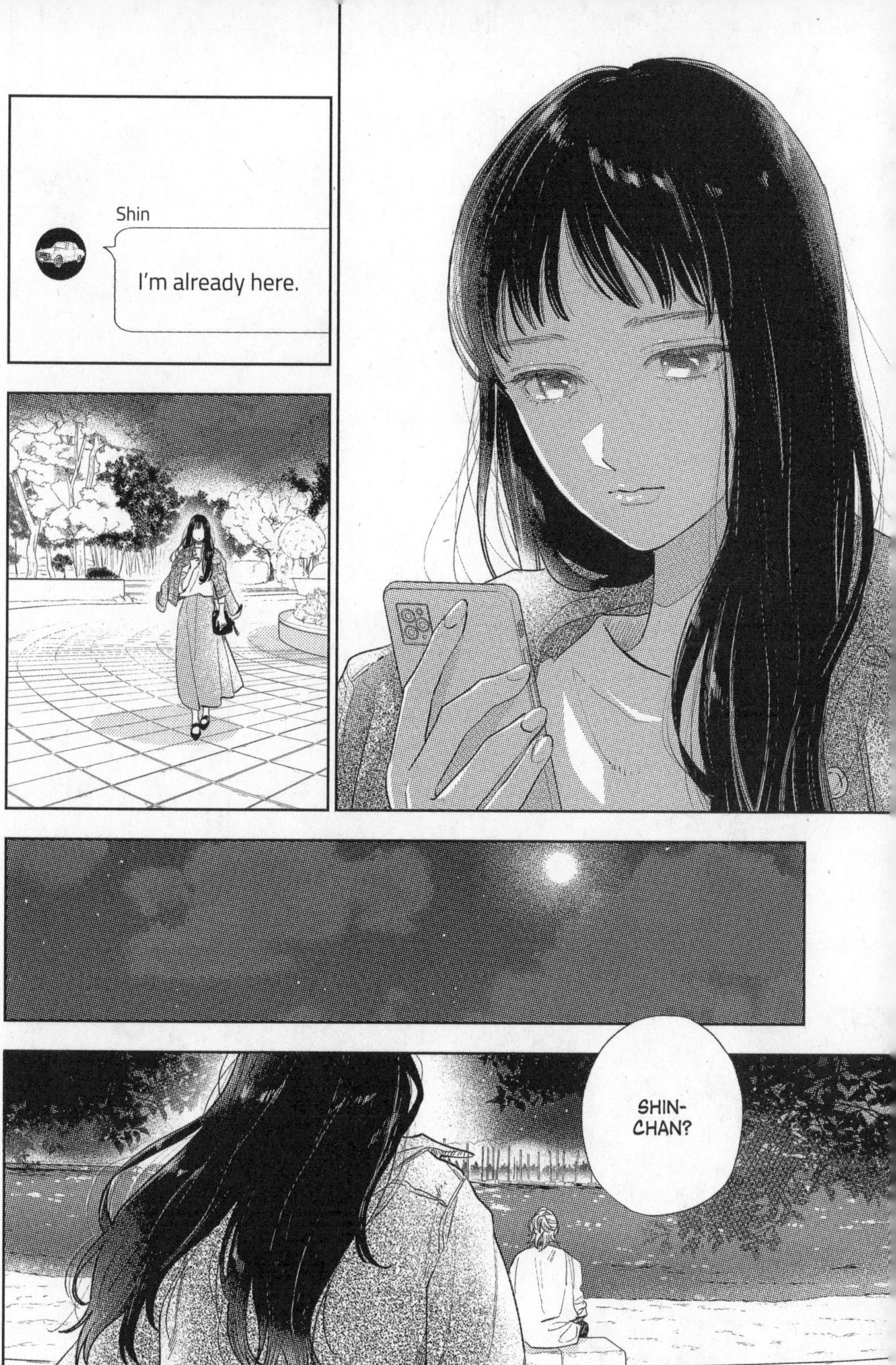
Shin
I'm already here.
SHIN-CHAN?

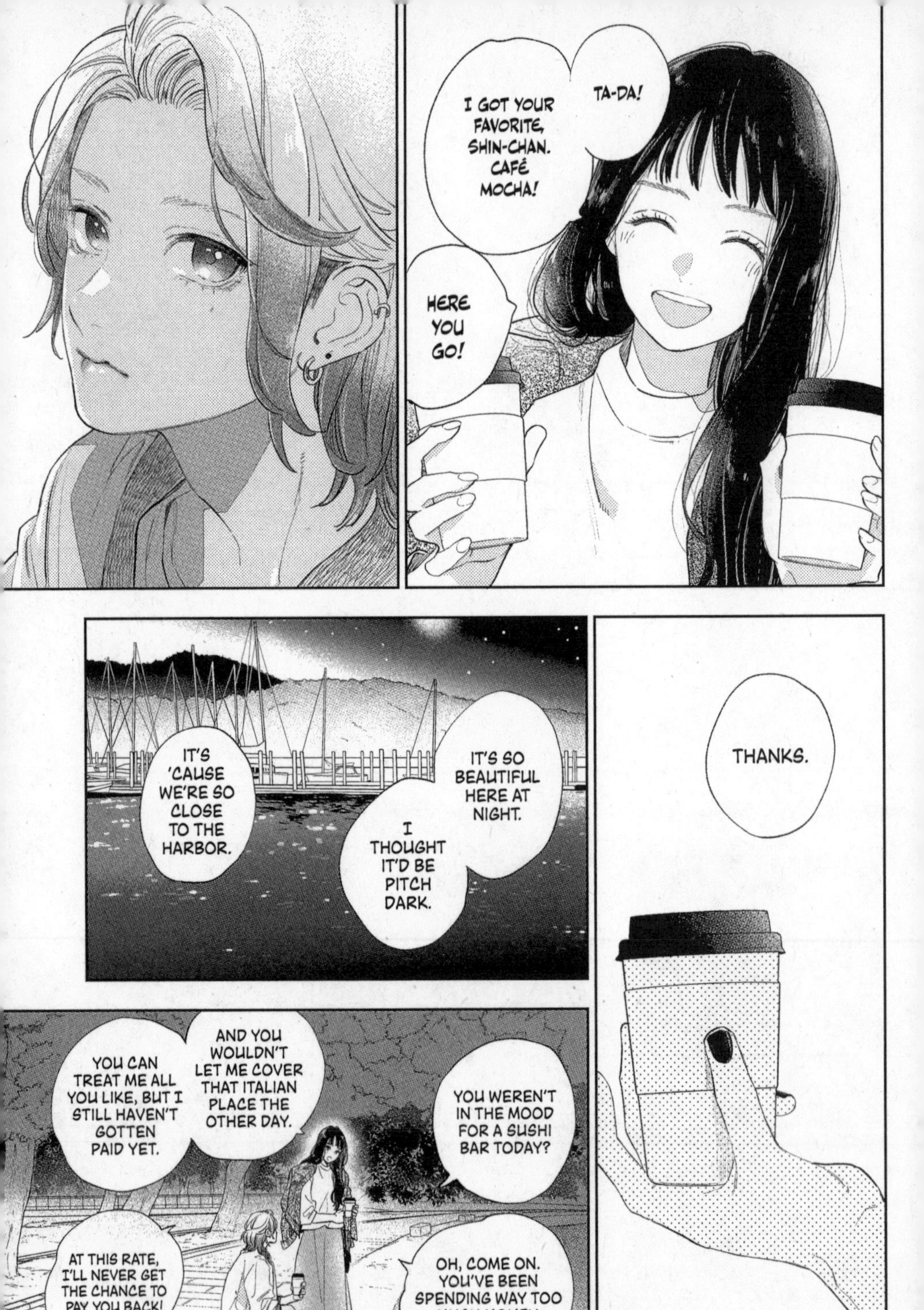
TA-DA!
I GOT YOUR FAVORITE, SHIN-CHAN. CAFÉ MOCHA!
HERE YOU GO!
THANKS.
IT'S SO BEAUTIFUL HERE AT NIGHT.
I THOUGHT IT'D BE PITCH DARK.
IT'S 'CAUSE WE'RE SO CLOSE TO THE HARBOR.
YOU WEREN'T IN THE MOOD FOR A SUSHI BAR TODAY?
OH, COME ON. YOU'VE BEEN SPENDING WAY TOO MUCH MONEY, SHIN-CHAN.
AND YOU WOULDN'T LET ME COVER THAT ITALIAN PLACE THE OTHER DAY.
YOU CAN TREAT ME ALL YOU LIKE, BUT I STILL HAVEN'T GOTTEN PAID YET.
AT THIS RATE, I'LL NEVER GET THE CHANCE TO PAY YOU BACK!

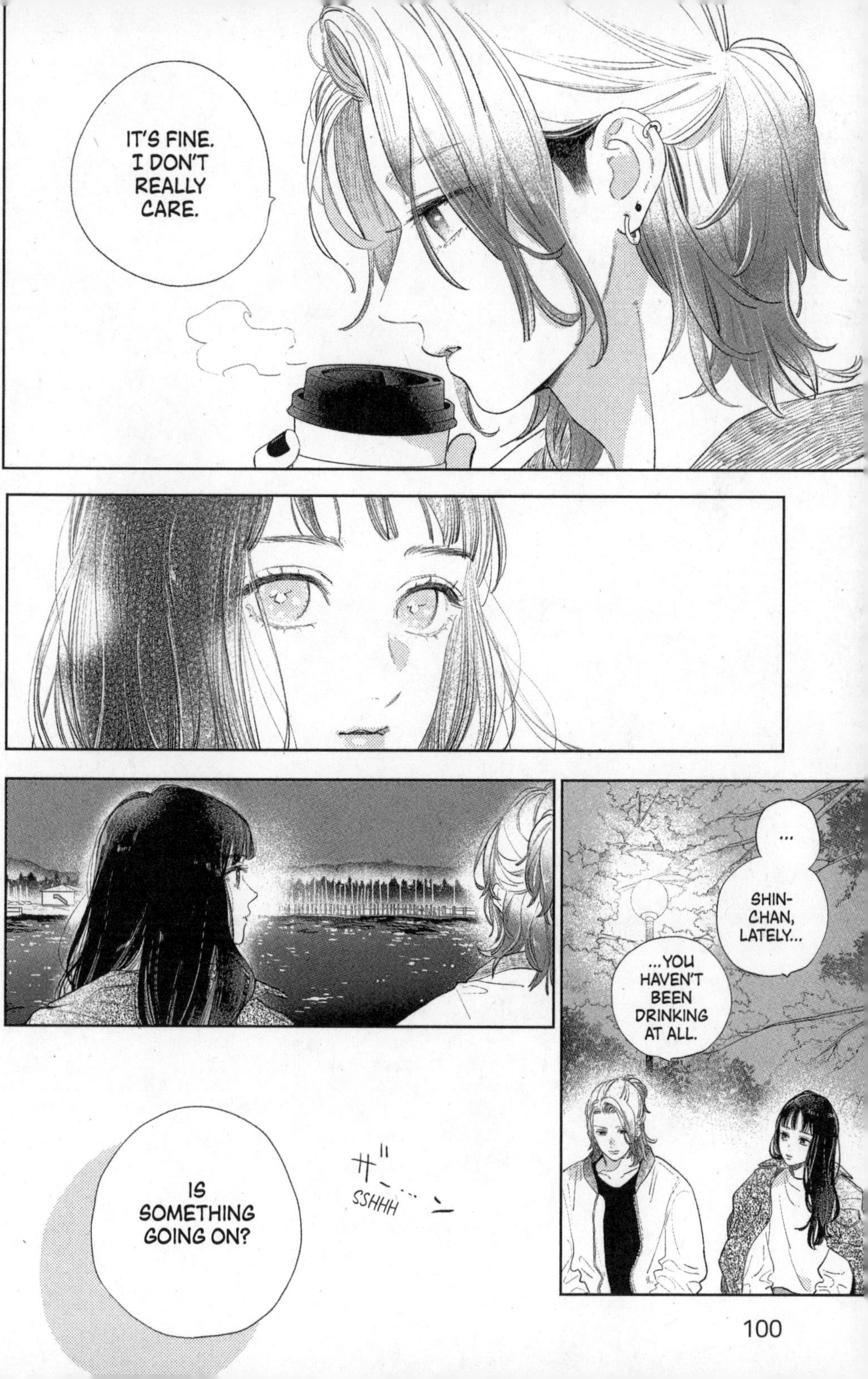
IT'S FINE. I DON'T REALLY CARE.
...
SHIN-CHAN, LATELY...
...YOU HAVEN'T BEEN DRINKING AT ALL.
ザー...
SSHHH
IS SOMETHING GOING ON?

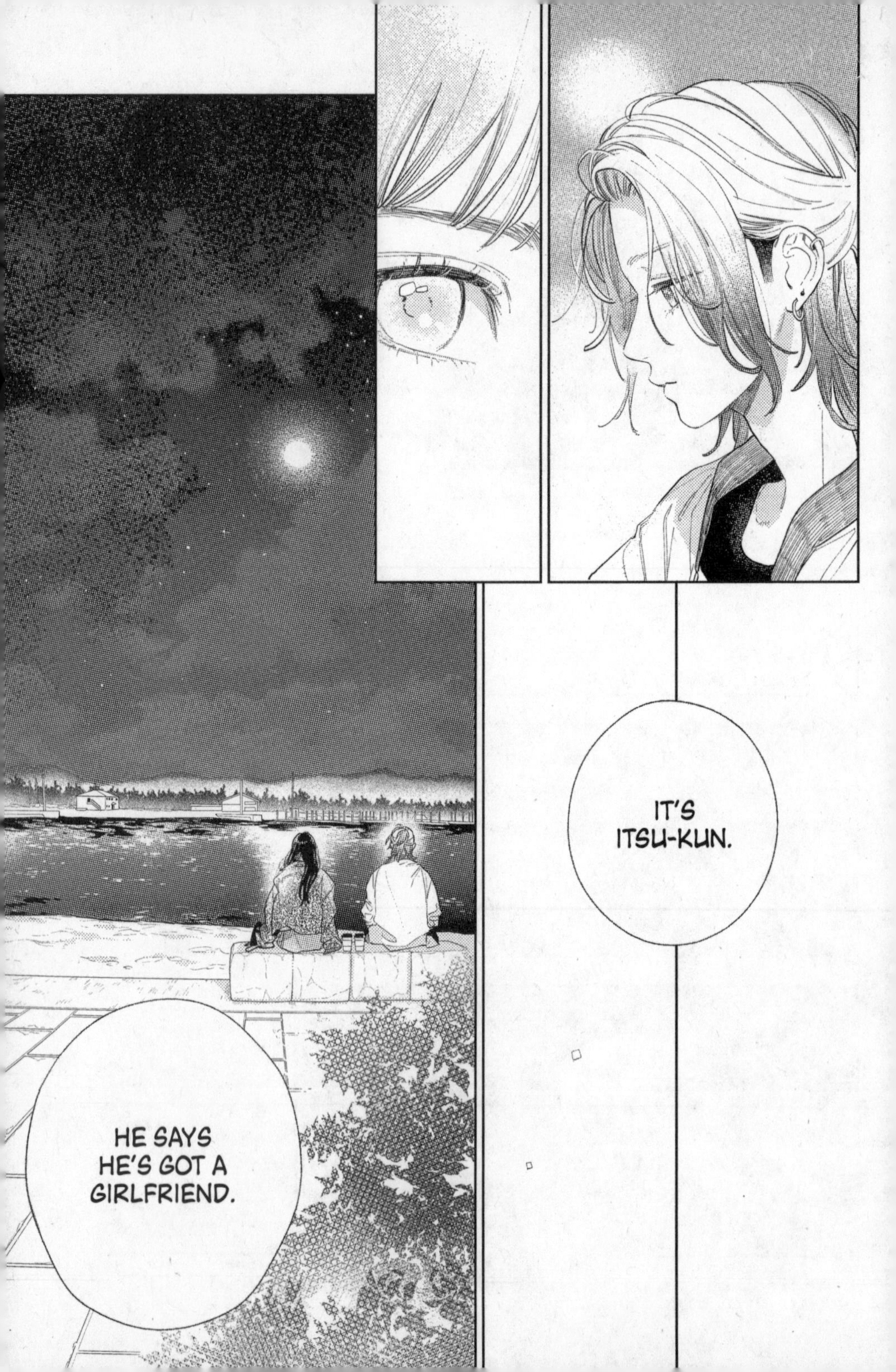
IT'S ITSU-KUN.
HE SAYS HE'S GOT A GIRLFRIEND.

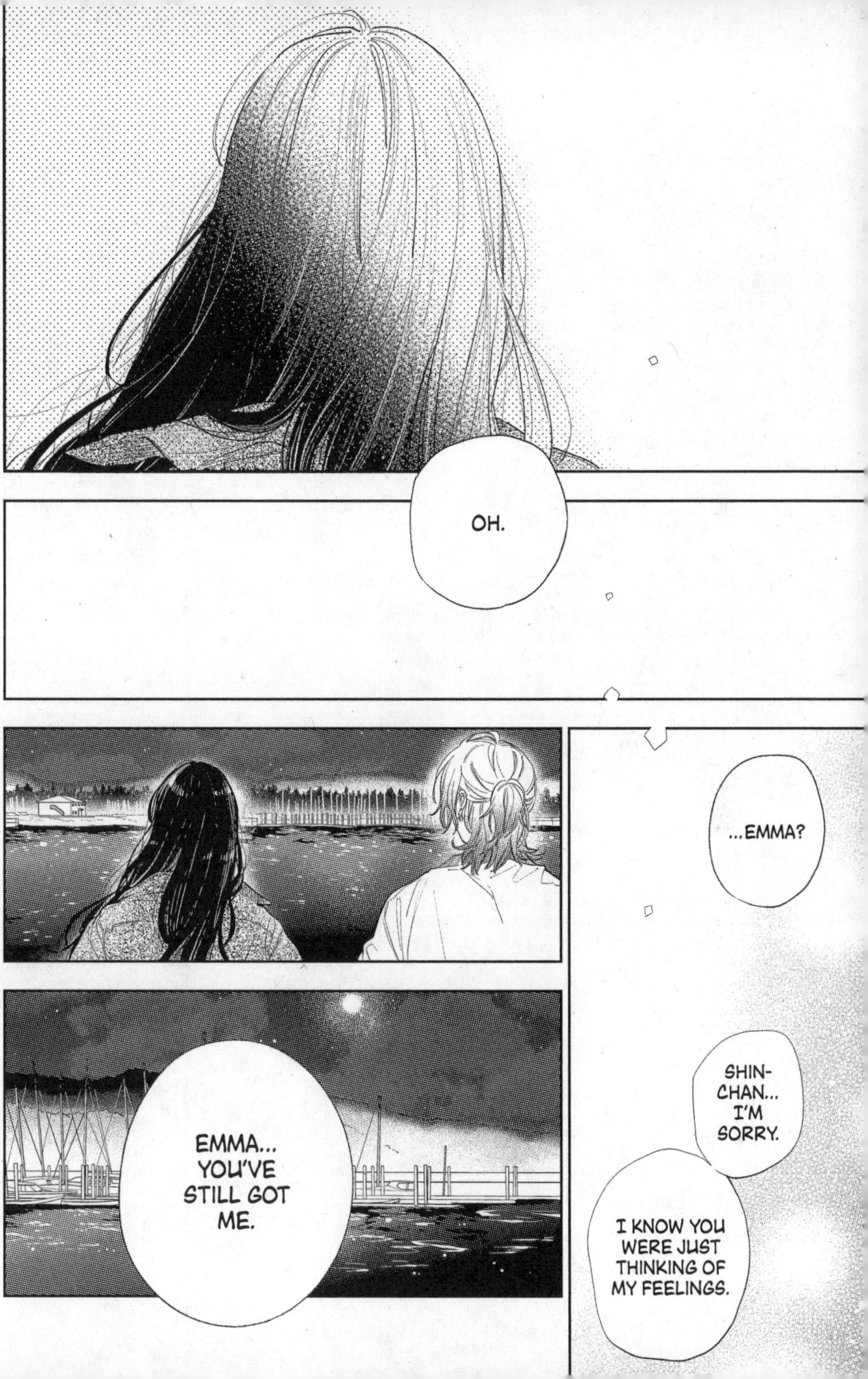
OH.
...EMMA?
SHIN-CHAN... I'M SORRY.
I KNOW YOU WERE JUST THINKING OF MY FEELINGS.
EMMA... YOU'VE STILL GOT ME.

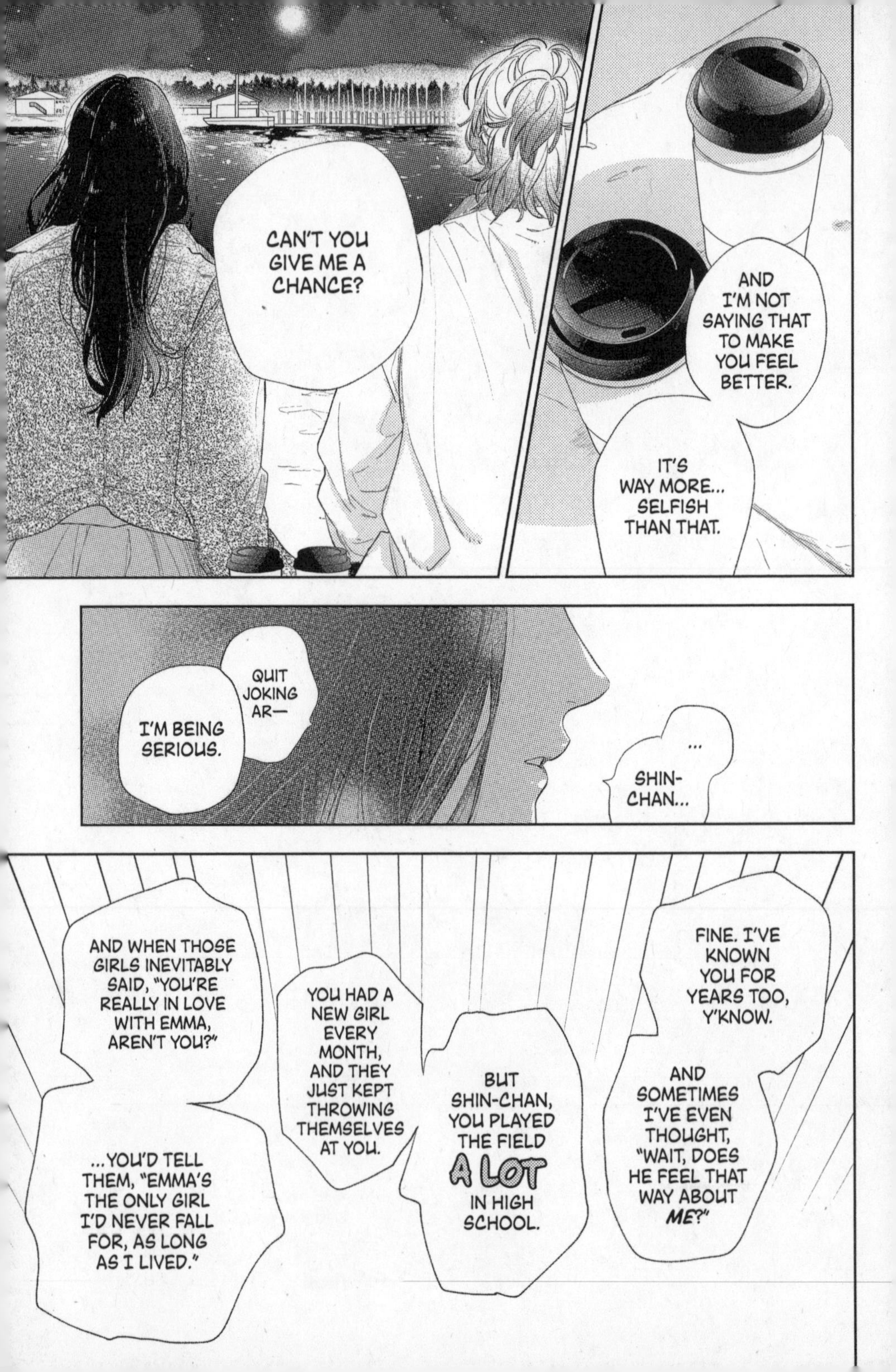
AND I'M NOT SAYING THAT TO MAKE YOU FEEL BETTER.
IT'S WAY MORE... SELFISH THAN THAT.
CAN'T YOU GIVE ME A CHANCE?
...
SHIN-CHAN...
QUIT JOKING AR—
I'M BEING SERIOUS.
FINE. I'VE KNOWN YOU FOR YEARS TOO, Y'KNOW.
AND SOMETIMES I'VE EVEN THOUGHT, "WAIT, DOES HE FEEL THAT WAY ABOUT *ME*?"
BUT SHIN-CHAN, YOU PLAYED THE FIELD A LOT IN HIGH SCHOOL.
YOU HAD A NEW GIRL EVERY MONTH, AND THEY JUST KEPT THROWING THEMSELVES AT YOU.
AND WHEN THOSE GIRLS INEVITABLY SAID, "YOU'RE REALLY IN LOVE WITH EMMA, AREN'T YOU?"
...YOU'D TELL THEM, "EMMA'S THE ONLY GIRL I'D NEVER FALL FOR, AS LONG AS I LIVED."

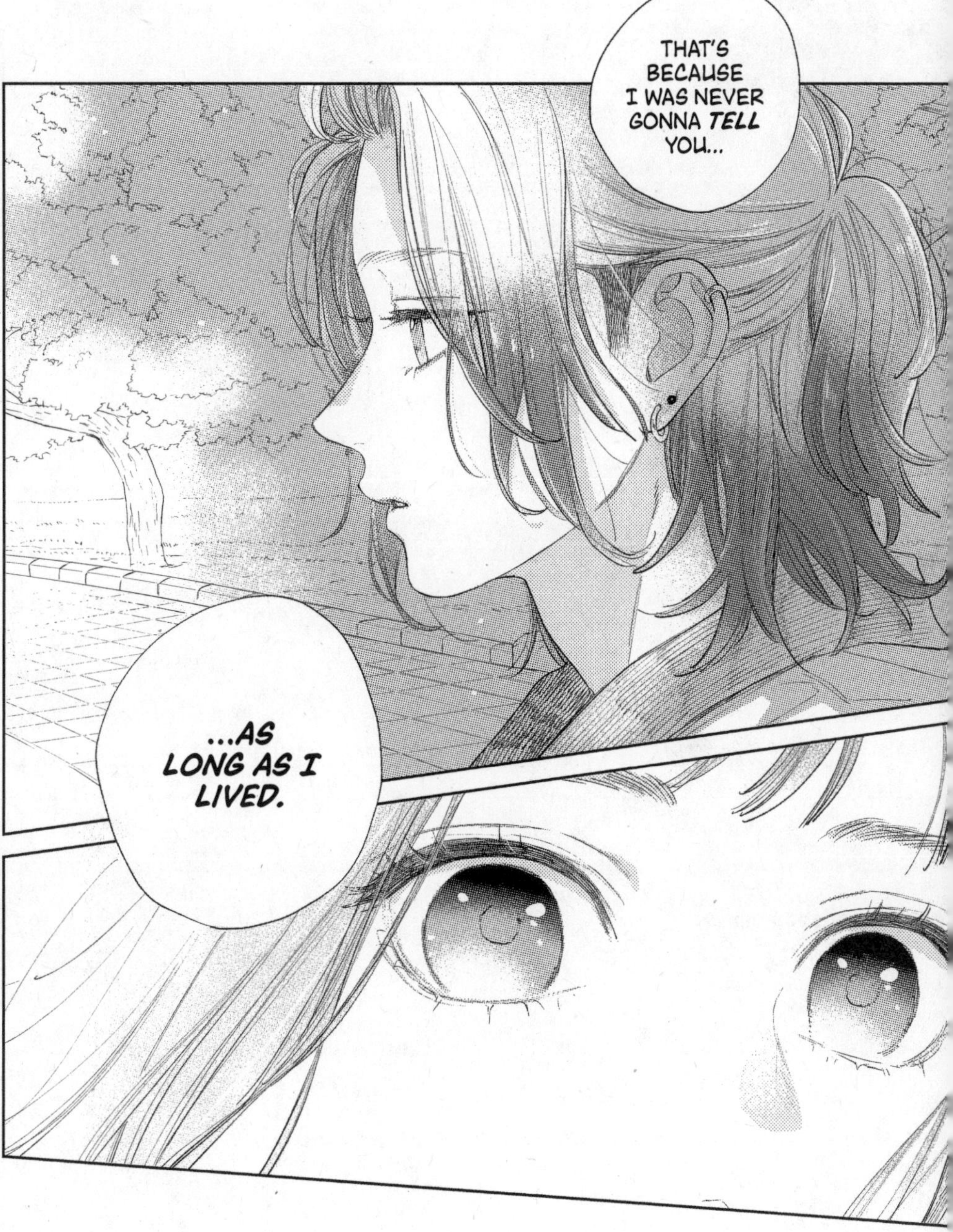
THAT'S BECAUSE I WAS NEVER GONNA *TELL* YOU...
...AS LONG AS I LIVED.

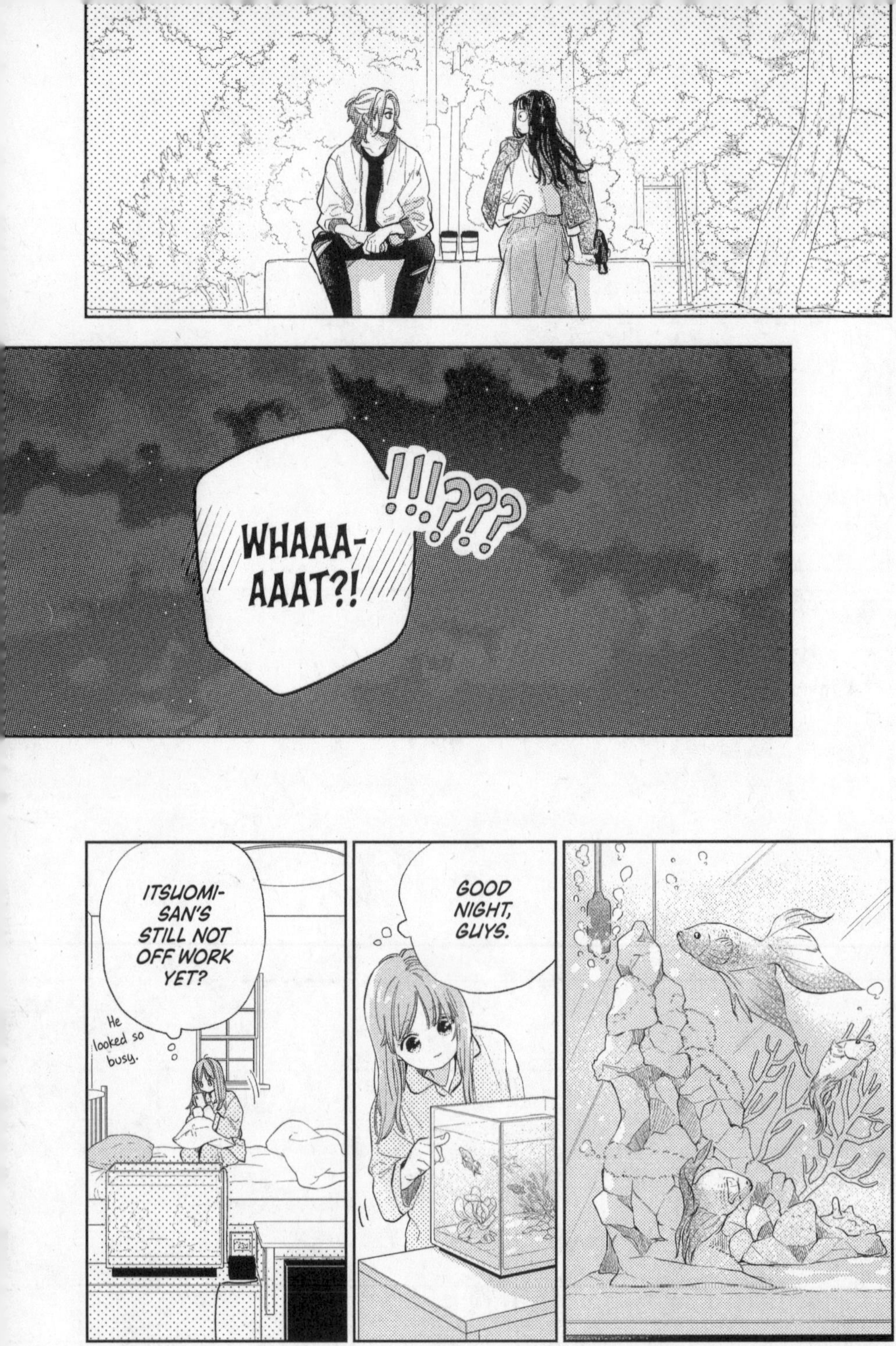
!!!???
WHAAA-AAAT?!
GOOD NIGHT, GUYS.
ITSUOMI-SAN'S STILL NOT OFF WORK YET?
He looked so busy.

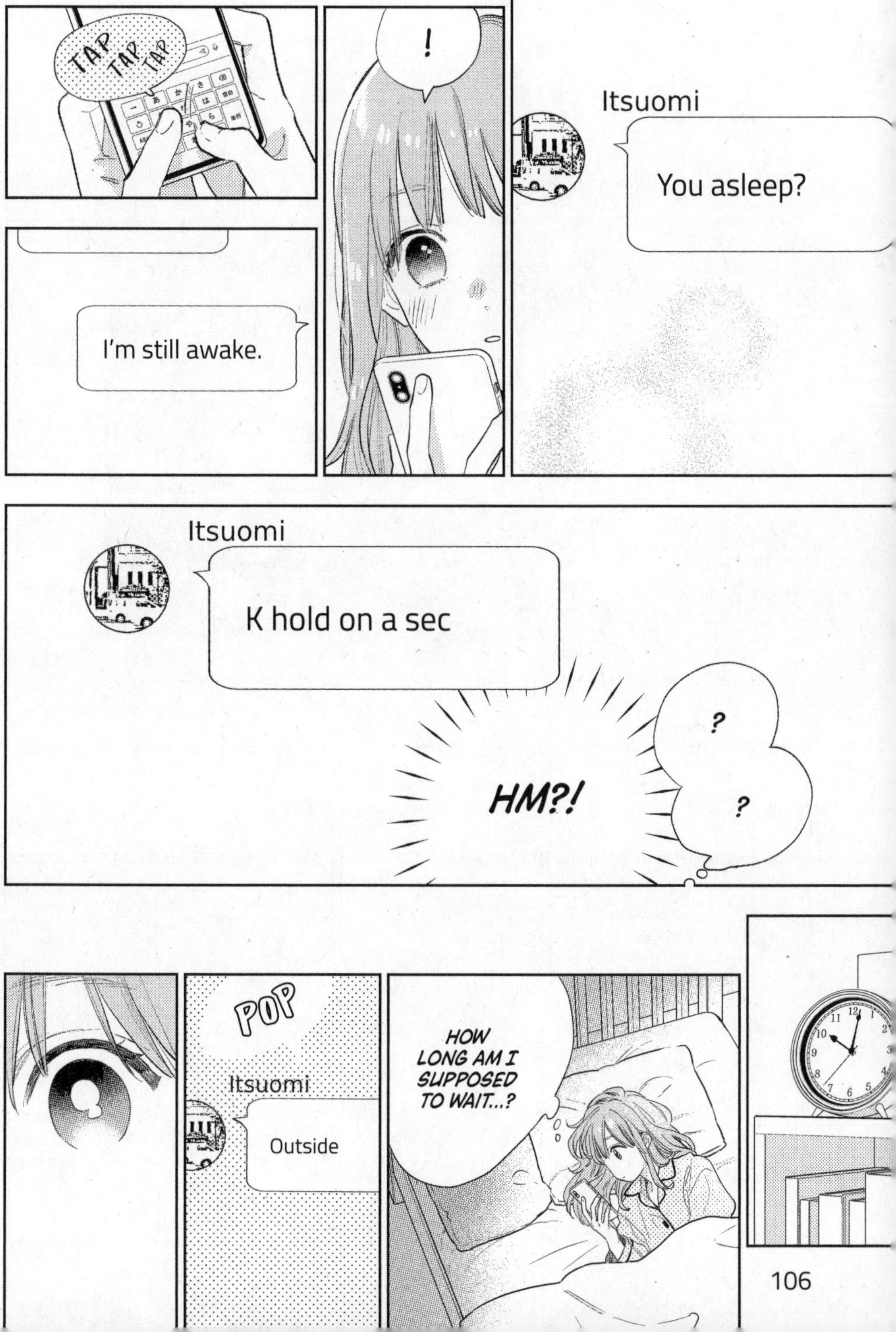
Itsuomi
You asleep?
!
TAP TAP TAP
I'm still awake.
Itsuomi
K hold on a sec
HM?!
? ?
HOW LONG AM I SUPPOSED TO WAIT...?
POP
Itsuomi
Outside

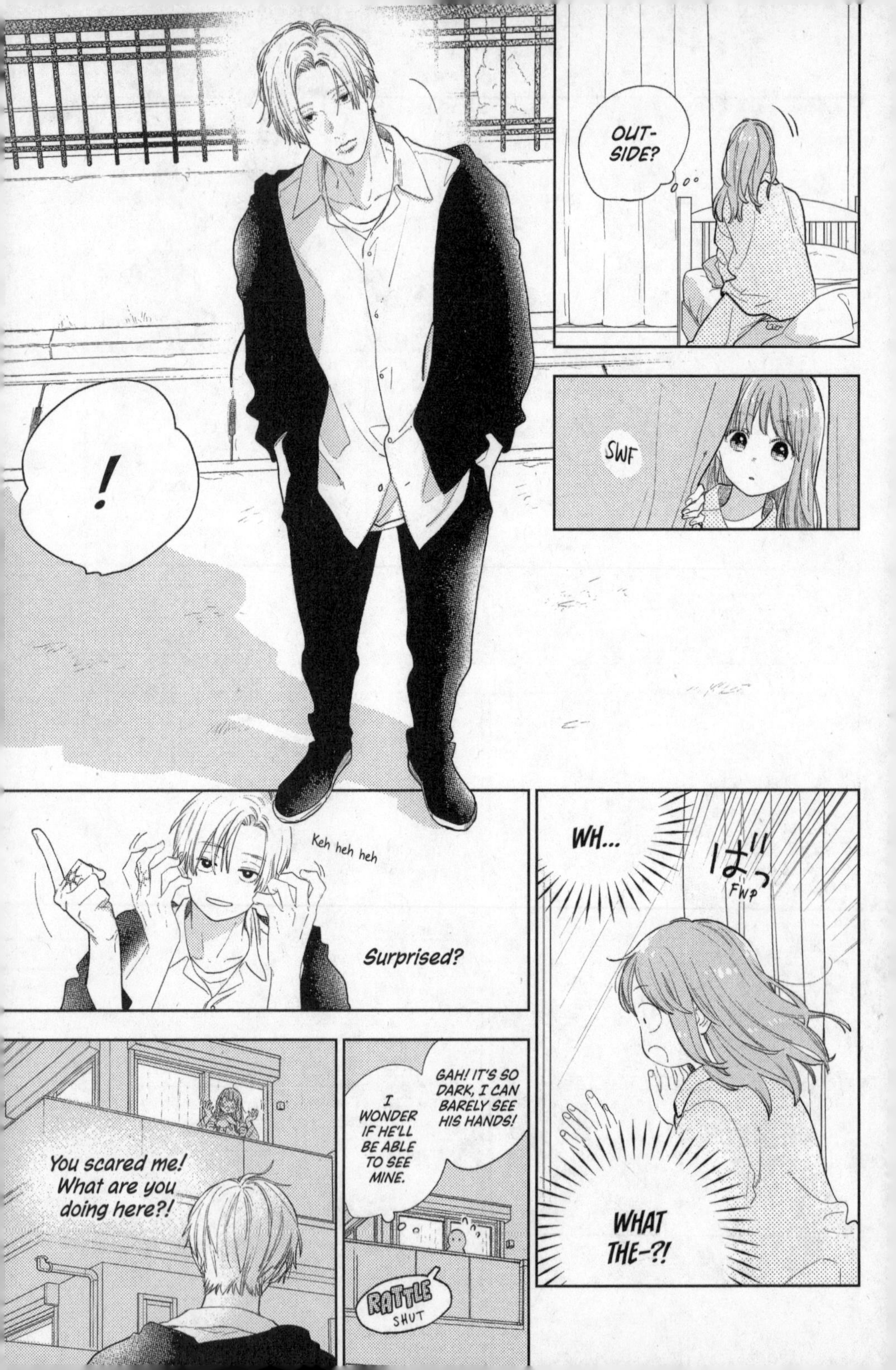
OUT-SIDE?
SWF
!
WH...
ぱっ
FWP
WHAT THE-?!
Keh heh heh
Surprised?
GAH! IT'S SO DARK, I CAN BARELY SEE HIS HANDS!
I WONDER IF HE'LL BE ABLE TO SEE MINE.
RATTLE
SHUT
You scared me! What are you doing here?!

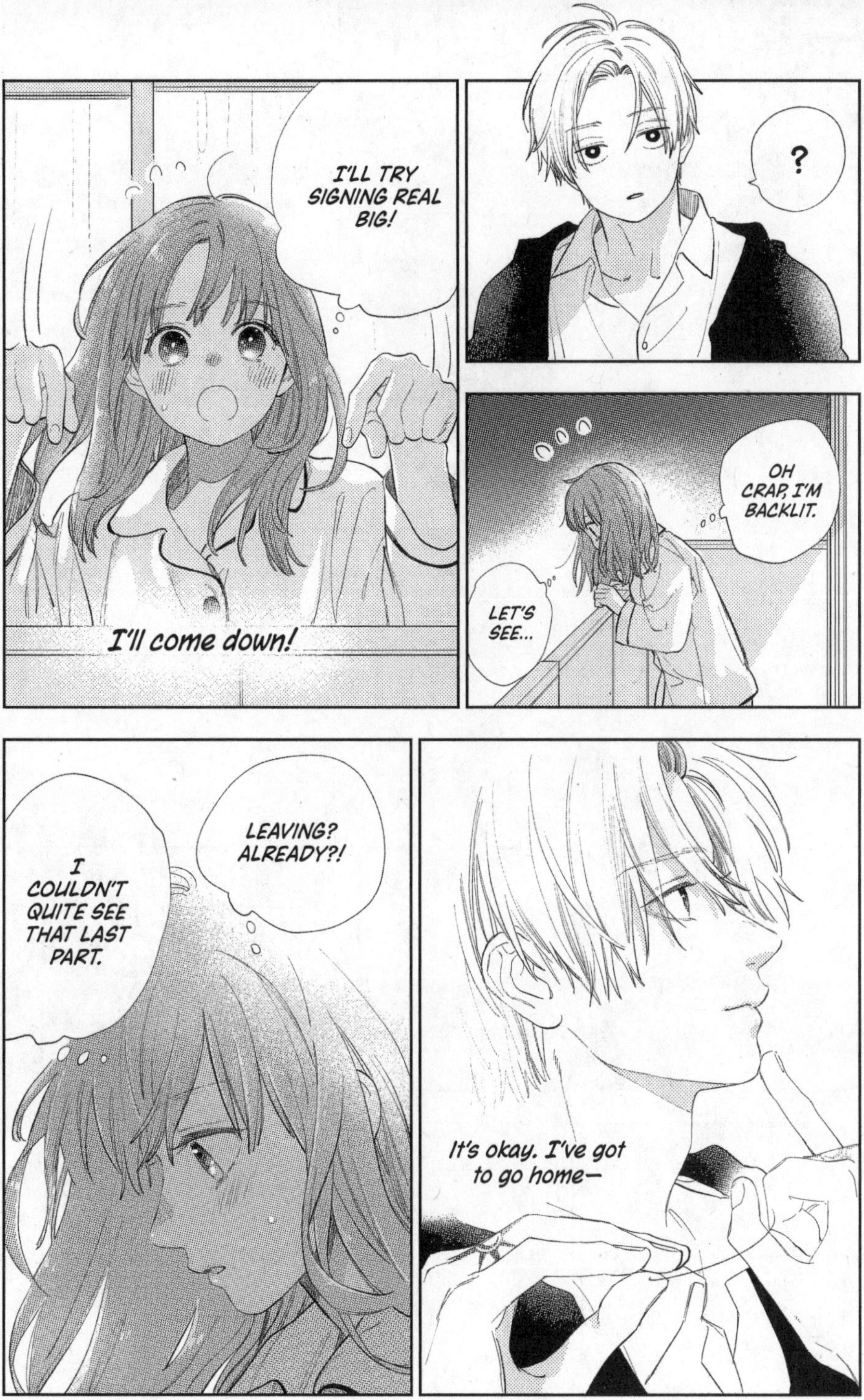
?
OH CRAP, I'M BACKLIT.
LET'S SEE...
I'LL TRY SIGNING REAL BIG!
I'll come down!
It's okay. I've got to go home—
LEAVING? ALREADY?!
I COULDN'T QUITE SEE THAT LAST PART.

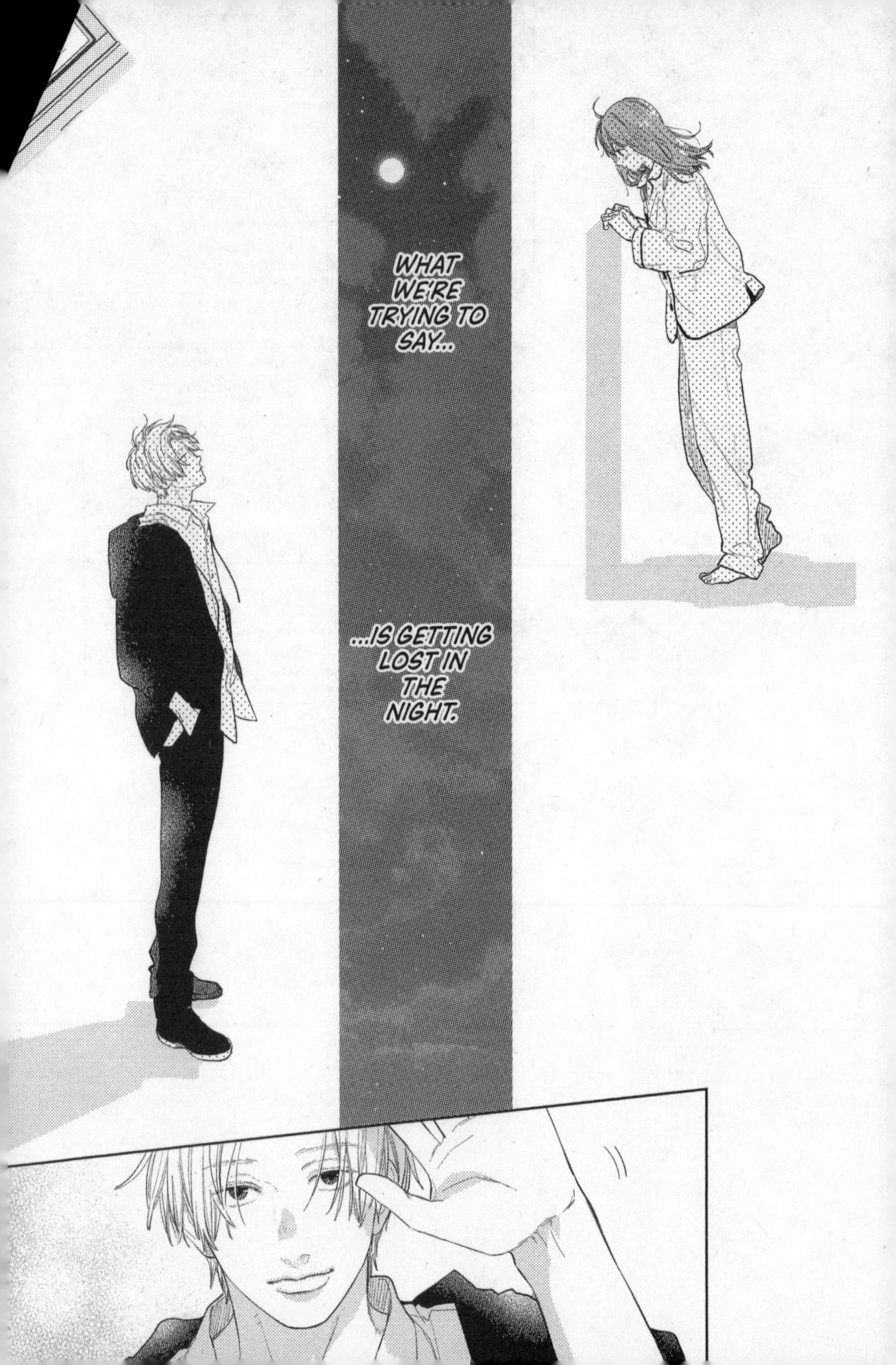
WHAT WE'RE TRYING TO SAY...
...IS GETTING LOST IN THE NIGHT.

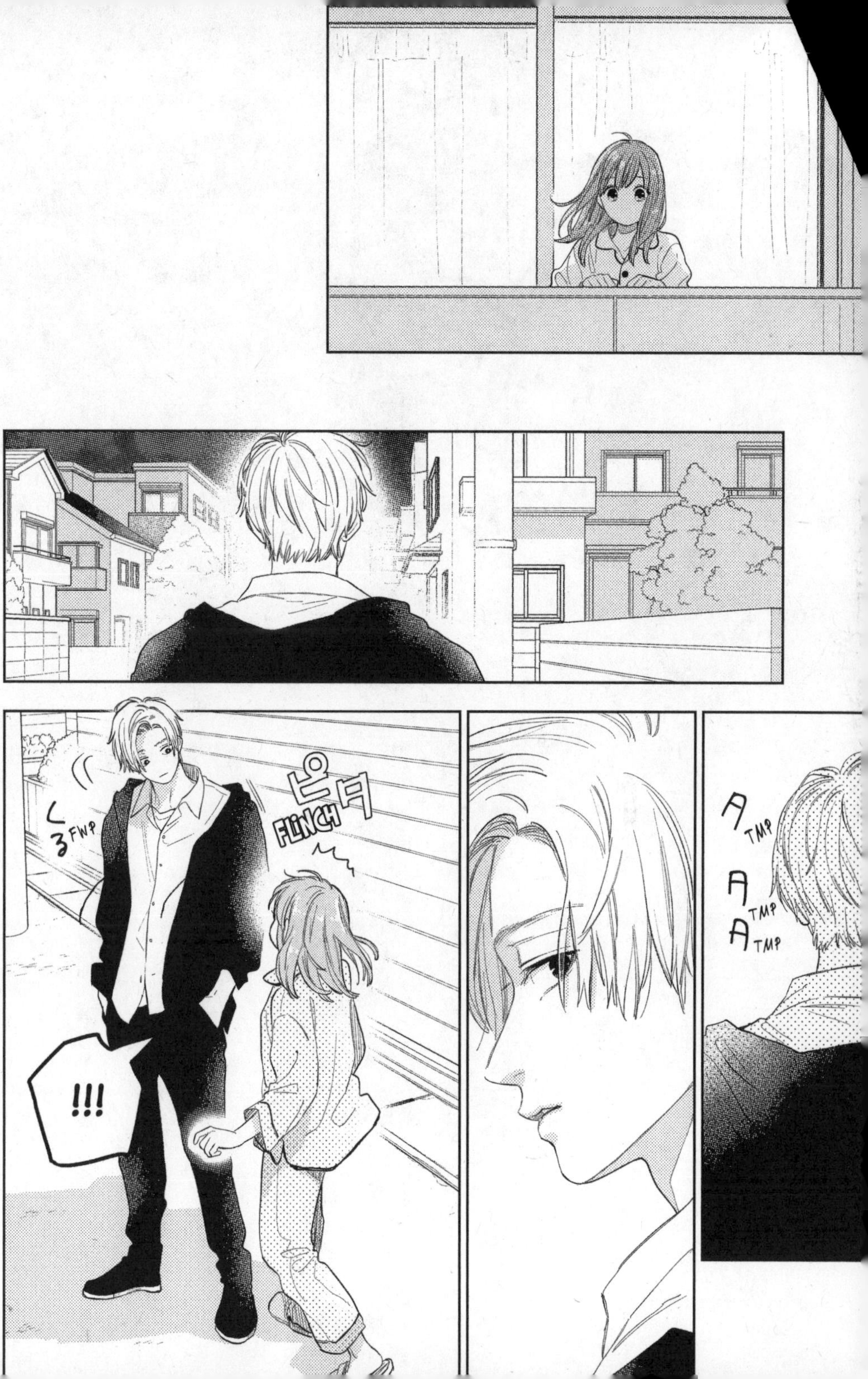

くる
FWP
ピクッ
FLINCH
!!!
TMP
TMP
TMP

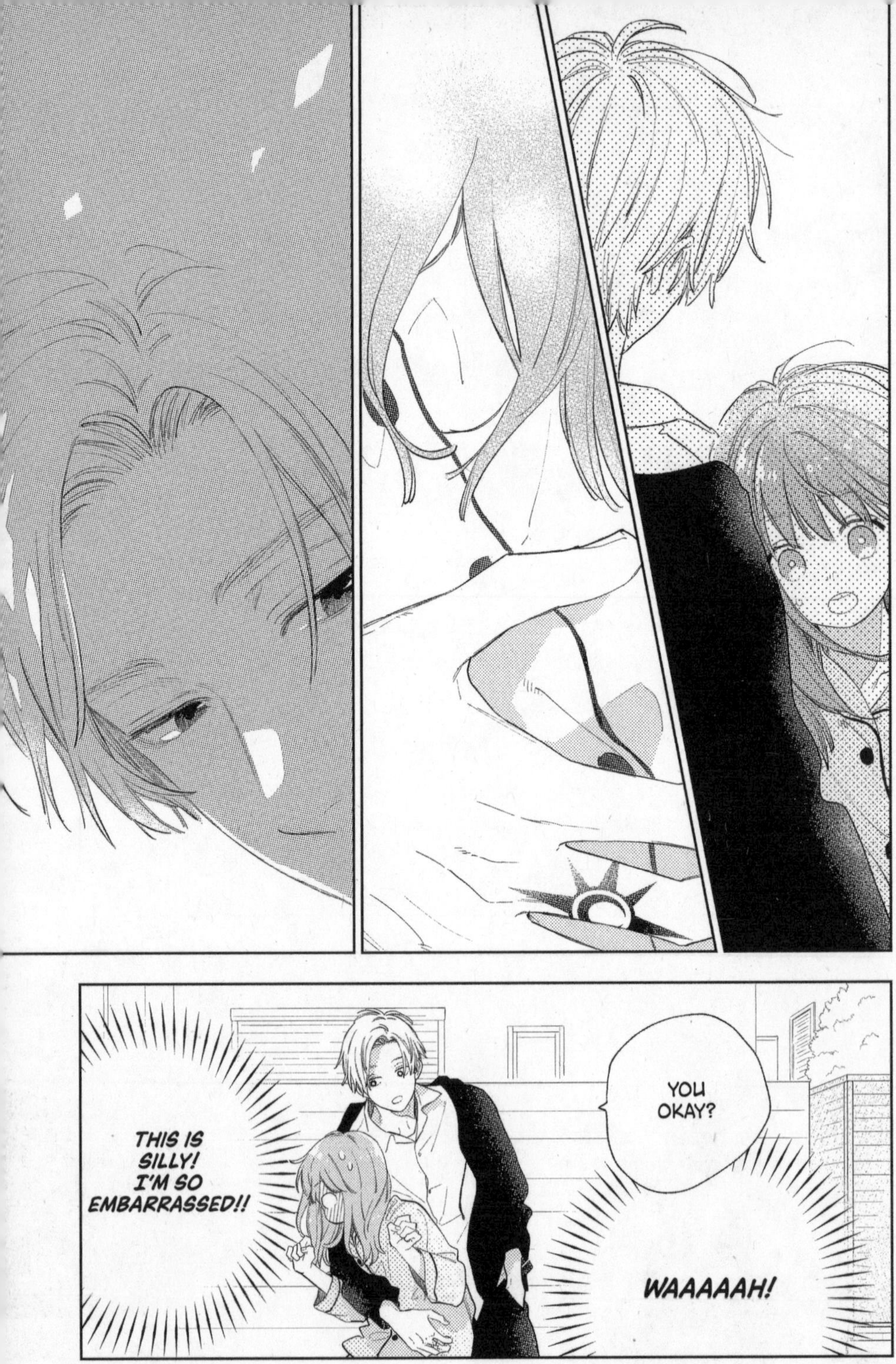
YOU OKAY?
WAAAAAH!
THIS IS SILLY! I'M SO EMBARRASSED!!

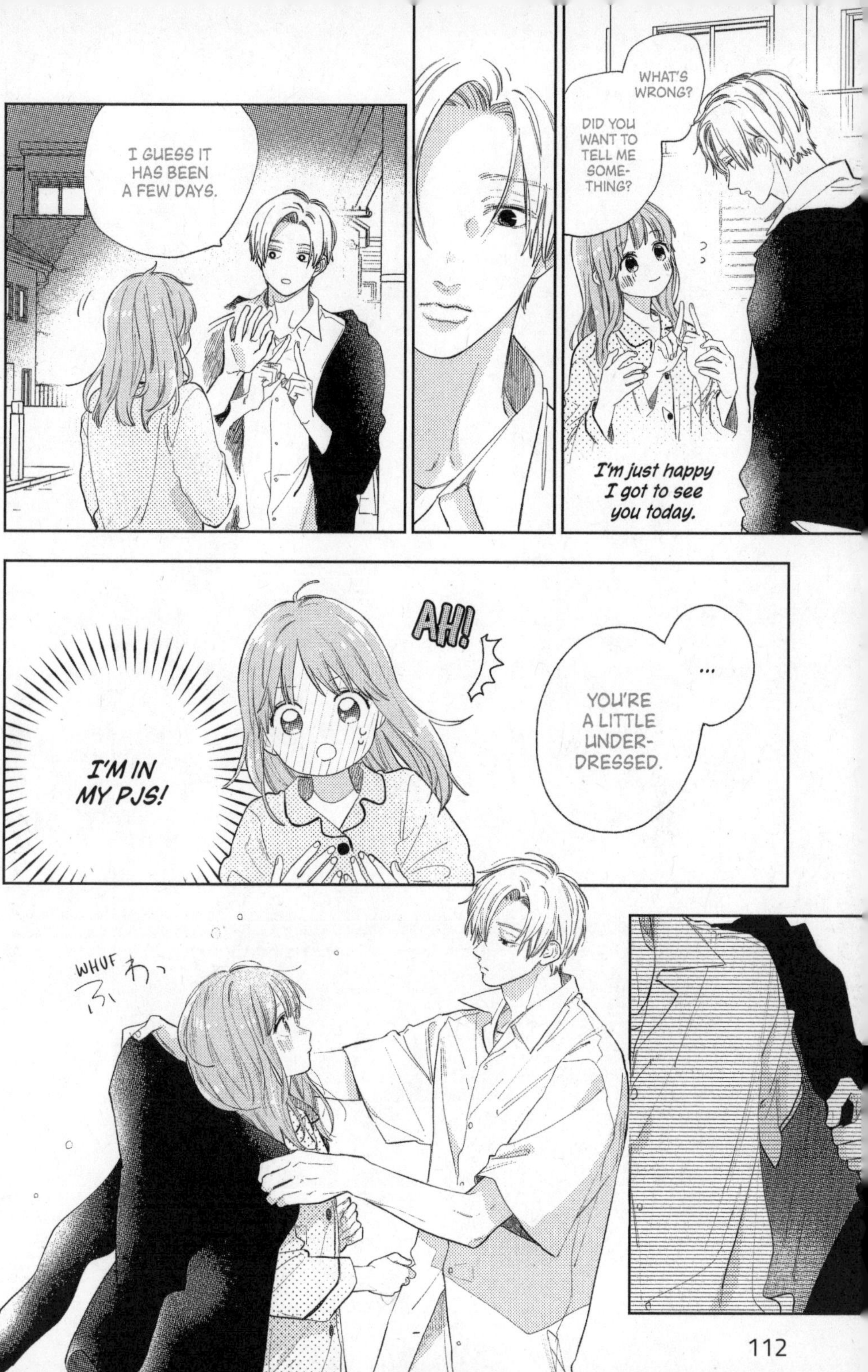
WHAT'S WRONG?
DID YOU WANT TO TELL ME SOME-THING?
I'm just happy I got to see you today.
I GUESS IT HAS BEEN A FEW DAYS.
...
YOU'RE A LITTLE UNDER-DRESSED.
AH!
I'M IN MY PJS!
WHUF
ふわっ

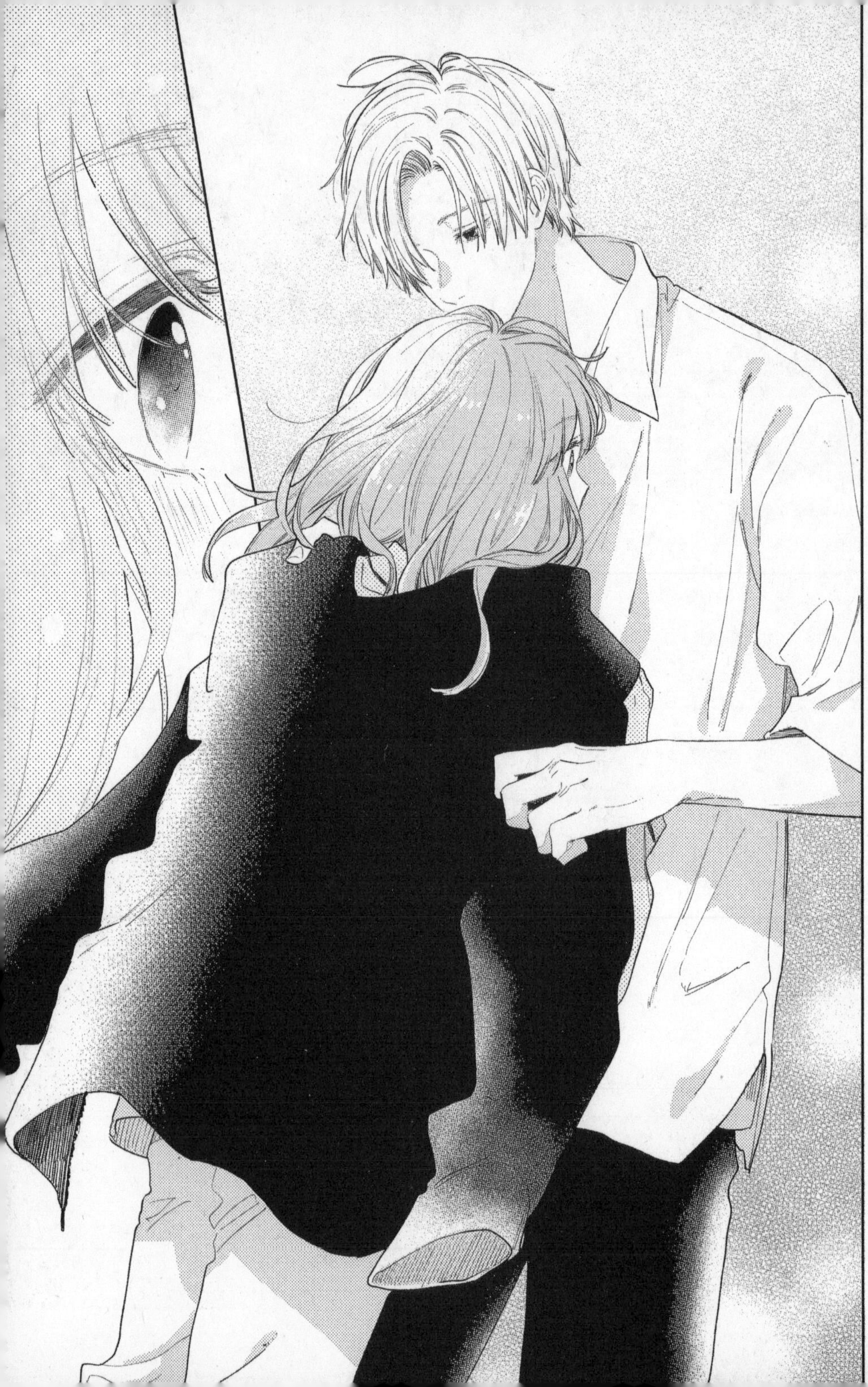

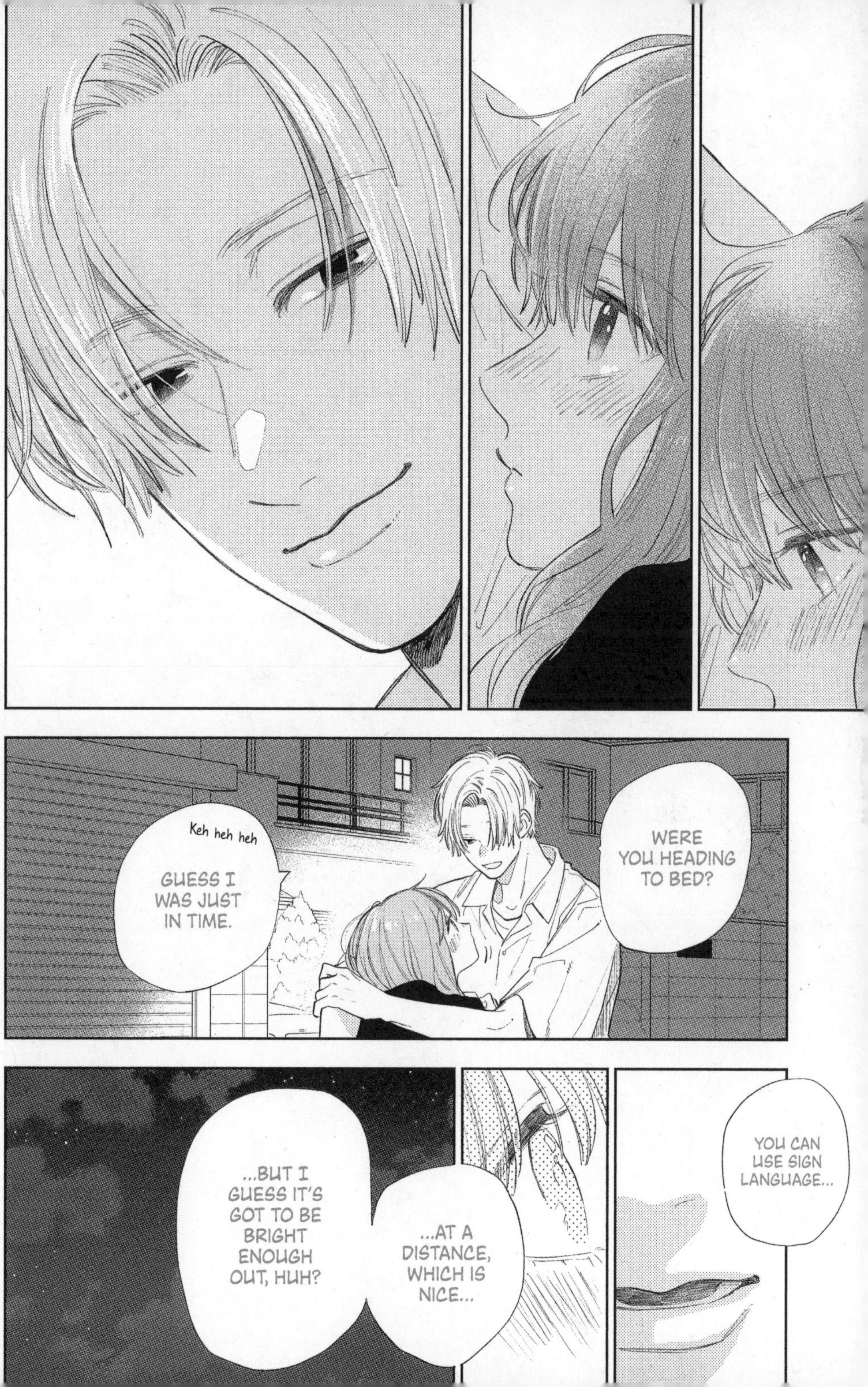
WERE YOU HEADING TO BED?
Keh heh heh
GUESS I WAS JUST IN TIME.
YOU CAN USE SIGN LANGUAGE...
...AT A DISTANCE, WHICH IS NICE...
...BUT I GUESS IT'S GOT TO BE BRIGHT ENOUGH OUT, HUH?

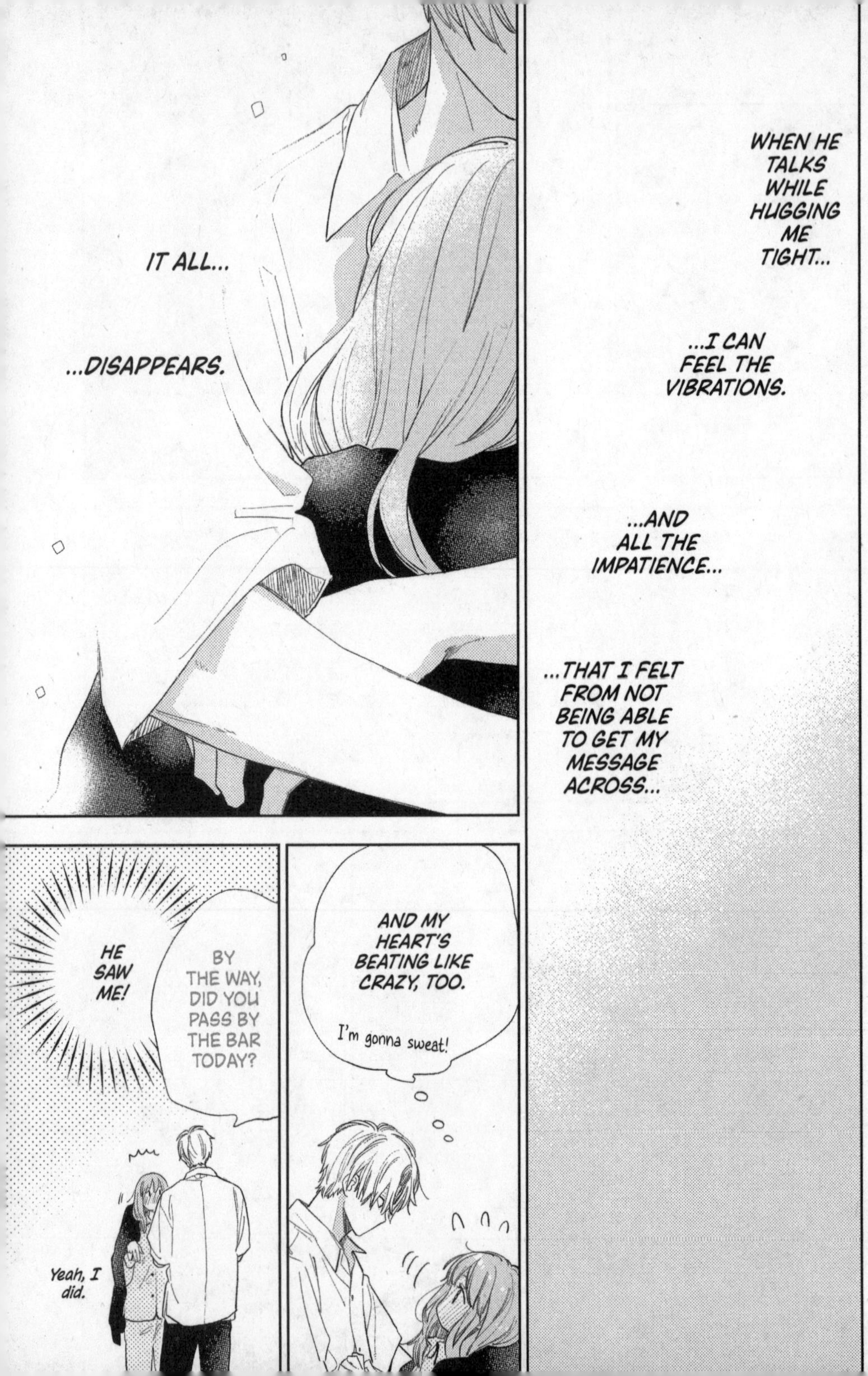

WHEN HE TALKS WHILE HUGGING ME TIGHT...
...I CAN FEEL THE VIBRATIONS.
...AND ALL THE IMPATIENCE...
...THAT I FELT FROM NOT BEING ABLE TO GET MY MESSAGE ACROSS...
IT ALL...
...DISAPPEARS.
AND MY HEART'S BEATING LIKE CRAZY, TOO.
I'm gonna sweat!
BY THE WAY, DID YOU PASS BY THE BAR TODAY?
HE SAW ME!
Yeah, I did.

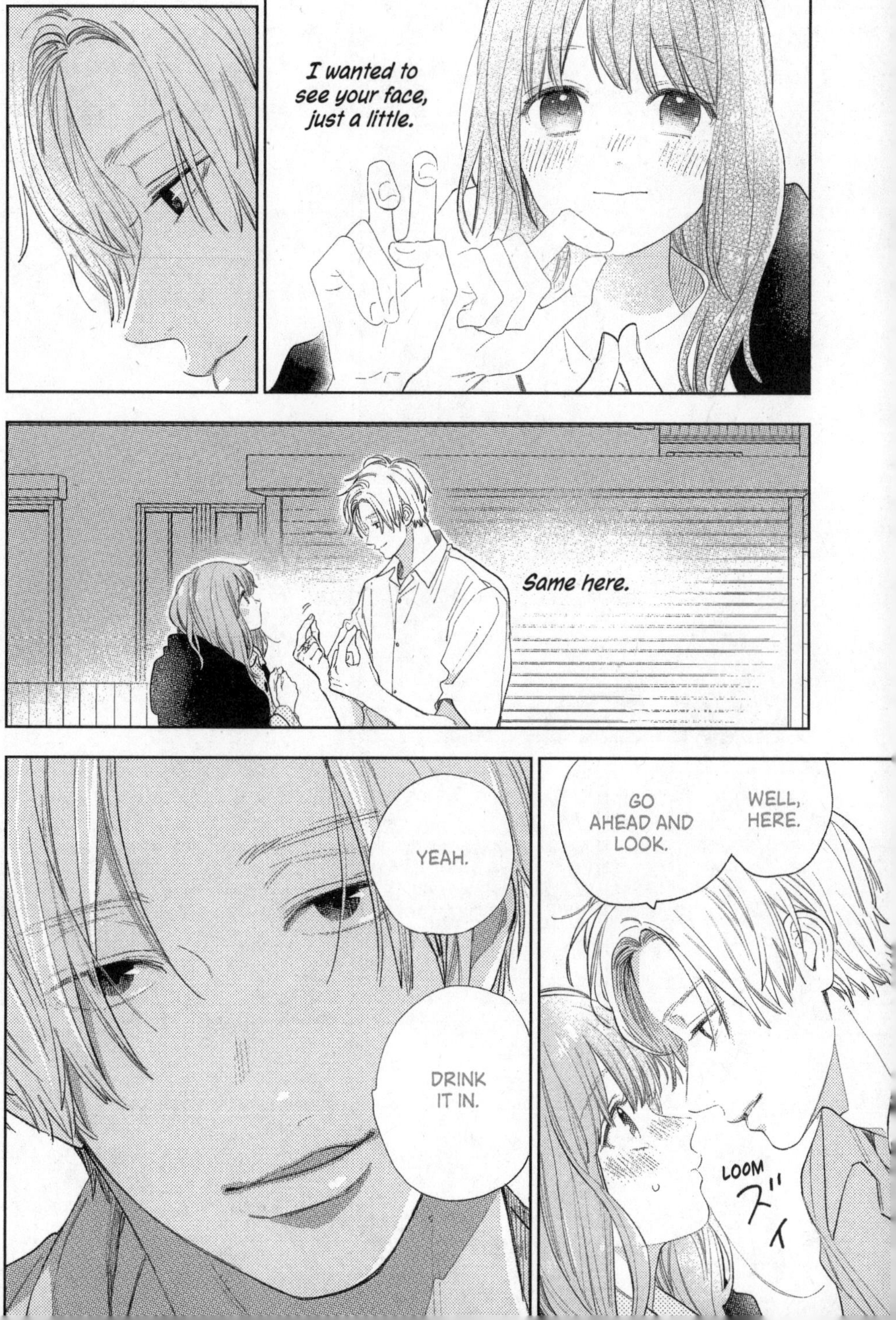
I wanted to see your face, just a little.
Same here.
WELL, HERE.
GO AHEAD AND LOOK.
LOOM
ズイ
YEAH.
DRINK IT IN.

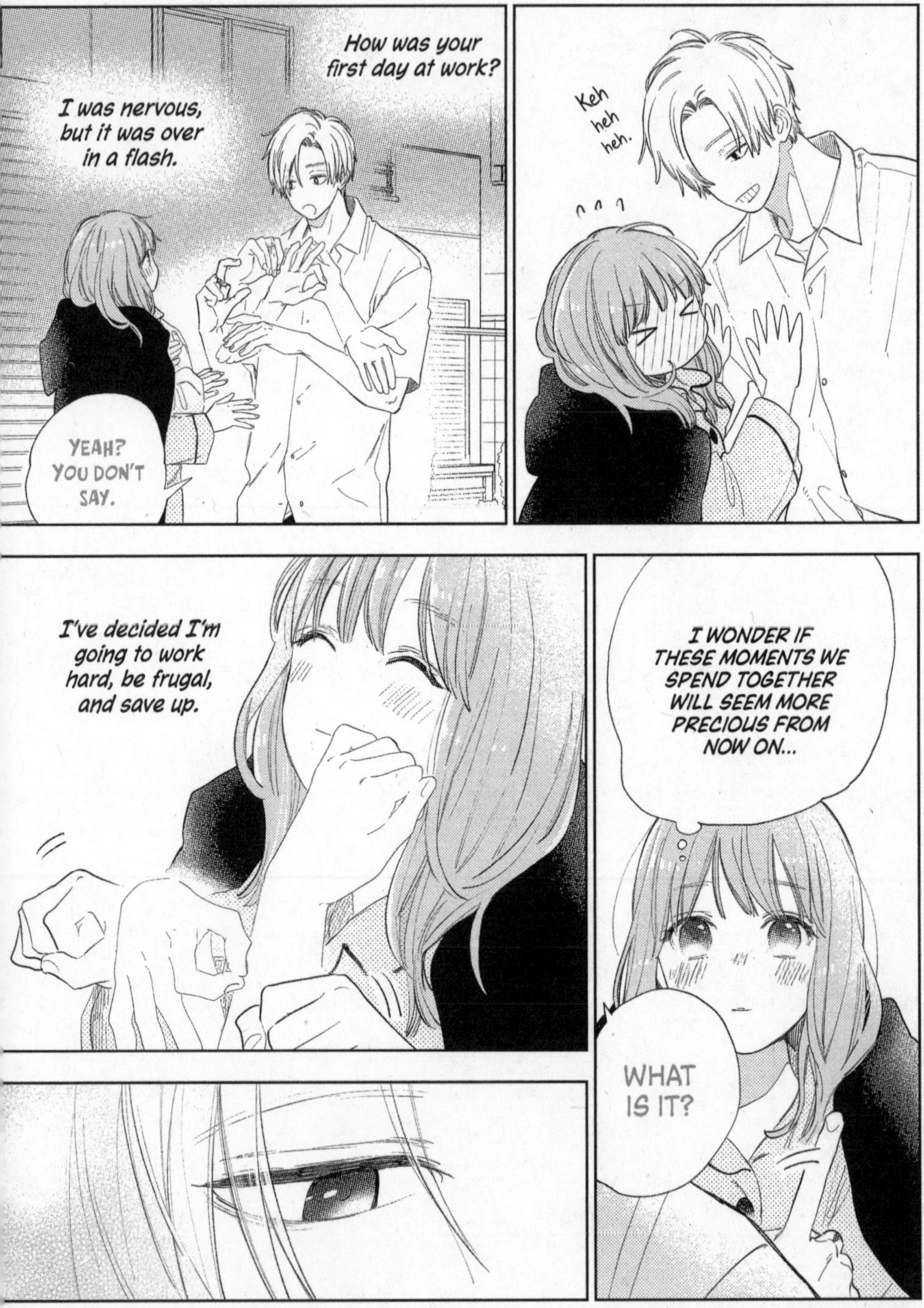
How was your first day at work?
I was nervous, but it was over in a flash.
YEAH? YOU DON'T SAY.
Keh heh heh.
I've decided I'm going to work hard, be frugal, and save up.
I WONDER IF THESE MOMENTS WE SPEND TOGETHER WILL SEEM MORE PRECIOUS FROM NOW ON...
WHAT IS IT?

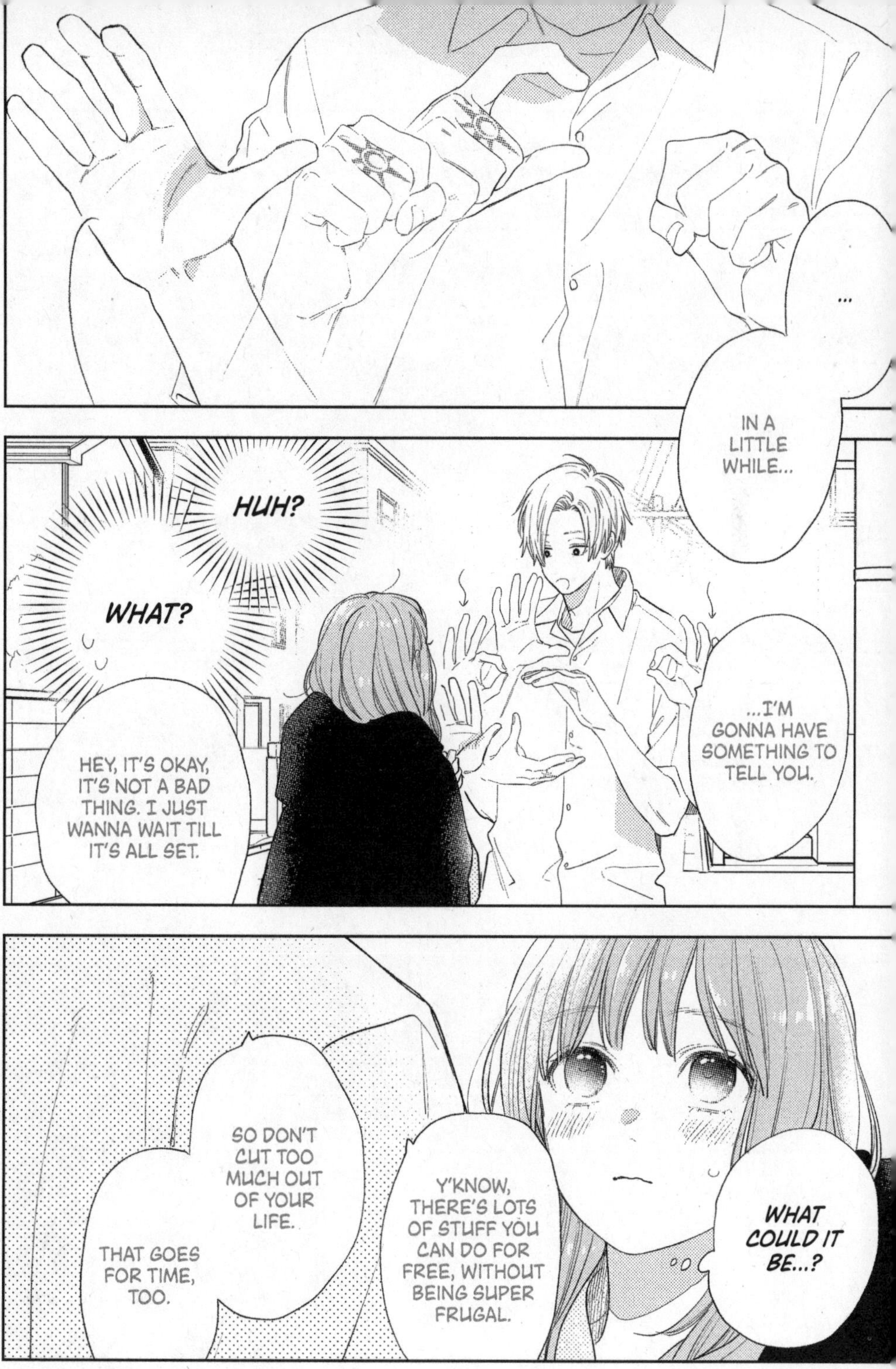
...
IN A LITTLE WHILE...
...I'M GONNA HAVE SOMETHING TO TELL YOU.
HUH?
WHAT?
HEY, IT'S OKAY, IT'S NOT A BAD THING. I JUST WANNA WAIT TILL IT'S ALL SET.
WHAT COULD IT BE...?
Y'KNOW, THERE'S LOTS OF STUFF YOU CAN DO FOR FREE, WITHOUT BEING SUPER FRUGAL.
SO DON'T CUT TOO MUCH OUT OF YOUR LIFE.
THAT GOES FOR TIME, TOO.

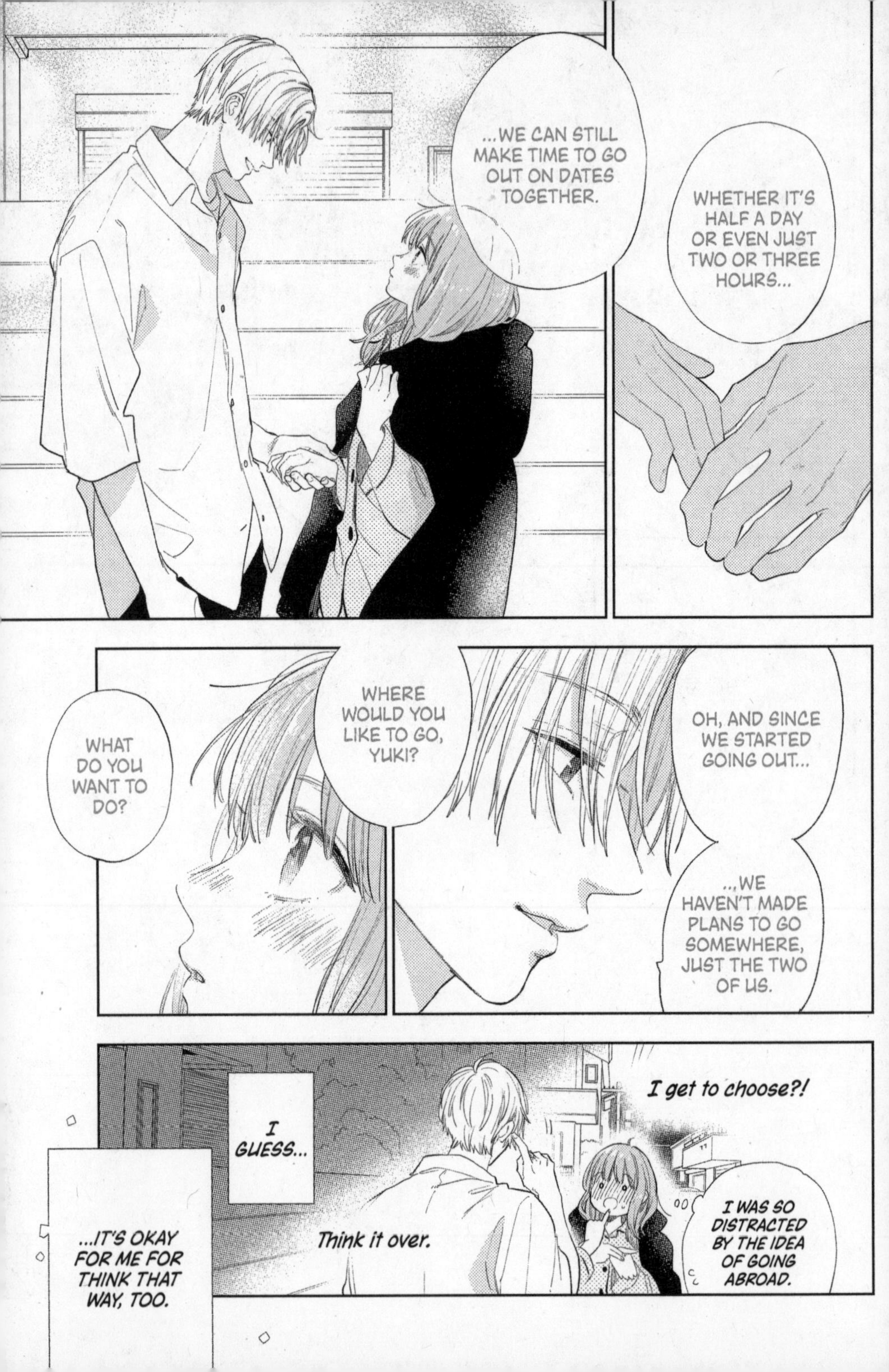
WHETHER IT'S HALF A DAY OR EVEN JUST TWO OR THREE HOURS...
...WE CAN STILL MAKE TIME TO GO OUT ON DATES TOGETHER.
OH, AND SINCE WE STARTED GOING OUT...
...WE HAVEN'T MADE PLANS TO GO SOMEWHERE, JUST THE TWO OF US.
WHERE WOULD YOU LIKE TO GO, YUKI?
WHAT DO YOU WANT TO DO?
I get to choose?!
I WAS SO DISTRACTED BY THE IDEA OF GOING ABROAD.
Think it over.
I GUESS...
...IT'S OKAY FOR ME FOR THINK THAT WAY, TOO.

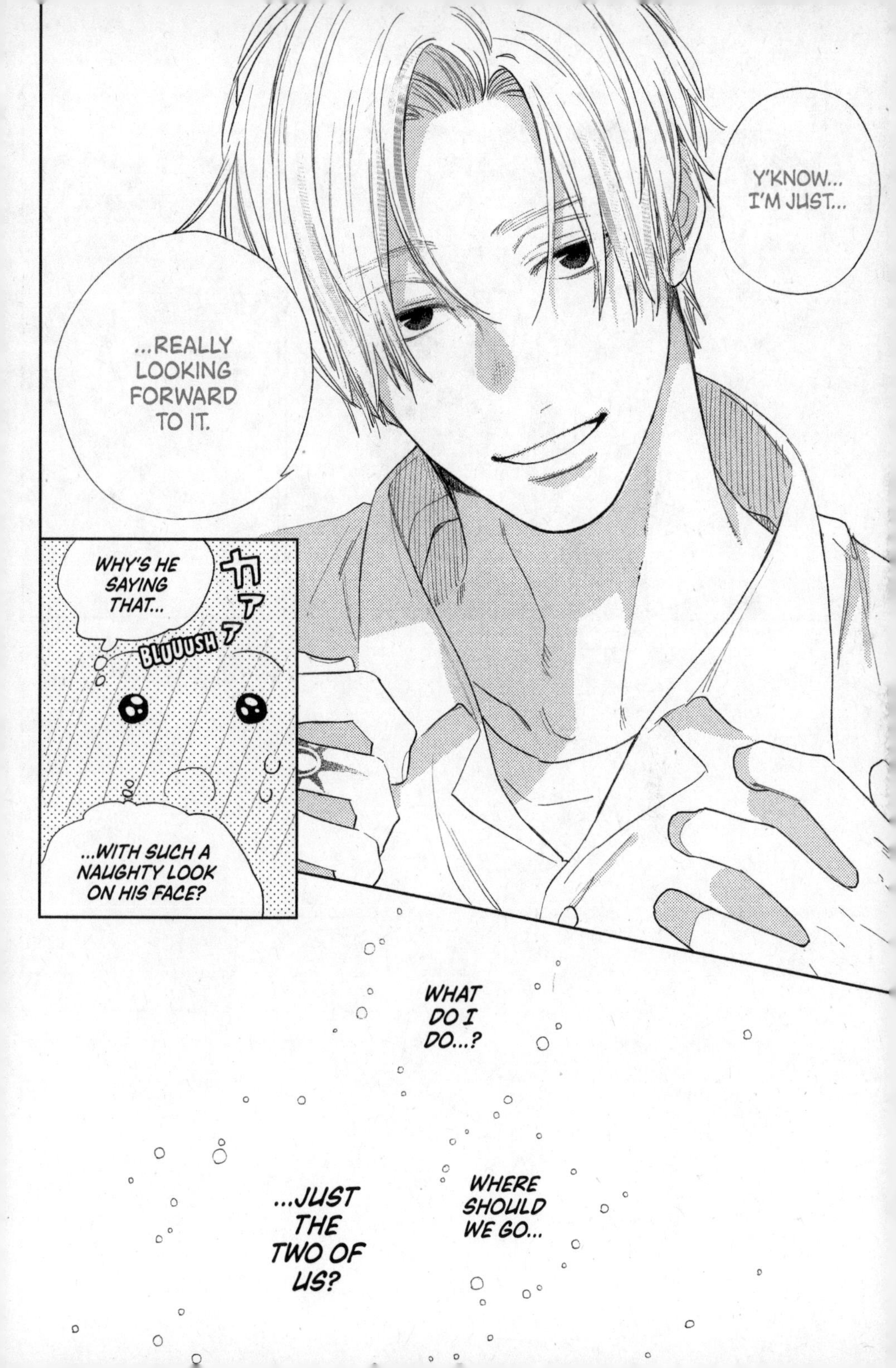

Y'KNOW... I'M JUST...
...REALLY LOOKING FORWARD TO IT.
WHY'S HE SAYING THAT...
カァァ
BLUUUSH
...WITH SUCH A NAUGHTY LOOK ON HIS FACE?
WHAT DO I DO...?
WHERE SHOULD WE GO...
...JUST THE TWO OF US?

Sign.20

A Destination Together

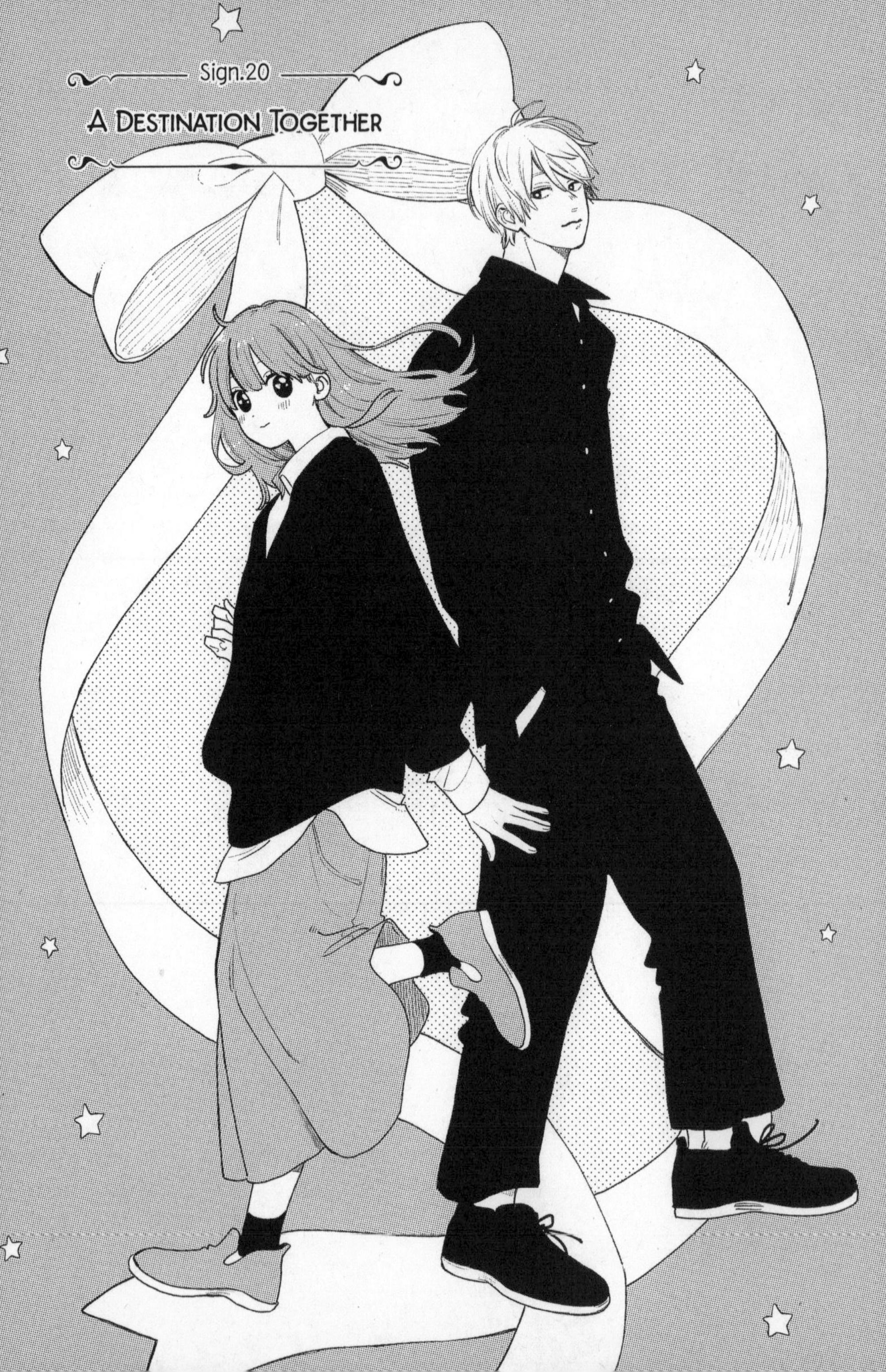

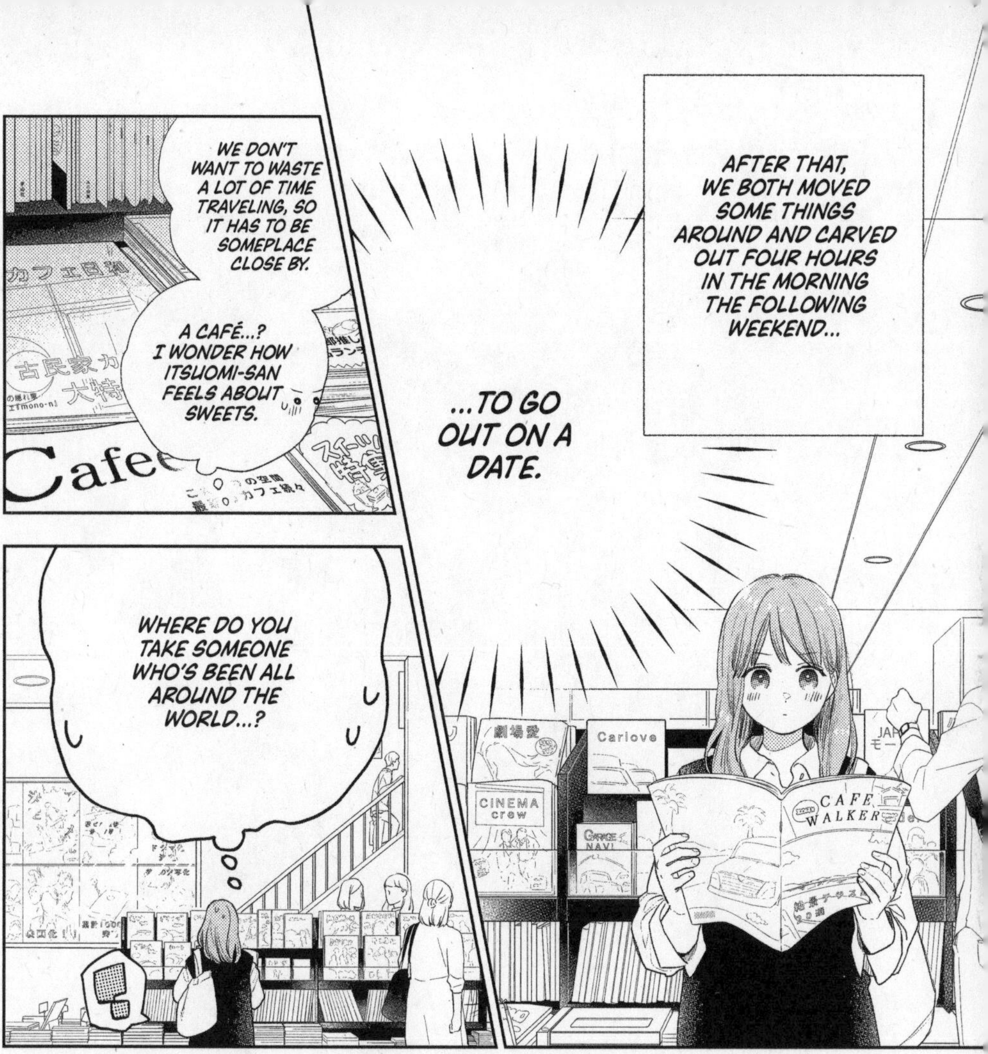
AFTER THAT, WE BOTH MOVED SOME THINGS AROUND AND CARVED OUT FOUR HOURS IN THE MORNING THE FOLLOWING WEEKEND...
...TO GO OUT ON A DATE.
WE DON'T WANT TO WASTE A LOT OF TIME TRAVELING, SO IT HAS TO BE SOMEPLACE CLOSE BY.
A CAFÉ...? I WONDER HOW ITSUOMI-SAN FEELS ABOUT SWEETS.
WHERE DO YOU TAKE SOMEONE WHO'S BEEN ALL AROUND THE WORLD...?

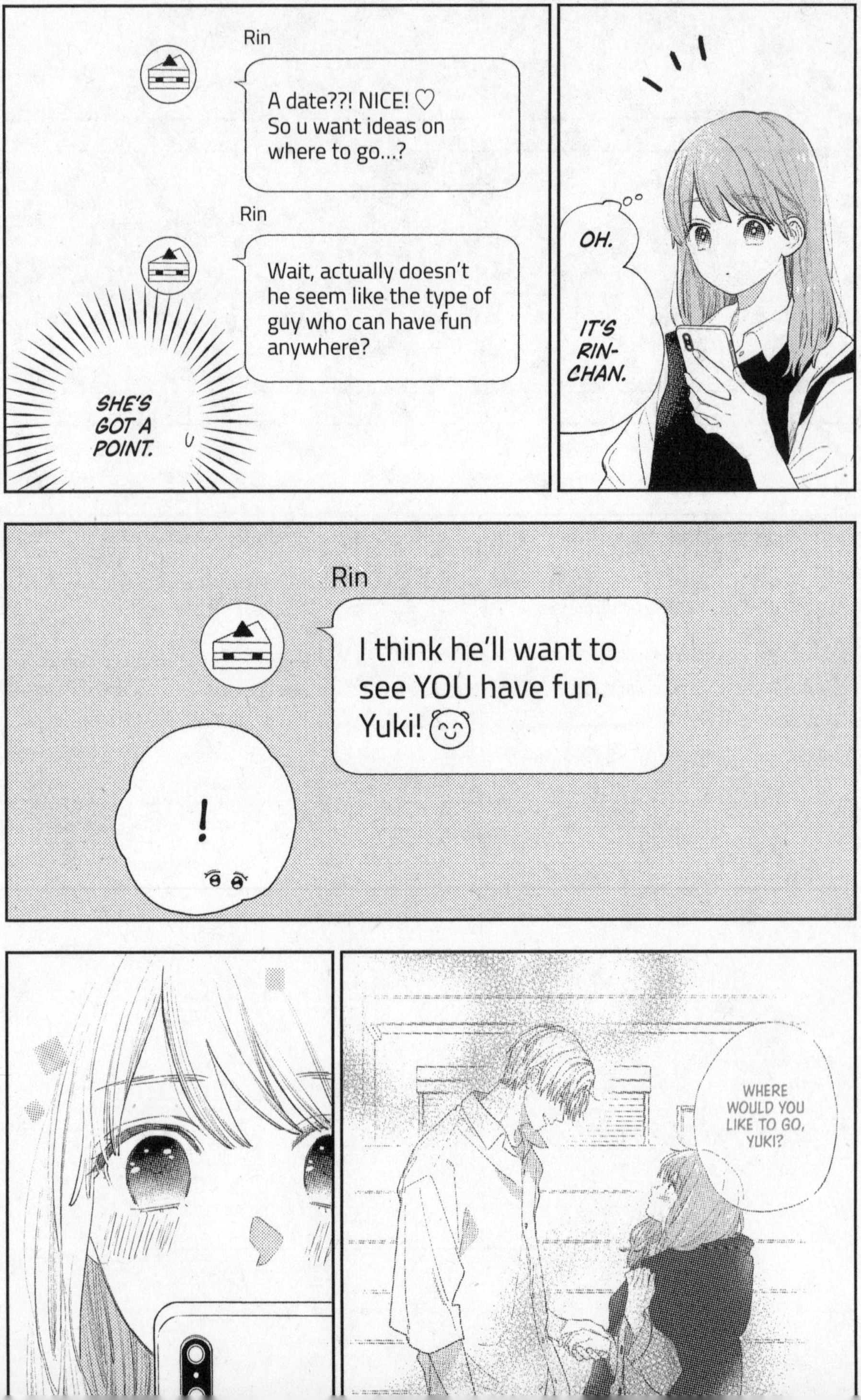
OH.
IT'S RIN-CHAN.
Rin
A date??! NICE! ♡ So u want ideas on where to go...?
Rin
Wait, actually doesn't he seem like the type of guy who can have fun anywhere?
SHE'S GOT A POINT.
Rin
I think he'll want to see YOU have fun, Yuki!
!
WHERE WOULD YOU LIKE TO GO, YUKI?

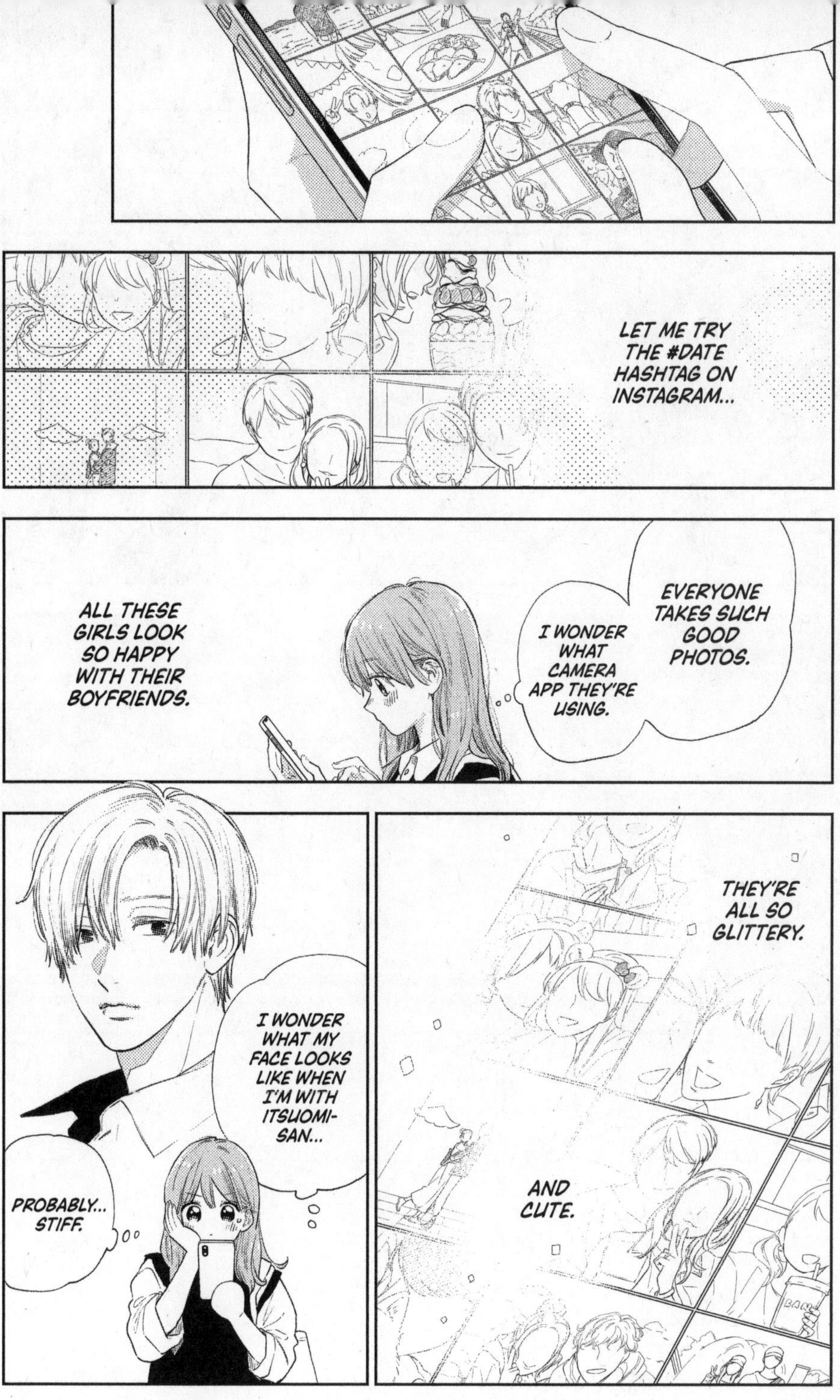
LET ME TRY THE #DATE HASHTAG ON INSTAGRAM...
EVERYONE TAKES SUCH GOOD PHOTOS.
I WONDER WHAT CAMERA APP THEY'RE USING.
ALL THESE GIRLS LOOK SO HAPPY WITH THEIR BOYFRIENDS.
THEY'RE ALL SO GLITTERY.
AND CUTE.
I WONDER WHAT MY FACE LOOKS LIKE WHEN I'M WITH ITSUOMI-SAN...
PROBABLY... STIFF.

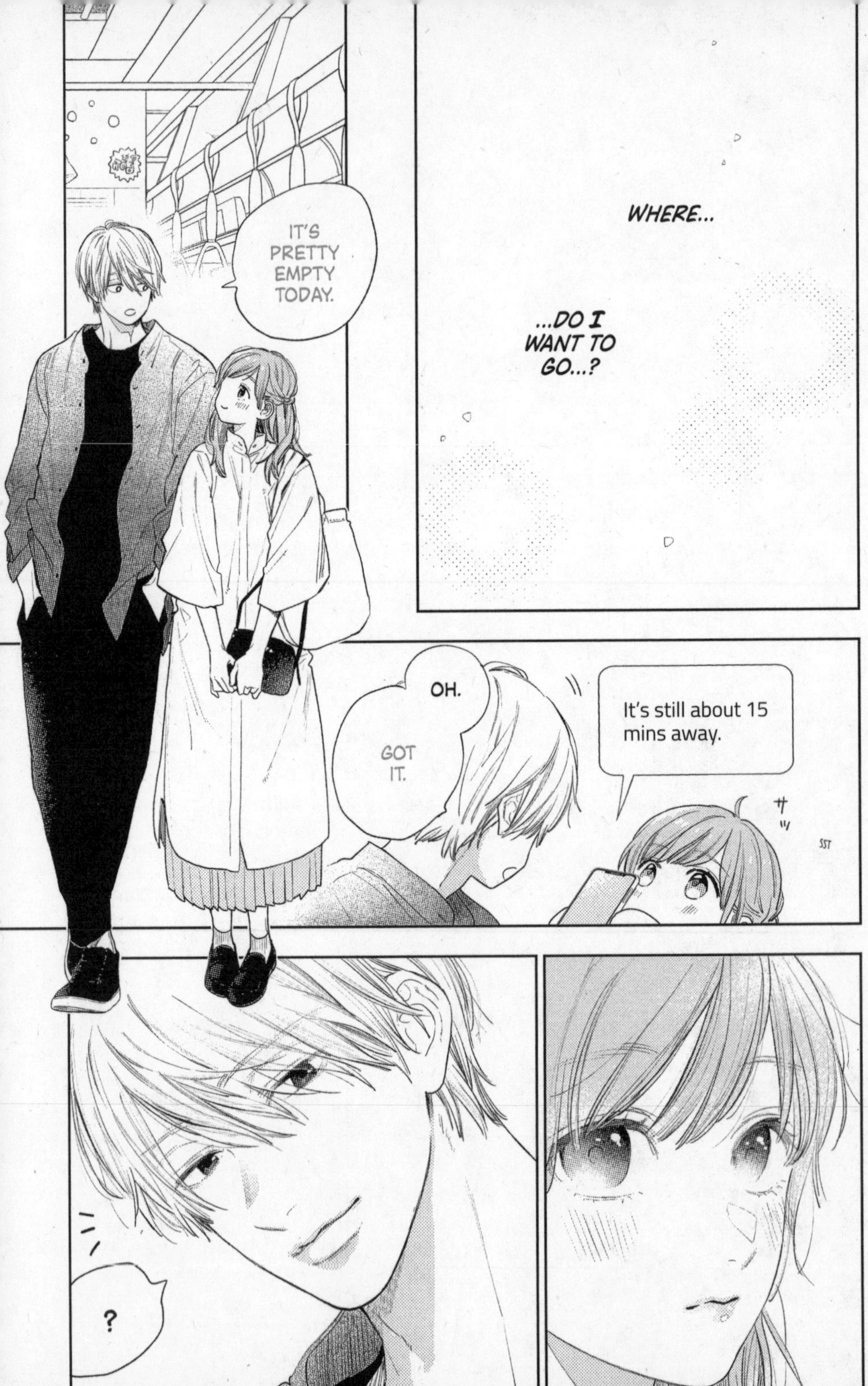
WHERE...
...DO I WANT TO GO...?
It's still about 15 mins away.
SST
OH.
GOT IT.
IT'S PRETTY EMPTY TODAY.
?

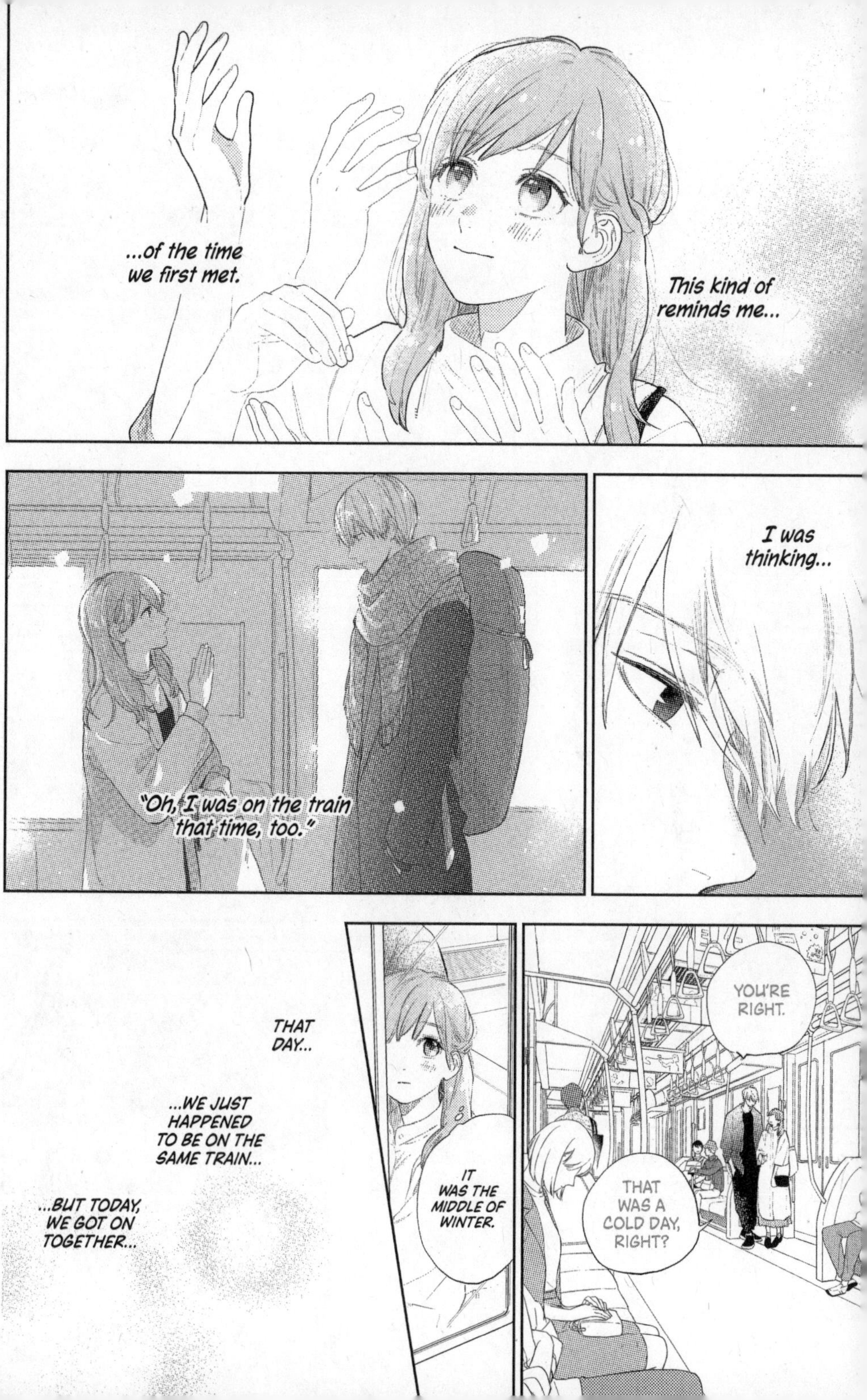

This kind of reminds me...
...of the time we first met.
I was thinking...
"Oh, I was on the train that time, too."
YOU'RE RIGHT.
THAT WAS A COLD DAY, RIGHT?
IT WAS THE MIDDLE OF WINTER.
THAT DAY...
...WE JUST HAPPENED TO BE ON THE SAME TRAIN...
...BUT TODAY, WE GOT ON TOGETHER...

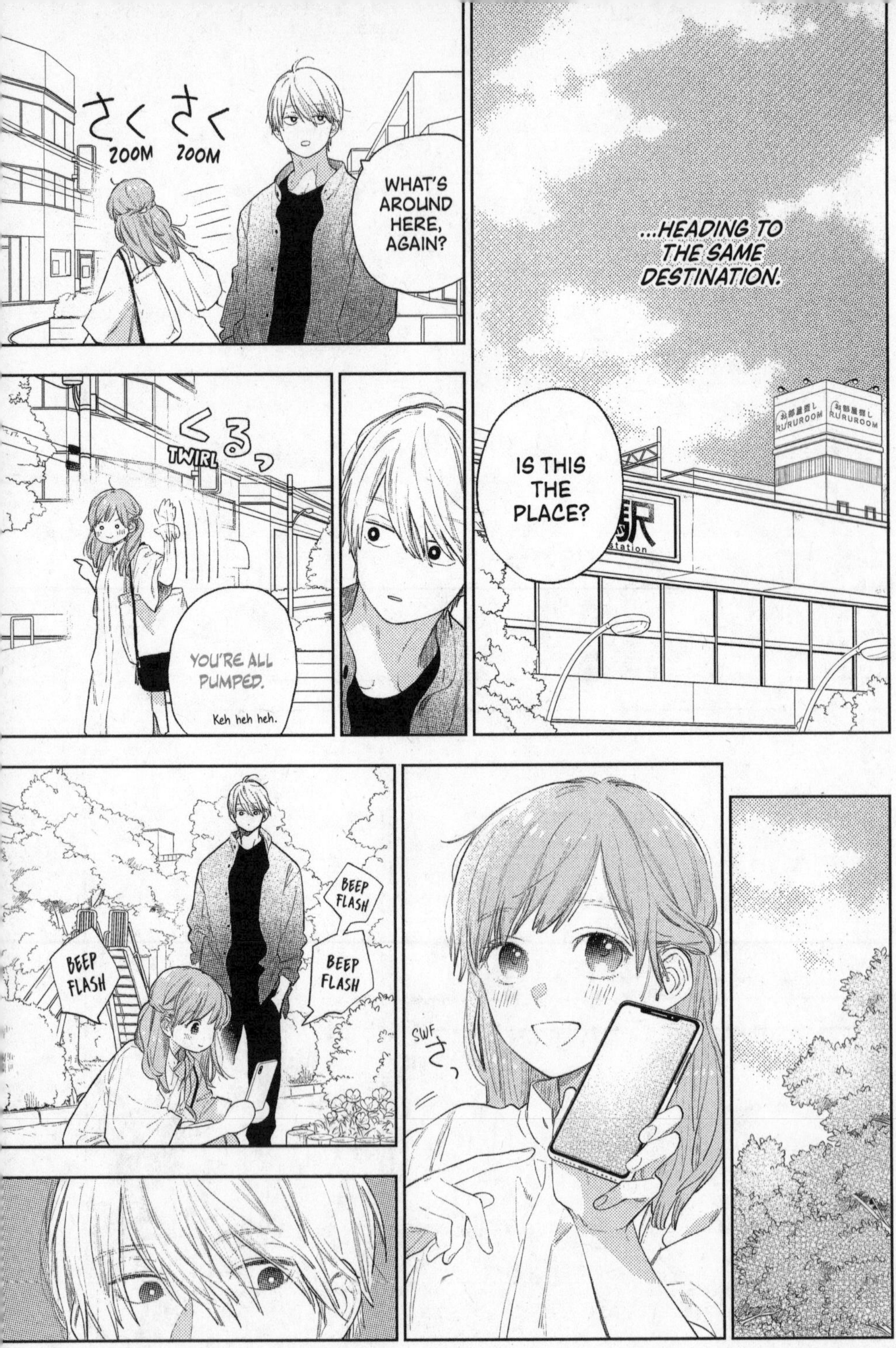

...HEADING TO THE SAME DESTINATION.
IS THIS THE PLACE?
駅
station
RURUROOM
RURUROOM
さくさく
ZOOM ZOOM
WHAT'S AROUND HERE, AGAIN?
くるっ
TWIRL
YOU'RE ALL PUMPED.
Keh heh heh.
さっ
SWF
BEEP FLASH
BEEP FLASH
BEEP FLASH

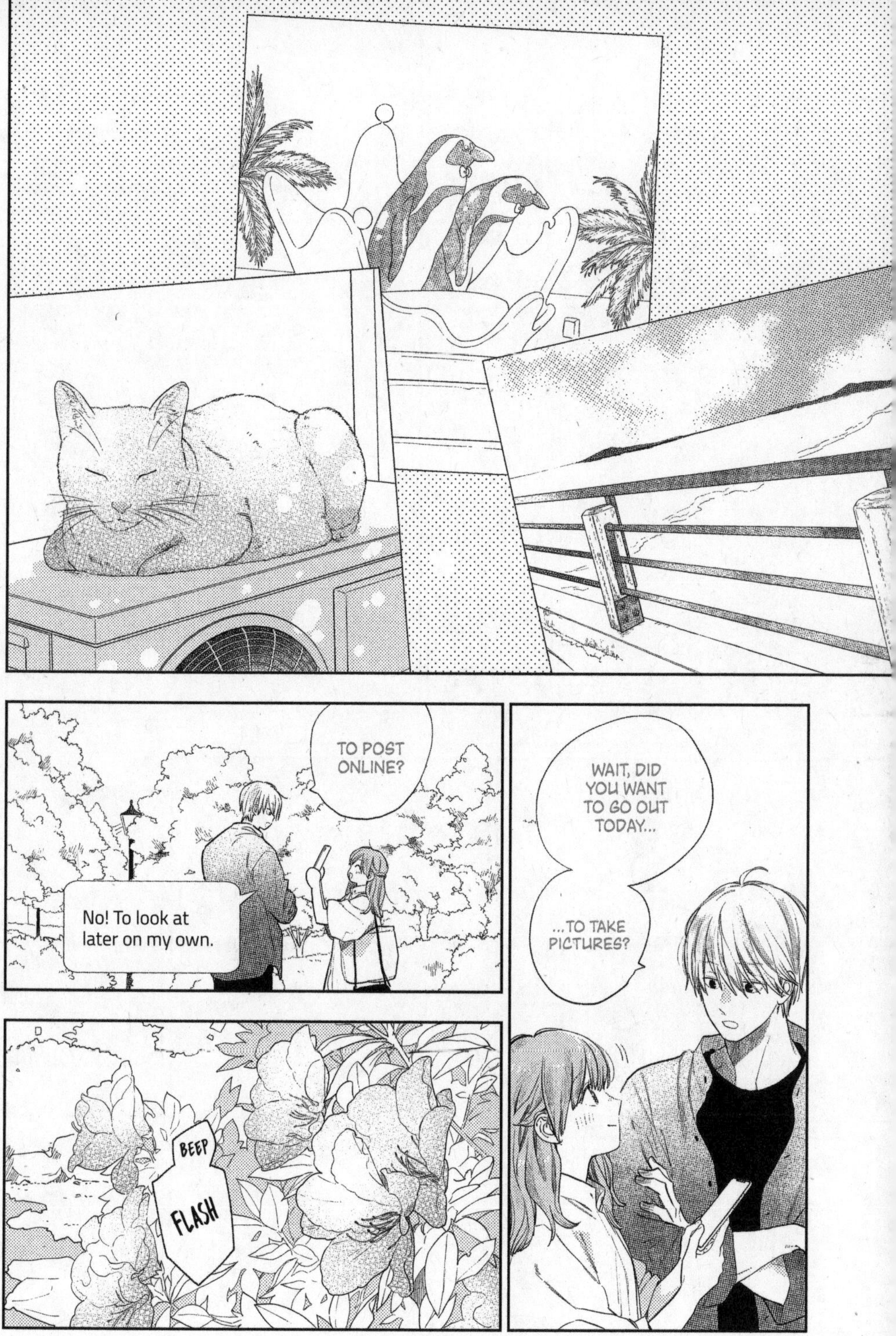
WAIT, DID YOU WANT TO GO OUT TODAY...
...TO TAKE PICTURES?
TO POST ONLINE?
No! To look at later on my own.
BEEP
FLASH

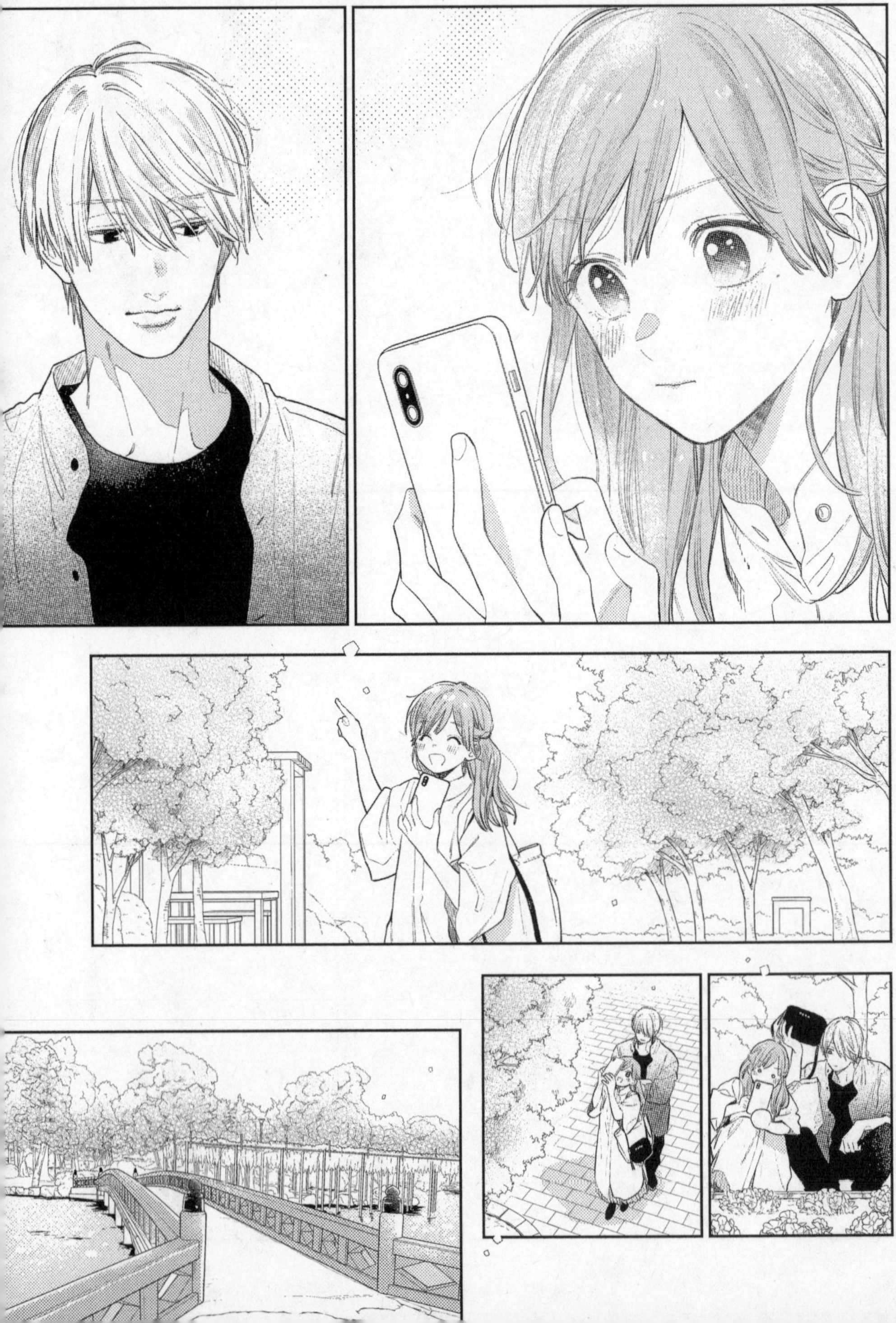

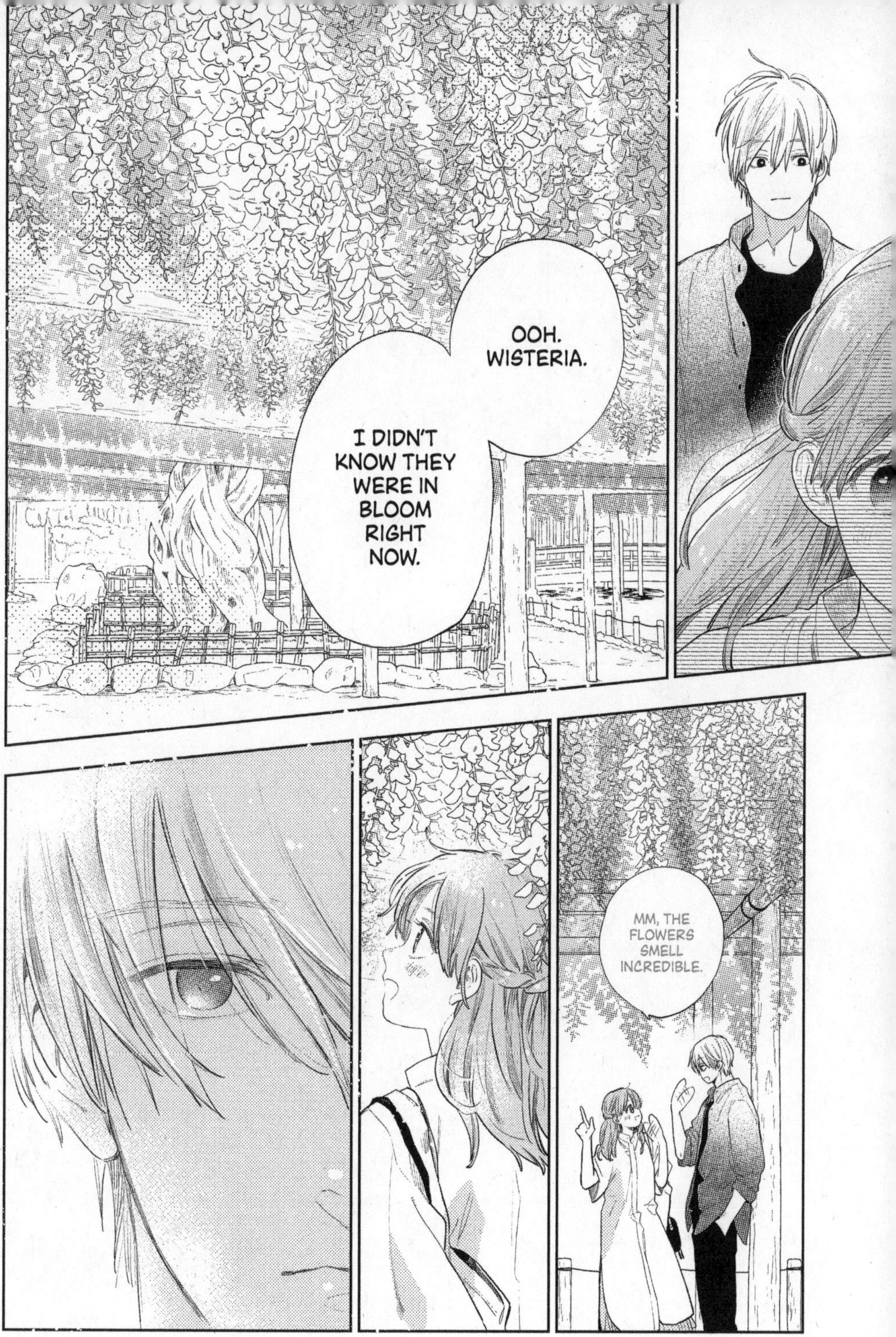
OOH. WISTERIA.
I DIDN'T KNOW THEY WERE IN BLOOM RIGHT NOW.
MM, THE FLOWERS SMELL INCREDIBLE.

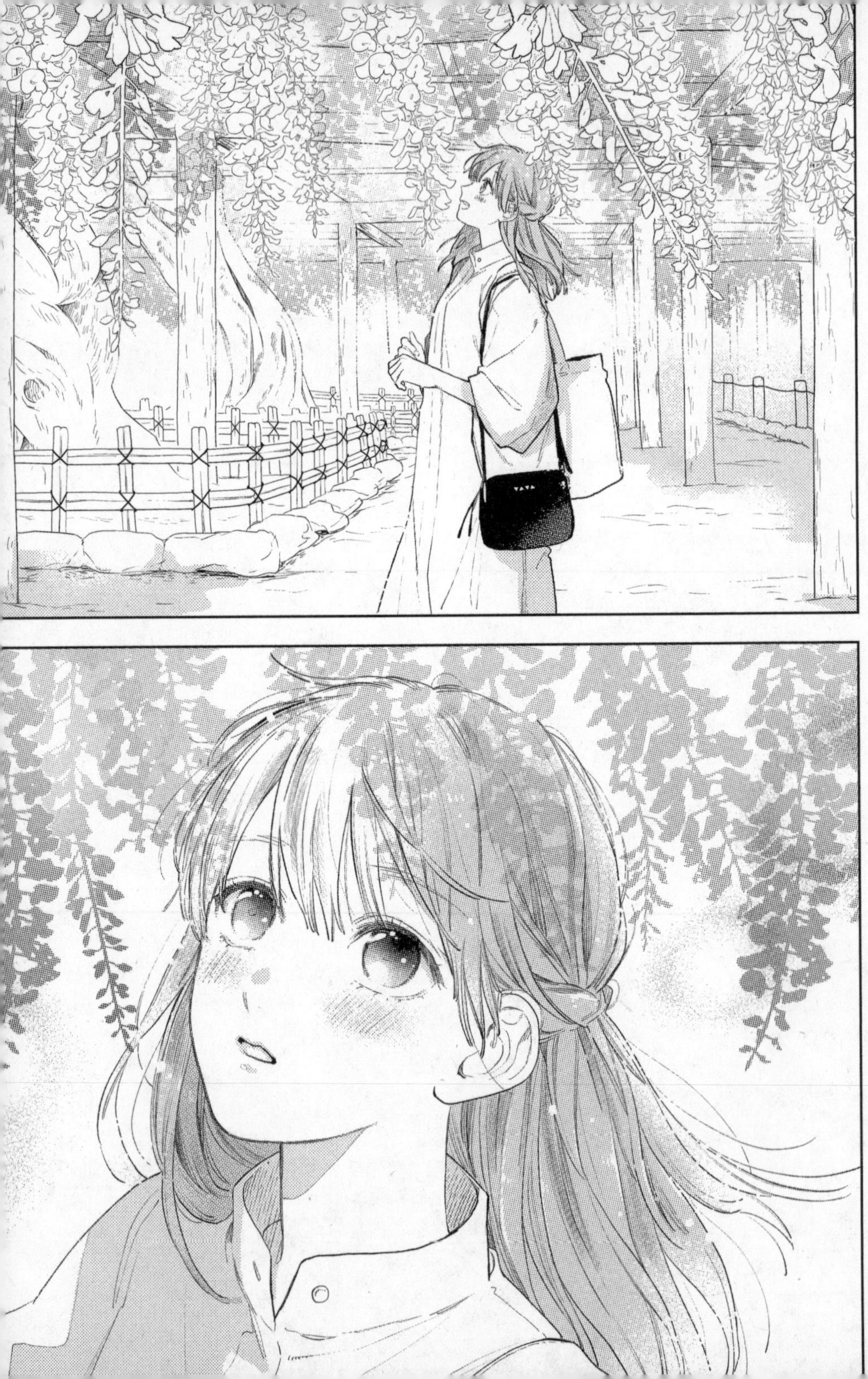

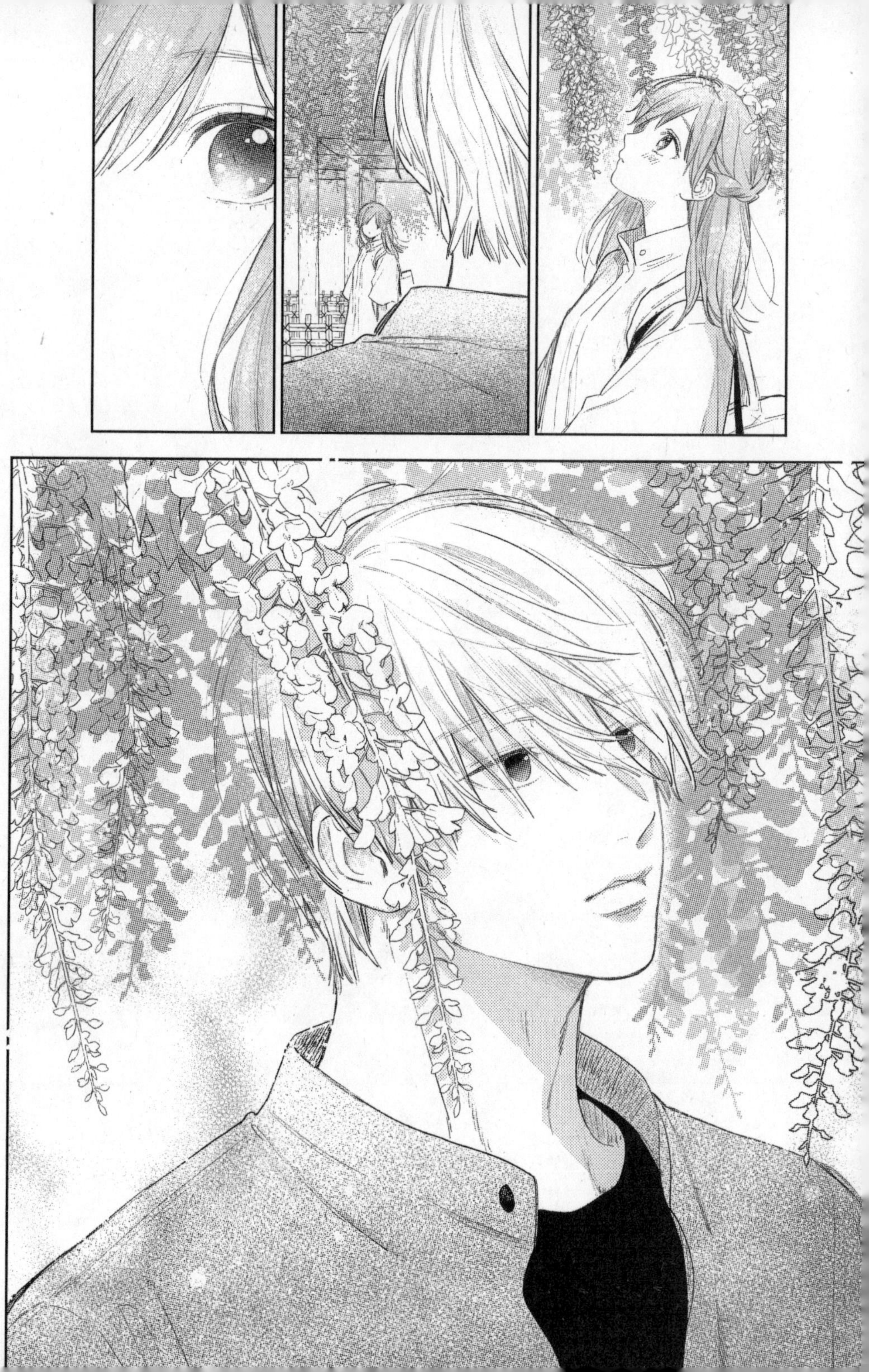

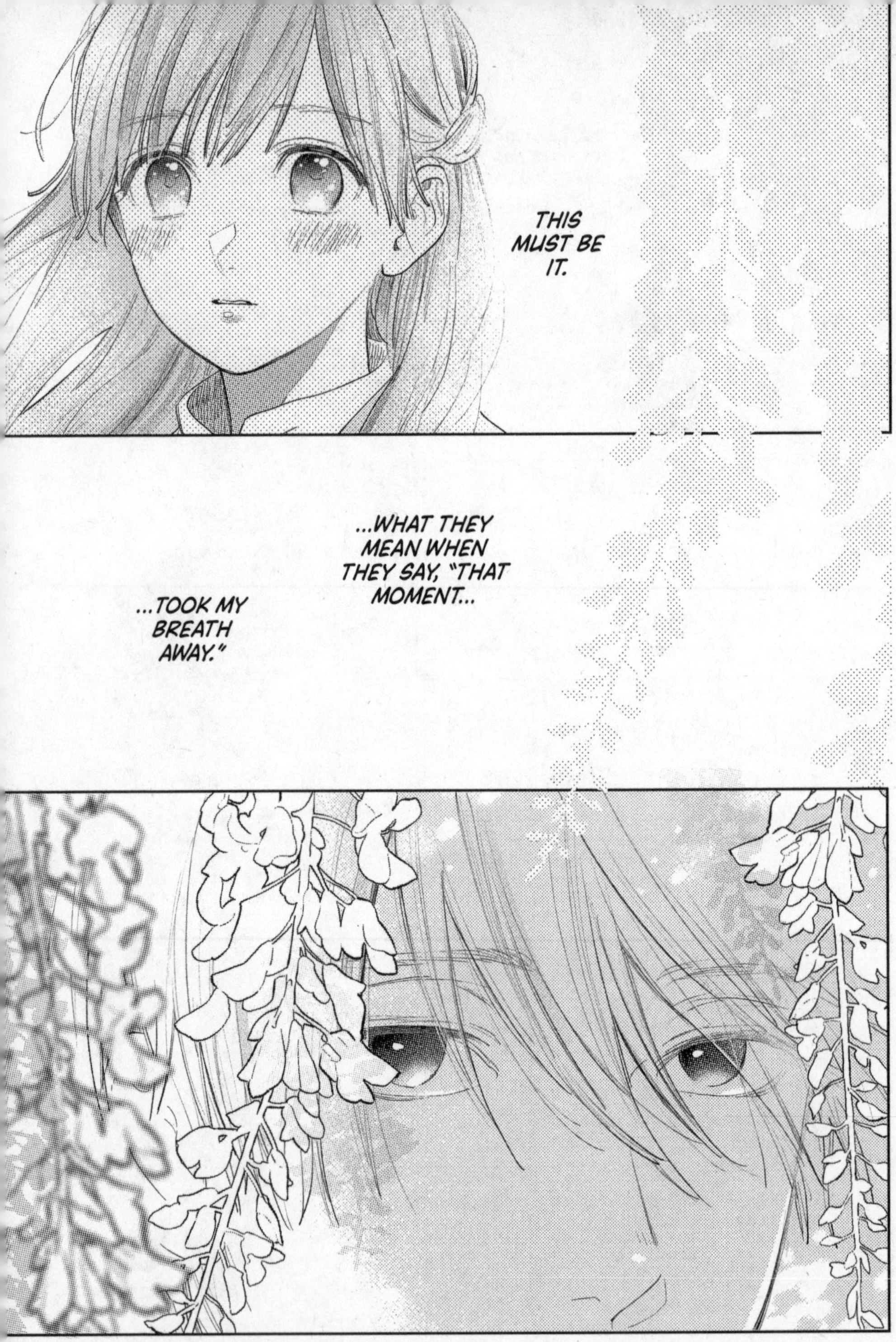
THIS MUST BE IT.
...WHAT THEY MEAN WHEN THEY SAY, "THAT MOMENT...
...TOOK MY BREATH AWAY."

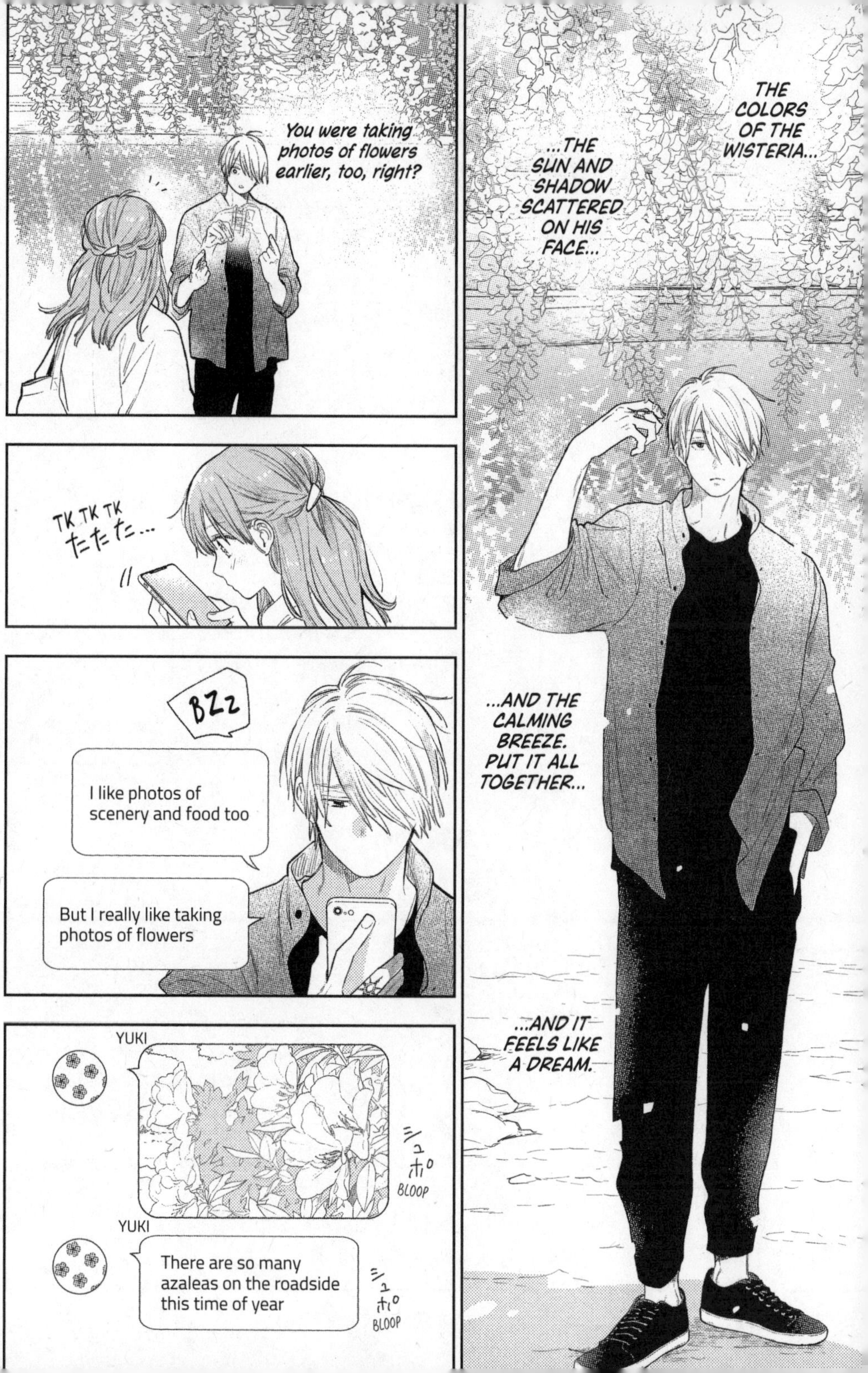
THE COLORS OF THE WISTERIA...
...THE SUN AND SHADOW SCATTERED ON HIS FACE...
...AND THE CALMING BREEZE. PUT IT ALL TOGETHER...
...AND IT FEELS LIKE A DREAM.
You were taking photos of flowers earlier, too, right?
TK TK TK
たたた...
BZz
I like photos of scenery and food too
But I really like taking photos of flowers
YUKI
シュポ
BLOOP
YUKI
There are so many azaleas on the roadside this time of year
シュポ
BLOOP

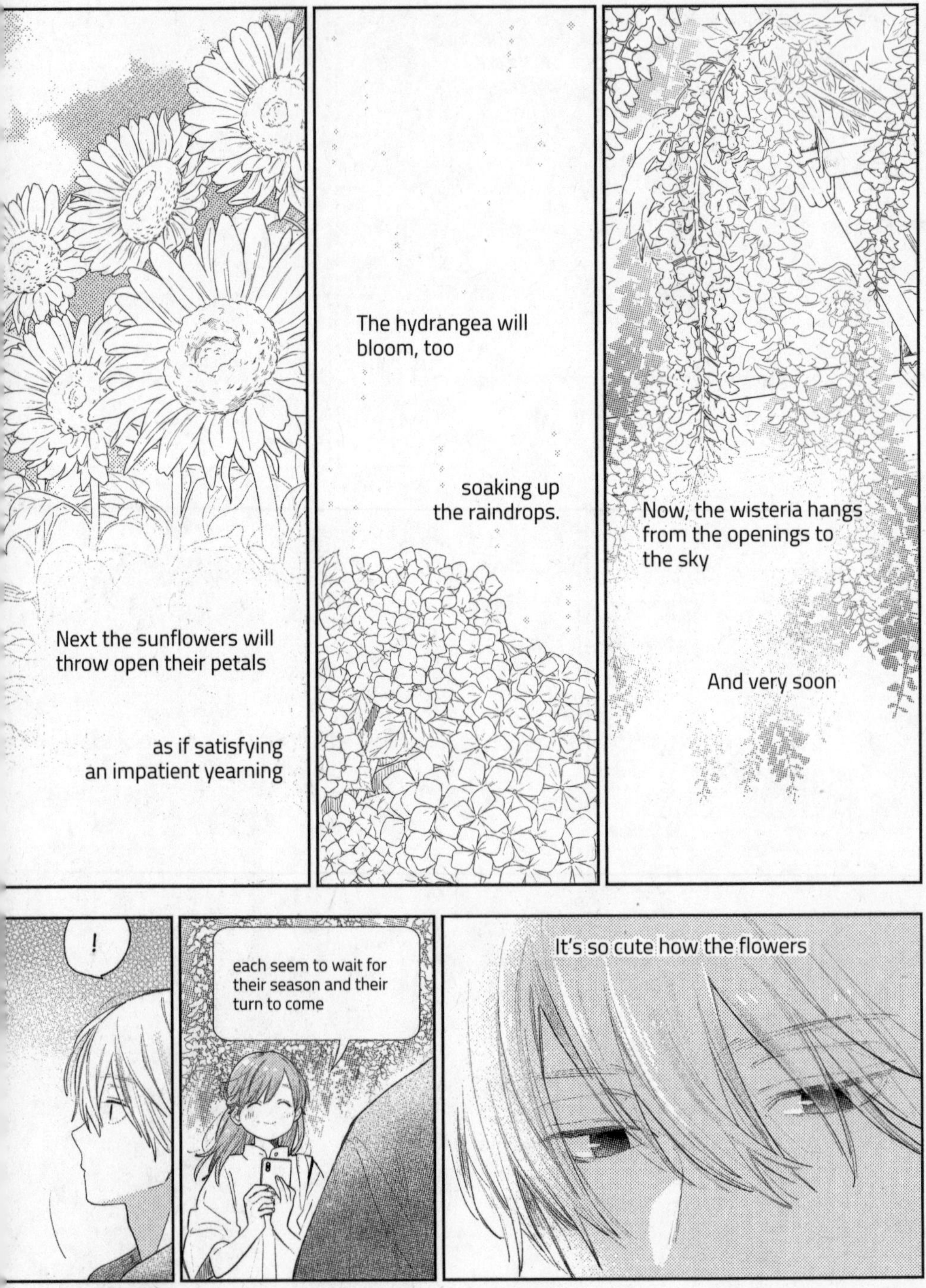
Now, the wisteria hangs from the openings to the sky
And very soon
The hydrangea will bloom, too
soaking up the raindrops.
Next the sunflowers will throw open their petals
as if satisfying an impatient yearning
It's so cute how the flowers
each seem to wait for their season and their turn to come
!

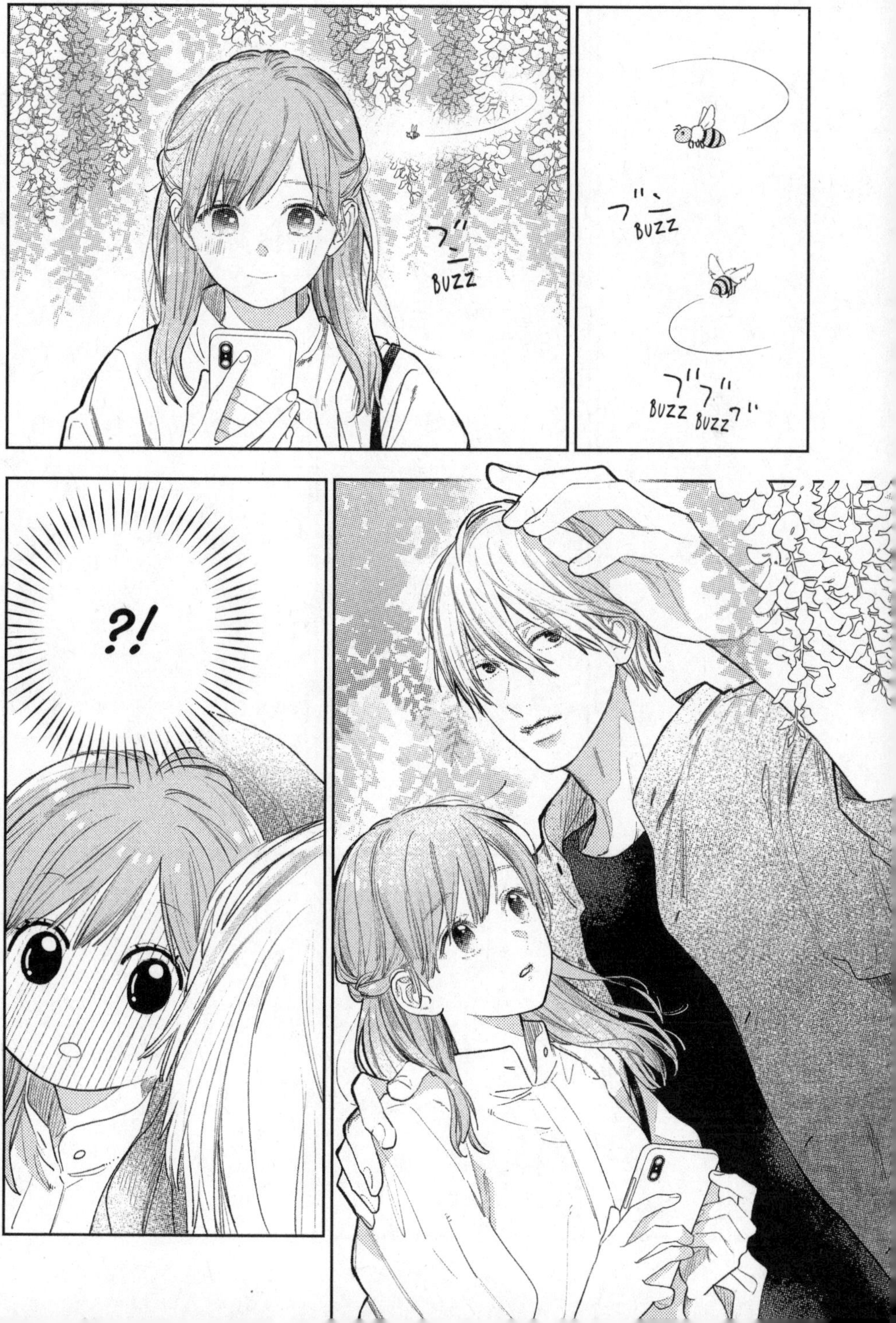
ブン
BUZZ
ブブブ
BUZZ BUZZ
ブン
BUZZ
?!

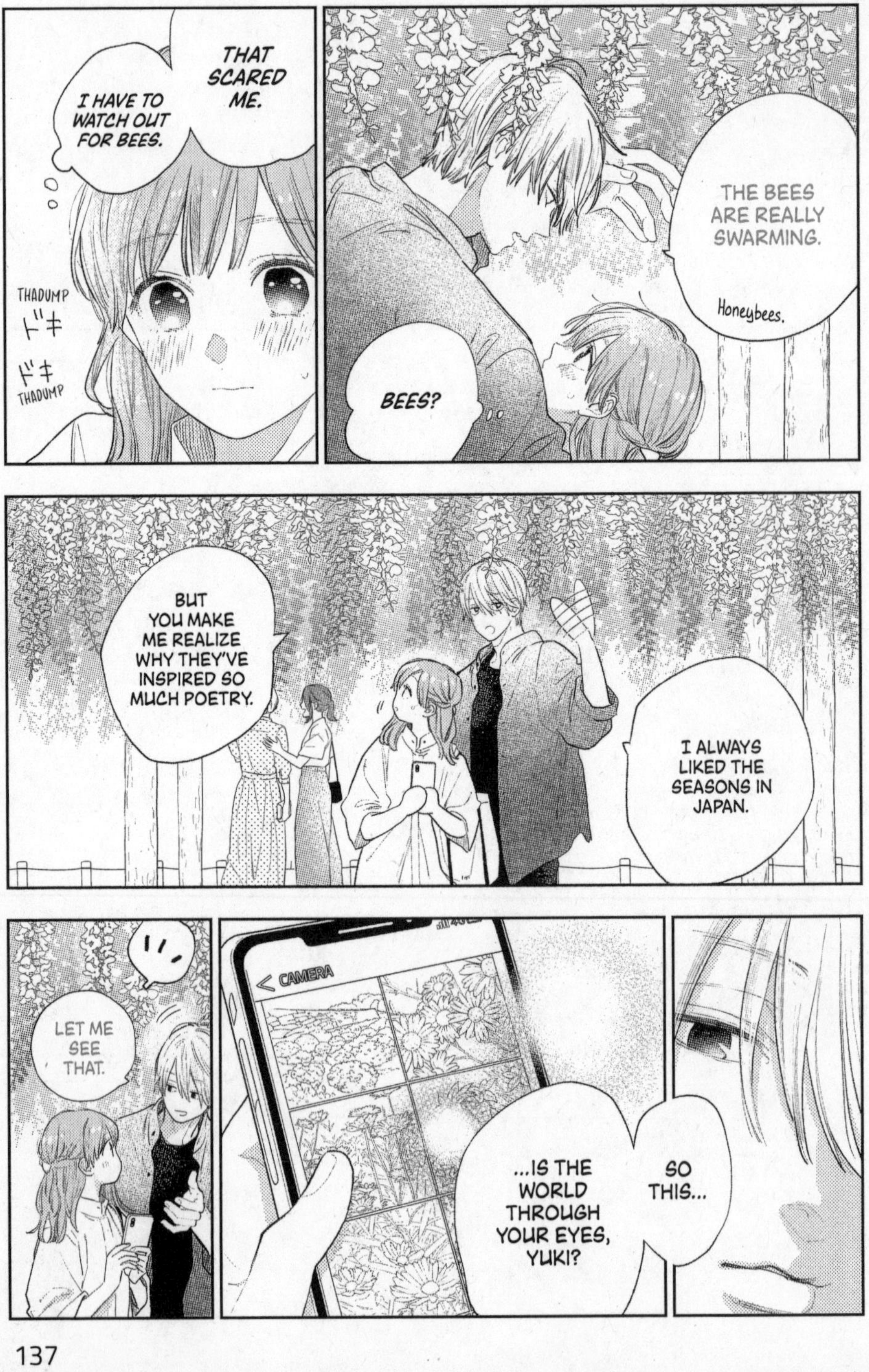
THE BEES ARE REALLY SWARMING.
Honeybees.
BEES?
THAT SCARED ME.
I HAVE TO WATCH OUT FOR BEES.
THADUMP ドキ
ドキ THADUMP
I ALWAYS LIKED THE SEASONS IN JAPAN.
BUT YOU MAKE ME REALIZE WHY THEY'VE INSPIRED SO MUCH POETRY.
SO THIS...
...IS THE WORLD THROUGH YOUR EYES, YUKI?
CAMERA
!!
LET ME SEE THAT.

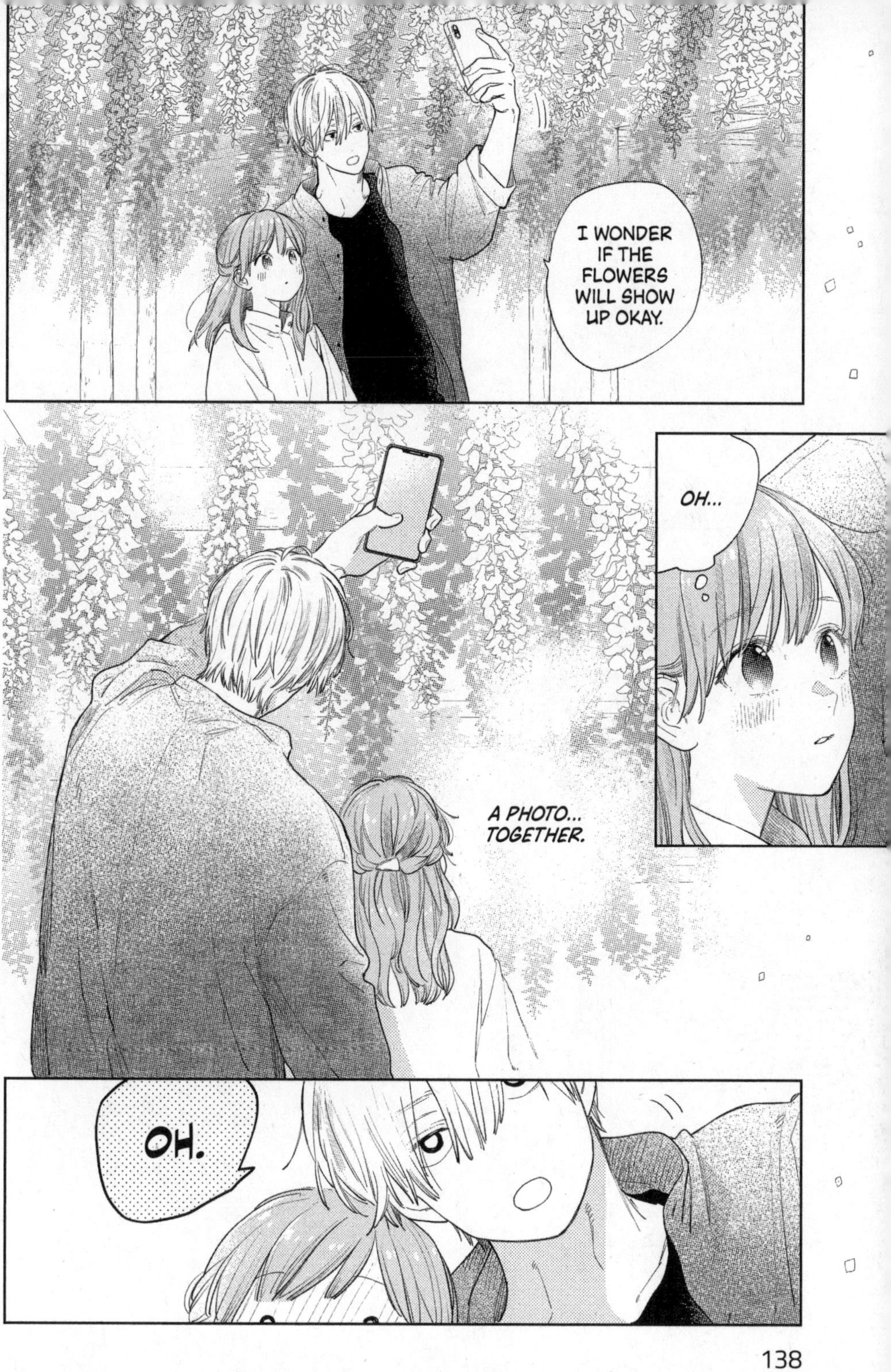

I WONDER IF THE FLOWERS WILL SHOW UP OKAY.
OH...
A PHOTO... TOGETHER.
OH.

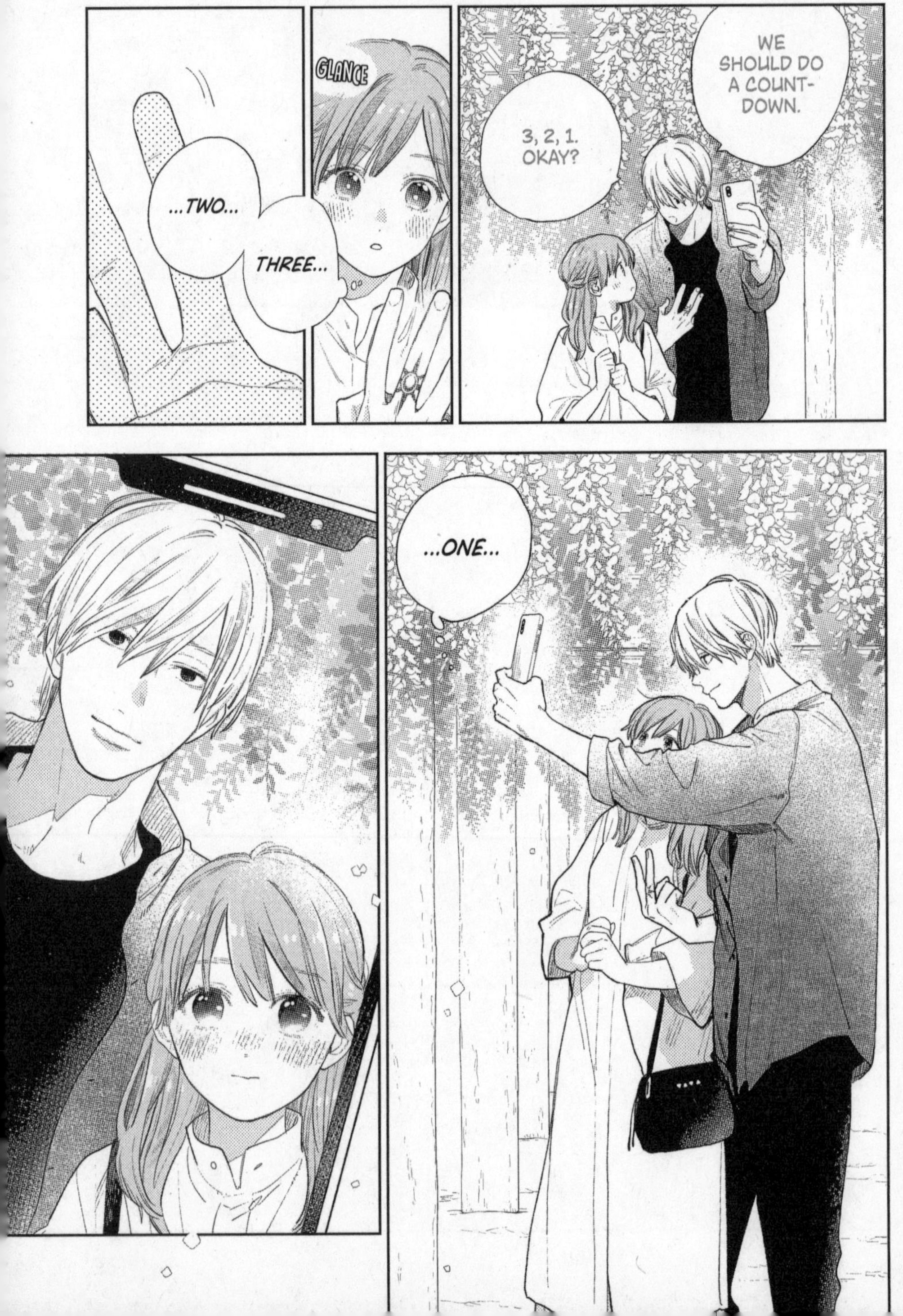
WE SHOULD DO A COUNT-DOWN.
3, 2, 1. OKAY?
GLANCE
THREE...
...TWO...
...ONE...

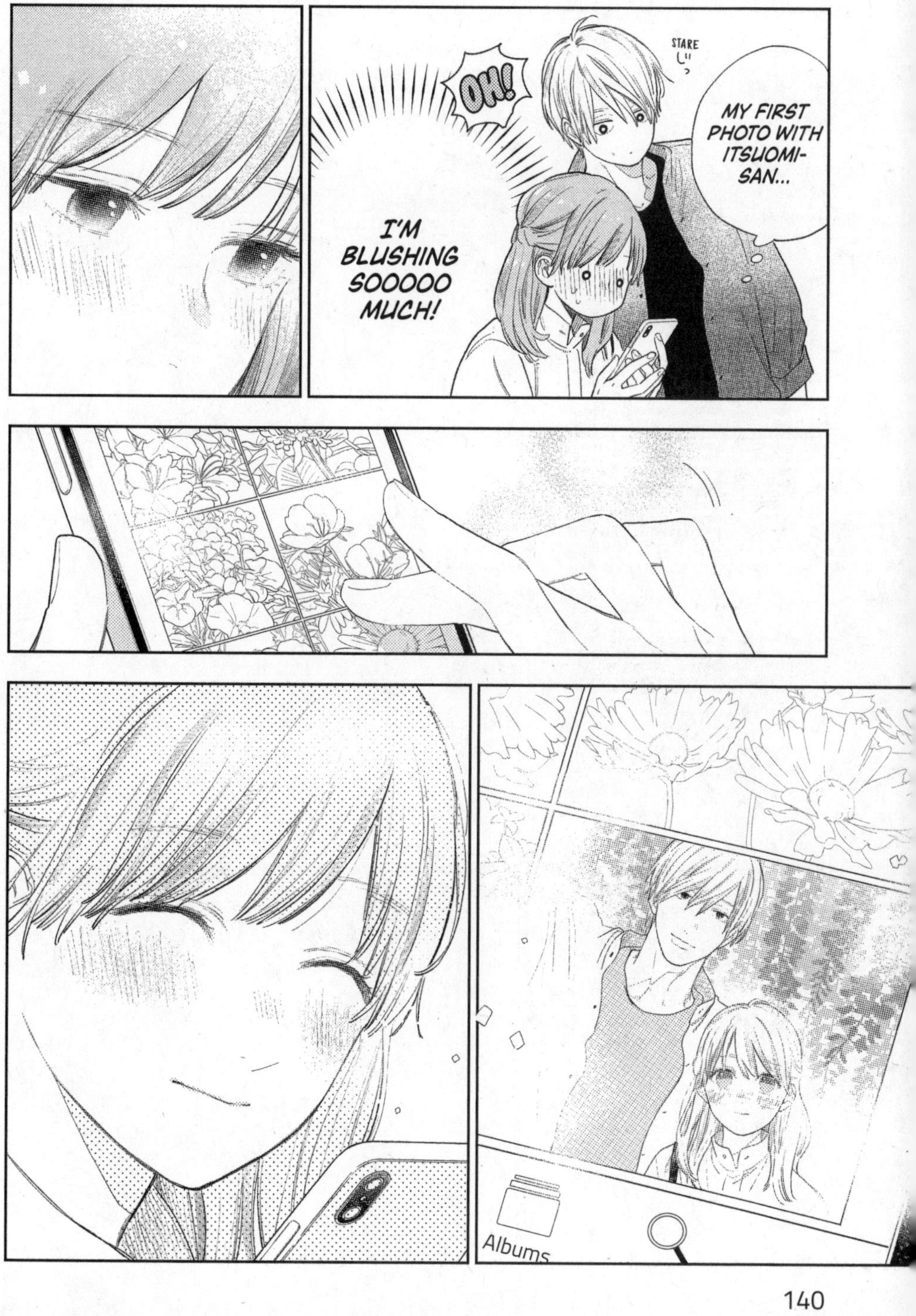
STARE
MY FIRST PHOTO WITH ITSUOMI-SAN...
OH!
I'M BLUSHING SOOOOO MUCH!
Albums

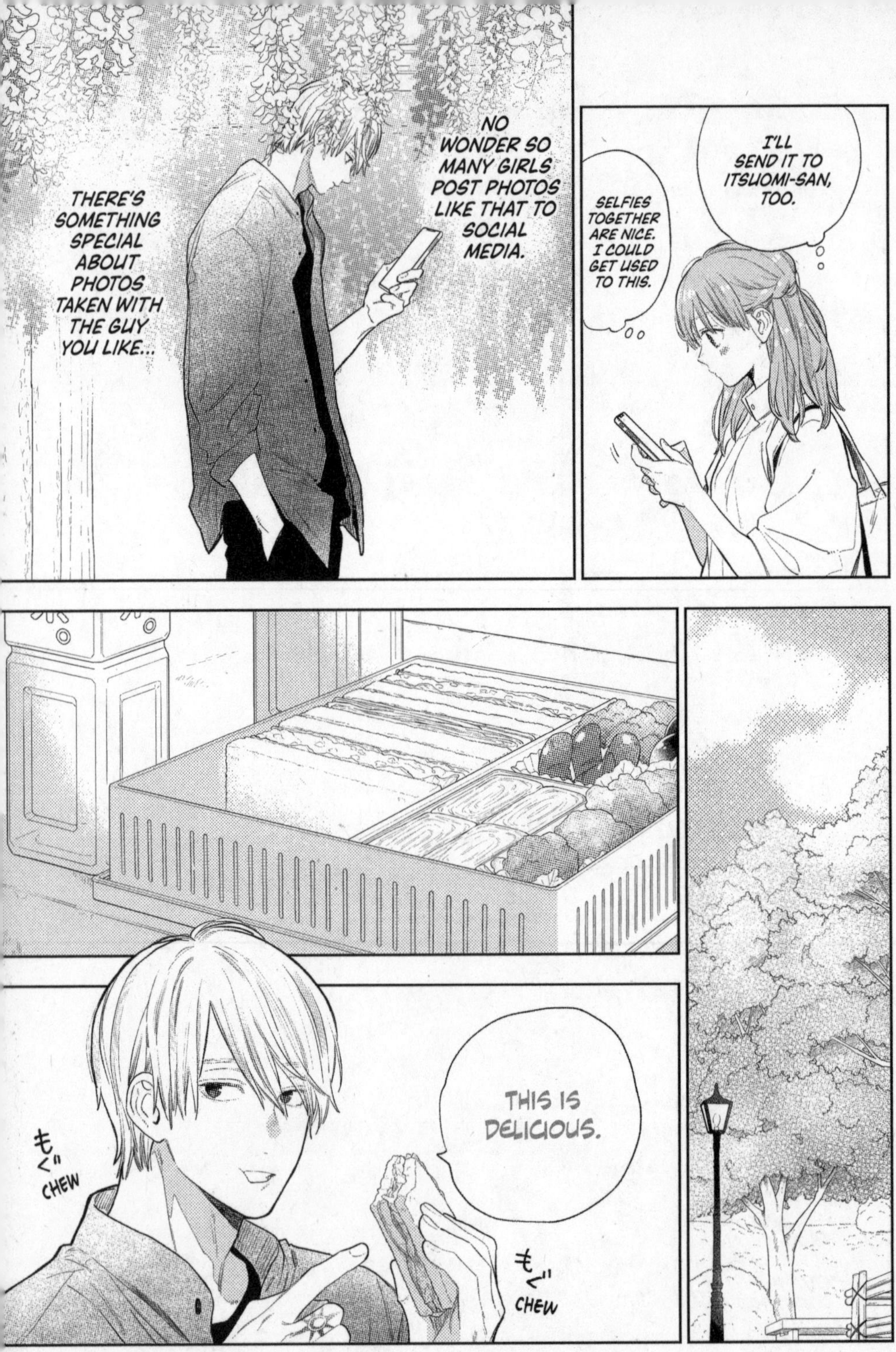
I'LL SEND IT TO ITSUOMI-SAN, TOO.
SELFIES TOGETHER ARE NICE. I COULD GET USED TO THIS.
NO WONDER SO MANY GIRLS POST PHOTOS LIKE THAT TO SOCIAL MEDIA.
THERE'S SOMETHING SPECIAL ABOUT PHOTOS TAKEN WITH THE GUY YOU LIKE...
THIS IS DELICIOUS.
もぐ CHEW
もぐ" CHEW

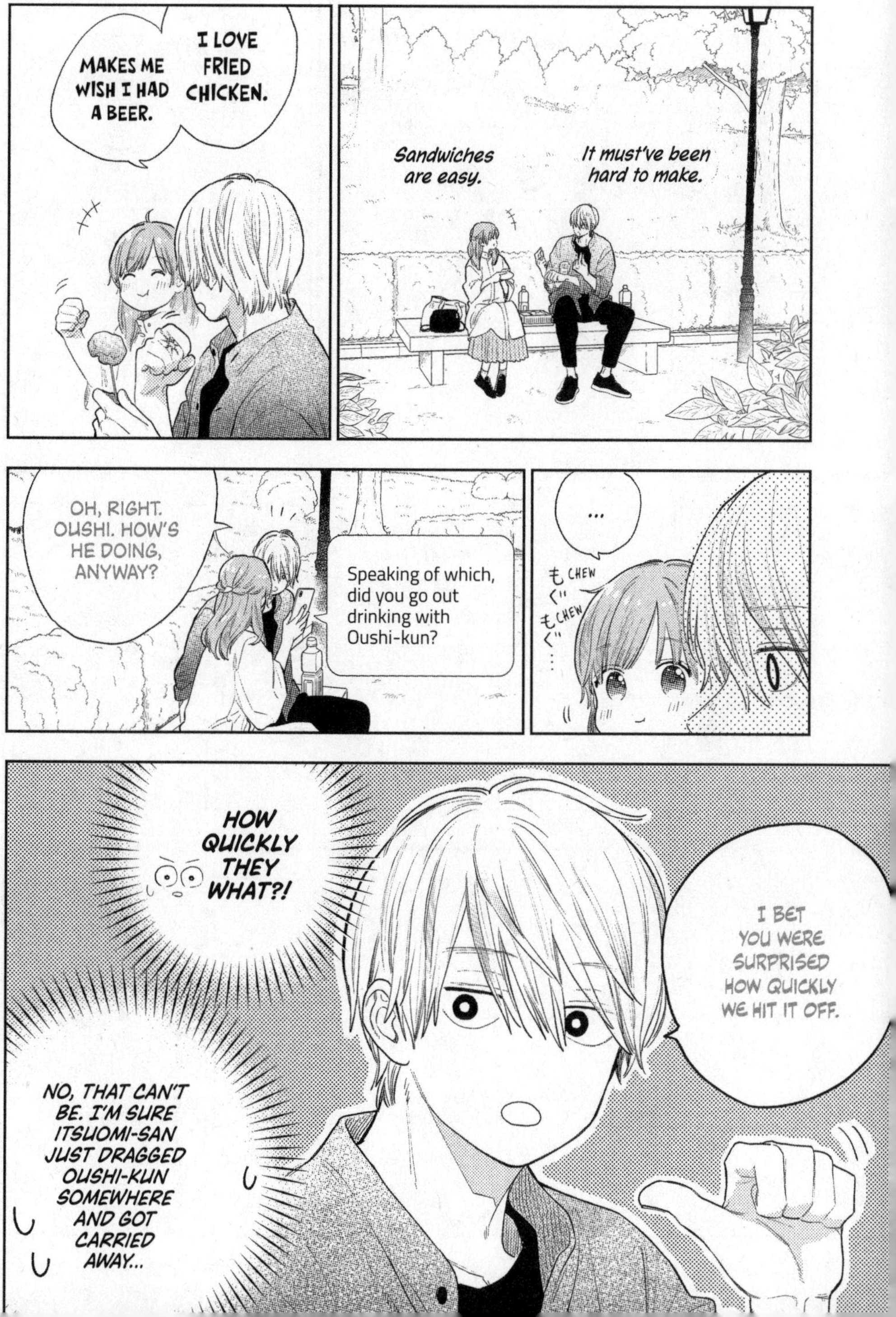
It must've been hard to make.
Sandwiches are easy.
I LOVE FRIED CHICKEN.
MAKES ME WISH I HAD A BEER.
...
もぐ CHEW
もぐ CHEW
Speaking of which, did you go out drinking with Oushi-kun?
OH, RIGHT. OUSHI. HOW'S HE DOING, ANYWAY?
I BET YOU WERE SURPRISED HOW QUICKLY WE HIT IT OFF.
HOW QUICKLY THEY WHAT?!
NO, THAT CAN'T BE. I'M SURE ITSUOMI-SAN JUST DRAGGED OUSHI-KUN SOMEWHERE AND GOT CARRIED AWAY...

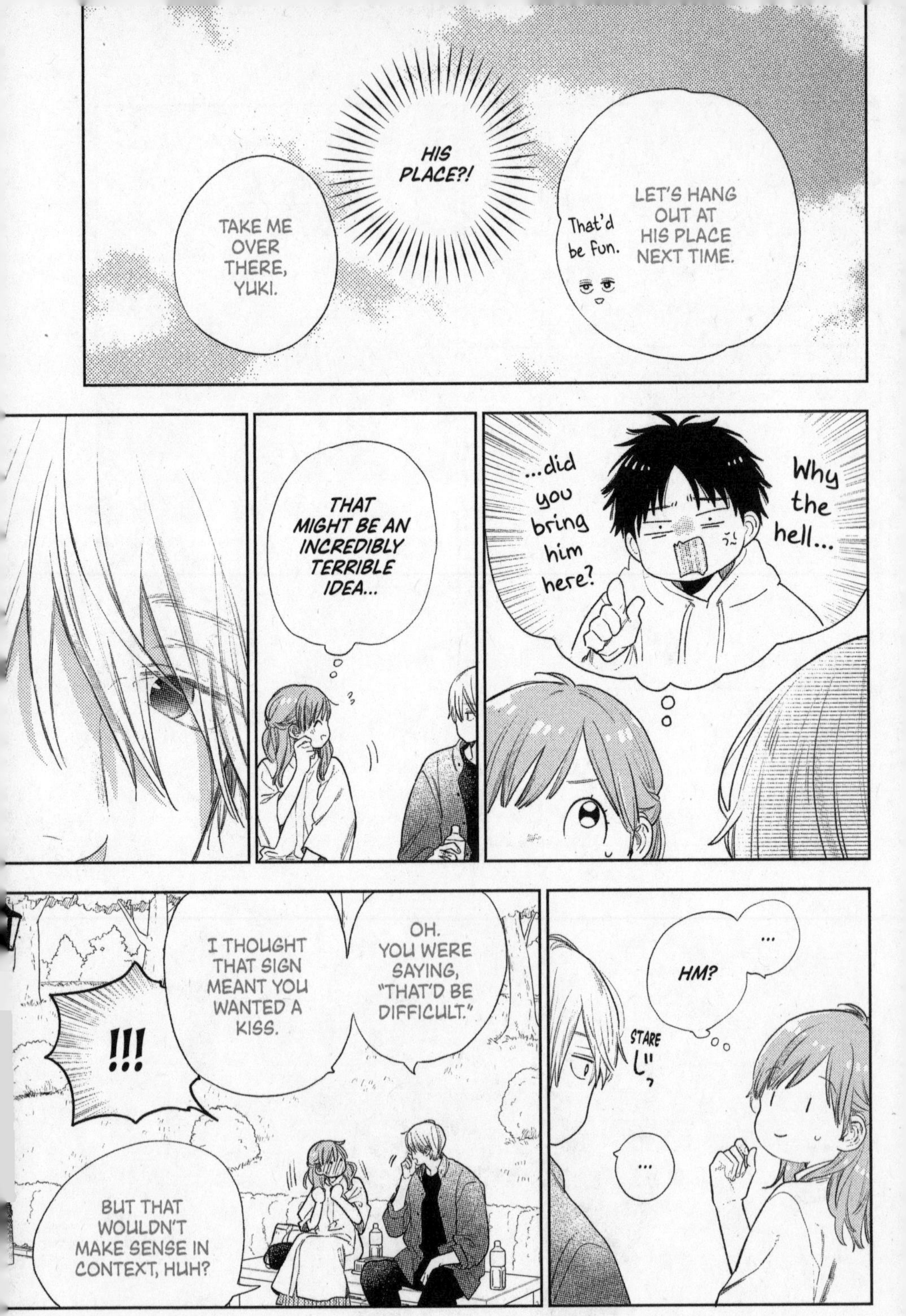
LET'S HANG OUT AT HIS PLACE NEXT TIME.
That'd be fun.
HIS PLACE?!
TAKE ME OVER THERE, YUKI.
Why the hell...
...did you bring him here?
THAT MIGHT BE AN INCREDIBLY TERRIBLE IDEA...
...
HM?
STARE
...
OH. YOU WERE SAYING, "THAT'D BE DIFFICULT."
I THOUGHT THAT SIGN MEANT YOU WANTED A KISS.
!!!
BUT THAT WOULDN'T MAKE SENSE IN CONTEXT, HUH?

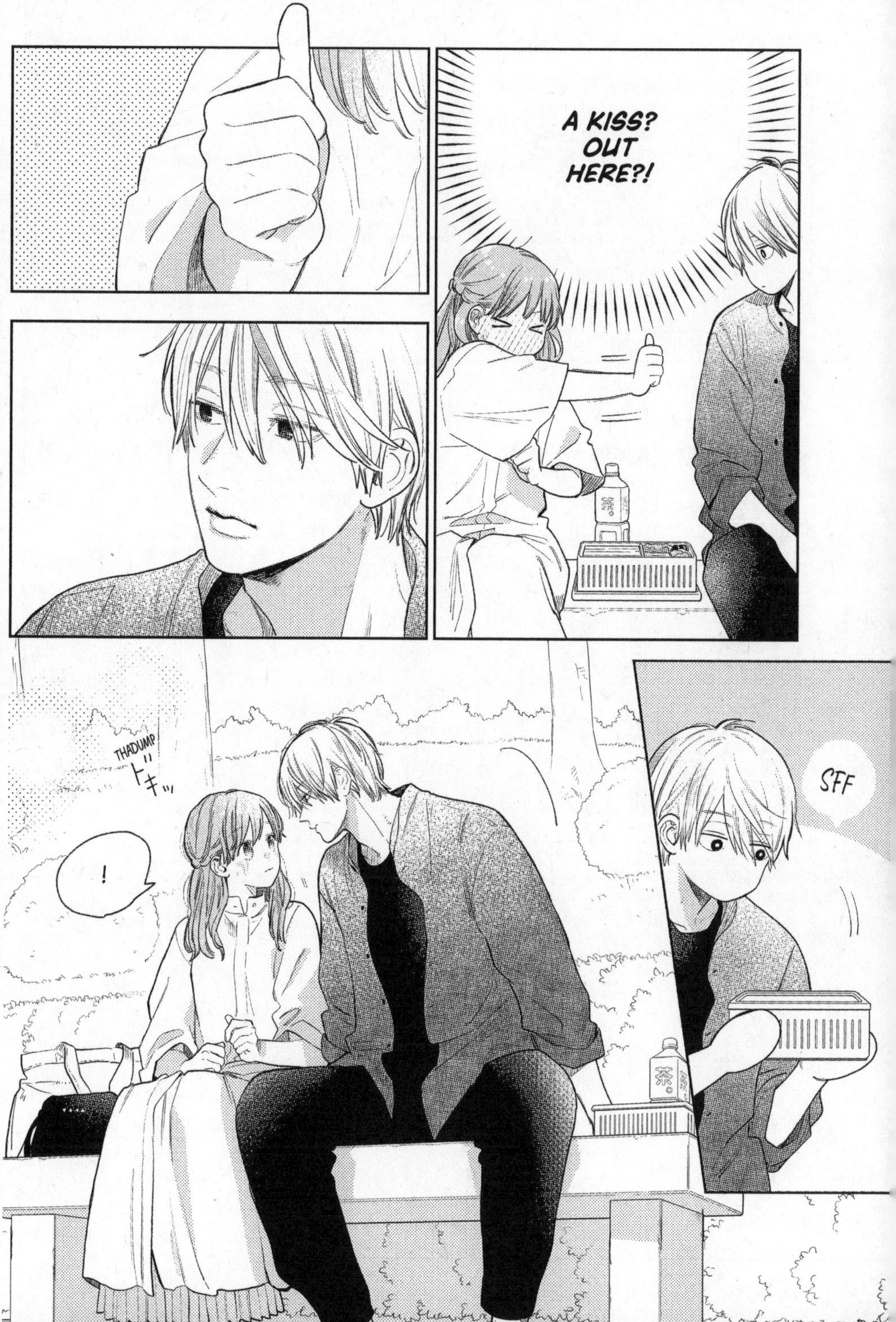
A KISS? OUT HERE?!
SFF
THADUMP
ドキッ
!

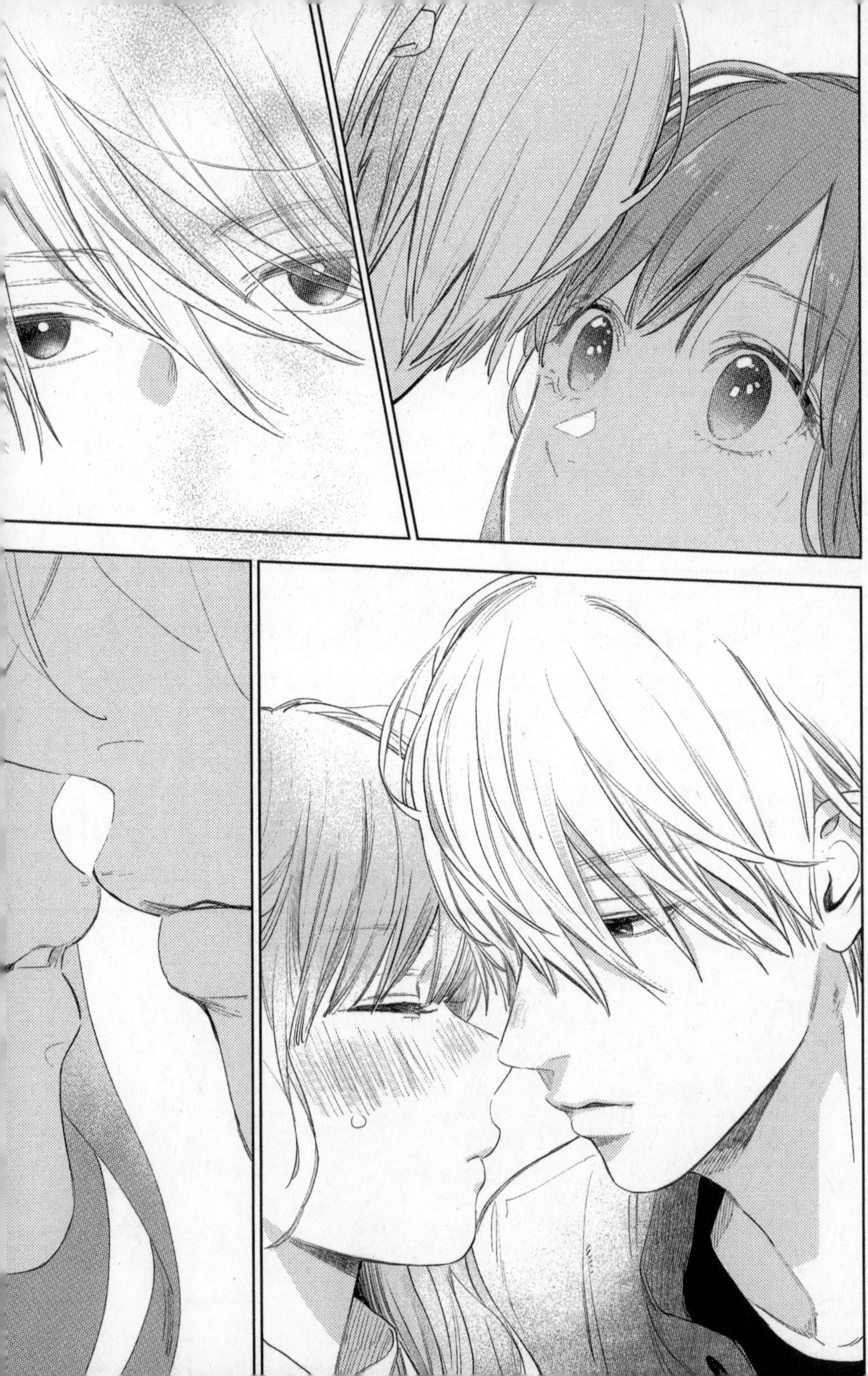

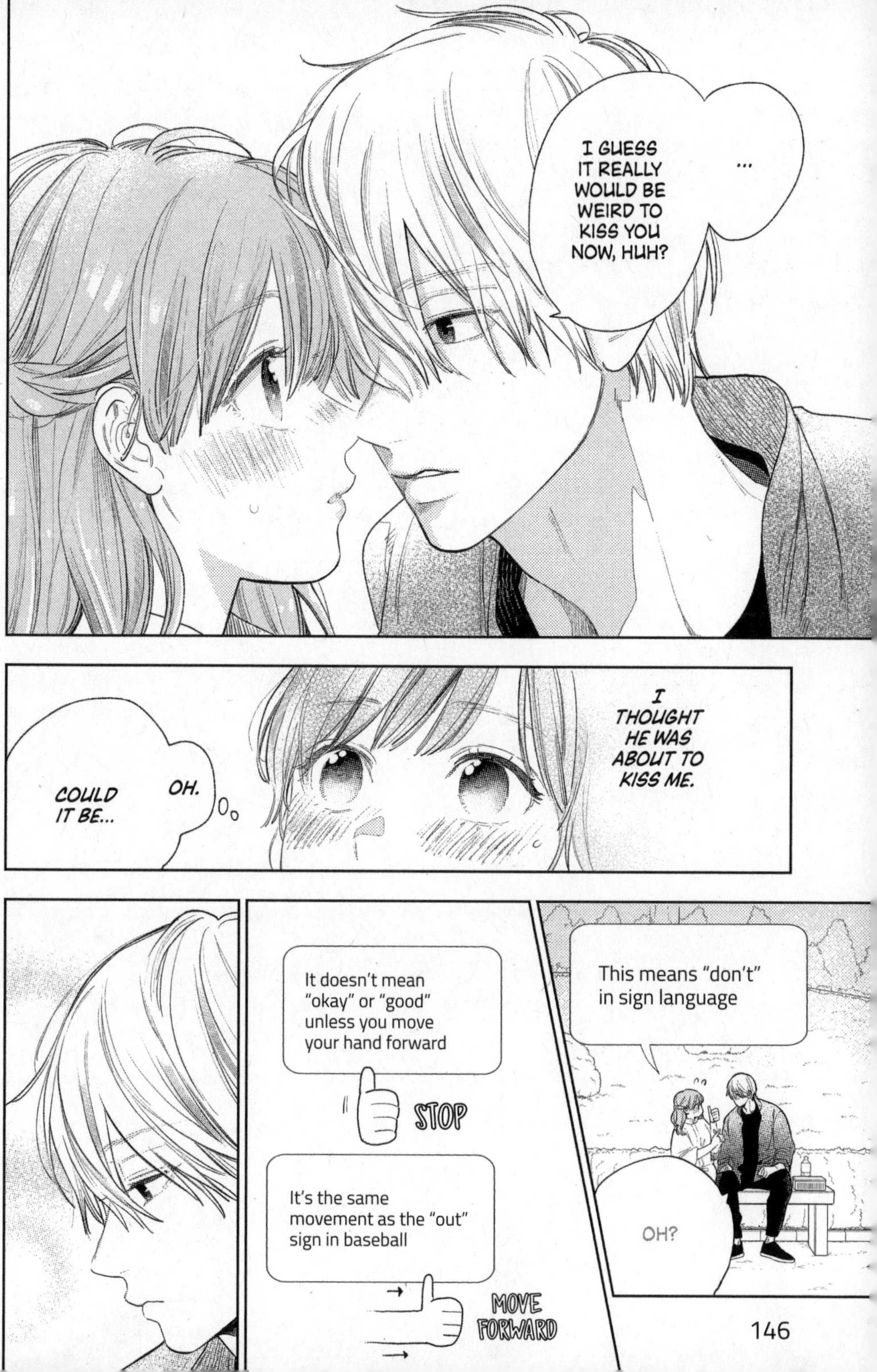
...
I GUESS IT REALLY WOULD BE WEIRD TO KISS YOU NOW, HUH?
I THOUGHT HE WAS ABOUT TO KISS ME.
OH.
COULD IT BE...
This means “don’t” in sign language
OH?
It doesn’t mean “okay” or “good” unless you move your hand forward
STOP
It’s the same movement as the “out” sign in baseball
MOVE FORWARD

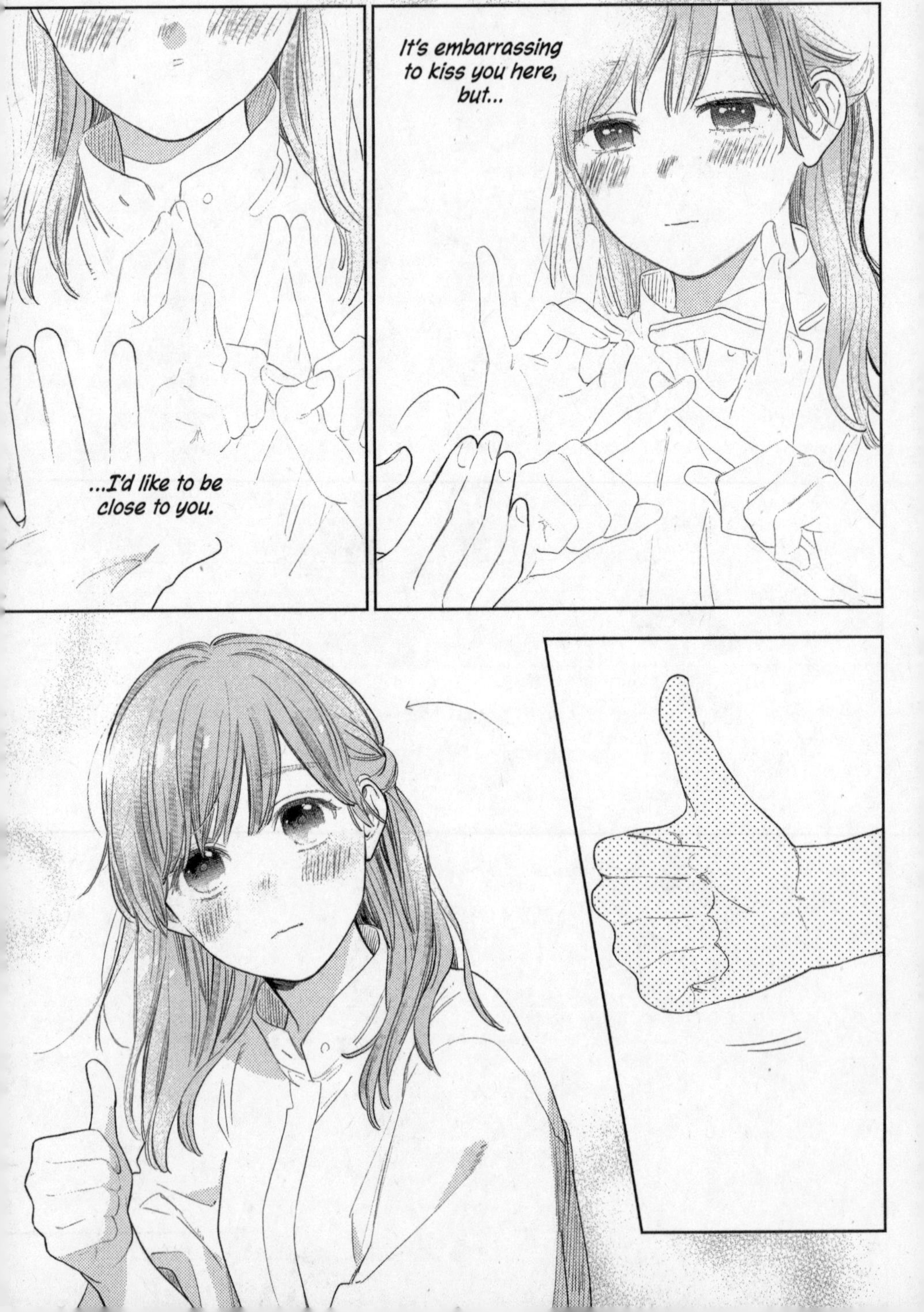
It's embarrassing to kiss you here, but...
...I'd like to be close to you.

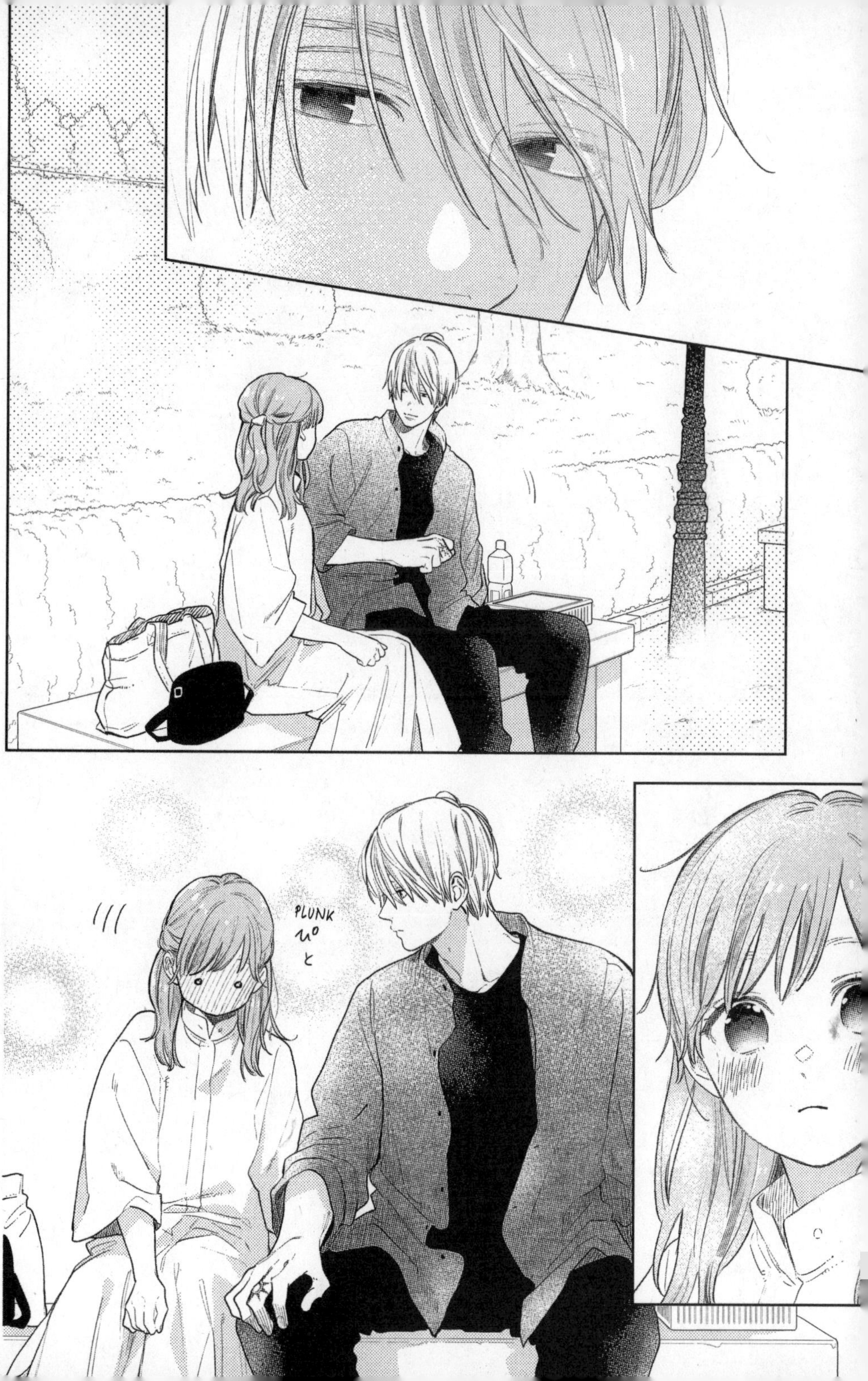
PLUNK
ぴと

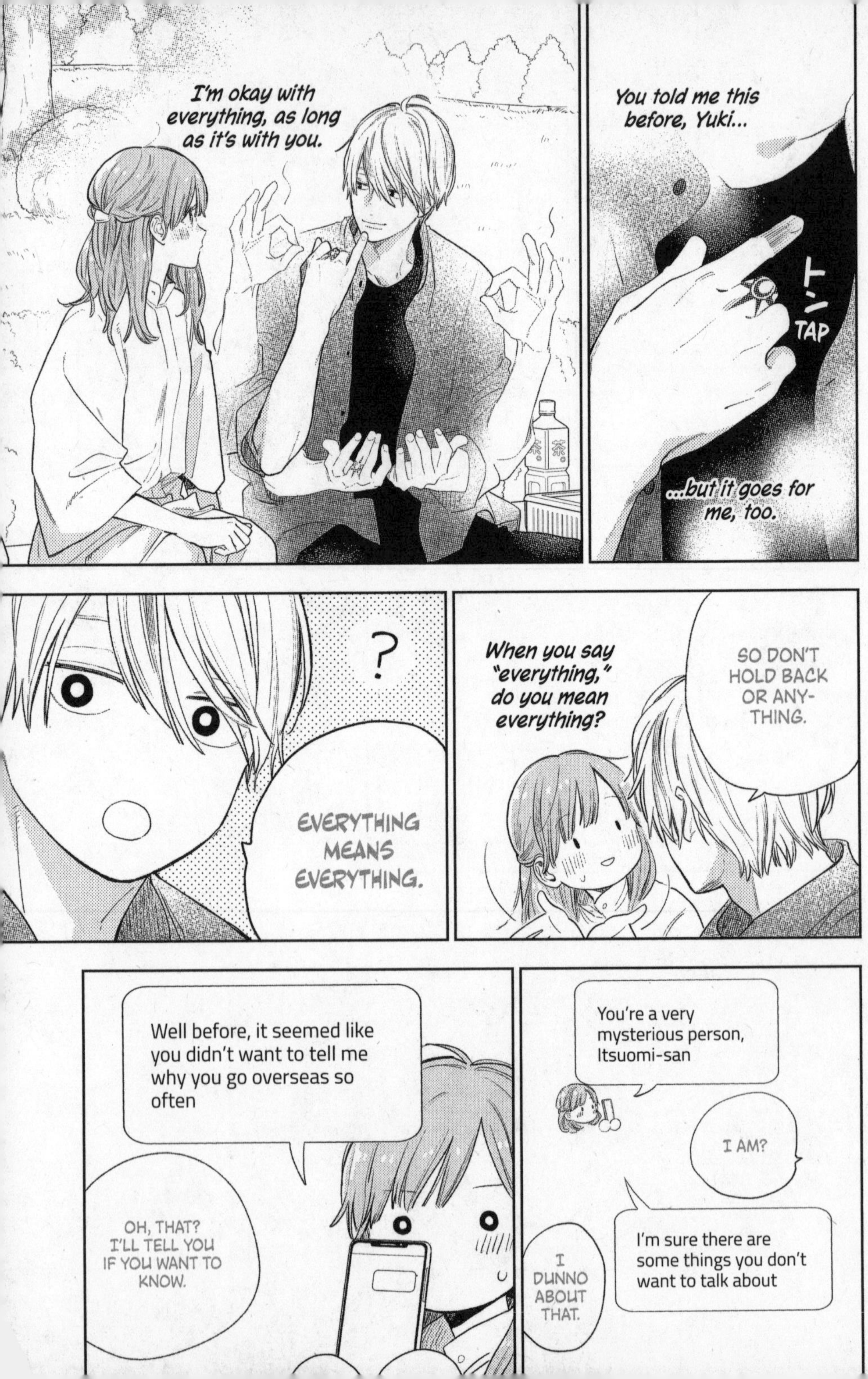
You told me this before, Yuki...
トン
TAP
...but it goes for me, too.
I'm okay with everything, as long as it's with you.
SO DON'T HOLD BACK OR ANY-THING.
When you say "everything," do you mean everything?
?
EVERYTHING MEANS EVERYTHING.
You're a very mysterious person, Itsuomi-san
I AM?
I'm sure there are some things you don't want to talk about
I DUNNO ABOUT THAT.
Well before, it seemed like you didn't want to tell me why you go overseas so often
OH, THAT? I'LL TELL YOU IF YOU WANT TO KNOW.

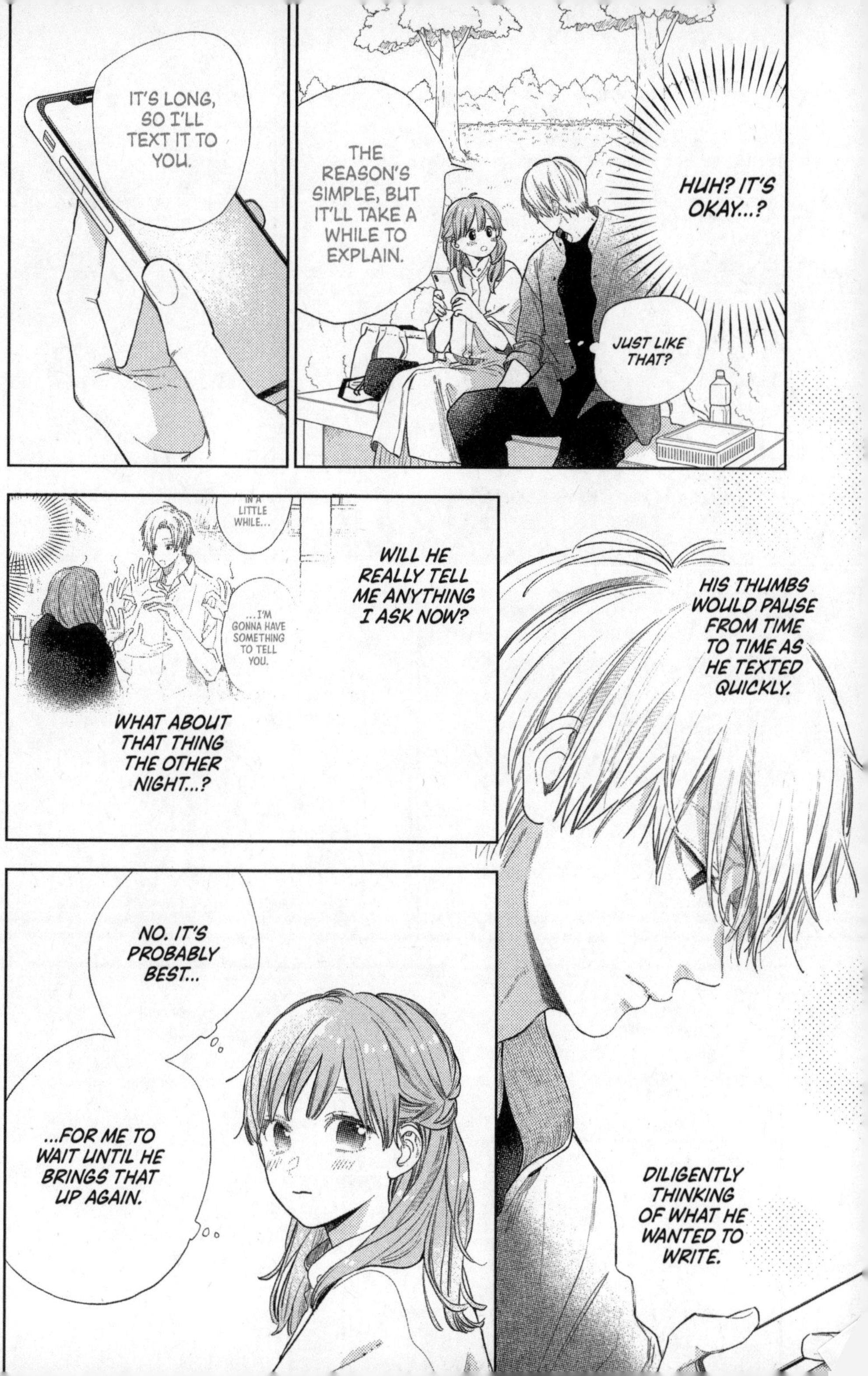
HUH? IT'S OKAY...?
JUST LIKE THAT?
THE REASON'S SIMPLE, BUT IT'LL TAKE A WHILE TO EXPLAIN.
IT'S LONG, SO I'LL TEXT IT TO YOU.
HIS THUMBS WOULD PAUSE FROM TIME TO TIME AS HE TEXTED QUICKLY.
DILIGENTLY THINKING OF WHAT HE WANTED TO WRITE.
WILL HE REALLY TELL ME ANYTHING I ASK NOW?
IN A LITTLE WHILE...
...I'M GONNA HAVE SOMETHING TO TELL YOU.
WHAT ABOUT THAT THING THE OTHER NIGHT...?
NO. IT'S PROBABLY BEST...
...FOR ME TO WAIT UNTIL HE BRINGS THAT UP AGAIN.

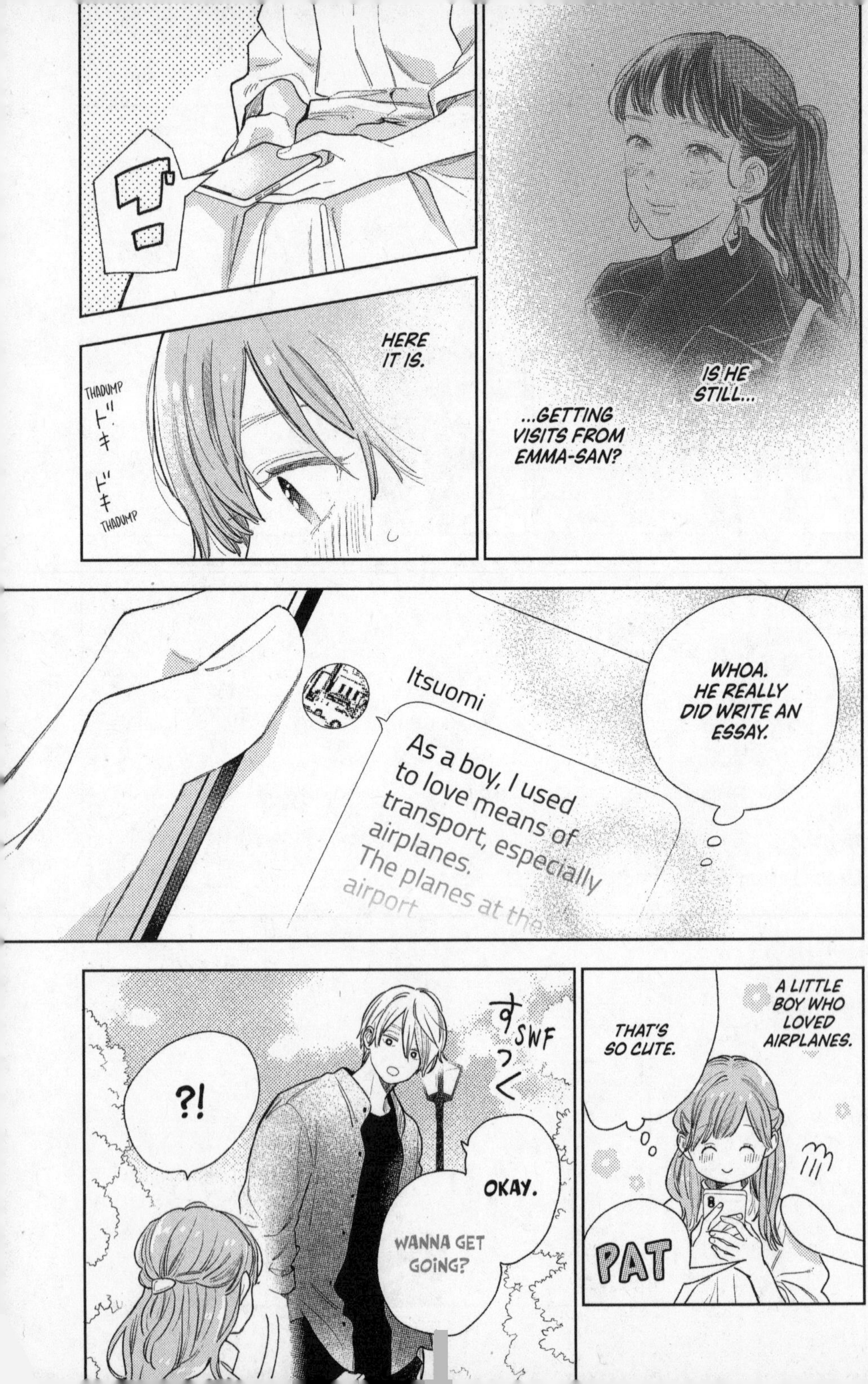
IS HE STILL...
...GETTING VISITS FROM EMMA-SAN?
?
HERE IT IS.
THADUMP ドキ
ドキ THADUMP
WHOA. HE REALLY DID WRITE AN ESSAY.
Itsuomi
As a boy, I used to love means of transport, especially airplanes. The planes at the airport
A LITTLE BOY WHO LOVED AIRPLANES.
THAT'S SO CUTE.
PAT
すっく SWF
OKAY.
WANNA GET GOING?
?!

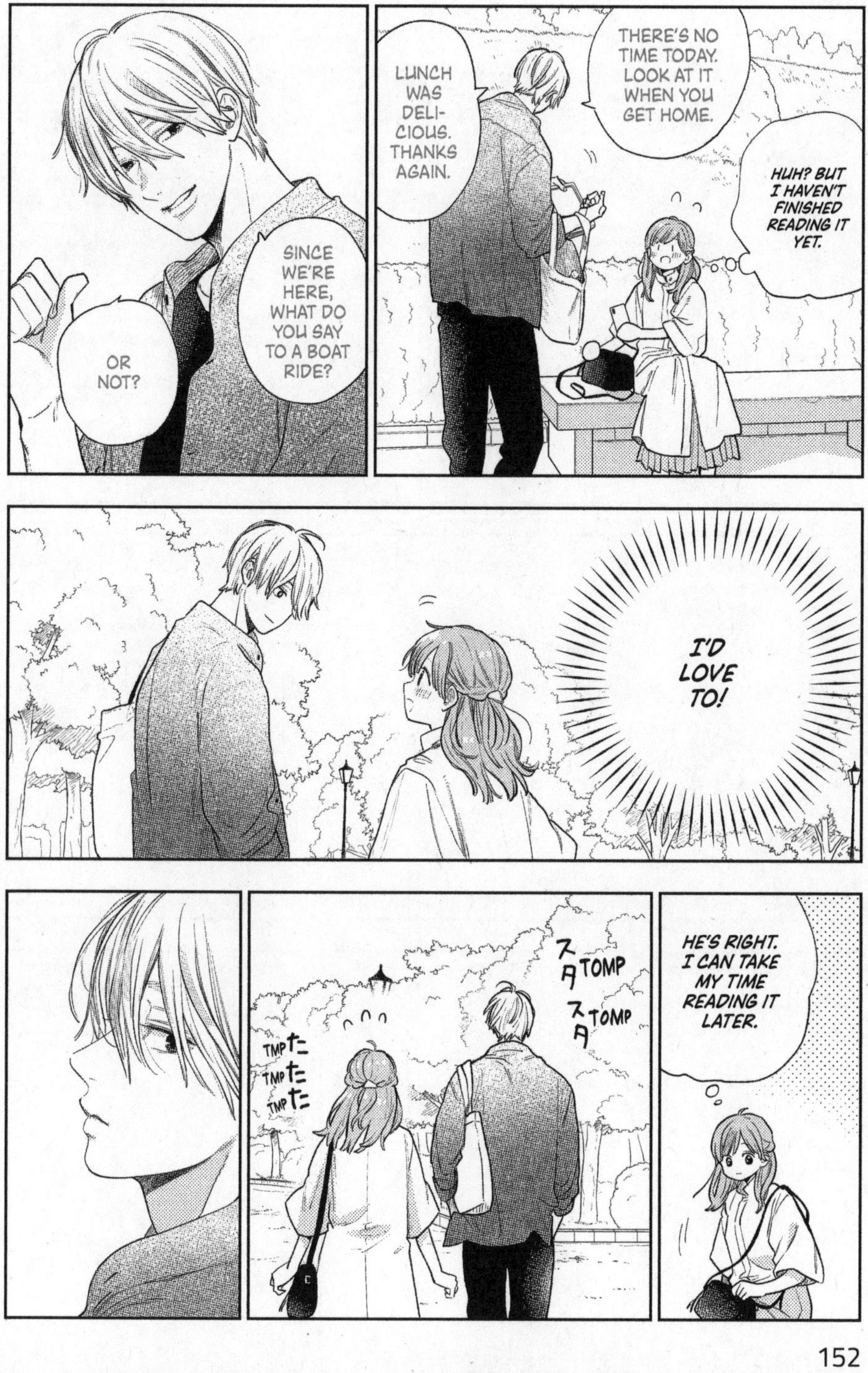
THERE'S NO TIME TODAY. LOOK AT IT WHEN YOU GET HOME.
LUNCH WAS DELI-CIOUS. THANKS AGAIN.
HUH? BUT I HAVEN'T FINISHED READING IT YET.
SINCE WE'RE HERE, WHAT DO YOU SAY TO A BOAT RIDE?
OR NOT?
I'D LOVE TO!
HE'S RIGHT. I CAN TAKE MY TIME READING IT LATER.
スタ TOMP
スタ TOMP
TMP た
TMP た
TMP た

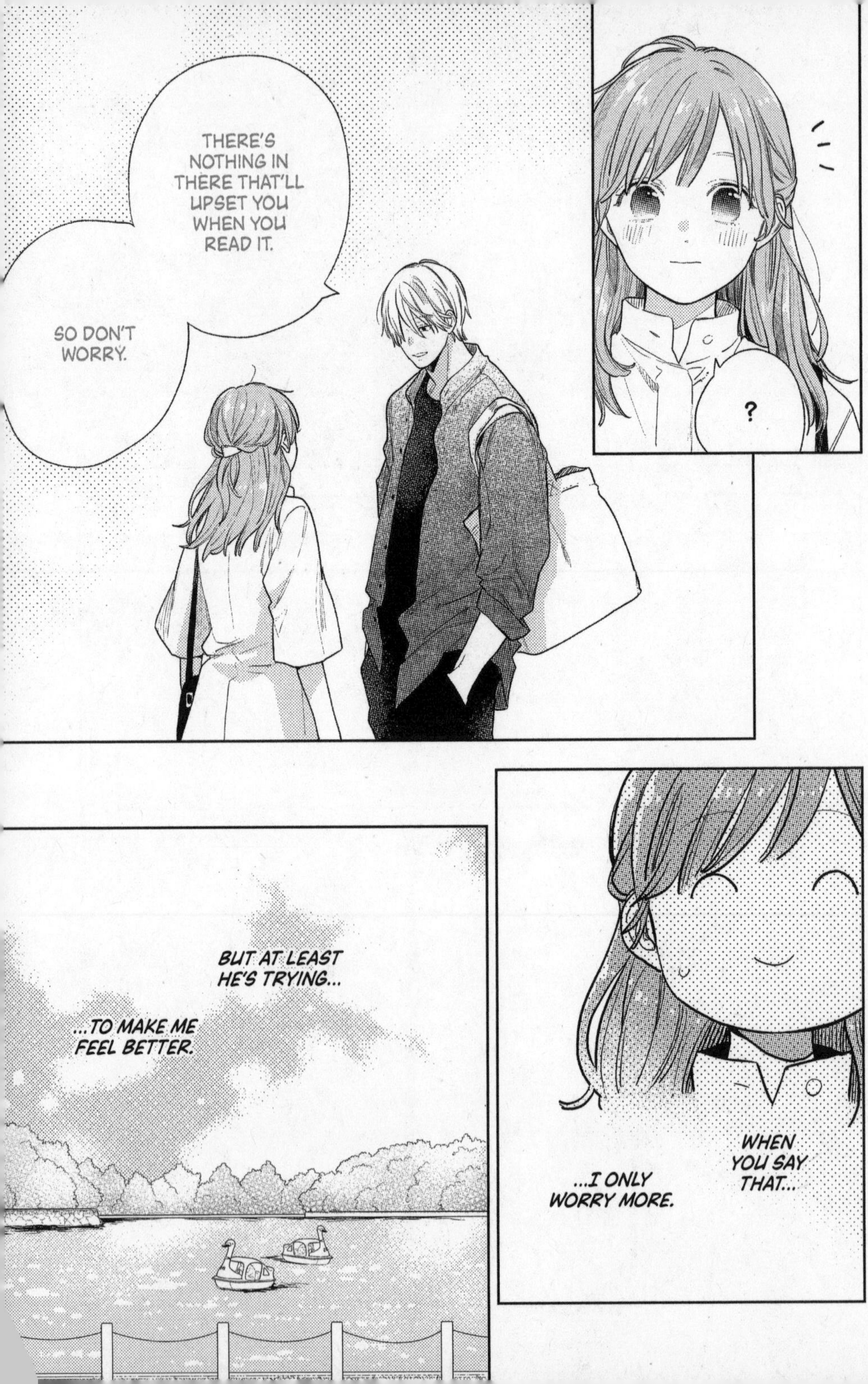
?
THERE'S NOTHING IN THERE THAT'LL UPSET YOU WHEN YOU READ IT.
SO DON'T WORRY.
WHEN YOU SAY THAT...
...I ONLY WORRY MORE.
BUT AT LEAST HE'S TRYING...
...TO MAKE ME FEEL BETTER.

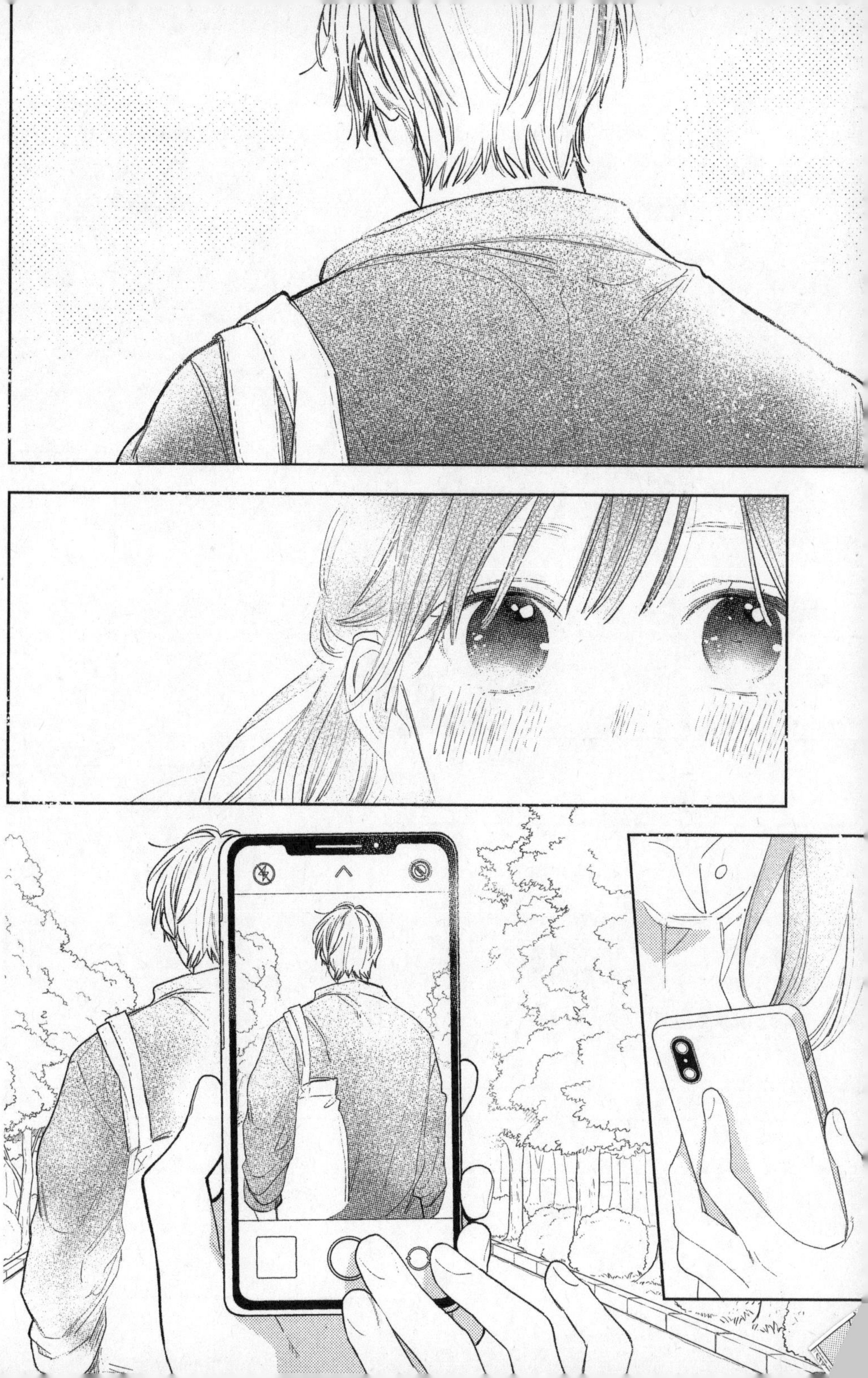

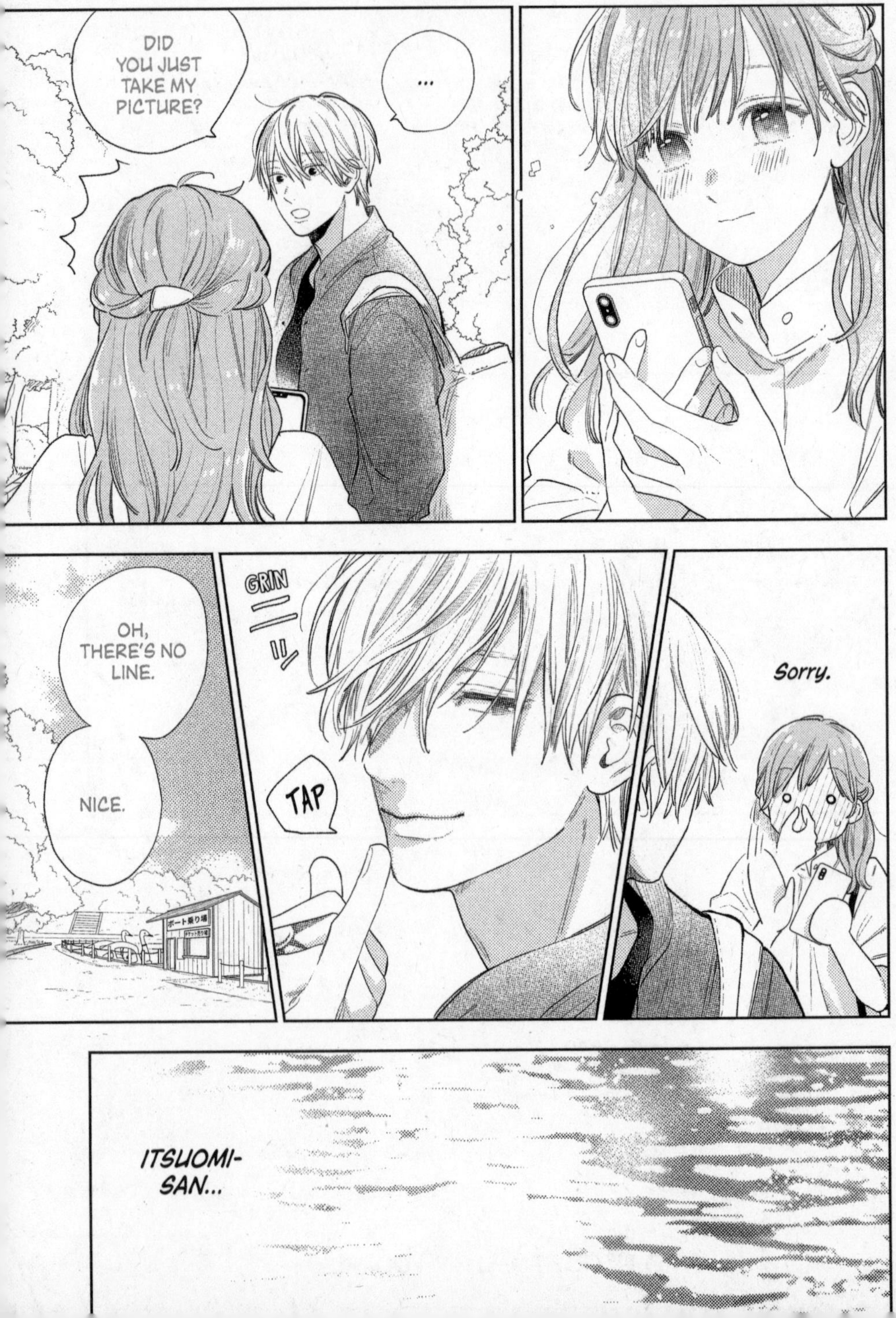
...
DID YOU JUST TAKE MY PICTURE?
Sorry.
GRIN
TAP
OH, THERE'S NO LINE.
NICE.
ボート乗り場
ITSUOMI-SAN...

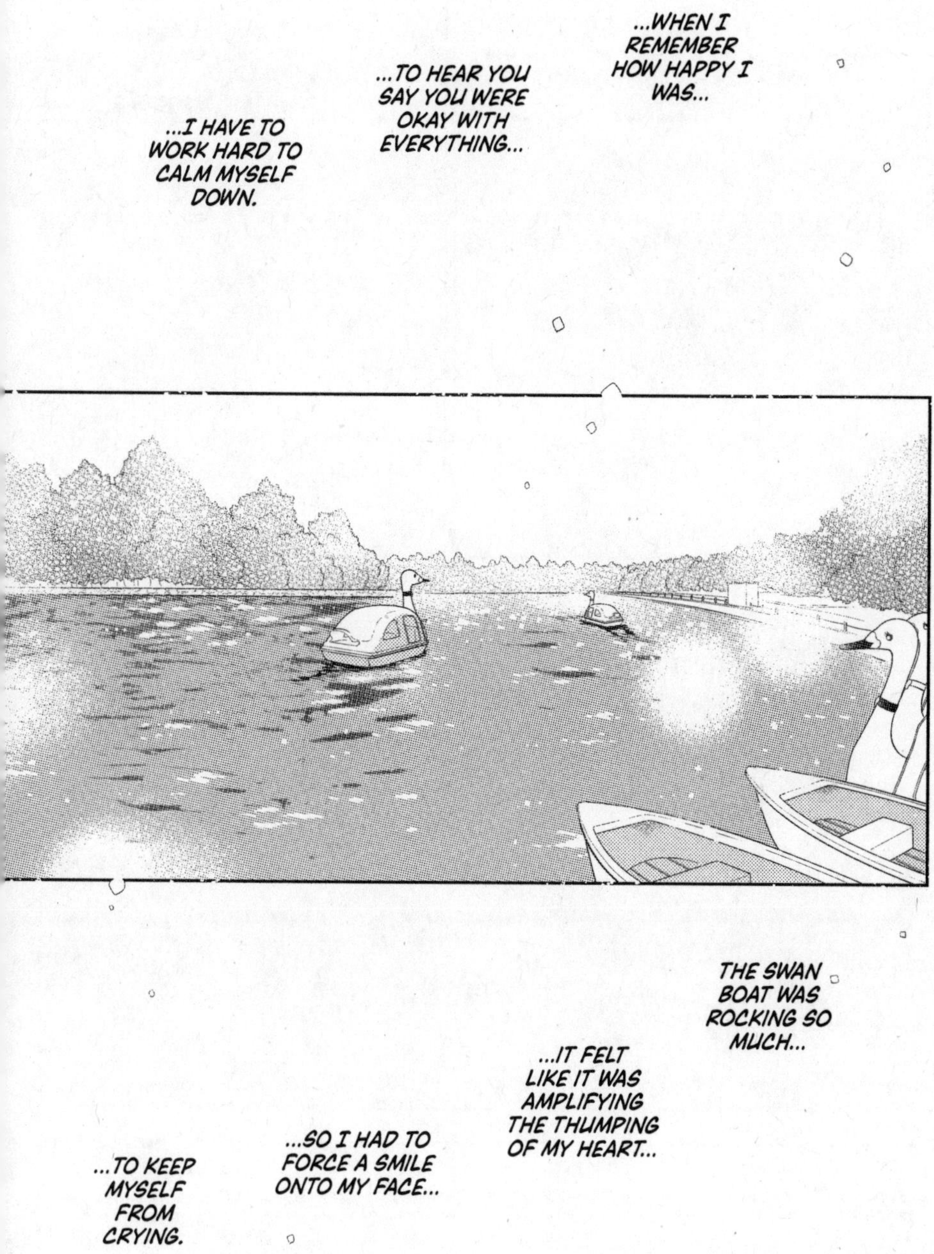
...WHEN I REMEMBER HOW HAPPY I WAS...
...TO HEAR YOU SAY YOU WERE OKAY WITH EVERYTHING...
...I HAVE TO WORK HARD TO CALM MYSELF DOWN.
THE SWAN BOAT WAS ROCKING SO MUCH...
...IT FELT LIKE IT WAS AMPLIFYING THE THUMPING OF MY HEART...
...SO I HAD TO FORCE A SMILE ONTO MY FACE...
...TO KEEP MYSELF FROM CRYING.

TO BE CONTINUED IN VOLUME 6

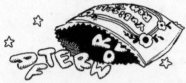

Thank you for reading Volume 5 of
A Sign of Affection. With the musical
and merchandise now released,
there are more ways than ever for
A Sign of Affection to touch people's lives,
for which I am beyond grateful. ☻
The comments on my social media
accounts and fan letters I receive give me
so much encouragement, too. Thank you.◊◊
Well, see you again in Volume 6! ♡

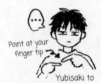

Point at your
finger tip ➤

Yubisaki to

Make two
hearts

Ren

Ren

We chose the
most unexpected
character to
bring you these
directions

♣The signs for the Japanese title,
  Yubisaki to renren ("fingertips and love")

(Of course you
can finger spell
it, too)

Special Thanks

- Editor: Shiigeru-san
- Balcolony's Takeuchi-san, Ichiki-san, Baba-san
- Everyone at spica works
- The editorial staff of *Dessert*
- The int'l rights department

- Sign Language Collaborator: Yuki Miyazaki-chan
- In Cooperation with: Naomi Nishimiya-san, Karen-san, Johannes
- Translation Help: Sakda Pakawan-san

- Backgrounds Materials Collaborator: Rockin' Robin, Osu shop-sama, Grand-Blue-sama

Staff
- Finishing Touches: Nao Hamaguchi-chan
- Background: Saya Aoi-san

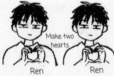All of my readers! ♡

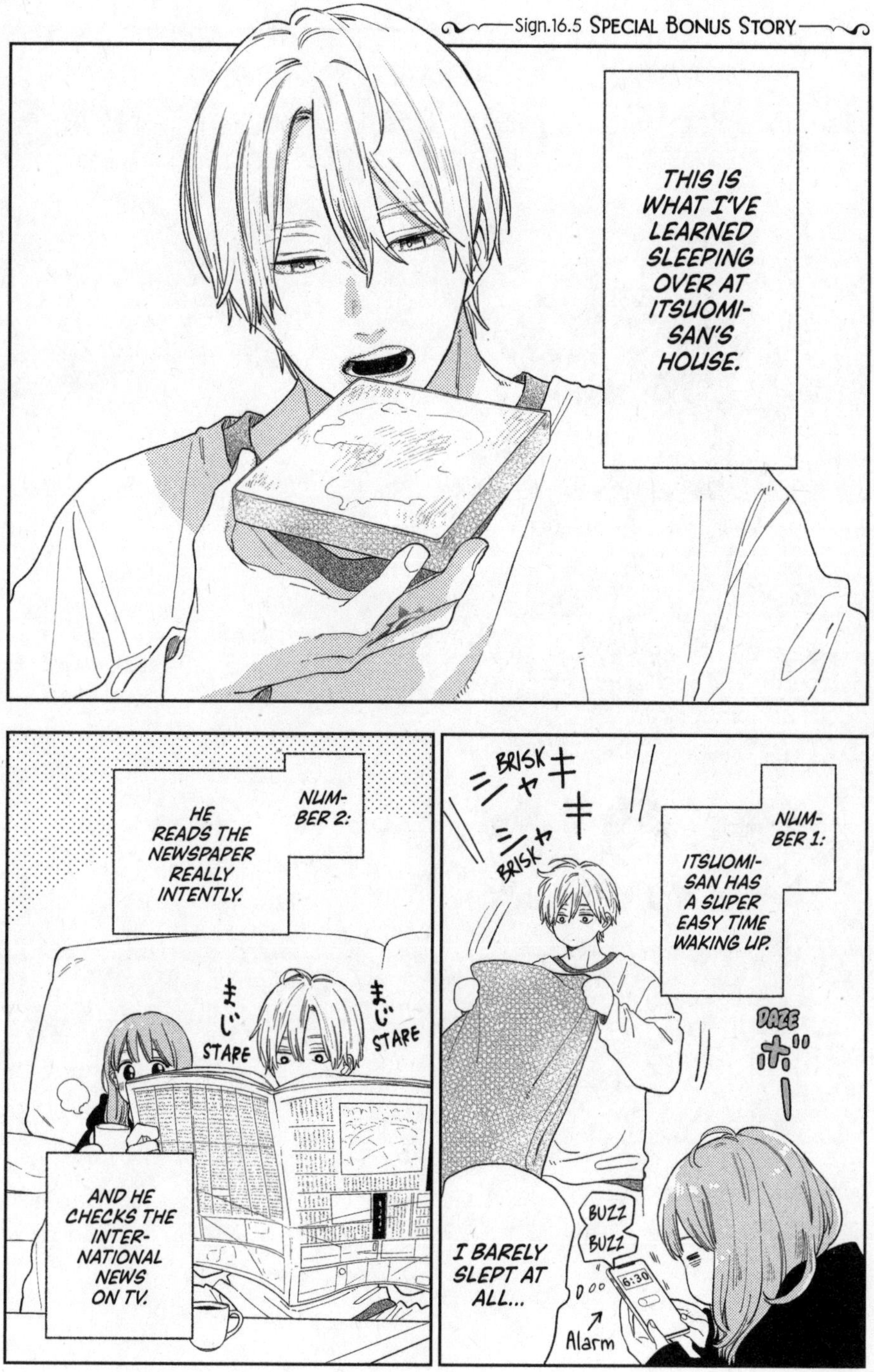
THIS IS WHAT I'VE LEARNED SLEEPING OVER AT ITSUOMI-SAN'S HOUSE.
シャキ
BRISK
シャキ
BRISK
NUMBER 1:
ITSUOMI-SAN HAS A SUPER EASY TIME WAKING UP.
ボー
DAZE
I BARELY SLEPT AT ALL...
BUZZ
BUZZ
6:30
Alarm
NUMBER 2:
HE READS THE NEWSPAPER REALLY INTENTLY.
まじ
STARE
まじ
STARE
AND HE CHECKS THE INTERNATIONAL NEWS ON TV.

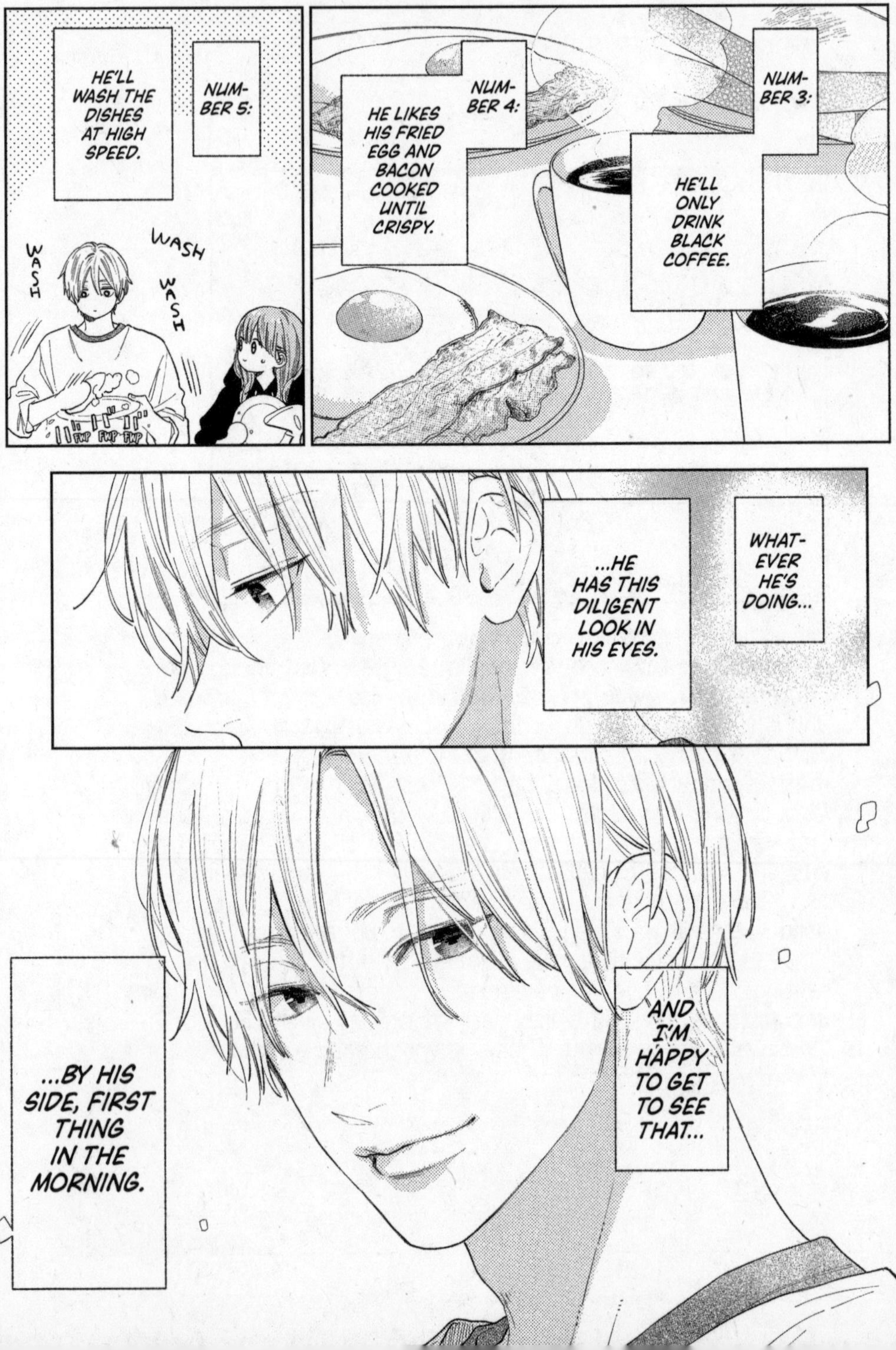
NUMBER 3:
HE'LL ONLY DRINK BLACK COFFEE.
NUMBER 4:
HE LIKES HIS FRIED EGG AND BACON COOKED UNTIL CRISPY.
NUMBER 5:
HE'LL WASH THE DISHES AT HIGH SPEED.
WASH
WASH
WASH
FWP FWP FWP
WHATEVER HE'S DOING...
...HE HAS THIS DILIGENT LOOK IN HIS EYES.
AND I'M HAPPY TO GET TO SEE THAT...
...BY HIS SIDE, FIRST THING IN THE MORNING.

TRANSLATION NOTE

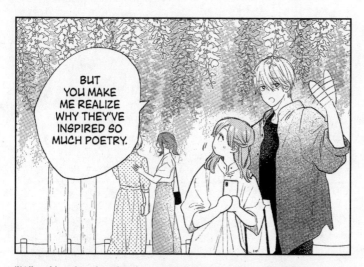

BUT YOU MAKE ME REALIZE WHY THEY'VE INSPIRED SO MUCH POETRY.

"Why they've inspired so much poetry," page 137
In the original Japanese version, Itsuomi says, "It's enough to make me realize why people use the phrase *setsugetsufuuka*." This is an idiom made up of four Chinese characters, like many Japanese sayings. *Setsu* means snow, *getsu* means moon, *fuu* means wind, and *ka* means flower. These four words are common *kigo*, or "season words," associated with winter, autumn, summer, and spring, respectively. Kigo are some of the most important elements of traditional Japanese poetry: the famous haiku, as well as *tanka*, *renga* (linked verse), and others. They can be used in a variety of ways, including as symbols, for pathos, or as synecdoche to invoke a variety of details about the setting, such as the temperature, weather, and location. Their accumulated meaning is especially important given the short length of many Japanese poems, in which each word must convey as much as possible.

A SIGN OF AFFECTION

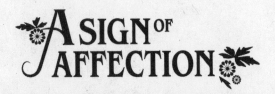

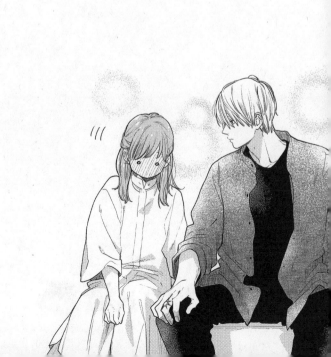

A SIGN OF AFFECTION

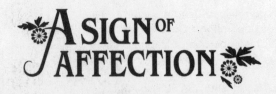

A Kodansha Comics Trade Paper
A Sign of Affection 5 copyright © 2C
English translation copyright © 20:

Published in the United States by Kodansha Comics, an imprint of Kodansha USA Publishing, LLC, New York.

Publication rights for this English edition arranged through Kodansha Ltd., Tokyo.

First published in Japan in 2021 by Kodansha Ltd., Tokyo.

ISBN 978-1-64651-418-2

Original cover design by Sari Ichiki (Balcolony)

Printed in the United States of America.

www.kodansha.us

9 8 7 6 5 4 3 2 1
Translation: Christine Dashiell
Lettering: Carl Vanstiphout
Additional Lettering: Lys Blakeslee
Editing: Ben Applegate, William Flanagan
Kodansha Comics edition cover design by Adam Del Re

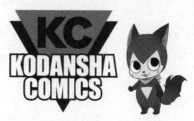

Publisher: Kiichiro Sugawara

Director of publishing services: Ben Applegate
Director of publishing operations: Dave Barrett
Associate director of publishing operations: Stephen Pakula
Publishing services managing editors: Alanna Ruse, Madison Salters
Production managers: Emi Lotto, Angela Zurlo
Logo and character art ©Kodansha USA Publishing, LLC